SOUTHEAST ASIA

Illusion and Reality in Politics and Economics

LENNOX A. MILLS

UNIVERSITY OF MINNESOTA PRESS, MINNEAPOLIS

PRINTED IN THE UNITED STATES OF AMERICA AT NORTH CENTRAL
PUBLISHING COMPANY, ST. PAUL

Library of Congress Catalog Card Number: 64-17805

PUBLISHED IN GREAT BRITAIN, MALAYA, INDIA, AND PAKISTAN
BY THE OXFORD UNIVERSITY PRESS
LONDON, KUALA LUMPUR, BOMBAY, AND KARACHI

The quotation from *Western Enterprise in Indonesia and Malaya*, by G. C. Allen
and Audrey G. Donnithorne, copyright George Allen & Unwin Ltd., is used with
the permission of the publishers.

Preface

I have attempted in this book to study some aspects of the economic and political situation which has evolved in the states of Southeast Asia since they became independent. The aim has been to discover whether the changes are so fundamentally similar that one can regard them as general trends of development which are common to the whole area. It is not possible to dogmatize since the period studied is brief, and conditions have not only altered rapidly but are still in process of evolution, so that it is easy to mistake the transient for the permanent. When everything is in a state of flux it is not possible to prophesy what shape it will ultimately assume. Nevertheless it does appear that some of the forces at work are so basic that tentative conclusions can be drawn.

All the countries of Southeast Asia want to raise their standard of living, and none of them can accomplish this without very substantial financial and technical assistance from abroad. By far the greater part of this help has come from the United States and the United Kingdom, although of recent years Indonesia in particular has received aid from Soviet Russia. The American and British governments have always maintained that their grants and loans could only be a minor part of the whole, supplementing the funds invested by private enterprise. The opposite has happened: apart from the ploughing back of profits by long-established firms little new private capital has entered Southeast Asia since 1941. The reasons are of such a nature that it is clear there will be no change in the foreseeable future, and that financial help must continue to be primarily governmental. The states of Southeast Asia are demanding much larger amounts than they have hitherto been

v

given. Whether they will receive them is part of the larger problem of how much in loans and grants a limited number of Western countries can give to the whole of the underdeveloped part of the world, and how far their policy should be affected by the competition in foreign aid which has developed with the Communist states. The wisdom with which the Asian governments have used foreign aid and their own resources in local capital and foreign exchange has varied widely, and it is clear that often the funds available could have been more effectively employed.

The basic problem is whether the standard of living can be raised when a high birth rate and a falling death rate are everywhere producing a rapid growth of population. The lack of statistical information makes it impossible to give a definitive answer, and one is forced to rely upon the opinions of people such as the government officials who have had a part in carrying out the projects financed by the Colombo Plan. Their belief is that the principal achievement so far has been to prevent the low standard of living from falling still further, and that much heavier expenditure will be essential if it is to be raised substantially. On the most optimistic calculation this will be a very slow as well as an expensive proceeding. It seems clear also that far and away the greater part of the cost will have to be borne by the United States. The burden could be much lessened if a radically different policy were adopted by most of the new governments which would change the conviction of private business that when a country attains independence it is likely to be a good place not to invest in.

Whenever a newly independent state has arisen in Southeast Asia it has at once been acclaimed by Americans and British as a democracy. This has been done on the strength of a paper constitution and the professions of its leaders. Any deviation between constitutional theory and practice has been explained away as temporary growing pains due to youth and inexperience. The various governments have been examined in this volume from the point of view of how they actually operate and two conclusions have been reached. All of them are dictatorships or oligarchies controlled by small groups of Western-educated, urban nationalists. Nothing else was to be expected, given the economic and social conditions and the tradition of government from above which prevail throughout Southeast Asia. It is of course possible to hope that the present forms of government will alter when fundamental changes have taken place in the structure of society. It would however be wishful thinking to take it for granted that a democratic future is assured.

The economic position of the Chinese and the hostility which this has created are the same in all the countries of Southeast Asia except Burma. The usual policy of the post-war governments has been to curb their activities by discriminatory legislation. This might be regarded as another general trend, if it were not that the Federation of Malaya and to a lesser extent Thailand follow the opposite policy. A Communist party is active in all of these countries and a study has been made of its tactics and the groups in society to which it appeals. There is no uniformity in the degree of success attained. This is due in part to variations in government policies, and partly to the differences in economic and racial conditions which exist in the various states. A chapter discusses the role of Southeast Asia in international affairs. There is a basic similarity in the underlying factors such as the existence of strong nationalism and of anti-Westernism in varying degrees. Foreign policy shows no uniformity, some governments being neutralist while others prefer alliances with the United States or the United Kingdom.

The whole of Southeast Asia is markedly alike in its economic situation and the uncertainty of raising the standard of living. The same can be said of the hesitancy of Western private capital to invest, though this is least evident in the Federation of Malaya and most pronounced in Indonesia. The whole area lacks the necessary prerequisites for democracy, and the governments which are evolving are the natural outcome. The problems of the Chinese and of Communism confront all the governments, but there is no uniformity in the policies adopted.

The chapters on private investment and government aid are in the main the result of research carried on in the United States and the United Kingdom. Most of the information was obtained from interviews or correspondence with American and British business and banking executives and government officials. I am very grateful for the help which they so generously provided. Almost invariably they stipulated that the firms they represented must not be identified, which explains the paucity of source references in these chapters. The rest of the book is based on the writings of others, including some of my former students. To cover the whole of Southeast Asia I have gone beyond the bounds of my own particular field of study, Malaya. This was done to satisfy my own need for a broader comparative study. Writers in the field have like myself prepared monographs on a single country or topic. For a long time I have been greatly interested in how far one could speak of general trends of development. To answer my own question I had to read something over a hundred detailed studies, not to mention articles, and then draw my own conclusions. It seemed to me that others might be interested in the results, and so I wrote this book.

I am much indebted to Professors Jan Broek and William C. Rogers and Captain Cary Hall, U.S.N., for the helpful criticisms which they made of several chapters, and to William Loy of the Cartographic Laboratory, University of Minnesota Geography Department, for the map which he prepared. Finally I gladly acknowledge my gratitude to the Guggenheim Memorial Foundation for its generous assistance, and to the Graduate School of the University of Minnesota for its grant toward the cost of drawing the map.

University of Minnesota

Table of Contents

Map of Southeast Asia, page 2

SOUTHEAST ASIA

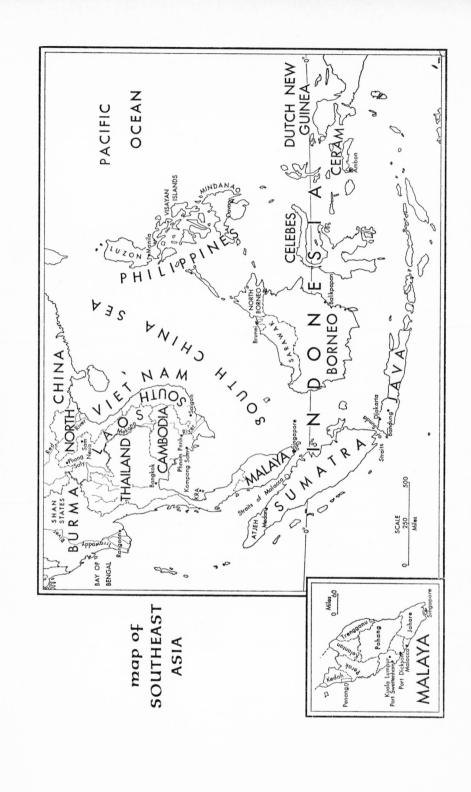

map of
SOUTHEAST
ASIA

PACIFIC

OCEAN

DUTCH NEW
GUINEA

CERAM

Ambon

MINDANAO

VISAYAN
ISLANDS

Davao

CELEBES

I N D O N E S I A

LUZON

Manila

PHILIPPINES

Balikpapan

NORTH
BORNEO

SOUTH CHINA SEA

Brunei

SARAWAK

BORNEO

NORTH CHINA

VIET NAM

LAOS

SOUTH

Red River

Sam Neua

Phong Saly

Mekong River

Saigon

JAVA

Djakarta

Bandung

Sunda Straits

SHAN
STATES

BURMA

THAILAND

CAMBODIA

Bangkok

Phnom Penh

Kompong Speu

KRA

MALAYA

Singapore

SUMATRA

Straits of Malacca

ATJEH

Medan

Irrawaddy River

Rangoon

BAY OF
BENGAL

SCALE
250   500
Miles

0

MALAYA

Miles
0   60

Trengganu

Kelantan

Perak

Pahang

Johore

Singapore

Kedah

Penang

Kuala Lumpur
Port Swettenham
Port Dickson
Malacca

I

Nationalism and Democracy

The Revolt against the Old Order

The usual explanation of the political revolution in Asia is that it is a revolt against European imperialist control. This description does not explain the revolution in Thailand which overthrew the absolute monarchy. The country was not a colony but an independent state, and the monarch was not a foreign ruler but the descendant of a long line of kings. He was retained as a royal figurehead, but apart from this he suffered the same fate as the British, Dutch, and French governments of Southeast Asia. It would seem to be more accurate to write that Asia is in revolt against the old order, whether that happens to be a native monarchy or a foreign colonial government.

The new leaders to whom power was transferred were a creation of the old order, a Western-educated middle class. It was only rarely that they came from the aristocracy or the peasantry. The majority were lawyers, doctors, civil servants, business men, intellectuals, and students. Some of them had received their higher education in Europe or the United States, and most of the others in the universities established in the colonies by the colonial governments. Students were an important element in the revolt against the old order. Like students everywhere they had a youthful enthusiasm for the cause which they had taken up, and this was heightened by the monotony of their lives. The Asian undergraduate spends long hours in poring over his books and lacks the social activities which enliven the life of the Western student. Much study was a weariness to the flesh, and a strike, a political demonstration, or an occasional riot were a welcome break

3

in the dull routine of life. They had prestige and an influence over their fellow countrymen which were far greater than those of students in most Western nations. The Federation of Malaya was an exception to the general rule in the character of its leadership. Here the majority of the leaders of the United Malay National Organization (U.M.N.O.), the principal Malay political party, were members of the aristocracy. Most of the leaders of the Malay Chinese Association (M.C.A.) were the successful business men who were the traditional heads of the Chinese community.

The principal following of the leaders prior to World War II came from the working class in the towns. The support of the peasant eighty per cent was uncertain and spasmodic. They were discontented but it is probable that they did not know exactly what they wanted. They did not like the changes which were taking place in their traditional way of life, and they felt that their foreign rulers were responsible. From the nineteenth century onward the formerly static village community was in a transition which is still in progress. This was brought about by the impact of Western economic forces and the development of the social services during the last century of colonial rule. There were memories mellowed by the lapse of time of the good old days when the village was unaffected by the booms and slumps of world trade, when handicraftsmen followed their traditional vocations, and the peasant was not plagued by earnest-minded officials who were determined to sanitate and generally uplift him by forcing on him new-fangled ideas about latrines, garbage removal, changes in his farming methods, and other unheard-of innovations. The peasant and the Western-educated had little in common. The latter lived in the towns and were extremely reluctant to bury themselves in the country-side. Frequently the only educated man in the village was the school-teacher. The urban middle class had little knowledge of the problems of the farmer. To the peasant his world was the village, and he had little interest or information about what went on outside it. His duty was to raise the crops, manage village affairs, and obey the orders of higher authority. From time immemorial national problems had been left to a remote and incalculable power called the government. Experience had taught the peasant that the less contact he had with it the better. It was to be feared and avoided and certainly not resisted.

On the eve of the Japanese invasion Kennedy, an American with a wide knowledge of the Dutch East Indies, estimated that of the 70,465,000 inhabitants perhaps 250,000 would have understood what was meant by a free and independent sovereign state of Indonesia. The urban Western-educated found it very hard to enlist the support of the rural population, or to retain it when they temporarily won it. This gap between the leaders and the peasants is still very wide, and is one of the principal hindrances to the establishment of democracy. In the interwar period it was estimated that those who led the revolt against the old order could not count on the support of more than about ten per cent of the population.

Nationalism and Self-Government

The Western-educated had the natural human ambition to rule their native countries, but always the road to the summit was blocked by a European or American in supreme control. The education established by the colonial rulers explained the secret of the power of the West. It revealed that nationalism was the concentrated force behind the will of Europe and the United States to conquer and control. No one could overlook this lesson, for the achievement and maintenance of national unity and independence were the central themes of much of their literature and political traditions. Western education bred nationalists where formerly no nations had existed in Southeast Asia.

The Americans, British, and Dutch had begun to grant self-government to their dependencies long before the outbreak of World War II. Each hoped to set up a democratic government after its own pattern, and all adopted the policy of self-government on the instalment plan. Political power would gradually be transferred from a Western bureaucracy to elected native leaders. Eventually the colonial authority would be abolished and the people of the country would control their own government. The reason for advancing gradually was the realization that of all the forms of government which man had invented democracy was the most difficult to operate. Even in the West only a minority of the nations were reasonably successful practitioners — if not a museum specimen, democracy was at least a comparative rarity. In Asia it was an exotic, for no Asian state had ever evolved government by the people on a national scale. The colonial powers believed that before their subjects could govern themselves democratically they must serve a period of apprenticeship. By 1941 the Americans in the Philippines were closest to the goal and had set 1946 as the date for complete independence. The British in Burma had gone almost as far, and the Dutch in the East Indies were a long way behind. In Indo-china the French had made practically no advance toward colonial self-government and had no intention of doing so. Their policy was that France and the colonies should be drawn closer together, and of set purpose they rejected autonomy which they believed would foster separation and not unity.

If the war had not intervened the British and Dutch dependencies would have had complete self-government in a generation at most. The Japanese conquest hastened independence because the prestige of the colonial powers was shattered by their failure to defend their subjects.

The spirit of nationalism and anti-imperialism which Japan had aroused was not diminished by her downfall; and the successive blows which she had inflicted on the White Man's prestige . . . had left one lasting impression on those whose lands had been overrun by the Japanese. This was that never again could they rely on their Western masters to protect them. Moreover the spell of relative independence which most of these countries had been accorded by the Japanese had whetted their appetites for full and complete freedom from foreign control. When peace was restored nationalist sentiment in the countries of South and East Asia was stronger than ever.[1]

Even though the Japanese retained control in the background the natives who staffed the puppet governments had more power than they had held under the colonial regimes. This increased their appetite for real independence and gave them greater confidence in their ability to govern.[2]

Nationalism is basically responsible for the widespread distrust of the West which still exists. There is an easily aroused suspicion that the former European rulers are plotting to restore their control. The United States is particularly suspect as the strongest of the capitalist powers and because, as Nehru pointed out in his history of the world, she is the exponent of a more subtle form of domination. The European colonial powers sent in their armies and conquered an Asian country. The United States disclaims all idea of conquest, but gradually its

6

business men win so much control that the country discovers that it has lost its independence. Further suspicion has been aroused by the American insistence on the retention of bases in the Philippines and Japan. Another characteristic of post-war nationalism is the sensitive demand for equality, respect, and prestige. This attitude makes the new states ready to react violently against any Western proposals which seem to infringe their absolute independence.

Self-Government and Democracy

The Western-educated leaders were only a small minority but they always claimed to voice the aspirations of the whole people. Their proclaimed goals were freedom and democracy. Western liberals strongly supported them, and took it for granted that a victory for nationalism meant also a triumph for democracy. The history of nationalism should have taught them that the two need not go together. The goal of nationalism is always self-government but this does not necessarily mean democratic government. As against the United States, the United Kingdom, or France where the two were inseparable there were Imperial and Nazi Germany, Fascist Italy, or Soviet Russia. It is perfectly possible to support government by one's own people and at the same time be indifferent to popular sovereignty. The revolt of the American colonies from Spain led to dictatorships and not democracy. Patriotism and the ballot box are not inevitably related. But disregarding the experience of history, it was assumed that in Asia where democracy was a recent colonial import nationalism would be a democratic and progressive force. The possibility was ignored that what the mass of the people wanted was government by men of their own race and economic betterment.

After independence was attained the new states set up democratic governments, usually of the parliamentary rather than the presidential type. Written constitutions, universal suffrage, secret ballot, a legislature responsible to the voters, an executive accountable to the legislature, an independent judiciary, and a bill of rights were the usual elements. To some extent this was brought about by the influence of their Western education upon the Asian elite. All the colonial powers were democracies at home, and no one could be educated in their schools without being imbued with democratic ideas. The Western-educated acquired a belief in democracy, and considered that it was a superior form of government, a symbol of maturity and modernity. Democracy was thus a proof of equality with the West whereas autocracy was outmoded. Self-interest dictated the same policy. The doctrines of government by popular consent and majority rule were the arguments used to justify the demand that power be transferred from a small number of foreign officials to the people of the country. The Western-educated were certain that if this were done the real authority would lie with them and not with the ignorant and tradition-bound peasantry. Indeed they were often rather contemptuous of the masses whom they claimed to lead. At the same time they tried to win the support of as many as possible of the people. This was an obvious political necessity in their struggle against the imperial powers. A demand for democracy was also necessary if the Asian leaders were to have the support of the Western liberals. It would never have been given if the proposal had been to set up an autocracy.

Definitive judgments about the governments of Southeast Asia are difficult to make, because many of the essential facts are unknown. It is easy to read their constitutions, parliamentary debates, and the published speeches of the leaders, but none of them tells the full story of how the constitutions work in practice. Studies have been made of elections — how many voted, whom they voted for, and how the elections were conducted. What one would like to know is why the people voted as they did. Are there any parallels to the Filipino *cacique* who leads his band of debt slaves to the polling booth and sees to it that they vote as he directs? To what extent does the villager make up his own mind, and how far does he do what the village headman or someone with local influence orders? Was the discovery unique which was made in Singapore in 1958 by the By-Election Corruption Commission, that members of the Chinese criminal secret societies had become an integral part of democratic elections? Apparently they were employed by several Chinese politicians to influence voters.[3] Information on points like these would give a much clearer picture of the situation.

Judging by what information is available it would seem that the governments of Southeast Asia could be described as follows. Philippine democracy appears to be controlled by an oligarchy of landowners, money lenders, and *caciques*, although more attention must be paid to the peasants since Magsaysay's presidency. Ngo Dinh Diem of South Viet Nam was head of a family autocracy. The twin supports of Thai democracy are the army and an extensive and complicated distribution of financial favors which makes opposition to government imprudent. Cambodian democracy is Premier Prince Sihanouk, whether he happens to be premier or temporarily resigned from office. Federation of Malaya democracy is a marriage of convenience between Malay aristocrats and Chinese big business men, with Hindu trade union leaders as the Number Two Wife. Indonesia is a guided democracy, a camouflage for the dictatorship of President Sukarno which will last as long as he retains the support of the army and the Communists. Burman democracy of recent years has been the pro-U Nu rump of the Anti-Fascist People's Freedom League, with interludes when the army takes over control to clean up the mess made by the politicians. The constitutional monarchy of Laos has been an anthropologist's paradise of primitive tribes, where rival factions led by a small number of French-educated Lao intrigued and fought for control of the government.

If democracy is evolving in Southeast Asia it is not developing in accordance with the orthodox Western pattern. This is only to be expected for democratic constitutions cannot be exported like standard size, ready-to-wear clothing. They must be evolved to suit the characteristics of the people. Perhaps the idea can be exported, but if it is acclimatized in its new environment the results will not be the same. Asia has been influenced by Western ideas, but at the same time no nation can escape from its past. This will have its effect upon the way in which the government operates. Professor Rupert Emerson is pessimistic about the outlook for democracy in the underdeveloped countries. "What we are witnessing is the failure of a series of experiments in grafting an alien form of government on peoples whose background and circumstances are totally dissimilar from those among whom it originated, and who were on virtually every count demonstrably ill prepared to make it work." His prediction is that dictators will replace the sham democracies of today, and he is sceptical whether they will ever willingly relinquish their power in spite of their protestations that their rule is strictly temporary. He believes however that they will have to pay more attention to the people than in the past by plebiscites

9

with a 99.7 per cent supporting vote and other similar "familiar frauds of our age." [4] When one surveys the Afro-Asian world from Iraq, Egypt, and Ghana to Indonesia and South Viet Nam only a robust optimist would deny the possibility that he is right. It might be argued that the failures of the last decade are merely due to inexperience, but it is clear that many of the elements which were vitally important in the evolution of Western democracy are lacking in Southeast Asia, and that it will take a long time to supply them.

Prerequisites for Democracy

The history of democracy in the West appears to show that a large middle class is essential. In Southeast Asia it is very small, too small to play the role of its Western counterpart. Its principal components are professional men, particularly lawyers, civil servants, intellectuals, and professors. The business men who are so large a part of the Western middle class are very few, although they are beginning to appear owing to government encouragement. In the past Europeans and Chinese and to a minor extent Indians controlled business. The people of the country will never accept their leadership, and so the middle class remains too small to do its political work effectively. This is the group which furnished the Western-educated leaders who led the revolt against the old order. Below them comes a much larger element which Professor Tinker for want of a better term describes as the lower middle class.[5] By this he means all those who are literate in some Western language and have to some extent acquired Western ideas. Among them are office clerks, small shopkeepers, newspaper reporters, and school teachers. They passed their examinations by memorizing text books, and their minds hold an unassimilated mixture of half understood Western and traditional Asian ideas and a smattering of Marxism. They are poorly paid, worse off than skilled artisans, and they feel that their social status and prospects are far below what their education gives them the right to expect. They are probably the most discontented class in Asia, and having nothing to hope for from the present order of society they are susceptible to Communist propaganda. Their number steadily grows, for the new governments have energetically expanded the school system. There has been quite a large

10

output of partly educated youths who find that their economic opportunities fall far short of their expectations.

Government in Asia was absolute and despotic, while democracy was confined to the village, so far as it existed even there. Although the village governed itself it was not necessarily a school for democracy. Often the position of headman was hereditary, and the village elders who exercised great influence were frequently drawn from the more prominent families. The humbler villager learned to be content with the station in life to which it had pleased God to call him. Actions were governed by custom and innovators and rebels were duly suppressed. This did not encourage the individualism and self-reliance which underlie Western democracy.[6] To counterbalance a long tradition of autocratic rule there were a hundred years or less of Western education which reached only a small fraction of the population, and the policy of gradually introducing democratic government which was followed during the final generation of colonial rule. The group principally affected was the small, Western-educated, urban middle class. Some of them fully accepted the democratic ideal and strove to realize it in practice, while others did not. Their Westernization and their urban life cut them off from the peasants. If democracy is to be acclimatized a bridge must be built between this elite and the peasant eighty per cent who have the vote but as yet have no understanding of their rights and obligations in a democracy and no conception of national as opposed to village problems. The gap between the masses and the Westernized few who control the new governments is immense. This gap will probably narrow as politicians appeal to the peasants to swell their following. The Communists are doing this in Java. It is not certain that this will make for democracy in view of the gullibility of the peasants. In the Philippines they were persuaded that freedom from American rule meant the abolition of taxes and higher prices for their crops.

The peasant has always believed that when he had tilled the crops, attended to village affairs, and paid his taxes he had done all that was required. The government was a remote and alien autocrat with which he had nothing to do save to obey. Its manifestations in the shape, for example, of tax collectors were feared and evaded if possible. The ideal ruler was the benevolent despot who gave his people justice and prosperity. That the peasant should be the source of authority and give government its orders never entered his head.

The democratic constitutions of Southeast Asia were drafted by the Western-educated leaders and imposed on the peasants. The evidence appears to show that universal suffrage has not miraculously changed their point of view, and they continue to be docile to authority. Here is one place where one wishes that studies could be made of why rather than how they vote. Only fragments of evidence are available. Sjahrir declared that in the Indonesian election of 1955 the majority of the peasants voted as their village headman or Muslim priest directed them. It was stated that they usually regarded any member of the elite as Authority, the successor of the Dutch official and his predecessor the sultan.[7] There is some evidence that in Burma voting in the village is swayed by whoever has local influence, spiritual or temporal. Thai cultivators said that voting was a meaningless ritual which they performed when they were ordered to do so. The general impression gained is that since the war the peasants have become nationalists but not democrats. They want to be governed by people of their own race and not by their former colonial rulers. Their support of their government however is passive: they accept its orders and it does not occur to them to take the initiative.

The attitude of the leaders toward the peasantry is one of rather impatient condescension. They take it for granted that it will be a long time before the cultivators will be capable of deciding what is good for them. The politician and the civil servant know best. Their motives are mixed — a desire to raise the standard of living, the determination to increase the power and prestige of their country, and an equal resolve to create more adequate scope for their own ambitions. They are determined to crowd into a brief span of time the sweeping economic changes which took the West a century or more. This involves rapid and drastic changes in the traditional way of life, and they are resolved to force the peasant up the painful ascent of progress. No colonial government would have dared to initiate so revolutionary a break with the past. So far as one can ascertain, the bulk of the peasants do not want to alter their customs. They wish for a change to the extent that they want to own farms large enough to support their families, and to be freed from rent to the landowner and debt to the money lender. For the rest it is not at all certain that they desire any alteration in their traditional way of life.[8] This raises the speculation whether the present elite would ever voluntarily resign its power. Apart from its sense of mission which has been advanced as the justification for a good many oligarchies from the Senate of republican Rome downwards, there are many material rewards for a ruling group. Western liberals assume that because the middle class in the West did not resist the rise to power of the workmen, therefore the same thing must happen in Asia. Since history never repeats itself exactly, but at most with variations, one wonders.

Some observers have doubted whether democracy is compatible with the high percentage of illiteracy in Southeast Asia. This is hard to answer, for the Germans were well educated and yet the Weimar Republic was a failure. So much depends on the attitude of mind of those who are literate, whether they are inquiring and sceptical or believe uncritically everything they read. If the latter, literacy merely increases the number who can be reached by propaganda, although this is less important with the increase of radio broadcasts in Asia. Perhaps the most one can say is that a fair amount of literacy seems necessary for a successful democracy. The importance of whether elections are technically free has been somewhat overrated as an evidence of progress toward democracy. It is incontestable that such an election as the one in the Philippines in 1949 where armed bands employed by the governing class beat and killed opponents showed a brutally frank disregard for democracy. More subtle methods, however, can be equally effective with an unsophisticated electorate, and yet no one can say the law is infringed. The Hindu peasantry supported the Congress Party because Gandhi told them to. He was a holy man and the mouthpiece of their gods, and when your gods tell you to vote for a party you obey. There have been instances in the Philippines where candidates were elected because their hereditary position in the community gave them the right to office. A word in season from village headmen or other persons of influence may make overt interference with a free election unnecessary. A sense of social equality is probably a minor factor. The United Kingdom was a democracy during the nineteenth century, and yet it was true to say that all men were equal except lords, who were a necessity.

The Asian characteristic of voting for a man rather than for his party principles is sometimes given as another evidence that the new states are undemocratic. Everywhere the personality of the leader is much more important than what he stands for, and the decisive factor is whether he has that indefinable personal magnetism which can be described as political sex appeal. Political parties are not like those of the West: they are factions following a leader. What holds them together is loyalty to the individual, and also the expectation that if he rises to power he will have many desirable favors to bestow. The West, however, is not free from this phenomenon though in a less exaggerated form. The cult of personalities plays quite an important part in American politics.

One condition which is of the utmost importance is that the leaders and the led must be firmly determined to uphold toleration and respect for the rights of the minority. The parties in opposition must have complete freedom to became the majority so long as they use normal constitutional methods. Judged by this standard South Viet Nam did not pass the test. Allied with the principle of toleration is the existence of a strong tradition of independence and willingness to oppose the government in order to uphold one's personal rights. This is lacking among the peasantry. A very important point is whether the civil authority can control its armed forces. In Thailand it has failed since a few years after the revolution of 1932. In Indonesia the government has never been fully in control and now partly depends upon the armed forces for its continuance in power; and in Burma the army twice took over the government when it decided that the politicians could no longer be trusted to promote the interests of the nation.

A single-party system which suppresses the opposition is not a democracy. To do this breaks the fundamental principle that the opposition must be allowed complete liberty to advance its views and try to win the support of the voters, so long as it does not abuse its freedom to obtain control of the government by force. Professor Emerson put the argument clearly in his *Empire to Nation*.

Only if an opposition party is available and is equipped with the rights essential to its free functioning can the ordinary citizen have any assurance that he is being presented with the facts and alternatives on which informed judgment can be based. Without the existence of an opposition he is inevitably forced to rely largely on the information which comes to him from the government and the governing party and to vote for the single slate of candidates officially laid before him. The freedom of choice which democracy implies is effectively denied him.[9]

No Asian state with the exceptions of North and South Viet Nam has gone as far as Ghana in the direction of single-party rule, though the flagrant interference by the Liberal party with the Philippine elections of 1949 showed at any rate a lack of repugnance to this course. It was prevented from repeating its tactics by a combination of aroused public opinion — an encouraging sign — American pressure, and Magsaysay's use of the army to prevent intimidation on election day. In Burma there was an approximation to single-party rule under the Anti-Fascist People's Freedom League (A.F.P.F.L.) from 1947 until the party broke into two factions in 1958.

The low standard of living is a potential danger. The people are not democrats, and there is no widespread demand for popular government. One does not miss what one has never known. This does not mean that the masses are indifferent to their condition: they insist that the government raise their standard of living, and if it fails to do this they may turn to the Communists. The essential point is that most Asians are far more interested in economics than in democracy. A full stomach and a reasonable certainty of its continuation have a far stronger appeal than political ideals.

The governments of Southeast Asia are not democratic at the present time whatever they may become eventually. The ideas and conditions which led to the development of democracy in the West cannot be expected to establish themselves quickly. For the near future the countries of Southeast Asia will be governed by oligarchies of the new Western-educated class, provided that they control their armed forces. So far they have succeeded in Malaya and the Philippines. In Indonesia faction and incompetence opened the way for dictatorship, in Burma the army took over control, and in Thailand a military dictatorship is in control behind the façade of a democratic monarchy.

II

The Philippines, Burma,
and Malaya

The Philippines

The constitution of the Philippine Republic set up a democracy of the American type based on separation of powers between the executive and the legislature. The vote is held by all adults aged twenty-one, male and female, who are literate. This disenfranchises many of the poorer peasants, leaving roughly half the adult population qualified. The president is elected directly by the people, and has considerably greater powers than his American counterpart. The legislature has two houses, and the Supreme Court decides constitutional disputes. There are fifty-six provinces, each made up of a varying number of municipalities. Their power is very limited, since almost all authority is centralized in the Insular Government at Manila. The actual working of the central government is very different from that of its American prototype. Prior to World War II the President, Manuel Quezon, was a quasi-dictator. He was master of the government and of his party, the Nationalists, for he could break any politician who opposed him. He was shrewd and farsighted, and his gifts of oratory were such that when it suited his purpose he could persuade his audience that black was white. He had the support of over two thirds of the voters. His popularity was greatest when he came closest to infringing the constitution, for then the people felt that this was the strong ruler doing what needed to be done, without allowing legal niceties to hamper him. Quezon had exceptional gifts whereas his post-war successors apart from Magsaysay were mediocrities. So after 1946 the government changed from an incipient dictatorship to an oligarchy of the governing class. Magsaysay was able partly to impose his will upon this oligarchy owing to his ability and his immense popularity, and it is an interesting speculation what might have happened if he had not been killed in mid-career in an airplane accident.

In 1935 Senator Juan Sumulong wrote a description of Philippine democracy that is still substantially accurate. "The majority and minority parties represent almost exclusively the intelligentsia and what we would call the Philippine plutocracy, and the needy classes have no representation in these parties, and for this reason they have neither voice nor vote, even only as minorities, in the formulation of government policies."[1] By plutocracy and intelligentsia Senator Sumulong meant the American-educated landowners, money lenders, and *caciques*. In 1938 eighty-two out of ninety-eight members of the National Assembly were landowners or lawyers whose interests were allied with theirs. The landowner cultivated his estate by renting it in small farms to tenants, the usual rental being half the crop. The tenant was unable to live on his share and was compelled to borrow from his landlord at an extortionate rate of interest. Many fell so hopelessly in debt that they became debt slaves. The landowner *cum* money lender was a *cacique* or local political boss and controlled the votes of his tenantry. He was the mainspring of democracy in the rural areas and his object was to make the Philippines safe for caciquism. Since the politicians wanted to be elected there was harmonious cooperation between them and the landowners.

Since Senator Sumulong wrote, the group has widened to include some Filipinos engaged in commerce and manufacturing, many of whom are members of the old landowning families. From their wealth and position in society this was the group which profited most from American rule economically and politically. When democracy was introduced it was they who supplied the leadership and control, and were on intimate terms with the American administration. Before World War II there was only one political party of any importance, the Nationalist, since the opposition was too weak and transient to have much significance. The Nationalist party was the governing class incorporated for political control.

17

Liberals and Nationalists

In 1946 the Nationalists divided into two parties or rather factions. The majority seceded to form the new Liberal party under Roxas, while the remainder stayed in the Nationalist party. The division was not a matter of principle but of expediency. During the war a great part of the Nationalists had collaborated with the Japanese in the puppet government which they set up, and Roxas was accused of having been a leader of this group. There was a strong demand that he and they be tried as war criminals, and Roxas decided that it was darkest under the light. The United States would acknowledge the Philippines as an independent republic in 1946, and an election was to be held to choose the president and legislature. The Americans could not inaugurate the new republic by hanging the president, so Roxas was safe if he could be elected. He launched his candidacy as the founder of the new Liberal party, the other collaborators joined him, and the remnant who stayed in the Nationalist party were overwhelmingly defeated. Two years later Roxas died of heart failure and was succeeded by the Vice President, Quirino. Born of humble parents and not a member of one of the wealthy and influential landowning families, Quirino was honest and well intentioned but mediocre; his principal qualification was that he had always been a good party man. He did not control the party machine and those who did made it clear that if they supported him as president he must approve their formulation of policy. Among other things this meant no effective agrarian reforms, and an indulgence in graft by the members of the government and their friends which broke all previous records. Quirino was forced to agree, though toward the end of his career he was able to strengthen his position through the methods of financial persuasion which are the perquisite of Philippine presidents.

The Nationalists inveighed against the corruption of the Liberal government, but on the whole there was no significant difference between the programs of the two parties. They were equally opposed to agrarian reforms which would lessen their wealth and political power. When President Magsaysay introduced his measures to improve the position of the peasants he met bitter opposition from his own Nationalist party as well as from the Liberals. Both parties were dominated by the American-educated wealthy landowning and commercial class. Urban labor

18

and the peasantry had few spokesmen, and there was little middle-class representation, since the majority of the merchants and manu-facturers were alien Chinese and Westerners. The political role of the Chinese was to be the principal source of funds for both parties. Their only means of exerting influence was through their money, and they used it individually and as a community to obtain personal favors or prevent the passage of a law detrimental to their interests. Hayden's comment, written twenty years ago, is still substantially accurate. He asked what the effect upon American democracy would be if three quarters of the business men throughout the country were

aliens who had no votes, no interest in government save to protect themselves from it or to use it, and no devotion to the political institu-tions of the nation? What would American politics be were 75% of all taxes on business to be paid by this same group of aliens who possessed no legitimate control over government agencies for the levying and collection of taxes and the regulation of business? [2]

Incidentally many Western companies hinted delicately that periodi-cal gifts in the proper quarters formed part of their normal costs of operation.

The emergence of two parties has not meant that a two-party system has evolved, with different policies. All that happened was that the governing class split into two rival factions, each desirous of power. This was nothing new in Philippine politics. Periodically the pre-war Nationalists had divided into rival factions, but after a trial of strength the weaker had always submitted and returned to the party fold. Each of the post-war parties has been divided into groups which contended with one another for control. A dissatisfied group was quite likely to join the opposing party if it saw a prospect of increased patronage and influence. There was no telling when some of a party's members might move to the opposite camp. In this game the president had the ad-vantage that he could offer more than anyone else, and it was essen-tial that he do so to increase his following and retain his position. [3]

Personality vs. Party

The key to the understanding of much of the working of the political system is that from top to bottom men follow a leader. The twentieth-century party leader is the spiritual descendant of the *datu* who ruled

19

his tribe before the arrival of the Spaniards. He was the father of his people and their leader, he settled their disputes, and he gave them rewards for good service. A government of laws and not of men has little attraction for the majority: they prefer one which is controlled by one dominant personality. What they want is the strong ruler who protects them against injustice and dispenses favors. Government is personal and paternal; and generally speaking the voters will follow a popular leader whatever party label he may have adopted at the moment. Filipinos

require strong individual leadership. Most of our political issues are resolved partly on the merits of the case but even more by the extent of public confidence in a particular leader. If such confidence is strong the people generally do not go deeply into the pros and cons of a particular issue but rather take the attitude — we believe in this leader, he is wise and good, let him have his way and we will judge his leadership by the results.[4]

The supreme leader is the president, and Filipinos of all ranks go directly to him if possible, rather than to the appropriate government department. One reason for the immense influence of Magsaysay over the peasants was that he encouraged them to visit him in person in his presidential palace at Malacañang and dealt with their petitions on the spot. When the number of petitioners became too large for him to see each one personally, he employed a staff of assistants to take down particulars of their requests. These were filed, and whenever Magsaysay visited a province he went in person to the villages of some of the petitioners and dealt with their cases on the spot. This practice was not peculiar to him; it is as old as recorded Asian history. In India it was known as *durbar*. When Solomon gave his verdict on the parentage of the baby he was holding *durbar* in his palace in Jerusalem, and the two women who claimed the infant argued their case before him.

How to Win Friends and Influence People

Durbar is not confined to the president: every politician down to a member of a municipal council is besieged by those who want favors or the redress of grievances. In return the client does everything he can to further the interests of his patron. This is one recognized way of building up a following. A frequent request is for a civil-service position, and the result is that though appointment and promotion depend theoretically on ability, influence is a determining factor in practice. Other forces which conduce to this result are nepotism and friendship. A man with influence is expected to use it first to promote the interests of his own family, secondly of his friends, and thirdly of those who come from his own town or province. Fourth place is held by well-qualified outsiders. The art of politics is for the leaders of the groups that make up the Liberal and Nationalist parties to ally themselves with the lesser leaders outside Manila, such as the provincial governors, and so down the line to the municipalities. When a group leader in Manila makes a political move he mobilizes his supporters throughout the islands. The provincial governor is a very important cog in the party machine because of his influence locally.[5] Sometimes this influence is strengthened by his inherited position if he is a member of an old family which traditionally has played an important part in local affairs. The *caciques* are a force to be reckoned with because they can control the votes of their tenants in support of their chosen candidate.

The "pork barrel" is important in elections. Following a custom of many years' standing from ten to fifty per cent of the funds allotted to public works are divided each year among the legislators. In 1948 the amount was $100,000 apiece, and in 1956 it was $50,000 to a representative and $125,000 to a senator.[6] Each legislator decides how to spend his "pork" on roads, schools, and the like so as to get the best results in the next election. The president's control over the disbursement of this fund is an important part of his influence over his party. Opposition members also receive their share, but may meet interminable delays before obtaining it.

The high cost of politics has its effect. The Election Code forbids a candidate to spend on his campaign more than a year's salary of the office he seeks. It specifically proscribes buying votes and providing free food, drink, and transportation. The Code has been a dead letter for many years and merely serves to describe what has become common practice. At the present time legislators usually spend from four to forty times their annual salary of $3,600. A candidate who is not rich or financed by wealthy interests is under a heavy handicap. If he is elected he must promote the interests of his supporters, and "rare is the individual who enters Congress a free man." [7] Furthermore the cost of living in Manila is higher than in most parts of the United States, and the majority of elected members maintain a standard of living far out of proportion to their official salary. To relieve their chronic shortage of money the presiding officers of both houses have large funds not subject to audit which they spend at their discretion to help the needy. The really deserving poor, which means the party faithful, receive much more than those who have failed in their duty. The effect of this gentle pressure is that a member must be rich or strong-minded or very ascetic in his habits to belong to the opposition.

The perquisites of office have long been an established tradition, but since 1945 the conception has become more liberal. President Quezon was far from puritanical: he knew that holders of public office were not inspired solely by disinterested zeal. He realized, however, that a country with a small revenue could not afford too wholesale a process of self-enrichment, and he disciplined those of his followers who did not exercise reasonable self-restraint. After 1945 and particularly during the Liberal regime a much more uninhibited code of conduct prevailed. An American journalist with long personal experience wrote that

This creeping corruption began at the very lowest levels of government and extended all the way to the top, except for the president himself [Quirino]. It soon became generally accepted that a suppliant could not enter a government office without being prepared to pay some sort of bribe. There were little deals at the bottom, big deals at the top. . . . Democracy was rapidly coming into disrepute. [8]

A typical example was the disposal of $100,000,000 of American government surplus property which brought $40,000,000 to the Philippine Treasury, and large profits to influential supporters of the Liberal party. Filipinos do not expect their public men to be saints, but the wholesale corruption aroused so much condemnation that greater moderation was practiced thereafter. One curious phase of the subject is the connection between law and politics. The Philippines has so many lawyers that there are not enough cases to go around, and since the words lawyer and politician are almost synonymous almost all the legislators belong to this profession. The amount of their income and the size of their fees depend less on their legal qualifications than on their influence in government departments. If an official is uncooperative the lawyer-legislator can move to delete his salary from the next appropriation bill. And so a leading legislator who has obtained a large import license or a certificate of naturalization for a Chinese client may present a lawyer's bill for $25,000 or more.

Malcolm, formerly an American Justice of the Supreme Court of the Philippines, wrote that the Filipino was a born politician who could give Tammany Hall all the aces in the pack and still win the game. Some of the methods by which a Filipino leader built up his following have been described. There were also tactics of a different kind, which became particularly prominent in the election of 1949. Padding the voters' lists was badly overdone, and the popular joke was that the birds, the bees, and the occupants of cemeteries must have gone to the polls in some districts since the number of voters almost equaled the total population. Armed gangs hired by members of the government roamed the streets and beat or killed supporters of the opposition. Judge Malcolm described the campaign as "the dirtiest and bloodiest in all Philippine history."[9] The result was a victory for President Quirino and the Liberal party. The two subsequent elections of 1951 and 1953 (which included that for the presidency itself) were on the whole conducted without violence or fraud, although there were sporadic cases of intimidation. Since the same Liberal government was in office on all three occasions, the marked contrast with its conduct in the 1949 election calls for investigation.

In 1951 President Quirino was personally in favor of a free election, and he allowed his Secretary of Defense, Magsaysay, to use the army to ensure this. It patrolled the polling areas and prevented the wholesale terrorization of voters. The Commission on Elections, the duty of which was to supervise registration and voting, investigated charges of fraud with an energy in marked contrast to its lethargy in 1949. This Commission was appointed by the President, but was powerless to act unless it had his active support. To some extent also public opinion had an influence. The flagrant abuses of the 1949 election had aroused indignation, and a National Movement for Free Elections was active in exposing electoral abuses. Its chief support came from business and professional groups in the larger towns, and to a great extent

23

it was financed and inspired by Americans. The change in electoral tactics was encouraging, though it was discouraging that so much depended on the attitude of the president. Without his support Magsaysay could not have used the army, and the Commission on Elections would have been unable to carry out its constitutional function.[10]

Magsaysay's Election

In 1953 Magsaysay resigned his position as Secretary of Defense in the Liberal Cabinet, and a few days later he was accepted by the Nationalists as leader of the party and their candidate for the presidency in the approaching election. The change was acceptable since Philippine politics emphasizes personalities and not party allegiance. Magsaysay genuinely wished to help the peasants and he was also ambitious of power. He realized that the men who controlled the Liberals would never allow him to accomplish either purpose. He could not hope to be elected without the support of a party machine and its campaign funds. Magsaysay was a leader in search of a party, and the Nationalists were a party in search of a leader. From their point of view he was the answer to prayer. His career had made him a national hero: his known incorruptibility gave him a strange and almost unique position: he was popular with the army, which might be important in the conduct of the election: and he had to a marked degree the political sex appeal which was essential for a politician. The landowners who controlled the Nationalists were as opposed to his ideas of agrarian reform as the Liberals. Once the election had been won, however, they believed they could keep him in order. Their confidence was not altogether misplaced: it took him nearly two years after his election to win a dominant voice in the party organization, and he was never able fully to carry out his plans for reform. A split in the Liberal party which took place at this time helped the Nationalists still further. A group of influential Liberals supported General Carlos Romulo in his ambition to displace Quirino as the party's candidate for the presidency. They were defeated by the Quirino clique, whereupon they seceded and eventually joined the Nationalists, after a bargain had been made on the allocation of seats in the next legislature.[11]

The election of 1953 was an overwhelming defeat for the Liberals. Magsaysay won the presidency and the Nationalists gained a large

24

majority in the legislature. This was the calmest and cleanest election since the creation of the Philippine Republic, despite some killings and numerous instances of violence. Popular support for Magsaysay was so obvious that it would have been dangerous for the government to use fraud and terrorism. His adherents were well organized: they investigated charges of fraudulent practices, combated attempts at coercion, and threatened to meet force with force. The Commission on Elections carried out its duties energetically. The Roman Catholic Church issued a solemn warning against electoral fraud, and threw the weight of its influence against Quirino. The apparent result was that the Nationalist Secretary of Education was more favorable to church schools than his predecessor.[12] About fifteen thousand soldiers policed the polling places and helped to ensure a free election. There were indications that some of the Liberal leaders would have been willing to risk a repetition of the tactics of the 1949 election. General Romulo stated and Magsaysay himself confirmed that if he lost the election by a repetition of these methods he would have used force to seize power by a *coup d'état*.[13] American pressure for a free election had an indirect effect. The government was scrupulously neutral, but made it clear that if the Liberals were re-elected by fraud and violence, they would be in no position to negotiate successfully for badly needed financial help. American correspondents in the Philippines covered the election and reported their findings in the United States. Domestic and foreign pressure combined to bring about a free election. Popular demand had a part in this result, but it was reinforced by the Filipino army and gentle pressure from the United States.

An important cause of Magsaysay's victory was the personal appeal which he made to the peasants, promising them redress of their grievances and winning their enthusiastic support.[14] He made a particular point of visiting the villages and speaking personally to a greater number of people than had ever before been reached by a presidential candidate. They were the majority of the voters, but in earlier elections few politicians had taken the trouble to visit the *barrios* or villages. They relied on their alliances with the landowners and *caciques* to control the rural vote and confined their efforts to the towns which they courted assiduously. It was the townsmen and not the peasants who received most of the "pork" and the other favors which the legislator had to bestow. Magsaysay introduced into Philippine politics the innovation of "a marathon nation-wide handshaking campaign." These tactics joined to his personal magnetism and his championship of peasant grievances won for him a mass following. He had also the support of the Nationalist party machine. It is an interesting speculation whether Magsaysay could have won if he had not had the help of an organized national party. All previous experience had shown that this was essential, and the election of 1957 bore this out. Manahan, who came closest to Magsaysay in policy and tactics but whose supporters were very poorly organized, was defeated by Garcia, a conventional politician who had the backing of the Nationalist party.

The new president was more of a "man of the people" than any of his predecessors, all of whom except Quirino had belonged to the governing class. He was not, however, of so poor and lowly an origin as he was represented to be by those who directed his election campaign. His father was at one time a teacher of carpentry in a trade school; later, though, he became the owner of a prosperous wagon works and furniture factory, and his family possessed about twenty-five hundred acres of land. But Magsaysay probably was the only president who ever worked with his hands: he began as a mechanic in a transport firm, and before the war he had become branch manager.[15] Apart from the peasants, his principal support came from some of the younger business and professional men in the towns.

The 1957 Election

On Magsaysay's death in an airplane accident he was succeeded by Vice President Garcia, an experienced politician but not one of the principal leaders. He gradually won control of his party machine by building up his own clique through the skillful use of presidential patronage and pork barrel. Once again the party represented the landowners and *caciques*, for most of the urban business and professional groups which had supported Magsaysay's reforms broke with Garcia. They formed the Progressive party and nominated as their presidential candidate for the next election Manahan, a newspaper publisher and prominent follower of Magsaysay. Senator Recto, a bitter opponent of the late president who had been by turns a Nationalist and a Liberal of sorts, came out as leader of a new and strongly nationalistic party, while the Liberals were also in the running. Apart from a few who were killed or injured and the spending of far more money by candidates than the law permitted, the election of 1957 was quiet and honest, and the people voted freely. Most of the candidates claimed to be the spiritual heirs of Magsaysay and promised to carry on his policies. In one sense at least this was true. Magsaysay's tactics of himself canvassing individual voters had given them an added sense of their own importance and compelled his successors to imitate him. It was no longer possible to rely on a combination of platform oratory and mutually beneficial arrangements with provincial governors and other local leaders. Manahan in particular surpassed even the late president in the number of villages he visited and of voters he spoke to personally. His party organization was weak, however, and neither he nor any of the Progressive candidates was elected. There were some indications that voters capitalized on their enhanced importance by demanding distributions of food or money in exchange for their support.

The Nationalists won a large majority in both houses of the legislature and Garcia was elected president. Most of the Liberal candidates were defeated, but they scored a unique success in winning the vice-presidency. Their candidate, Macapagal, defeated the Nationalist Laurel. Although a Liberal, he claimed to be Magsaysay's authentic spiritual successor, since he had voted for some of his reforms. This curious combination of a Nationalist president and a Liberal vice-president was cited as proof that the electors voted freely. It seemed to show that they did not understand their own constitution, for if Garcia had died the control of the executive would have been transferred from the victorious Nationalists, whom the voters presumably preferred, to the defeated Liberals.

Most of the victorious Nationalists were veteran politicians who could be relied upon to support the party machine. One American observer summed up his impressions by remarking that "power has returned to seasoned politicians who will rely upon trusted conservative policies . . . Parties retain their characters as cliques in which loyalties are based more on personal or sectional ties than on group interests." Agrarian reforms continued but without the vigor which Magsaysay temporarily infused into them. The popular belief was that the extent of official corruption had decidedly increased.[16] In the presi-

27

dential election of 1961 Garcia was defeated for the presidency by the Liberal Macapagal, but the Nationalist party retained control of both houses of the legislature.

Macapagal was the first president who had genuinely risen from the lower classes, and he had a good record of honesty in his political career. Even though he was a member of the Liberal party, he had supported some of Magsaysay's agrarian reforms, and in his electoral campaign he promised to enforce them vigorously. This made it certain that he would encounter the same opposition as Magsaysay from the Nationalists and from his own party. One principal reason for his victory over Garcia in 1961 was his election as vice president in 1957. Understandably Garcia did not want a Liberal to have any part in a Nationalist administration, and so for four years Macapagal had little to do except cultivate the voters. He visited and revisited more *barrios* and talked personally to more peasants than Magsaysay himself, and the same combination of political sex appeal and promises to redress agrarian grievances produced the same result. During his campaign Macapagal created his own personal political machine which defeated Garcia's Nationalist party machine. Some observers have seen in this the proof that the day of the party machine dominated by the landowners is ended, and that the age of Philippine democracy and reform is dawning. Against this is the certainty that the Nationalists retained control of both houses of the legislature, and that the nature of Filipino politicians, Nationalist and Liberal, has not changed. By the end of 1961 Macapagal had won the support of enough Nationalist members to have a majority in the lower house and create a deadlock in the senate. An observer of the Philippine democratic process explained his success as follows. "The constitutional prerogatives of the Philippine president are such that opposition offers few rewards," and legislators who have seen the light can find "ample precedents for political realignments." An explanation of these cryptic remarks can be found in the earlier part of this chapter. Despite Macapagal's success he was unable to overcome Nationalist opposition and induce the legislature to pass a law which would encourage foreign investment. He considered this essential to accelerate industrialization. It was impossible to predict whether he would be able to carry out the policy outlined in his state of the nation address of January 28, 1963. In it he declared that Magsaysay's attempts to help the tenants had been ineffective, and that he would vigorously press forward toward the conversion of sharecroppers into owners of their own farms.[17]

Burma

The government of Burma is in form an English-style democracy. The President, elected by a joint session of parliament, is little more than a constitutional figurehead. Parliament is bicameral, its dominant body the Chamber of Deputies. It is popularly elected, all citizens over eighteen having the vote. The Chamber of Nationalities or upper house is composed of elected representatives from the six states which make up the Union of Burma. The head of the government is the Prime Minister; prime minister and cabinet are collectively responsible to the Chamber of Deputies and must resign if they lose the support of a majority of the members.

Nominally the Union of Burma is a federation but in actuality it is dominated by Burma proper, which overshadows the other states in population and wealth. For most purposes the federal or Union government is the government of the whole country. When the Union was formed in 1947, Aung San, the Burman leader, persuaded the other peoples to join it in return for the creation of semi-autonomous states with the right of secession. Each state would have its own Council composed of its members in the Union parliament. In practice the degree of independence allowed the states is decidedly limited, and it is open to question whether they would be permitted to exercise their legal right of secession. The policy of the Union government is to unite all the peoples of Burma into a unified whole through Burmanization and the extension of the Buddhist religion. Whenever possible the leaders of the minority races who are appointed to office are those who are most pro-Burman.[18]

During the interwar period the British were carrying out their policy of granting self-government in instalments. Burman political life was made up of the kaleidoscopic shifts and permutations of the political parties or more accurately factions which attached themselves to the rival leaders. They were fluid groups held together by considerations of personal ambitions and profit, and there were no very distinctive programs. The governments were weak, highly unstable coalitions, and the practical working of the system established a tradition of bribery and corruption which survived the war. Members of parliament "weren't going to vote for ministers who didn't make it worth their while. Not that they were all mercenary, but they themselves were being subjected to pressure. The electorate regarded government as a cornucopia, an inexhaustible source of money and favours." Bribery and nepotism became widespread in the appointment and promotion of officials, especially in the lower grades.[19]

The Anti-Fascist People's Freedom League

The pre-war parties were combined in 1944 into the Anti-Fascist People's Freedom League (A.F.P.F.L.) under the leadership of Aung San, the head of the Thakin party. The purpose was to carry on underground resistance to the Japanese. A nation-wide organization was built up which included the countryside as well as the towns. This removed one of the greatest weaknesses of the pre-war parties. They were small cliques of English-educated, mostly living in the towns, and had little contact with the peasants. The Thakins seem to have been the dominant element in the formation of the A.F.P.F.L.[20] Their leaders were extreme nationalists who graduated from the University of Rangoon in the middle 'thirties, and became part of the Japanese fifth column after the British rejected their demand for immediate and complete self-government. When they discovered that Japan had no intention of giving Burma real independence they organized the A.F.P.F.L. They also made a secret arrangement with the British in India, by which they agreed to go over to the British side at a propitious moment. Early in 1945 a British-Indian army defeated the Japanese and began the reconquest of Burma. In March the Burmese National Army, which the Japanese had allowed Aung San to raise, deserted to the British and assisted in the closing stages of their victory.

The A.F.P.F.L. was by far the strongest political force in post-war Burma, and demanded immediate self-government in place of the British policy of gradual advance. On the British refusal the A.F.P.F.L. began to prepare for civil war, and Aung San created his private army, the People's Volunteer Organization (P.V.O.). The British Socialist Government accepted Aung San's demands, agreeing that a Constituent Assembly should be elected to draw up a constitution, and decide whether Burma should remain inside the British Commonwealth as a self-governing Dominion or leave it. The A.F.P.F.L. won ninety-six per cent of the seats, and the Assembly voted that Burma should secede and become an independent republic, the British government accepting the decision.

The Revolts

Events soon showed that the centrifugal character of Burman politics had not been ended by the formation of the A.F.P.F.L. U Saw, a pre-war prime minister, decided to take a short cut to power. He hired a group of criminals who in August assassinated Aung San and six of his ministers. Rance, the last British governor, saved the situation by arresting the assassins and appointing U Nu as prime minister. All that U Saw gained by his coup was the distinction of being the only British prime minister who was hanged. The loss of Aung San was irreparable: his influence was uniquely great and he and the other murdered ministers included most of the small number of able leaders in Burma.

The Communists seceded from the A.F.P.F.L. in 1948. They split into two factions, the Whites and the Reds, and each began a revolt against the A.F.P.F.L. government. Part of the P.V.O. also revolted from a variety of motives. Their late leader, Aung San, was the only man who could control them: to some extent they contained Marxist elements: and they were dissatisfied because they felt that an ungrateful country had not adequately rewarded their patriotic services by government appointments. A large part of the warlike Karens revolted because the government refused to allow them to form an independent state. They regarded the Burmans as enemies and oppressors, and were a curious mixture of primitives and American-trained Baptists. Thousands of *dacoits* (gang robbers) seized the unique opportunity, some operating as honest gangsters and others plundering and killing under the best Marxist auspices. The rebel armies followed the usual hit-and-run guerilla tactics which were used by the Huks, the Chinese terrorists in Malaya, and the soldiers of Ho Chi Minh in Viet Nam. The government controlled some of the towns but the

31

rebels dominated the countryside. Burma became an Irishman's paradise, with everyone fighting everyone else.

Pre-war Burma had developed a tradition of violence and contempt for law and order. The police had been unable to maintain order effectively in the countryside, dacoity had increased, and the country had the highest murder rate in the world. The A.F.P.F.L. came to power by the threat of civil war and by hamstringing the British administration through a police strike. The result was that the ideal which the British had tried to create of a government of law and order was replaced by the belief that the road to power lay through violence. In 1961 there were indications that the factions which made up U Nu's Union party government might use force against one another.

Most of the army remained loyal to the government, its numbers were increased, and by the end of 1951 all the rebel forces had been driven into the jungles and the foothills of the mountains. There was no longer any danger that the government would be overthrown. Its power, however, was limited: outside the towns its authority ceased at sunset. After dark the rebels collected food and taxes. By 1953 they had suffered further defeats and were degenerating into bandits. By 1958 thousands had surrendered but thousands remained in the jungles who lived by gang robbery. Over large areas the government was unable to restore law and order. Many peasants had abandoned their farms and fled to the towns for security. "The atmosphere of uncertainty and impermanence is ubiquitous. . . . All the work for a Welfare State and the plans for the future depend on ending the existing unrest." [21]

The A.F.P.F.L. Government

As the result of the secessions from its ranks the A.F.P.F.L. came to consist of Socialists, and until it split into two factions in 1958 Burma was virtually a single-party democracy. The parliamentary opposition was too small to be effective. This marked contrast to the multiple-party system of the British period did not mean that Burma had outgrown faction. The A.F.P.F.L. was itself a coalition of rival leaders, many supported by their own followings, who intrigued against one another for greater power within the party. The difference from the pre-war system was that until 1958 they usually contrived to stand together against opponents. Among the principal factions composing the A.F.P.F.L. were the Trade Union Congress led by U Ba Swe, the Federation of Trade Organizations, the Youth League, and the All Burma Peasant Organization. Each of them had its own organization, and its leader was a prominent member of the A.F.P.F.L. and often a cabinet minister. The A.F.P.F.L. also included subordinate communal parties among the minority races such as the Kachins, Chins, and Karens. U Nu, the Prime Minister, remarked that "political leadership is the monopoly of the educated middle classes." All the leaders were English-educated middle-class intellectuals. None of them came from the peasants or the manual laborers. Most were contemporaries in age, graduates from Rangoon University, and former members of the Thakin party. Their beliefs were a blend of ideas drawn from classical liberalism, socialism, and Buddhism. The A.F.P.F.L. was joined by many opportunists ambitious for a career, and it was Professor Tinker's opinion that the majority of the lesser leaders at any rate were "bullies and bosses" who were interested only in power, prestige, and financial advantages. J. S. Furnivall, who was adviser to the government of Burma, agreed with this opinion and quoted the belief of U Nu that there was a good deal of corruption. This extended to the civil service, where appointments were made by political influence.[22]

The peasants were the principal support of the A.F.P.F.L., and the All Burma Peasant Organization was set up to keep them within the fold. The party machine extended into the villages, with an agent in every district. A local man with wide influence in his own area, he was in close touch with the A.F.P.F.L. leaders in Rangoon. He had nothing to do with the formulation of policy, for this was determined by the central committee. The A.F.P.F.L. was not an example of "grass-roots democracy" but of control from the top; the principal duty of the local agent was to see to it that its members supported the party when called upon to do so. By way of compensation he was a petty autocrat in his own district. It was he who was the real ruler and not the Deputy Commissioner, the civil servant who was officially in charge of the district. The latter had learnt from experience that if he opposed the party boss the government would punish instead of supporting him and therefore he did what the A.F.P.F.L. agent ordered. Professor Tinker

33

described many of them as acting the tyrant in their own neighborhoods, giving orders to the Deputy Commissioner, harassing their personal enemies, and levying a quiet blackmail on all local economic and social activities. The home guard, created and armed by the government to protect isolated communities from the rebels, became the private army of local A.F.P.F.L. leaders and was sometimes used to terrorize the population. In 1958 U Nu ordered it disbanded.[23]

U Nu was a devout Buddhist and a believer in democracy. He had not organized a faction of his own, and he never fully controlled the party even though he was its leader. He often voiced the wish to give up politics and retire to a monastery. He was likewise a very astute and skillful politician, who realized that too idealistic a devotion to high principles was a luxury which he could not afford. He was genuinely convinced that only a revival of Buddhism with its insistence on non-violence could restore peace and save Burma from the delusion of worldly desire which produced hatred and warfare. Expressed in terms of practical politics, his belief was that to counter Communism the primary reliance must be upon Buddhism and not the army. He appreciated the very great influence which the monks had over the laity, and saw that their support would bring in many votes to himself and the A.F.P.F.L. He restored the church to the position which it had held before the British regime, but he refused to allow the monks to interfere in politics apart from counseling the people to refrain from violence and obey the government's orders. His devotion to Buddhism and his support of the monks were one principal reason for his wide popular support. In U Nu's mixture of sincere belief and realization that faith and political expediency went hand in hand he resembled Gandhi, who was a combination of Hindu holy man and astute politician.

Elections

The first election after the establishment of the republic took place in 1951, when the government was gaining the upper hand in the civil war. The A.F.P.F.L. won three quarters of the seats in the legislature, and despite some charges of dishonesty the result seems to have been a fair approximation to the actual state of public opinion. In the next election, in 1956, the A.F.P.F.L. ran against the Communist-dominated

National Unity Front (N.U.F.) and several weak conservative groups. The dominating element in the N.U.F. was a left-wing Socialist faction in the A.F.P.F.L. which seceded from the party in 1950, called itself the Burma Workers' and Peasants' Party, and became a Communist-front party. The A.F.P.F.L. had strong advantages owing to its well-developed machine and its control of government funds. In spite of this the opposition did much better than had been expected, especially in the rural areas. Of the votes actually cast the A.F.P.F.L. received 55.9 per cent and 173 seats, the opposition 36.9 per cent and 55 seats, and independents 7.2 per cent and 22 seats. There was a background of violence with a few murders committed by each side, but this had been standard practice in elections ever since the British began to introduce self-government in 1922. The salient point was the challenge to the claim of the A.F.P.F.L. that it was the sole voice of the Burmese people, and that any opposition to it could be ignored as factious. The reason why it fared worse than it had expected seems to have been "the arrogance, self seeking and indifference of most of the lesser A.F.P.F.L. leaders, which separated them from the party's rank and file and from the electorate." Discontent with the inability of the government to restore peace and prevent the plundering raids of rebels and dacoits was also widespread.[24] As a result of the election U Nu resigned his position as prime minister in order to purge his party of corruption and reorganize it. He does not seem to have been successful in this endeavor.

The Division of the A.F.P.F.L.

The centrifugal tendency in Burman politics reached its climax in 1958 when the A.F.P.F.L. split into two factions, one headed by U Nu and the other by U Ba Swe. The underlying reason was that each suspected the other of intriguing to oust him from his position of power in the party and the government.[25] Personal rivalries and not serious differences of policy were the cause. U Nu and U Ba Swe had been allies in their fight against British and Japanese rule and the rebellions against the republic. This had created a bond of union, but gradually it weakened and broke under the strain of personal ambition for power and conflicting ideas about which measures were most important at the moment.

A parliamentary division on June 9, 1958, showed that the majority of the A.F.P.F.L. supported U Ba Swe against U Nu. In the course of debate the opposing groups vied with one another in accusations of corruption, nepotism, and undue influence. U Nu won by eight votes because he received the support of the opposition N.U.F. From then onwards his retention of office depended upon Communist support. U Nu's faction took the name of the Clean A.F.P.F.L. and U Ba Swe's the Stable A.F.P.F.L. U Nu offered to all Communist rebels who surrendered an amnesty and the restoration of full rights of citizenship. The Communists had been demanding for some time that they be allowed to form a political party, since their attempt to overthrow the government by force had failed. U Nu also released many political prisoners, and ordered the army to abandon determined operations against the Communists.[26] Public security had been poor even before the issuance of these orders. Conditions now became worse because while many bandits surrendered, others began to terrorize the villages in order to increase the power of the Communist party. The Socialists and other factions began to strengthen their private armies.

In September 1958 U Nu announced over the radio that he had asked General Ne Win, the commander of the army, to assume the prime ministership and re-establish order so that free elections could be held. The general stipulated that the Chamber of Deputies must elect him and that his cabinet should include no members from the political parties. He was to hold office for six months, but later at his request parliament extended the period by another six months, since he found himself unable to carry out his task in the time originally allotted to him. It is not certain whether military intervention was at the request of U Nu, who was alarmed at the results of his concessions to the Communists, or whether the army, which was strongly anti-Communist, decided that the state of the country required it to act. Both U Nu and the general insisted that it was the former's idea. At any rate U Nu resigned in October, and Ne Win became prime minister.

The Ne Win Dictatorship

Army officers were appointed to many of the most important positions in the administration, but Ne Win respected constitutional forms and tried to work with parliament. The army took vigorous action against the rebel bandits, and their number as well as that of the *dacoits* was greatly decreased. To a large extent law and order were restored. Ne Win attacked corruption in the government and arrested some supporters of U Nu on charges that ran the gamut from murder to petty graft. The army enforced various measures which were essential but highly unpopular. It rehoused the fugitives who were living in insanitary hovels in Rangoon, and it compelled the local citizens to remove the accumulated refuse of years from the streets. The economic measures introduced by Ne Win are discussed elsewhere. The army also established the National Solidarity Association of citizens, with branches in the towns and villages, and two senior officers as leaders. Its purposes were to assist the army in combating lawlessness and to educate the people in their civic rights and duties. The Association was to be non-partisan and to take no part in party politics. It was widely disliked and became politically unimportant soon after U Nu returned to power.

Restoration of Civil Government

In 1960 a free election was held and no officers were candidates, in accordance with Ne Win's belief that the army should take no part in government and leave this to civilian politicians. U Nu's Clean A.F.P.F.L. won an overwhelming victory. In Burma proper it obtained 57.2 per cent of the votes and 149 seats: the Stable A.F.P.F.L. received 30.7 per cent and 30 seats: and the N.U.F. got a mere 4.8 per cent and no seats. In 1956 it received 36.9 per cent of the vote and 55 seats. Apparently a large number of those who voted for it in 1956 did so as a protest against the A.F.P.F.L. and not out of support for Communism. Several factors contributed to U Nu's victory, of which the most important seem to have been his personal popularity and the support of the Buddhist monks. What has been called his "religious aura" was a great asset. The average voter and perhaps particularly the women regarded him as a good man, and they liked his simple and unostentatious way of life and behavior. He won the support of the monks by promising to make Buddhism the state religion. Each party used a color as its symbol during the election, and U Nu thoughtfully chose yellow, the sacred Buddhist color, with which to paint his ballot boxes, and also put his picture on them. This recalls an election years ago in Ceylon when a Buddhist Sinhalese running against a Hindu Tamil won an overwhelming majority by using the same color and conveying the impression that he was the favored candidate of the Lord Buddha. The religious appeal was reinforced by the astute manner in which U Nu made capital out of the unpopularity which the army had gained by compelling the Burmans to do things they did not want to do. U Nu was careful not to oppose Ne Win in parliament, but in his speeches he conveyed the impression to the public that he was against such fascist regimentation. He likewise contrived to identify the Stable A.F.P.F.L. with army rule, because it had tended to support Ne Win's policy. In the fourth place U Nu had a better party machine than his opponents, and also a large campaign fund.[27]

The election gave Burma a second chance to establish democracy. Some observers believed that Ne Win had eliminated the worst of the corruption in political life, and part of the inefficiency. His relinquishment of power seemed to show that he was sincere when he said that the soldiers should be the servants of the state and not its masters. It was true that the army did not hold the dominating position which it had in Indonesia, and that its rule had become unpopular. Generally, however, military dictators were not overly influenced by such considerations, and Ne Win had the support of some sixty thousand well-trained and well-equipped soldiers. All things considered it appeared that the politicians were free to show whether they could do better next time. But it was impossible to believe that conditions could ever be quite the same again. The politicians would have been wise to remember that the army had intervened to rectify their shortcomings, and that this could be a precedent for the same thing happening again.

From its inception the government of Burma was controlled by a small English-educated elite, most of whom worked together and sometimes intrigued against one another for some twenty years. They often seemed out of touch with the peasants and rather contemptuous of them. Sometimes they meted out highhanded treatment to political opponents who opposed them in a constitutional manner.[28] One link between the elite and the peasants was the Buddhist monks, and another the local A.F.P.F.L. leader. The latter could not be described as a democratic institution, though he was preferable to the *cacique* in the Philippines. On the whole the press was uncensored, and elections free from bribery, intimidation, and fraudulent voting. The peasants had the traditional attitude that government was a power above and outside them and not one which they had the right to control. At the same time they were individualistic to the point of anarchy. The traditional practice was to follow a local leader whose moral authority was respected. He might be a Buddhist monk, a local A.F.P.F.L. agent, or the village headman, and not necessarily at all a civil servant. If he counseled support of the government the peasants followed his lead, and equally so if he led a revolt. This psychological trait was one reason for the lawlessness in the rural areas which marked the British period. The same proneness to violence was shown in the revolts against the republic. Whether Burma would eventually become a democracy depended in part on whether the propensity to factiousness and intrigue could be held in check more than in the past. Here much was expected from U Nu who himself was a believer in democracy. It was hoped that with his wide influence he would be able firmly to establish it. As against this there was some slight evidence that many educated Burmans were disillusioned about the applicability of democracy as it had been practiced in Burma, and contrasted it unfavorably with the efficiency and honesty of Ne Win's government.[29] U Nu's renewed tenure of power was not calculated to reassure them.

The *Coup d'État* of 1962

In March 1962 General Ne Win again took over control, and this time it was clear that he was not acting in response to the prime minister's invitation. He did not show the same careful respect for constitutionality which had marked his earlier intervention. U Nu was arrested along with a large number of other politicians, the legislature was suspended, and a cabinet was installed almost all the members of which were army officers. Ne Win became both prime minister and chief of state. Burma was placed under military rule, and the political parties were told that they could continue their activity on the condition that they supported the dictatorship. It was intimated that eventually the country would be given back to civilian rule, but that first of all the constitution must be rewritten and extensive reforms carried out. The impression was given that the return of the politicians to power was likely to be postponed for quite a long time.

General Ne Win gave as the reason for his intervention that U Nu's government had brought about an "economic and political crisis" from inefficiency and weakness. The principal accusation was that he had been weak in dealing with the pressure of the Shans and other minorities for greater autonomy as opposed to the policy of Burmanization and central control which the government had followed in the past. The Kachins and Karens made common cause with the Shans and revolts broke out. At first U Nu refused all concessions, but in October 1961 he agreed to negotiate. He also promised separate states to the Arakanese and the Mons. The army was afraid that the unity of the republic would be endangered if the government became genuinely federal instead of virtually unitary. This was the immediate occasion for the *coup d'état*. Another cause was the renewal of the struggle for power between the rival factions that made up the Union party, as U Nu's supporters now called themselves. In 1961 reports began to circulate that local leaders were afraid that U Nu planned to get rid of those who did not fully support his leadership and reunite the A.F.P.F.L. These malcontents were reported to have collected arms and engaged in plots. The bandits too seemed to be recovering their strength, and law and order to be deteriorating. The army officers were also dissatisfied with the way in which the government was carrying out its Socialist policy. A description is given in Chapter XI of the very moderate degree of success achieved in the years prior to the first military intervention in 1958. The army was not opposed to socialism: on the contrary it wanted to go faster and farther than U Nu thought expedient. It was, however, critical of the inefficiency and corruption which were among the reasons for the failure of the civil administration to reach its goals. In 1961 Brigadier General Aung Gyi, the second in command, apparently declared that after a dozen years of civilian rule "we still cannot manufacture a needle . . . At this rate our country will go to the dogs." After his return to power in 1960 U Nu extended the field of state socialism by nationalizing import trade. There were reports that one at least of the motives was the profit which accrued to some of U Nu's supporters. The result was a sharp rise in prices and the cost of living which alarmed the army. It lost patience with the combination of mismanagement, inefficiency, and weakness which it regarded as the hallmarks of government by the politicians and imposed its own control. For the second time U Nu had failed to acclimatize democracy.

40

The result was that the politician was subordinated to the soldier for an indefinite time to come.[30]

Malaya

The government of the United Kingdom announced in 1917 that its policy in India and the dependencies was gradually to transfer power from British officials to elected native leaders until eventually complete self-government was established. By 1941 India and Burma were close to the goal. The government of Malaya was, as it had been in 1917, a benevolent despotism controlled by British officials. The explanation was that there was no Malayan people to whom power could be transferred. In the Philippines the Americans were able to hand over the reins to the Christian Filipinos, ignoring the two small minorities of the Moros and the Pagan tribes. In Indonesia there were the Indonesians, and in Burma the Burmans were two thirds of the population. But in Malaya there were three separate and antagonistic communities, the Malays, Chinese, and Indians. None had even a simple majority of the population, and each disliked and contemned the other two. If democratic self-government were built on this foundation every election would record that the electorate divided three ways according to race, and that the spirit of cooperation and compromise was totally absent. A very probable result would be civil war.

Singapore had been predominantly Chinese in population from the date of its foundation in 1819, but the Malay States of the Peninsula had had only a small minority of Chinese until the British took over control in the eighteen seventies and later. Once they had established law and order Chinese immigrants entered on so large a scale that they radically transformed the racial character of the country. The Indians arrived in much smaller numbers as laborers especially on the European rubber estates. Before World War II the bulk of the Chinese and Indians were transients: they came to Malaya because economic opportunities were far better than in their native countries, and eventually returned home with their savings. A minority had settled permanently in Malaya, but part even of these regarded China or India as their native country and Malaya as a temporary place of exile which they would leave when they could afford to return home. The Malays were the only permanent element in the population.

41

The situation has changed in the past quarter of a century. From 1930 onwards the entrance of male Chinese was restricted by quota, but no limitation was imposed on women and children. They arrived in large numbers and transformed the Chinese sex ratio. In the peninsula the proportion of females to males changed from 384 per thousand in 1931 to 833 per thousand in 1947.[31] Enormous numbers of Chinese homes were established. The parents usually came as laborers and probably had no intention of settling permanently. In 1937, however, Japan invaded China, and this was followed by World War II and the civil war which ended in the victory of Mao Tse-tung. For a quarter of a century it has been difficult and often impossible to return to China, and many of the Chinese now appear to regard Malaya as their permanent home. By 1957 70 per cent of them had been born there. This does not mean that they have a Malayan patriotism: indications point rather to the growth of Chinese nationalism.

The reasons for the unpopularity of the Chinese are the same as those in the other countries of Southeast Asia, and are discussed in another chapter. The Malays dislike the Indians for similar reasons, but the problem is much less serious since they are only a small proportion of the population. The size of the Chinese community makes the situation in Malaya unique. In 1948 the proportion of Chinese to the people of the country was .5 per cent in the Philippines, 1.6 per cent in Indochina, 2.1 per cent in Indonesia, and 15.6 per cent in Thailand. In Malaya as a whole the Chinese in 1947 were 44.9 per cent of the total population, the Malays 43.3 per cent, and the Indians 10.4 per cent. In the Federation of Malaya the Malays were 49.2 per cent and the Chinese 38.6 per cent, while in Singapore the Chinese were 77.4 per cent and the Malays only 12.1 per cent.[32] The Malays had become a minority in their own country.

The Benevolent Despotism

A further complication prior to World War II was that the Malays had a strong aristocratic tradition, and believed that the control of government was the prerogative of the Sultan. Their attitude was summed up in the remark, "We like government to consult our interests; but when government gives an order we like to obey it." Unfortunately the Sultans with very few exceptions were incapable of grappling with the problems of the twentieth century. The Chinese were very much more advanced, astute, and aggressive. To a large extent the Malays were under their economic control. If democracy were set up it would not be long before the Chinese had political control as well. The British government felt a special responsibility toward the Malays since it had taken over control of the peninsula at the invitation of the rulers and not by conquest. Its policy was that parliamentary democracy could not be established until they had be-come capable of holding their own against the other communities.

Meanwhile the government must continue to be carried on by Euro-pean and to a growing extent Malay administrators under the control of the Governor of the Straits Settlements (Singapore, Penang, and Malacca), who was also High Commissioner for the Malay States. He was assisted by advisory councils which contained a minority of unofficial or popular members nominated by him to represent the different races and economic interests. Constitutionally he was an autocrat but in practice he rarely used his legal powers and ruled by compromise and persuasion. This conciliatory attitude explained in large part why before the war the demand for self-government was negligible. There was general agreement that the government was hon-est, impartial, reasonably efficient, and conscientious. The Malays felt that it protected them against the Chinese and safeguarded their special rights. The Chinese, Indians, and Europeans approved a regime which promoted their economic interests, and most of them were far too engrossed in their own business affairs to pay much attention to anything else. Altogether the general feeling was that any change would probably be for the worse.

Post-war Reforms

After the war the United Kingdom government resolved drastically to alter its policy. One decision was that it was preposterous to have eleven governments in a country the size of Florida, and that they should be reduced to two. Before the war each of the nine Malay States had its own government: four of them were joined in the Federated Malay States: and the eleventh government was the Crown Colony of the Straits Settlements. Under the new arrangement Singapore would be a separate colony, while the nine Malay States, Penang, and

Malacca would be combined in the Malayan Union. Virtually all power would be concentrated in the Union government, though each state would have a council with such authority as might be delegated to it. It was also decided to force the pace toward democracy, and give completely equal rights of citizenship to Malays, Chinese, and Indians. The whole policy of safeguarding the special position of the Malays was abandoned without consulting them. The Chinese and Indians had made no demand for citizenship, and showed no interest in the new proposals.

To facilitate the carrying out of the reforms the Malay sultans were compelled to sign treaties by which they transferred all their rights of legal sovereignty to the British crown. A special envoy, Sir Harold MacMichael, was sent out in 1945 to obtain their signatures, and he seems to have crashed his way through each royal court with all the delicacy and finesse of a runaway bulldozer. The significance of the treaties was this: Legally the sovereignty in each state lay with its sultan, and the authority of the British officials rested on the treaty by which he agreed to govern in accordance with the advice of his British adviser or resident. In practice this gave the British complete control, and the sultan had become a constitutional figurehead. Every act of government, however, had to be done in his name, as the source of all authority. By the MacMichael treaties he would cease to hold this position, and would occupy his throne as an insubstantial ghost.

MacMichael's mission and the reforms accomplished the miracle of making the Malays politically minded. Societies to oppose the new policy were set up all over Malaya, and in 1946 they joined to form the United Malay National Organization (U.M.N.O.). It was a communal party which only Malays could join, and its policy was Malaya for the Malays and no equal rights for Chinese and Indians. The leaders were not the sultans but the English-educated Malays, the majority of whom belonged to the aristocracy, including hereditary territorial chiefs who held high office in the state governments. The principal leader was Dato Onn bin Jaafar, *mentri besar* (chief minister) of Johore.

The Federation of Malaya

The British government now did what it should have done in the first place, and in 1946 consulted the Malays about the new constitution. The MacMichael treaties were abrogated, and the sultans regained their position as the legal sovereigns. The Union government was transformed into a federation. Power was divided between the federal and state governments, with the former as the dominant authority in legislation, finance, and the executive. This was inevitable in so small a country since many questions such as health transcended state boundaries and required uniform treatment. The special rights of the Malays were safeguarded. Citizenship was opened to Chinese and Indians, but the qualifications were defined so as to ensure that as few as possible could qualify. Since all Malays were citizens, this would give them a large majority when voting should be introduced for the federal Legislative Council. Temporarily it was to consist of seventy-five members, of whom fourteen were officials while the unofficials were nominated by the High Commissioner. He was the chief executive and was assisted by an Executive Council made up of official and unofficial members. Each state and settlement was to have an Executive Council and a Council of State, the sultan being the chief executive. The Federation of Malaya was established in February 1948.

Communal Politics

Prior to the war there had been outward harmony between Malays and Chinese, although there were signs that this was coming to an end. Working on the principle of divide and rule, the Japanese stirred up the latent hostility of the Malays, and the Chinese Communist guerillas aggravated it by killing and plundering unarmed Malay peasants to persuade them to cooperate. Following on this came the MacMichael treaties, the British proposals for a Malayan Union, and the formation of U.M.N.O. Malay nationalism and communalism became conscious and organized, and dominated the new federation. It was not long before the Chinese followed suit. They had been indifferent to the offer of equal citizenship in the Malayan Union scheme until it was modified under Malay pressure, whereupon they protested vigorously at the curtailment of the privileges originally extended to them. The Indians objected that insufficient attention was paid to their rights.

In 1949 Tan Cheng-Lock, a wealthy and influential Chinese, founded the Malayan Chinese Association (M.C.A.). One purpose was to agitate for the improvement of their status under the federal constitution.

The second was to unite their community in an organization which would try to counter the efforts of the Communists to win the support of the poorer Chinese for the revolt which had broken out in 1948. Membership was open to Chinese who had been born in Malaya or lived there for at least five years and intended to remain permanently. Non-Chinese might be admitted as associate members, but in practice the M.C.A. was a Chinese communal party. Its policy was equal rights for all, with the unwritten conclusion that with free competition the Chinese would win. The M.C.A. was led by a group of wealthy and influential Chinese business men, and resembled U.M.N.O. in the predominance of the conservative element of the community. The Malayan Indian Congress (M.I.C.) was organized to promote Indian interests. Representing a minority, its policy might have been summed up by the British socialist slogan of fair shares for all.

Malaya now had three communal and exclusive parties, which mirrored the threefold division of the population. Moreover, many of the Indians and Chinese felt that their loyalty was to their country of origin and not to Malaya. Chinese nationalism was much stronger than before the war and was growing. In the following years, communal antagonism became stronger and not weaker, despite the efforts of the British government to foster unity. The auguries for the acclimatization of democracy were not good. Before it could hope to succeed the three races must learn to work together, and two of them must think of themselves as Malayans and not as Chinese or Indians living in Malaya.

The Alliance

Dato Onn, the founder of U.M.N.O., tried to bridge the gap between the three races. He began to feel that communalism was injurious to all, and urged U.M.N.O. to admit non-Malays to membership. Failing in this he broke away and in 1951 founded the Independence of Malaya party (I.M.P.) which was non-communal and accepted members from all races. He was succeeded as president of U.M.N.O. by Tengku Abdul Rahman, a brother of the Sultan of Kedah. Dato Onn lost the support of the Malays and failed to obtain that of the Chinese. However, his venture had the curious result that it induced the two leading communal parties to cooperate in order to defeat the only non-communal party. U.M.N.O. and M.C.A. collaborated in the municipal elections of 1952–1953, with the result that they won an overwhelming majority of the seats and I.M.P. was disastrously defeated. Their success suggested to the leaders that their alliance might profitably be extended into the field of federal politics. U.M.N.O. had most of the votes, M.C.A. could provide the necessary funds, and both the Malay and Chinese leaders were hostile to Dato Onn. The difficulty was that in accordance with the federal constitution of 1948 none of the members of the Legislative Council were elected. The U.M.N.O.-M.C.A. Alliance demanded in 1953 that the majority of the seats be made elective. In 1954 the government announced that the members would be increased from seventy-five to ninety-eight, of whom fifty-two would be elected.

The election was held in 1955, and the U.M.N.O.-M.C.A. Alliance, which was joined by the M.I.C., won fifty-one out of the fifty-two elected seats. Dato Onn dropped his moribund I.M.P. and came out as leader of a new Party Negara which advocated Malay communalism and attacked the Chinese. His rapid reversals of attitude created the suspicion that he was an opportunist, and he did not win a single seat. Examination of the results of the election showed that this was a Malay rather than a Malayan victory. By far the greater part of those who voted were Malays, for not only were they the majority of the electorate but in addition something like three quarters of the Chinese and Indians who had the franchise did not go to the trouble of registering. This was in keeping with their usual apathy about taking part in public affairs. The allocation of seats among Malays, Chinese, and Indians was decided before the election by the leaders of the three parties, and the voters were informed that they must support the official Alliance candidate. This explained why most of the Chinese were elected in constituencies which had a Malay majority, and was a tribute to the control of U.M.N.O. over its community.

Legally the constitution of 1948 was still in force, but so far as its provisions allowed the control of the federal government was transferred to the Alliance. They had a majority in the Legislative Council, and ten of the fifteen members of the Executive Council were appointed from their number by the High Commissioner on the advice of the Alliance leader and Chief Minister, Tengku Abdul Rahman. The High Commissioner refrained from using his legal powers to override his councils and governed in accordance with their advice, so that in practice the Alliance virtually controlled the legislature and executive. In 1956 a conference was held in London, and it was agreed that the Federation should be granted independence by the end of August 1957. The program was carried out and in two years the Federation moved from a government with a nominated legislature under the ultimate control of the Colonial Office to the status of an autonomous and equal partner in the British Commonwealth. The speed of change exceeded all previous advances to self-government.

The Tempo of Advance

The pre-war method under the policy of self-government by instalments was that a period of years must elapse at each stage during which the dependency served its apprenticeship in learning how to govern itself democratically by using the powers progressively given to it. In India this plan was carried out in twenty-eight years (1919–1947) and in the Philippines in thirty-nine (1907–1946). There was always a difference between the pace at which the ruling power felt it wise to transfer authority to an inexperienced people and the speed with which the dependency demanded a larger measure of self-government. The imperial government had to choose between granting power faster than it genuinely felt was wise, and opposing the colonial demand, with the certainty that this would create hostility. No satisfactory halfway house was ever found between complete control and complete self-government. The demand for independence would appear first of all among the small minority of the Western-educated. Gradually they would enlist the support of more and more of the population. Eventually the ruling power would be confronted with a national demand which it would not resist even if it were possible to do so. The colonial powers were democracies at home, and their traditions and public opinion would not in the long run allow their governments to oppose a widespread popular demand for self-government. After World War II the tempo accelerated. Asian nationalism was stronger and more impatient and there was an attitude of suspicion and hostility toward Western powers much greater than before 1939. Any hesitation in granting demands met a far more explosive response than before the war, and a period of apprenticeship as long as those served by India and the Philippines was dismissed as preposterous.

Nationalism in Malaya appeared later than in most parts of Asia. What then developed was three antagonistic nationalisms, and the British government had little success in its attempts to create a Malayan nationalism which would unite them. As long as this continued it had to remain as an impartial arbitrator. Lyttleton, the Secretary of State for the Colonies, expressed an opinion widely held by Malayans as well as Europeans when he said in 1952 that if the British withdrew in six months the country would be plunged into racial conflict. The formation of the Alliance was the first indication of the willingness of the three communities to work together. It was not a union of the three races, but that was too much to expect. They would not amalgamate and intermarry, but one could hope that in time they would settle down to an attitude of live and let live. Meanwhile the leaders had arranged a marriage of convenience which was obviously to their advantage. If it survived, here at last was a party if not a Malayan people to which control of the government could be surrendered. It was disconcerting that the chief hope of overcoming communal antagonism lay in a bargain between the leaders of three frankly communal parties. The question was whether the self-interest which had brought them together would continue. There was also the problem whether they could control their followers. Under the surface the Chinese still regarded the Malays as ornamental incompetents, and the Malays disliked and feared the Chinese. The Alliance leaders however had the support of a policitically minded minority, and by acceding to them the government of Great Britain kept fairly well abreast of articulate public opinion.

The demand for self-government came from U.M.N.O. rather than M.C.A. The leaders of U.M.N.O. were drawn largely from the aristocracy and with their traditional right of leadership the probability was that they could hold the allegiance of the peasants. Their policy was to make considerable concessions to the Chinese to win their cooperation, and there was the danger that the Pan Malayan Islamic party might win over the Malays by arousing their hostility to the Chinese and their loyalty to their religion. This party had won one elected seat out of fifty-two in the election of 1955. It combined extreme Malay nationalism with the demand that the Federation become an orthodox Islamic state. There was a small group of Malay leftists which included

49

journalists and English-educated students who opposed the conservative leadership of U.M.N.O., but it seemed unlikely that they could attract enough of a following to threaten its predominance. The U.M.N.O. leaders were friendly to the British connection, and on the whole the chances seemed good that they would retain their control of the Malays.

The Chinese were a far from united community, and the English-educated leaders of M.C.A. had less control over their members than had those of U.M.N.O. The English-speaking Chinese included most of the wealthiest business men, many of them belonging to families which had lived in Malaya for several generations and were partially anglicized. To some extent they were affected by Chinese nationalism, but they were interested chiefly in making money. They also wanted political power, and they were the self-appointed leaders of M.C.A. Traditionally the Chinese looked up to successful business men as their leaders so that their position seemed assured, but actually it was under attack. Over against them were the later arrivals, many born in Malaya but others alien immigrants. After the war a marked growth of Chinese nationalism appeared, particularly among the younger generation. It was strongest among the Chinese-speaking, but was gaining ground among the English-speaking as well. Some of the Chinese-speaking opponents of the leaders of M.C.A. were coming forward as leaders of the nationalist Chinese. Others were the sons of wealthy English-speaking Chinese who were in revolt against their fathers' standard of values. The leaders of M.C.A. did not have the same control over their party as the Malay aristocrats had over U.M.N.O. There were serious internal dissensions and it is still uncertain whether the present conservative leaders will be able to maintain their position. The mass of the Chinese, however, are much too busy earning a living to trouble themselves about politics, and they are not interested in democracy.

The Federal Constitution

Federal nationality and citizenship were granted automatically to all born in the Federation on or after independence day, August 31, 1957. The same rights could be acquired without much difficulty by the majority of the large existing alien population of Chinese and Indians. The special rights of the Malays were safeguarded, and Malay would be the only national language, although for ten years English might be used for all official purposes. The demand was rejected that Chinese be given an equal status with Malay, and that speeches in the legislatures might be made in Chinese or in an Indian language.

The Federation was to be a constitutional monarchy, the head of state or Yang di-Pertuan Agong being chosen for a five-year term by the nine sultans from among themselves in order of seniority. He must in general act in accordance with the advice of the prime minister and cabinet. They were responsible to the federal parliament, which was bicameral. The Senate had thirty-eight members, twenty-two elected by the state and settlement legislatures and sixteen appointed by the head of state. The House of Representatives had a hundred members (a hundred and four in the first federal legislature), elected in single-member constituencies by universal suffrage. The Supreme Court had jurisdiction in disputes between states or between a state and the Federation. The government of each of the nine Malay states would consist of the sultan, the executive, and the legislature. The sultan would be a constitutional ruler acting on the advice of his *mentri besar* or chief minister. The *mentri besar* and the ministers chosen by him comprised the executive council and were collectively responsible to the legislative assembly, which was popularly elected. The governments of Penang and Malacca were similar, except that in place of a sultan there was a governor appointed for four years by the Yang di-Pertuan Agong. The division of powers between the federal and subordinate governments was very similar to what it had been in the previous constitution. Federal powers embraced almost all the major activities of government, and included the principal sources of revenue. The taxing powers of the states were so limited that they were dependent on federal grants to cover the bulk of their expenditure. The Federation continued to overshadow the states in the fields of legislation, the executive, and finance.

The Alliance was based on a tacit agreement that the Malays would be in a superior position in the political field and the Chinese in that of economics. Governmental action would continue to be taken to assist the Malays gradually to improve their economic position, but without any serious discrimination against the Chinese. If either community tried to override the compact it could disrupt the U.M.N.O.-M.C.A. Alliance. The federal constitution was attacked by extreme nationalists in both camps. U.M.N.O. was criticized for making it too easy for Chinese to obtain citizenship, and because it did too little to raise Malay living standards. Chinese complained because the Chinese language was not given an equal status with Malay. Many teachers in the Chinese private schools denounced as an attack on Chinese culture the Alliance decision that in order to get a government subsidy they must give their curriculum a Malayan emphasis in addition to teaching Chinese subjects. The teachers received considerable support from the Chinese-speaking.

The Election of 1959

In its election campaign the Alliance put its major stress upon the necessity for all three communities to abandon exclusive nationalism and put in their place a new Malayan nationalism based on cooperation and mutual tolerance. Speakers warned of the danger from the opposition parties which based their appeal on race, class, or religion. They argued from sheer reasonableness, but the argument was strengthened by an election device which was simple and on the whole effective, so long as the party leaders could control their followers. Instead of running against each other they eliminated competition by arranging how many representatives of each community should be allowed to stand for election. Thus there was only one Alliance candidate in each constituency, and the three party organizations did their utmost to ensure that their full voting strength supported the Malay, Chinese, or Indian who was nominated. The election was free and honest, and the democratic process was not assisted by intimidation or fraudulent voting.

An American observer remarked of the opposition that it "generally focuses upon issues which divide and not those which unite, and upon policies which would serve to disrupt rather than to promote good government and cordial relationships with the Western world." The most successful of the opposition parties, the Pan Malayan Islamic party, demanded an ultra-nationalist Malay state based on Islamic law and the abolition of imperialism as represented by the military alliance with the United Kingdom and the loss of Singapore. The party did not explain how Malay nationalism would be strengthened by regaining Singapore, since the addition of a predominantly Chinese population would mean that the Malays would be outnumbered in their own homeland. The party's strength lay among the uneducated, devout Muslim peasants of the conservative states of Kelantan and Trengganu, "who are apt to regard religious embellishments in political oratory as evidence of piety and probity." The opposition also included several small labor parties which drew their principal support from the towns and the tin-mining state of Perak. Small labor parties were weak in the villages where the decisive political power still lies. They tried to attract Chinese voters by condemning Malay nationalism and advocating equal rights for all Malayans. They also demanded a planned socialist economy, the nationalization of the tin and rubber companies, and the imposition of higher taxes upon them (which seemed somewhat contradictory). Dato Onn and his Party Negara gave the impression that their only clear aim was that they wanted to be elected.

The Alliance won seventy-seven of the hundred and four seats in the federal House of Representatives, but its percentage of the vote fell to 51.5 per cent as compared with 79.6 per cent in 1955. The vote of the Pan Malayan Islamic party rose from almost 4 per cent to nearly 21 per cent, and that of the labor parties from less than 1 per cent to 19 per cent. The M.C.A. vote was decreased since some members broke away and ran as independents because the party did not insist strongly enough upon the claims of the Chinese, especially in education.[33] Obviously the Alliance no longer possesses the overwhelming popular support which it had in 1955, although this is not surprising. A government which follows a sane and moderate policy in a country with acute communal antagonisms would be certain to lose the votes of the extremists. It is also evident that communalism continues and is a threat to the Alliance. What no one can foresee is whether its middle-of-the-road policy will continue to hold the majority of the voters, or whether extremism will defeat it. If this were to happen it might end in civil war, and a dictatorship might be the only way to prevent disaster. To avoid this it is essential that the Alliance continue to form the government for a long time to come.

Singapore

Singapore became a separate Crown Colony on April 1, 1946. The principal reason for its exclusion from the Malayan Union was that if it were added with its predominantly Chinese population the Malays

53

would be outnumbered. The government consisted of a governor, an executive, and a legislative council. The councils were composed of official and unofficial or popular members. Since British policy was the progressive establishment of self-government an increasing number of the unofficials were elected instead of being appointed by the governor. The vote was given to all British subjects over twenty-one, male and female, most of the voters being Chinese. Over half the adult population were alien immigrants from China and therefore did not have the franchise. It had been found that the large majority of the qualified voters would not take the trouble to register. So in 1954 it was announced that from then onwards they would be automatically registered, in the hope that this would induce more to vote. There was to be a Legislative Assembly where twenty-five out of the thirty-two members were popularly elected, three were officials and four unofficials appointed by the governor. The executive council would be replaced by a Council of Ministers composed of the governor, three officials and six members of the majority party in the Assembly appointed by the governor on the advice of a Chief Minister. A form of dyarchy was created where the governor controlled finance, foreign affairs, defense, and internal security, while the other departments were in charge of the six unofficial ministers.

The Labour Front Government

The Malay element in the population was so small that Singapore was virtually free from the communalism which plagued the Federation. In exchange, Chinese nationalism and sympathy for the Peking Government were strong, and there was a powerful Communist party which was predominantly Chinese. An election was held in 1955, and a newly formed socialist party, the Labour Front, won ten of the thirty-two seats. It formed an alliance with a minor party, the governor used his power of nomination to give it two additional seats, and it could rely on the votes of the three officials. This gave the party eighteen votes in an Assembly of thirty-two. The Labour Front advocated the rapid attainment of complete independence and the creation of a welfare state. Its leader, David Marshall, was the son of an Iraqi Jew and an eloquent and effective speaker of the emotional type.

The principal opposition came from the People's Action party (P.A.P.).

It was made up in part of Communists and fellow travelers and partly of left-wing socialists. The Communists controlled a group of trade unions and were strongly entrenched in the Chinese private schools, particularly the large secondary schools. P.A.P. was the only party with a good organization. The leader, Lee Kuan-yew, was an English-educated Chinese lawyer. While denying that he was a Communist he admitted that "Any man in Singapore who wants to carry the Chinese-speaking people with him cannot afford to be anti-Communist. The Chinese are very proud of China." P.A.P. used its trade unions and its following among the students to organize a series of violent strikes and riots in which several were killed, including an American newsman.

In 1956 Marshall led an all-party delegation to London and asked for independence within a year. The Secretary of State for the Colonies proposed instead that Singapore have domestic self-government, while the British government retained control of defense, foreign affairs, and internal security. The strength of the Communists had made him apprehensive lest P.A.P. come to power and "Singapore should become an outpost of Communist China." In view of the naval base and the island's strategic position on Australia's and New Zealand's communication routes with the United Kingdom, the government insisted that it must have the power to maintain internal order if the Singapore government should prove unable to do so. On this point the negotiations collapsed and Marshall resigned in protest. His colleagues did not support him and one of them, Lim Yew-hock, a socialist trade union leader, became Chief Minister.

He carried on a vigorous campaign against Communist subversion in 1956 and 1957, arresting a number of P.A.P. leaders, trade unionists, school teachers, and students. An amusing instance of the Communist ingenuity in setting up apparently innocuous organizations was that one of their creations was the Chinese brass-gong musical society. Lim Yew-hock published evidence to show the Communists had penetrated P.A.P., and Lee Kuan-yew admitted that it had been used as a Communist front. The Colonial Office was reassured by Lim Yew-hock's anti-Communist measures, and in 1957 an acceptable compromise was found for internal security. It was agreed that Singapore should receive internal self-government, including the control of security, while the United Kingdom retained control of foreign policy and defense. An

55

Internal Security Council of seven members would be established to decide whether the United Kingdom could intervene to maintain law and order within the colony. The British and Singapore governments would each have three members, and the decisive vote would be held by a representative of the Federation of Malaya. There would be an elected legislature of fifty-one members, and a cabinet responsible to it. A special Singapore citizenship was created to accommodate the three hundred thousand Chinese immigrants who wanted the rights of citizenship but were unwilling to become naturalized British subjects in order to obtain them. They would be required to take an oath of loyalty to Singapore and renounce their allegiance to China.

P.A.P. soon showed that more was needed than the arrest of some of its leaders to curb it. In December 1957 it won control of the municipal council of the city of Singapore. Meetings of the council under a P.A.P. mayor seem to have resembled debates of the French revolutionary assembly of 1792 in its more uninhibited moments. From this P.A.P. went on to a greater victory, defeating the Labour Front and gaining control of the government of the colony. Lee Kuan-yew insisted on the release of his party members arrested by Lim Yew-hock; but once he was in office he was much more moderate than when he was in opposition. He hoped to attract foreign capital and also to gain admission to the Federation as the only ways of finding employment for the rapidly increasing number of young Chinese who were coming on the labor market. The government of the United Kingdom favored the union of Singapore and the Federation, but until 1961 Tengku Abdul Rahman refused to agree. He then reversed his policy and strongly urged that the Federation of Malaya be expanded into the Federation of Malaysia by including Singapore and the British protectorates in Borneo of North Borneo, Brunei, and Sarawak. The federal House of Representatives with its Malay majority approved the proposal in October 1961, and Lee Kuan-yew warmly supported it. The British government agreed, and plans were made to consult the peoples of the dependencies on their willingness to join.

Federation of Malaysia

The inclusion of Singapore in the Federation was obviously most desirable if economic questions alone were considered. This would bring it inside the Federation's tariff, open a much larger market, and so help to find employment for the growing population. Singapore too was the port through which the Federation carried on most of its foreign trade. With the Malays of the Federation, however, political considerations were paramount, and this was why Tengku Abdul Rahman, whose position depended on the support of U.M.N.O., opposed the admission of Singapore until 1961. In 1959 the estimated population of the Federation of Malaya was 6,815,000, of which 3,405,000 or 49.9 per cent were Malays and Malaysians (immigrants from Indonesia who merge easily with them) and 2,520,000 or 36.9 per cent Chinese. This gave the Malays a considerable majority in votes, and the Federation was based on the tacit agreement that while the Chinese held most of the economic power the Malays were politically dominant. The situation would be completely altered and the Malays reduced to a minority if Singapore were admitted. Its total population was 1,634,000, of which the Chinese were 1,230,000 or 75.2 per cent and the Malays 227,000 or 13.7 per cent. The combined population of Singapore and the Federation would be 8,449,000, of which the Chinese would be 3,750,000 or 44.3 per cent and the Malays 3,632,000 or 43 per cent. The Chinese would have both economic and political control. This could lead to the fall of Tengku Abdul Rahman, the breakdown of the Alliance government, and a recrudescence of communal hostility.

The reason for the reversal of policy was the grave danger that Lee Kuan-yew's moderate P.A.P. government would be replaced by Communist control of Singapore. He lost two by-elections and thirteen of his supporters in the Assembly defected to form the Socialist Front (Barisan Socialis) party which was virtually a Communist-front organization. He was left with a majority of one in the Assembly, and seemed likely to be defeated in the 1963 elections if not before. An outpost of the Peking government on the Federation's southern doorstep was a danger which could not be ignored. Tengku Abdul Rahman was also influenced by the dangerous growth of Communist power in South Viet Nam. If it and Laos were overrun, the next line of defense would be Malaya and the British dependencies in Borneo. A Communist base at Singapore could not be allowed. Once Singapore joined the Federation, Tengku Abdul Rahman would control its internal security. He made it clear that Communists and fellow travelers would be arrested or deported if they were a danger to the peace.[34]

Tengku Abdul Rahman believed that the inclusion of the three dependencies in Borneo would counterbalance the addition of the Chinese from Singapore. In this he may have been overly optimistic. Rather more than half their estimated population of a million and a quarter are neither Malay nor Chinese, but Dayaks and other primitive indigenous races. If it could be assumed that they would support the Malays their numerical superiority would be restored. This cannot be taken for granted: they are not Malays, and from their past history they fear Malay domination of their country almost as much as Chinese penetration. They are so primitive that they have never voted in the embryonic democratic life of Borneo. One of the greatest difficulties which the British officials had to solve was how to ascertain their wishes about joining the Federation. The commission of inquiry appointed by the British government estimated that at a rough guess about a third of the population of each of the three dependencies in Borneo strongly supported joining the Federation. Another third favored it with safeguards: the Dayaks stipulated that they must be protected from dominance by the Malays or the establishment of an Islamic state. Of the remainder some preferred independence and the rest a temporary continuation of British colonial rule.[35] The commission unanimously reported the Federation was "an attractive and workable project." Eventually the Sultan of Brunei refused to join, and the Federation, enlarged to include Sarawak and North Borneo, was established on September 15, 1963.

The government of the United Kingdom was very eager that nothing should interfere with its use of the Singapore base, including the existing right to employ it in order to carry out obligations under S.E.A.T.O. Tengku Abdul Rahman wished to expand the Federation's defensive alliance of 1957 with Great Britain to cover the enlarged Federation. At first he was adamant that the Singapore base must not be used for S.E.A.T.O., but only for the defense of the Commonwealth; but finally he consented to a compromise. An agreement was announced that the alliance would be extended to the territories included in the enlarged federation. Great Britain would have the right to maintain the base at Singapore "and make such use of these bases and facilities as the United Kingdom may consider necessary for the purpose of assisting in the defence of Malaysia, and for Commonwealth defence and for the preservation of peace in South East Asia." The final clause meant that the United Kingdom could continue to use the base in order to discharge her obligations under S.E.A.T.O. She would no longer do so by virtue of her rights of sovereignty over the colony of Singapore but by agreement with the future Malaysian Federation to which the sovereignty was transferred. Tengku Abdul Rahman made it clear that before the base could be used to assist S.E.A.T.O. his government must be consulted. "Consultation must involve a degree of consent." Moreover the United Kingdom could not transfer control of the base to S.E.A.T.O. or any member of that alliance.[36] It was expected that Australia and New Zealand would join the enlarged Anglo-Malaysian defensive alliance with which they were already associated.

Agreement was reached that the federal government would control foreign affairs, defense, and internal security. Singapore would have more extensive powers than the other states of the federation: it would retain control of its own labor, education, and medical and health policies, and would keep 75 per cent of its taxes. On the other hand it would have only fifteen members in the House of Representatives, although it was entitled to twenty-five on the basis of population. As against this only about 384,000 out of its 624,000 voters met the qualifications for federal citizenship. This could be obtained by birth or naturalization, and aliens must have a knowledge of Malay. Something like 300,000 who had Singapore citizenship were Chinese alien immigrants, many of whom had never troubled to learn Malay. Furthermore, Singaporeans, although federal citizens, would not be allowed to vote outside Singapore in any federal election. The terms were ratified by the legislature despite the vehement opposition of the Communists, led by Lim Chin-siong. In addition Lee Kuan-yew held a referendum in August 1962 where voting was compulsory. The voters were required to choose among three alternative forms of merger with the Federation of Malaysia. Two of the three were certain to be rejected, and no choice was allowed for voters who were against any form of merger. The Communists countered by urging the electorate to turn in a blank ballot, and predicted that half would be blank votes. When the referendum was held only about 25 per cent of the votes cast were blank, while 397,600 or 70 per cent approved the form of merger negotiated by Lee Kuan-yew. In February 1963 Lim Chin-siong and 110 other Communists were arrested on the charge that they were plotting an uprising to prevent Singapore's merger with the federation. They had close connections with the leaders of the abortive revolt in Brunei and with the Indonesian Communist party which supported it. The arrests were described as "the most important security operation" since the end of the Communist revolt in Malaya.[37] In the election of September 1963 Lee Kuan-yew won thirty-seven of the fifty-one seats in the Assembly, whereas the Communist Barisan Socialis party won only thirteen. Early in October the Communists engineered a general strike, but Lee Kuan-yew immediately arrested the leaders and the strike soon collapsed.

The rebellion in Brunei and some neighboring parts of Sarawak and North Borneo in December 1962 left behind it a strong suspicion that Sukarno was involved in it. The charge was publicly brought against him by Tengku Abdul Rahman. Ostensibly it was an attempt to prevent the Borneo dependencies from joining the Federation of Malaysia, which was described as a manifestation of British neo-colonialism. It was suppressed in Brunei by troops sent from the garrison at Singapore, but part of the rebels held out in Sarawak. The leader, Azahari, was a Brunei politician who directed the fighting from the safe sanctuary of Manila. He was also believed to be of Indonesian descent, and had certainly been an officer in Sukarno's army during the revolt against the Dutch. It was difficult to see how he could have obtained arms and trained his followers without outside help. In earlier years prominent Indonesian officials had hinted that the Borneo dependencies might some day be liberated and joined to Indonesia. Sukarno himself had strongly opposed the merger of the dependencies in the Federation of Malaysia, and he and the Indonesian Communist party had openly sympathized with the rebels in Brunei. In a radio broadcast Sukarno called upon the Indonesians to support the revolt. Subandrio, the Foreign Minister, said that his government would give "full assistance" to the rebels to prevent the Borneo dependencies from joining the Federation of Malaysia. Veiled threats had been made in the controlled Indonesian press of guerilla warfare to prevent the merger.[38] There was a striking similarity between these tactics and the methods by which Sukarno gained control of Dutch New Guinea — threatening speeches, the creation of a fifth column of Indonesians and a few Papuans, and the landing of soldiers to fight an undeclared war. All of which led to American pressure on Holland, and the surrender of New Guinea via a United Nations trusteeship. Sukarno's motive might be the neo-imperialism which has been shown by other former dependencies which have achieved independence, such as India and Goa. Equally it could be a repetition of his New Guinea adventure — diverting the Indonesians from thinking about their worsening economic condition by rousing their anti-Western xenophobia. Tengku Abdul Rahman announced in February 1963 that the Malayan armed forces would be substantially enlarged because of the "hostile attitude" of Indonesia. He also said that if there were war he would have the armed assistance of Great Britain. Later in the year he tried to end the conflict by an agreement with Sukarno and President Macapagal of the Philippines that the United Nations would be asked to investigate and decide whether the population of North Borneo and Sarawak genuinely wished to join the Federation. Macapagal supported Sukarno's opposition to it because he demanded the cession of North Borneo to the Philippines by very tenuous and insubstantial arguments. The United Kingdom government sanctioned the arrangement, although it was absolutely unprecedented to allow the United Nations to intervene in the affairs of British territories.

This attempt to prevent further hostilities proved to be useless. A guerilla war continued in the jungle which covers a large part of Sarawak, and the government of Indonesia officially encouraged its citizens to take part. Diplomatic relations with the Federation of Malaysia were broken off and all trade forbidden. A mob was allowed to sack the British embassy in Djakarta, and the government took over control of British investments. Units of the Indonesian army were moved up to the frontier in Borneo. In the course of the fighting conclusive proof was obtained of Indonesian complicity in sixteen major incidents. The British soldiers fighting the guerillas captured Indonesian military equipment and uniforms. Prisoners stated that they had been recruited and trained in Indonesian Borneo, and some declared that they had been conscripted for service. A United Nations mission

61

headed by an American carried on investigations in Sarawak and North Borneo, and reported in September that the majority of the population wished to join the Federation of Malaysia. Sukarno at once refused to accept the findings of the mission and declined to change his policy. The United Kingdom and Malaysia face the prospect of a jungle war fed from outside which may last for years like the war against the Viet Cong in South Viet Nam, with Indonesian Borneo playing the same role as Laos and North Viet Nam.

In 1964 the American government sent the attorney general, Kennedy, on a mission of conciliation to Sukarno, Macapagal, and Tengku Abdul Rahman. Prince Sihanouk also intervened as a peacemaker. Kennedy was optimistic about the result of his efforts. The three governments agreed to send representatives to Bangkok to arrange a settlement. Sukarno promised to cease hostilities — and rather weakened the reassuring effect of his pronouncement by following it with a speech in which he reiterated his determination to crush Malaysia. He refused to withdraw his "freedom fighters" from Malaysian territory, and for the first time officially admitted that they were operating under his orders. He had the effrontery to demand that the British forces be withdrawn from Borneo, a part of the Commonwealth, and more than hinted that the Anglo-Malayan defensive alliance must be abrogated. He also insisted that Tengku Abdul Rahman must attend their meetings as a private person and not as prime minister of Malaysia. Tengku Abdul Rahman's attitude was that he would be delighted to see the end of a war which was not of his seeking. For the time being the Malayan and United Kingdom forces were strong enough to contain the guerillas, and he would not ask Australia for the armed help which had been promised.

III

Indonesia, South Viet Nam, and Thailand

The Constitution of Indonesia

The original constitution was drawn up in 1945. It provided for an elected president, a premier and cabinet responsible to him, and an assembly. The latter was to be elected by universal suffrage when this became feasible, and until then it was to be appointed by the president. The revolt against the Dutch ended in 1949, but the president continued to appoint the members until 1955. The principal reason for postponing the election for so many years appears to have been that some of the parties were afraid that a popular vote would give them fewer members than they obtained through presidential appointment, and they contrived to postpone that disagreeable necessity for as long as possible.[1] Sukarno was appointed president in 1945 by the other leaders of the revolt, and to date he has not found the times propitious for holding a presidential election to regularize his position. Recently he was appointed president for life.

Sukarno preferred the American type of constitution where the cabinet was responsible to him and not to the legislature, and this was the practice during the early years of the republic. When the revolt ended with the Dutch transfer of sovereignty to the republic, the legislature insisted on the parliamentary type of democracy, and the cabinet became responsible to it and not to the president. When Sukarno established his guided democracy in 1959 he reverted to the American type and again made the premier and cabinet responsible to himself. Even during the years when Indonesia had the form of a parliamentary democracy the president had wide powers. Besides being commander in chief of the armed forces and controlling foreign affairs he could dissolve the legislature, veto laws, and himself legislate in times of emergency. He could not be impeached or removed from office and was responsible to no one. The constitution was vague in defining the position and duties of the president, and Sukarno interpreted its ambiguities to his own advantage. This enabled him to exert an influence which was within the letter of the law, but far in excess of what most political leaders considered to be its intent. One illustration of this was that he sometimes powerfully affected policy by making a direct appeal to the people in public speeches over the heads of the cabinet and legislature. The most important reason for his success in enhancing his constitutional position was that he was himself the strongest political force in Indonesia. He claimed to be the principal leader of the nationalist revolution and was accepted as such by the Indonesians. As a politician he far surpassed all the rest in his personal magnetism and oratorical skill, and this combination of gifts gave him a mass following which none of his rivals could equal.[2]

The Politically Effective Class

Machiavelli coined a useful phrase, the politically effective class, by which he meant the elements in the state which had a preponderant influence on the course of government. The politically effective class in Indonesia is a strong contrast to that of the Federation of Malaya in its antecedents and outlook. Both are the Western-educated group but in the Federation of Malaya they are the traditional ruling class of Malay aristocrats and wealthy Chinese. Before the war many of the Malays were government officials and supported British rule, but their connection with the colonial power did not lessen their traditional influence over the peasants. They are conservative in policy and well-disposed toward the former ruling power. In Indonesia many of the Dutch-educated leaders come from the middle class, although some belong to the aristocracy. Sukarno is the son of a village school teacher. The Indonesian· branch of the Dutch administrative service was recruited from the nobility, and contrary to what happened in Malaya this alliance with the colonial power weakened their position as the traditional ruling class. The middle-class nationalist leaders attacked them as well as the Dutch, and strove to abolish the old social order at the same time as Dutch rule. During the twentieth century the allegiance of the masses was in large measure transferred from the aristocracy to the middle-class leaders. The latter were more revolutionary in their policy than the U.M.N.O. leaders, since they were trying to rise to power and were not born to an established position. During the postwar colonial revolt many of the regents and other aristocratic government officials joined the struggle against the Dutch. In this way they retained a position of authority in the civil service and the political parties of the Indonesian Republic. To some extent they have also kept their influence over the peasantry as the traditional ruling class. The politically effective class is a Western-educated mixture of aristocratic and middle-class elements.[3]

The estimate has been made that the politically effective class numbers about a thousand, nearly all of whom have a Western education which went at least as far as the secondary school. The majority took part in the colonial revolt, and many of the older men like Sukarno were engaged in the political struggle against Dutch rule during the interwar period. From this group come the politicians, the senior civil servants and army officers, the principal leaders of the trade unions and the youth and student organizations, the editors, bankers, professors, and importers. They have many interests in common, and the political views of most of them are similar. They are intensely nationalist, nearly all are socialists, and very few are Communists. Often they are linked by marriage or by years of close political association. As time passed they divided more and more into rival factions called political parties which struggled with one another for control of the government.[4]

The Army

Apart from the Communists the army is the only comparatively well organized and disciplined body in Indonesia. It has never been fully under the control of the government. During the years of fighting against the Dutch many senior officers had political as well as military duties, and after the war was over they continued to regard themselves as semi-independent of the civil authority. The loyalty of the privates is to their officer rather than to the state, and if he rebels or intervenes in civil affairs they tend to follow him as they did in the revolts of 1958. The frequent weakness and corruption of the government led the officers to feel that they were justified in intervening. Thus in 1956 one army clique in Java arrested Abdulgani, the Foreign Minister, on charges of corruption. The army itself has been divided into rival cliques, and a political party sometimes formed an alliance with one faction or another in order to strengthen its own power. Gradually the higher command acquired wide powers of control over the civil administration. They were used only intermittently, and the result was an ill-coordinated dual administration where power was shared between the civil and military authorities. The army seems also to have been infected by the corruption against which it inveighed in the civil administration.

One reason for the formation of cliques was that the army was a combination of diverse and conflicting elements. The nucleus was the semi-guerilla force which was raised to fight the Dutch after 1945. This included the youth militia recruited and trained by the Japanese, the "teenagers armed with rifles," to keep the country quiet. Their officers tended to be authoritarian, and to believe that they had the right to keep the government in order. After 1950 the guerillas were amalgamated with the Dutch colonial army against whom they had been fighting. A third element was the officers who received their commissions after the fighting was over and were sent abroad for their military education. They were better trained than the previous groups, and wanted the army to be reorganized and made more efficient. This was strongly opposed by the officers of the former Japanese militia who realized that so exacting a standard was beyond them. Still another cause of factions was regionalism. During the revolt soldiers were raised in the areas where they fought and had close links with the civil population. After the war was over a large part of the garrisons stationed in many of the islands and particularly Sumatra continued to be recruited locally. They sympathized with the complaints of their friends and relations against the policy of the government in Java, and in the end this was an important cause of the revolts of 1958.

Divisions in the army were partly responsible for some of the revolts in Java, Borneo, and Celebes which have plagued the republic since it was first established. During the war with the Dutch, local leaders raised independent guerilla bands which were not part of the regular army that was more or less under the control of the government. They were estimated to number a hundred thousand, and after the war the government ordered them to disband and return to civil life. Some of them obeyed, others were given civil-service positions for which they were totally unfitted, and yet others turned bandit. Hard and monotonous labor had no charms for guerillas who had discovered that a young man with a rifle and no inhibitions could live pleasantly without work.[5]

The Trade Unions

Apart from the army, the trade unions have been a political force which the politicians must take into account. Most of the leaders have not been workmen or peasants but middle-class professional men or politicians. They and not the members have controlled the unions. The majority have been under Communist domination and were combined into the Central Organization of All-Indonesian Labor (S.O.B.S.I.) with reputedly 1,500,000 members. Most of those in the S.O.B.S.I. trade unions were not Communists, but they were led by a minority of well trained and well paid Communist organizers and agitators. They spent far more than they received in membership dues, and presumably have been financed by Russia or China. The policy of the trade-union leaders was described as "irresponsible, adventurist, class struggle demagogy." Especially on the foreign-owned estates they succeeded in extorting concessions which sometimes made further production unprofitable, and thus helped to contribute to the present critical economic situation. Usually the government supported the unions, from xenophobia and also from an appreciation of their political power.[6]

The Peasants

The revolutionary upheavals of the past twenty years changed life in the villages from what it was under the Dutch. The peasants became much more aware of the outside world, and the nationalist leaders aroused expectations of better living conditions which were not fulfilled. In Java at least the standard of living is still lower than before the war.

Tremendous population pressure exists alongside economic stagnation, with peasants owning, share owning or working as labourers tiny and uneconomic plots of an average size of about two acres and often less than half an acre. These moreover were constantly subject to further subdivision with the further growth of the agricultural population.

Unemployment was widespread, and this led to heavy migration to the towns where the peasant often found that his economic prospects were equally precarious. The failure of the governments to give effective help to the peasants finally played into the hands of the Communists and markedly increased their rural support in Java.

The village has in some ways become more democratic than before the war: the headman has usually been elected, and has often been compelled to come to terms with the more politically conscious villagers. But where national as opposed to petty local matters are concerned, the peasants continue to be ignorant and submissive to the orders of their educated leaders. They expect the government to command them, and it does not occur to them that democracy gives them the right to give orders to their rulers. They are nationalists but not democrats, and their ideal is still the benevolent autocrat who will make life better for them. "The elite has generally exercised its leadership without the necessity of any great amount of consultation with the mass of the population." Preoccupied with political intrigues in the capital, Djakarta, they have limited contact with the peasants, have little understanding of their needs and make small attempt to find out. Their attitude is one of slightly condescending impatience with their benighted fellow countrymen who must be remade on a twentieth-century model. The politically conscious public whose opinion the politicians must consider has been estimated at two million more or less out of the ninety million Indonesians. They have had at least an elementary education and read a newspaper. Most of them are urban but they include some prominent villagers. They are members of trade unions, peasant organizations, political parties, and the like, and through them they exert considerable influence on politics.[7]

Political Parties

No fewer than twenty-seven parties won representation in the national legislature of 273 members in the election of 1955. There was little difference between the policies of most of them, and the reason for their separate existence was the rival ambitions of their leaders. The multiplication of parties has been typical of most Asian democracies, but nowhere has it attained such gargantuan proportions as in Indonesia. It has been primarily responsible for the weakness and instability of the governments. A political party has been a faction organized by a leader to support him in his struggle for power. Party principles have been of minor importance, and the cement which held it together has been the personality of the leader and his ability to reward his followers with the loaves and fishes of office. This led to widespread and growing corruption, for example in the awarding of government contracts which in the end helped to discredit democracy. It also explained in part the growth of the civil service until it numbered approximately a million badly paid officials. Appointment was a very convenient way of rewarding deserving followers and ensuring their future loyalty, and the government service became notorious for incompetence, endless procrastination, and dishonesty. With the exception of the Communists, organization was poor and discipline weak. Each party tried to win the support of those who had local influence such as district officials, village headmen, and religious leaders, and through them obtain the votes of the public. Most elected representatives had only tenuous contact with the party organization in their constituencies. Every party was made up of rival cliques which put its own interests above those of the party. A leader who had become a cabinet minister could never be certain that his followers in the legislature would support him. Some might do so while others voted against him, or part of them might even secede to another party if this seemed to offer better prospects of personal advancement. Opposition parties were frequently completely irresponsible in their subordination of national interests to those of their own faction.[8]

Many of the parties were dominated by politicians who had spent the better part of their lives opposing the colonial government in the interwar period. Their policy was to attack everything that the Dutch proposed, and since they were a permanent opposition without hope of office they were able to advocate measures which were completely impracticable without any risk that they might be called upon to carry them out. This bred an attitude of permanent hostility to government and of irresponsibility which survived the end of Dutch rule. Suddenly they found themselves catapulted into a new world where chronic opposition was pointless and the urgent need was to find solutions for the problems that confronted the new republic. With many of the politicians the habit of years was too strong to be overcome. They tended to continue opposing whatever proposals an Indonesian government put forward, and to avoid the responsibility of advancing a workable policy of their own.

The unity which the leaders managed to maintain during the war against the Dutch did not survive their victory. The decade of the 'fifties was marked by a growing division which made cooperation for the good of the country more and more difficult. Divergencies over policies were only a minor cause, for most of them had more similarities than differences. The real reason was the conflicting ambitions of the politicians. Instead of grappling with the economic and political problems which demanded solution they plunged into a competitive scramble to win the positions of authority formerly held by the Dutch. The struggle became more intense since it was personalities and not differences over policy which were the decisive factor. Antagonism was sharpened and made more bitter because the contestants knew each other so well and often were connected by marriage. Frequently allegiance to a party or the attitude of a leader toward major questions was determined by personal friendship or hostility.[9]

Factiousness and Government Stability

The effect of factiousness upon governmental stability was calamitous. Owing to the multiple party system every government had to be a coalition in order to obtain a parliamentary majority. Each cabinet was a collection of rival prima donnas all of whom wanted to occupy the center of the stage simultaneously. Each measured jealously the importance of the position assigned to him compared with those given to his competitors, and sought for means to enhance his importance. There was the added complication that no cabinet minister could count on the loyalty of the cliques in his party if personal considerations made a change in allegiance expedient. As a consequence governments were weak, unstable, and short-lived. Often the cause of their fall was not so much a conflict of policies as a clash of personal ambitions. Whenever an important and contentious issue arose and a government took resolute action it almost invariably fell, since some of its supporters went over to the opposition. The result was that a decision was postponed, sometimes for years and at others indefinitely. A European observer noted in 1955 that "the apparent futility of government by debate is robbing Parliament of its authority. The result is growing impatience and a sense of drift." By the end of the nineteen fifties the parties or factions had become more divided than ever, and more bent than ever on self-glorification and self-enrichment. A decade of democracy was a record of one failure after another to agree on a working coalition or an acceptable program. There had been nine cabinets in ten years, and for all of them the chief preoccupation had been not the government of Indonesia but the never-ending maneuvers and intrigues that were essential to postpone their fall. Meanwhile the army had intervened increasingly in civil affairs, and the Communists had very greatly increased their strength. No other democracy of Southeast Asia had given so close an imitation of organized bedlam.[10]

The end of the whole matter was growing disillusionment with democracy. This attitude was discernible as early as 1955, but at that time there was still the hope of an improvement when an elected legislature replaced the one that was nominated by Sukarno. The elections were held, and the result was exactly the same as before. There was something to be said for Sukarno's declaration that political parties were better buried, and that Western democracy was unsuited to Indonesia. Granted that he was an ambitious man who sought greater power, it still remained true that Indonesia was an immature political society which lacked the traditions that made democracy workable in some of the Western countries.

The Nationalist Party

The four largest parties were the Partai Nasional Indonesia (P.N.I.), the Masjumi, the Nahdatul Ulama (N.U.) which seceded from it, and the Partai Komunis Indonesia (P.K.I.).[11] In the election of 1955 they received votes as shown in the accompanying table. In the subsequent local elections in Java the Communists increased their following and emerged as the largest party.

Parties	Votes Received	Members Elected
P.N.I.	8,434,653	57
Masjumi	7,903,886	57
N.U.	6,955,141	45
P.K.I. (Communists)	6,176,914	39

The Nationalists (P.N.I.) were not a continuation of the Nationalist party which was founded by Sukarno in the interwar period and suppressed by the Dutch. The majority of the leaders of the P.N.I., however, were members of the earlier party and it was generally believed that Sukarno favored it, although as president he was supposed to be above party politics. The Nationalist party (P.N.I.) drew 86 per cent of its support from Java. It included a large number of Javanese officials of the middle and upper ranks, of whom the majority belonged to the aristocracy. They retained a substantial influence over the village headmen and the peasants. The P.N.I. was intensely nationalist and hostile to Western private investment, particularly Dutch. In foreign policy it advocated neutralism, implying no commitment to either the Western or Eastern bloc. It was hostile to imperialism but supported the annexation of Dutch New Guinea. The principal point in its domestic policy was Marhaenism which it had borrowed from Sukarno, who first enunciated it in 1930. The Marhaen were the 90 per cent or more of the Indonesians who lived close to the level of subsistence, and the aim of the policy was to increase their prosperity. Marhaenism condemned capitalism as an unmitigated evil and wished to substitute state or cooperative enterprises. In practice this policy was qualified by a willingness to assist in the creation of Indonesian capitalists, particularly if they were members of the P.N.I. The party was much more hostile to the Masjumi than to the Communists, and formed a loose working alliance with them to weaken its rival.

The Muslim Parties

During the early years of the Republic the Masjumi was considered to be the largest political party in Indonesia. It included the majority of the most prominent Muslim leaders and won much peasant support owing to its influence over religious leaders in the villages. Organization and party discipline were poor. The election of 1955 showed that about half its support came from the Outer Islands, particularly Sumatra and southern Celebes. It advocated that the state should be a democracy based upon the teachings of Islam. It supported neutralism in foreign policy, but unlike the P.N.I. it opposed Communism as undemocratic and incompatible with Islam. While nationalist it recognized the need for extensive investment of foreign capital for a long time to come. In domestic policy it was semi-socialist and advocated a guided economy with the nationalization of vital enterprises such as banks and public utilities. The second Muslim party was the Nahdatul Ulama. It was more conservative and influenced by Islamic tradition and less affected by Western ideas. Most of the leaders were learned religious teachers who had great influence over devout and uneducated villagers. In 1952 the Nahdatul Ulama seceded from the Masjumi on the ground that it was too worldly, and made its decisions on the basis of strictly political rather than religious considerations. This deprived the latter of most of its support in Eastern and Central Java.

The Communist Party

The Communist Party was founded immediately after World War I, but was driven underground by the Dutch because it instigated the premature and abortive revolts of 1926 and 1927. The party was revived after World War II and took part in the revolt against the Dutch. In 1948 it badly discredited itself because of its premature Madiun rebellion against the Indonesian government, and was almost wiped out by the republican army. In 1951 the party acquired a new and very able leader in D. N. Aidit, who had recently returned from a year in China and Indochina. His policy was to build up a large party with a mass following, and he expanded the membership from less than eight thousand to a claim of five hundred thousand in 1954 and one million five hundred thousand in 1957. The election of 1955 showed that the party was the fourth largest, and that 88.6 per cent of its vote came from Java, three quarters of it from the less prosperous parts of Eastern and Central Java. It also received considerable support from the peasants in the estate areas of Sumatra, where it had championed the cause of the squatters who had seized land belonging to Western companies. In addition to its size the P.K.I. was the best organized and disciplined party in Indonesia, and also the wealthiest. It was believed to receive large amounts from the Chinese business men as well as from the Chinese embassy.

The P.K.I. followed the usual Communist tactics of minimizing the doctrines such as nationalization of the land which would not appeal to a predominantly agricultural country. Instead it demanded farms for the peasants and other agricultural reforms. Another useful method was to champion existing grievances, as with the P.K.I. support of the squatters on the Western estates in Sumatra. Still more followers were obtained through Communist controlled organizations such as the Indonesian Peasant Front and S.O.B.S.I. Since Masjumi attacked Communism as incompatible with Islam, the P.K.I. took particular care to present its principles as entirely consistent with the Muslim religion. Extreme nationalism was the dominant emotion of Indonesia, and no other party could excel the P.K.I.'s protestations of fervent patriotism, its demands for the annexation of Dutch New Guinea, and its xenophobia against the West. Gone and forgotten were the days of the Madiun revolt. Another godsend was the jealous antagonism between the political parties, and particularly the hostility of the P.N.I. and Sukarno toward the Masjumi. An alliance was formed between the P.N.I. and the P.K.I., and from 1953 onwards the Communist members of the legislature provided the votes that were essential to keep Sastroamidjojo's Nationalist-dominated government in office. When Sukarno proposed his guided democracy the P.K.I. was his vociferous supporter.

Disaffection and Revolt

From the time of its establishment in 1950 the republic was beset by revolts and regional secessions. All the rebels had fought on the side of the republic against the Dutch with the exception of the natives of Ambon and Ceram in the Moluccas who tried to set up an independent republic in 1950. They were the most pro-Dutch of the Indonesians, many were Calvinists, and they had been favored in recruitment for the Dutch colonial army and civil service. The republican soldiers soon broke the back of the revolt, but it lingered on as a minor guerilla war. The Darul Islam revolts were much more extensive and serious. The first outbreak occurred in West Java in 1949, some months before the conclusion of peace between Holland and

Indonesia. Atjeh in northern Sumatra revolted in 1953. The Darul Islam rebels were the holy terrorists who showed the intensity of their yearnings for a Muslim theocratic state by killing and looting the peasants and terrorizing wide areas. "They prove their cause is orthodox / By apostolic blows and knocks." They were reinforced by disbanded guerillas of the republican army. The rebels were not numerous and were hampered by lack of arms, supplies, and money. They survived despite continuing surrenders because they operated in terrain which was difficult of access to regular soldiers. Moreover the government hesitated to wage an all-out war against them for fear of estranging the more conservative Muslim elements in Indonesia. So each year some scores or hundreds of rebels were killed, captured, or surrendered: hundreds of thousands of peasants lived in constant danger of guerilla attacks, and law and order virtually ceased to exist. Other rebellions broke out in southern Celebes and southern Borneo in 1950–1951. The rebels who professed to support Darul Islam were disbanded guerillas of the republican army who felt that they were insufficiently rewarded for their patriotic exertions. Another reason for these revolts as well as that in Atjeh was that the leaders, who were local men, had been replaced by officials sent over from Java. These rebellions caused heavy losses through destruction of property, paralysis of economic life and a constant drain on the treasury.

The widespread disaffection which culminated in the rebellions of 1958 in Sumatra and Celebes was far more serious than the earlier uprisings. To describe the later outbreaks as regional revolts against the unitary state would be an oversimplification, although it contains a good deal of truth. The East Indian Archipelago is composed of a great number of islands, and the larger of these are themselves divided by mountains, forests, and swamps into smaller sections often difficult of access to each other. The inhabitants comprise many subraces of Indonesian stock, each with its own language, customs, social structure, and, in certain cases, religion. Until the beginning of the present century there were large parts of Sumatra, Borneo, Celebes, the Lesser Sunda Islands, and New Guinea where no Dutch control of any sort existed. Effective rule over the whole of the East Indies was at the very most fifty years old at the time of the Japanese conquest. This was too short a period to weld the islanders into a single united people. In 1941 the memory of independence from outside control was still fresh. The Dutch often retained the old territorial divisions, and left the day-to-day conduct of affairs to the former rulers and local chiefs under the general supervision of European officials. The old loyalties to the local governing classes remained unbroken.

The Dutch imposed administrative unity upon subject peoples, but like the British in India they did not succeed in making them a single nation. It is true that despite their diversity the peoples of the islands in some ways felt themselves to be linked together as Indonesians. Islam was a unifying force. The principal influence, however, which brought them together was apparently discontent with Dutch rule, and the desire to be governed by men of their own race. At the same time the peoples of the Outer Islands had developed regional loyalties, and they did not want to substitute Javanese for Dutch rule.[12]

After 1945 the Dutch tried to combine the grant of self-government with the retention of some measure of influence by creating fifteen states each with a wide measure of local autonomy. These were to be joined by the parts of Java and Sumatra controlled by Sukarno's Indonesian Republic in a federation with limited powers. In this way unity would be reconciled with island loyalties and interests, and the Outer Islands would be safeguarded from Javanese control. To a large extent each state was made up of the pre-war territorial divisions and the former rulers retained their position, although they were made responsible to elected representative councils. The plan seems to have had the support of the governing class in the Outer Islands. Sukarno and the other leaders of the revolt were determined from the first that Indonesia should be a unitary state. At the Hague conference in 1949 they reluctantly accepted a federation, but in 1950 they abolished it and put in its place a central government in which all effective power was concentrated over the whole of Indonesia. This meant that Java would control the Outer Islands, since it had 48,400,000 out of the total population of 70,465,000. Federalism was discredited because it had been sponsored by the Dutch, but later events seem to show that Indonesia might have been spared many troubles if it had been adopted. The republic was divided into ten provinces, which were to be given the largest possible measure of local autonomy. The whole emphasis, though, was upon centralizing authority in the government at

Djakarta, and particularly in taxation the power of the provincial governments was negligible. They were entirely dependent upon the
annual block grants from the national government and these were
completely inadequate to meet their needs.

The Outer Islands complained that the government was dominated
by Java, and that their interests were sacrificed for the benefit of the
Javanese. They paid far more in taxes than they received in grants.
Another grievance was that the Outer Islands produced 89 per cent
of the exports and Java only 11 per cent but the bulk of the foreign
exchange was used for its benefit. Owing to its large population Java
was a heavy importer of consumer goods. Except when there was a
particularly good harvest of rice, it consumed far more than it produced, and the deficit had to be paid by the Outer Islands. Since Java
had the bulk of the votes the government disregarded the protests of
the Outer Islands and continued to spend most of its financial resources on the former. The result was that the roads, schools, and other
social services of the Outer Islands were starved of funds and were in
a deplorable condition. Discontent was intensified by the reports of
corruption and mismanagement which radiated outwards from the
capital, and the growing conviction that the government was weak
and impotent. The Outer Islands complained that goods could only
be imported under government licenses, and a disproportionate percentage of them and of loans to finance the transactions went to Javanese business men who had political influence.[13]

Eastern Indonesia and Borneo had the special grievance that the
National Copra Purchasing and Marketing Board at Djakarta, which
had the monopoly of the export of copra, gave the producer a low
price and resold at a high profit. Owing to incompetent management
and possibly corruption the Board was unable in 1956 to pay its heavy
debts for the copra which it had bought from Indonesians. Moreover
the national shipping companies which the government had sponsored to squeeze out the Dutch K.P.M. were unable to provide cargo
space when and where it was needed, so that heavy losses were incurred by copra producers.

There were also political grievances dating from the adoption of the
unitary constitution. In order to bring the islands under effective control the old territorial divisions retained by the Dutch were abolished

and merged into ten provinces, so that regional loyalties and traditions should be eliminated. Local officials were replaced by others appointed by the government at Djakarta. Many of them were Javanese since it was believed that their loyalty to the central government was stronger. The displaced leaders became hostile when they were deprived of the local political spoils. Their antagonism was a principal reason for the revolts in Atjeh and Celebes, and in other parts of the Outer Islands similar resentment smouldered beneath the surface.[14] The garrisons in the Outer Islands complained strongly that they were starved of funds for equipment and barracks. In many islands the privates and often the officers were recruited locally, and in addition to their own grievances they sympathized with those of the local population. Still another cause of discontent was that the Masjumi, which drew most of its support from the Outer Islands, was out of power for most of the time after 1953. The governments were dominated by the Nationalists, a predominantly Javanese party. Furthermore, to retain power the Nationalists depended more and more heavily on Communist support, and both the army and the civil population in the Outer Islands were strongly opposed to Communism. The final incident which precipitated the revolt in northern Celebes was Sukarno's announcement that Communists would be included in the government under his scheme for guided democracy. A formidable volume of disaffection gradually arose in the Outer Islands against Javanese control.

One of the first overt signs was the gigantic Celebes and Sumatra copra and rubber "smuggles." In 1956 it was publicly admitted that for years the local army command in these islands had bypassed the government's monopoly by smuggling copra to British Borneo, Mindanao, and Singapore and retaining for its own use the foreign exchange earned by the sales. Private individuals followed suit, and the government felt itself too weak to take effective action.[15] The next development in 1956 and 1957 was that the army commanders in central and south Sumatra, Borneo, and eastern Indonesia took over control of the administration and proclaimed the autonomy of their areas. They refused to recognize the authority of the government at Djakarta, affirmed their loyalty to President Sukarno and the Republic, and withheld all the funds which they should have sent to the national government until their demands were complied with. They demanded provincial autonomy and the right to retain 70 per cent of the local revenues. Central Sumatra and north Celebes went further, and insisted upon the formation of a new government from which Communist influence was eliminated. Apparently none of the rebels wished to secede and establish separate states: the object was to force the government to grant constitutional and fiscal reforms.

Sukarno had no intention of granting the demands of central Sumatra and north Celebes, but eventually he was able to come to terms with the other provinces and decrease the disaffected areas. He then seized upon the United Nations' rejection of his claim to west New Guinea to arouse the hostility to the Dutch which was never far below the surface, and confiscated their property in Indonesia. This increased his popularity, and he also won the support of General Nasution, the Chief of Staff. In 1958 he brought over an army and defeated the rebel forces in Sumatra and North Celebes. They retreated to the jungle and a bitter and destructive guerilla war continued until 1961, when Sukarno on the advice of his generals offered an amnesty to all who surrendered. By August the large majority of the rebels in Celebes "returned to the lap of the republic." The Celebes guerillas were promised that some of them would be taken into the army and the rest rehabilitated and returned to civil life with full rights of citizenship. Both sides stressed that the negotiated peace was not a surrender but "a return to the motherland," and General Nasution in person thanked the rebels for giving him the happy opportunity of seeing them all again. He did not feel victorious but merely grateful at "the return of our brothers." Shortly afterwards one of the principal leaders in Sumatra surrendered and the government accepted his "official return to the army." Only a small number of guerillas continued to resist.

The government paid a heavy economic price for its victory. The rebels shipped large quantities of rubber and copra to Chinese merchants in Singapore to buy arms, and it was estimated that the government lost between ten and twenty per cent of its earnings from foreign exchange. It was also compelled to buy arms, and it was believed that 48 per cent of the budget and 45 per cent of the foreign exchange were spent to defeat the rebel armies. The result in Java was a particularly bad bout of inflation, which was made worse by the government's printing large amounts of paper money to meet its expenses. Furthermore, the suppression of the revolt did not end the political and economic causes which brought it about.

Sukarno's Guided Democracy

Sukarno is by far the most powerful politician in Indonesia, but unfortunately he is not a statesman. He became a professional revolutionary in 1915, and from that time onwards agitation against Dutch rule was his lifework. He illustrates an observation made earlier in this chapter that many of the older nationalist leaders who spent the best years of their lives opposing the colonial government continued their role of negative opposition after the Indonesian Republic had secured its independence. Sukarno's habit of mind has been purely destructive: he had an important share in destroying the power of Holland in the East Indies, but as President of the Republic he has had no constructive ideas.[16] His panacea for all the political and economic problems of the past decade has been larger doses of revolutionary nationalism. He has shown no understanding of economic questions, and indeed it has been remarked that his speeches have rarely referred to them. His doctrine has been that Indonesian independence is still endangered by the three evil forces of Western and particularly Dutch colonialism, imperialism, and capitalism. The country will not be really free until revolutionary nationalism has liberated Indonesia from its domination by Western private capital and has annexed Dutch New Guinea. It is a moot point whether he himself believed this last assertion or whether his frequent references to it were due to opportunism. What is clear has been that again and again he brought up the liberation of New Guinea when it was politically expedient to distract public attention from urgent domestic problems.

Sukarno's strong points are his prestige as the leader of the nationalist revolution, his flair for political intrigue, and his control over the masses which he owes to his consummate gift for hypnotic oratory of an emotional type. Some observers have been reminded of Hitler's powers of demagogy and his intuitive understanding of what was in the minds of his listeners. They have remarked that Sukarno's speeches do not make any clear proposals, but appeal to the emotions of his audience by talking eloquently and persuasively of independence, national pride, the need for unity and vigilance against Western capitalist im-

80

perialists, and the necessity for revolutionary nationalism. One foreigner confessed that he was always "fascinated and swayed" by Sukarno's powers of persuasion, but that when he considered the speech the following morning he always wondered why he had thought it so stirring and profound. Of recent years a growing number of Indonesian politicians have doubted his wisdom, but his popularity with the masses seems to have been unimpaired.

The principal motive of Sukarno's career seems to have been desire for personal power. When he visited Communist China he was greatly impressed with the success of Mao Tse-tung in organizing and driving the Chinese to increase the strength and material development of the country. He contrasted this with the futility of Indonesian parliamentary democracy, and came to the conclusion that it should be replaced by some variant of Chinese dictatorship, with himself as the supreme authority. In 1957 he publicly proposed that Indonesia should abandon Western liberal democracy as a failure and substitute guided democracy of a distinctively Indonesian type. A functional National Council appointed by Sukarno and with himself as chairman would be superimposed on the cabinet, which itself would include all the major parties. The Council would have representatives of all sections of Indonesian society — occupational (labor, peasants, and employers), social, religious, and cultural — as well as the leaders of the armed forces and the police and the principal cabinet ministers. The original proposal was that Communists who had been "unjustly" deprived of their rights would be included, but owing to the opposition of the army in the Outer Islands he was forced to omit them and substitute well known fellow travelers. The scheme was exceedingly vague as to the powers of Sukarno, the Council, Cabinet, and legislature, and their relation to one another.

Decisions in the Council and Cabinet would not be reached by the Western device of the majority vote but by the distinctively Indonesian method of *mufakat*. This was the traditional way in which the villages settled their problems. They avoided dividing into a majority and minority by continuing the discussion until at last a common point of view or a compromise acceptable to all emerged. Apparently Sukarno would decide when this state of general agreement had been achieved, and the duty of the cabinet and legislature would be to find ways of

81

carrying out the advice given to them. The defect of *mufakat* was the time that it took to reach a consensus of opinion. It was doubtless satisfactory for the leisurely deliberations of a village meeting, but a modern cabinet could not afford the time for endless discussion. Under *mufakat*, too, a contentious problem was sometimes shelved because it was felt that the preservation of harmony was more important than a settlement.[17]

Sukarno's proposal was supported by the Nationalist party, the Nahdatul Ulama, and the Communists who naturally approved a scheme which entrenched them at the seat of governmental authority. It was opposed by the Masjumi, the Socialists, and some of the other smaller parties; but despite the threat to their position their rivalries were too strong to enable them to combine against it. Soon afterwards martial law was proclaimed, which increased the power of Sukarno and the army. He contrived to gain the support of General Nasution and the army in Java. The latter was now the strongest force in Indonesia next to the President himself. It had been completely alienated by the futility of Indonesian parliamentary democracy, and blamed the political parties for its inefficiency and corruption. The politically conscious Indonesians had come to the conclusion that democracy meant corruption and inability to agree on any major issue, and held it responsible for the shortage of rice and consumer goods. In May 1957 Sukarno established his National Council, which acted very largely as his mouthpiece. While it was announced that the Council could only advise the Cabinet, it was hinted that the advice must be received as authoritative.[18] The Masjumi party was discredited because some of its leaders had taken part in the revolt in Sumatra.[19]

In 1959 Sukarno demanded that the attempt to draft a constitution be abandoned and the original constitution of 1945 be reinstated and made permanent. He failed to get the necessary two-thirds majority owing to the opposition of the Muslim parties. General Nasution thereupon forbade all party activity by virtue of his authority under the proclamation of martial law. This hamstrung the opposition, and in July 1959 Sukarno tore up the constitution which was being drafted and restored that of 1945. This meant that the cabinet became responsible to him and not to the legislature, the powers of which were severely curtailed. Sukarno now had complete control of the executive, and he could also legislate by decree since a state of emergency had been proclaimed. He next appointed a Supreme Advisory Council as a successor to the National Council which he had set up in 1957. It contained regional and functional representatives, and since he accepted the political parties as functional, there were two members apiece from the Communists, Nationalists, and Nahdatul Ulama, and six from the minor parties. Sukarno had achieved his aim of including Communists in the government. The Masjumi and the Socialists, who had opposed him, were given no representation. In March 1960 Sukarno dismissed the legislature, and set up a successor the members of which were chosen and appointed by Sukarno himself. His opponents such as the Masjumi were eliminated, and the Communists were liberally represented.[20] Sukarno could now say with a good deal of accuracy "I am the state," if he added "with the consent of the army and the Communists." As a finishing touch he banned his principal opponents, the Masjumi and Socialist parties, and in 1962 arrested some of their leaders. He announced the formation of a mass political organization to be headed by himself and called the National Front. There would also be a Provisional People's Congress, declared to be the supreme governmental authority, with its members appointed by himself.

Sukarno as dictator has the valuable assets of his prestige, his demagogic control of the masses, and his skill in political intrigue. The army is the only efficient force in Indonesia, and the officers are a picked group since able and ambitious young Indonesians regard it as the most desirable career. General Nasution is a capable officer and appears to control the armed forces, though there are persistent reports that factiousness continues. Nasution has been won over to support Sukarno, and has obtained substantial representation in the government. The army retains its overriding authority in many fields of civil administration. As previously this power is used spasmodically and at its own discretion. The army is hostile to the Communists, although Nasution himself says that it is neither for nor against them but merely non-Communist. The Communists have gained greatly in numbers and influence from Sukarno's favor, and are rumored to have infiltrated into the army. For the time being their policy is to support him since they need his help to increase their power in face of the strong opposition of the army. They often attack failures of the government, e.g., the inability to raise the low standard of living, but so far they always blame cabinet ministers and never Sukarno. It should be remembered that their leader Aidit contends that the Communists can obtain control of the government by constitutional means. They probably hope that their opportunity will come with the further deterioration of economic conditions. The Nationalists and the other political parties have declined sharply in influence. The distribution of power appears to be based on an unstable coalition between the politician, the soldier and the Communist. Sukarno trims adroitly between his rival supporters. In view of the shifts and compromises which have characterized Indonesian political and army life in the past decade, it is possible that this alliance might continue for a considerable time, because none of the three seems to be strong enough to ignore the other two.[21] So far as Sukarno is concerned the decisive factor may be whether he is able to cope with the economic and political problems which confront his country. Under parliamentary democracy there was always the premier to take the blame for the failure to solve them. Sukarno was in the background, however much his influence might have affected events. His establishment of guided democracy has deprived him of a scapegoat, and he himself bears the responsibility for the success or failure of his administration. Nothing in his previous career leads one to expect that he will show the necessary constructive ability. His policy has been a negative reiteration of old formulas, and at his age — he was born in 1900 — he is not likely to change. But whatever happens to Sukarno dictatorship in some form or other seems likely to continue.

South Viet Nam

Ngo Dinh Diem was appointed premier of the newly created state of South Viet Nam in July 1954. He was strongly nationalist and equally opposed to French rule and to Communism. Bao Dai, the Chief of State, and France were reluctant to make the appointment, but gave way under pressure from the United States. Ngo Dinh Diem's first fifteen months in office were taken up with defeating his domestic opponents and consolidating his position. He dismissed the commander of the army who supported Bao Dai and France and secured the loyalty of the soldiers. He crushed the Cao Dai and two other sects which had their own private armies, controlled part of the country, and formed an *imperium in imperio.* Military operations were conducted against the Communist guerillas, and their position was weakened. Ho Chi Minh had agreed to withdraw them to North Viet Nam in the peace treaty concluded at Geneva in 1954, but the promise had not been kept. Finally, on October 23, 1955, Ngo Dinh Diem eliminated Bao Dai. An overwhelming majority of the voters rejected him as Chief of State and elected Ngo Dinh Diem as president of the republic of South Viet Nam.

The new state could not have survived without economic and military aid, and for this the president turned to the United States. It supplied equipment and a military mission to replace French officers in training an army of 150,000. It also gave economic aid as described in another chapter. The large French army which had been concentrated in South Viet Nam after the loss of the northern part of the country was withdrawn on the demand of Ngo Dinh Diem. There was an exodus of French firms with their trained personnel, and a repatriation of a considerable amount of capital. Viet Nam severed the link between its currency and the franc, and a large part of its foreign trade was diverted from France to the United States. The result was to create in France strong resentment against the new state.[22] It was with difficulty that the deputies in the National Assembly were persuaded to approve a moderate grant of economic aid. The practical effect is that South Viet Nam has moved from the French into the American sphere of influence, and must look to its new protector for military and economic help.

The Constitution of South Viet Nam

In March 1956 a National Constitutional Assembly of 123 members was chosen by an electorate composed of all citizens of both sexes aged eighteen and over. The members came almost entirely from the same nationalist elite which made up the governments of the other states of Southeast Asia. The Assembly was dominated by the president's own party, the National Revolutionary Movement, together with a friendly Roman Catholic party. Apparently Ngo Dinh Diem had a good deal of influence over the drafting of the constitution.

The salient feature was executive leadership and control. The single-chamber legislature was given important powers and duties, but they

85

were overshadowed, at times even in the field of law-making, by those of the president. The constitution was based far more on the American than the French model, and emphasized the separation of powers between the executive and the legislature. Cabinet ministers might not be members of the National Assembly. The term of office of the president was five years, and he might be re-elected for two additional terms. He negotiated and ratified treaties, appointed and dismissed military and civil officials, submitted bills to the Assembly, had the power of veto, and might postpone elections in time of crisis. He could declare a state of emergency, and between sessions of the Assembly he might legislate by decree "for reason of emergency." A section of the constitution guaranteed the rights of the citizen, but they were hedged about with so many reservations that their validity was doubtful. For example freedom of public meeting and association were guaranteed, but the qualification was attached "within the limits set by law." Freedom of the press was also guaranteed and the censorship abolished. In practice the publication of anything of which the authorities disapproved was punished by fine, imprisonment or suspension of the publication. Despatches of foreign correspondents were strictly censored.[23]

The Government

The unusually extensive powers given to the president could easily be used to change a paper democracy into a dictatorship. An American observer wrote a description of the government in 1957 which remained true to the end.

From the beginning Diem has ruled virtually as a dictator. South Viet Nam is today a quasi-police state characterized by arbitrary arrests and imprisonment, strict censorship of the press and the absence of an effective political opposition. . . . there is little evidence that [he has] much understanding or sympathy for real democracy. . . . While unquestionably devoted to the welfare of his countrymen, whom he usually refers to as the "little people," he envisages the role of government as essentially paternalistic.[24]

The government in practice was a family affair. Virtually all power was concentrated in the hands of the president, his brothers, and his sister-in-law, assisted by a few trusted friends. He was suspicious of strangers, and refused to share power with other able and educated Vietnamese. Either they were too ambitious or hostile to the Ngo family, or they wanted too much.[25] Cabinet ministers were appointed and dismissed by the president, and they were careful to make no important decisions without referring to him.

An American university mission was brought in to train officials for the government service, but its puritanical standards are diluted by warm human emotions. In Asia a man with a proper sense of his responsibilities is expected to provide for his relatives and friends, and senior officials draw heavily on their families in filling positions. The example given by President Ngo Dinh Diem was loyally followed, and nepotism became rampant at all levels. The civil service was overstaffed and underpaid, and the traditional Asian practice of squeeze reasserted itself. Officials knew that they would be dismissed if they offended the government, and therefore they procrastinated in making decisions and when possible passed on the responsibility to someone in higher authority. Their support for the regime was often halfhearted. In the provincial governments the most important officials were army officers and not civil servants.[26]

So far as elections were concerned there was a fairly close approximation to a single-party system. It was possible but not probable for an opponent of the president to be elected as a non-party independent. When Ngo Dinh Diem was first appointed he set to work to build his own bloc of supporters. Besides appointing his own relatives and followers to the principal positions he won the support of the army officers. Before the Constitutional Assembly was elected in 1956 officials loyal to the president chose the candidates who were permitted to run and counted the votes. They also went from house to house and told the people how to vote. The candidatures of numerous independents were suppressed, and many cases were reported of intimidation or temporary arrest of suspected opponents of the administration.[27] The government had sponsored the organization of a nation-wide political party known as the National Revolutionary Movement. To belong to it was essential for anyone who hoped for a civil-service appointment or for a peasant who wanted a government loan. The membership was very large and it was in effect the official government party. The representatives of the Movement who were members of the National Assembly had to sign an undated letter of resignation in return for the government's assurance of election. There was also the Party of the Personality of the

Worker, the head of which was a brother of the president. Apparently it was not a political party but an intelligence service the duty of which was to make reports on Communist infiltration into the civil service and on official corruption.

There was no effective opposition party because none was allowed to exist. The law required that no party might be formed without official permission, and this was always refused to opponents of the regime. A candidate for election who opposed Ngo Dinh Diem had to run as a solitary independent. He could not form a party or in practice hold a public meeting. Other heavy handicaps were censorship of the press and control of the radio. The government had also the power under a presidential ordinance of 1956 to arrest "individuals considered dangerous to national defence and common security." The ordinance was supposed to apply only to Communists, but anti-Communists who opposed Ngo Dinh Diem were also arrested. No provision was made for a hearing, either judicial or administrative, and in 1957 it was estimated that the number of political prisoners was between seven thousand and eight thousand. The number in 1963 was unknown. When the Assembly met after the election of 1959 there was an empty chair. An opponent of Ngo Dinh Diem, Dr. Phan Quang Dan, the only successful opposition candidate, was elected in Saigon by an overwhelming majority, but was placed under house arrest when he tried to take his seat. This election was conducted in much the same fashion as its predecessor. Particularly in the country districts, most opponents of the government were prevented from running on trivial pretexts. Owing to the large number of Westerners living in Saigon they were permitted to stand in the hope of giving the election a democratic façade, but were given little opportunity to win.[28]

The Non-Communist Opposition

The result of Ngo Dinh Diem's policy was that anti-Communists who disapproved of his dictatorship had to choose between illegal activity and abandoning politics. In November 1960 a small group of army officers and civilian opponents of the president made an abortive attempt to overthrow him by a *coup d'état*. The greater part of the armed forces and the majority of his civilian opponents took no part in the revolt of the paratroops. Nevertheless many officers and officials chafed at the stringent and overcentralized control which Ngo Dinh Diem exercised. His failure to defeat the Communist guerillas made them still more discontented with his refusal to allow them more independence of action. Reforms were promised during and after the coup, but failed to materialize.[29] The president was unwise in confining power to so small a circle of relations and faithful friends. It allowed no outlet for the desire for power and it could not even claim the justification of success. It was impossible to believe that all the outstanding ability in South Viet Nam was confined to the president's relatives and intimates. As to his fear that some capable men were overly ambitious or were hostile to his family, to work with personal rivals and keep them in their place is an occupational hazard of all political leaders. On balance it would have been less dangerous to allow them reasonable scope than to frustrate them. It would also have been wise to relax the rigidity with which any opposition was stifled. To go from one extreme to the other, however, and convert the government into a paper democracy would equally have been a blunder.

The Vietnamese in all their history have had no experience of democratic government except sometimes in the election of village headmen. The central government was an absolute monarchy, the emperor administering the country through a civil service which was based on the model of the Chinese mandarinate. This was succeeded by French colonial rule, the aim of which was the exact opposite of the American and British policy of gradual training for self-government. The Vietnamese have not had even the short experience of democracy which was given the Filipinos and the Burmans, and in lesser measure the Indonesians. They lack the prerequisites which were discussed earlier. The overwhelming majority are peasants who look upon government as an outside power which commands them and enriches itself at their expense. They have no loyalty toward it: that is reserved for their families and villages. But they do not believe that it is proper for them to give orders to a force beyond their control. The opposition to Ngo Dinh Diem came from the tiny Western-educated middle class, a few thousand in number, who did not have positions in the civil service or the army. They were the teachers, lawyers, and other professional men, business men and students, and the majority lived in the city of Saigon. Significantly, most of them showed little interest in the condition of the peasantry which was the crucial problem in a predominantly peasant country. Democracy would be premature: Ngo Dinh Diem gave South Viet Nam the type of leadership for which it was fitted, though he went much too far in his rigid suppression of all opposition, his refusal to delegate authority to his military and civilian subordinates (especially when his own methods were failing to win the war against the Communists), and his establishment of a family dictatorship. His crowning folly was his mishandling of the Buddhist opposition.

The treatment of the Buddhist monks was the immediate although not the only cause of Ngo Dinh Diem's downfall. They inherited the traditional hostility to Roman Catholicism which had existed since the seventeenth century because missionary priests were regarded as agents of European imperialism. The greater number of the Vietnamese were Buddhists, and the monks had strong influence over them. The monks were enjoined by the rules of their order to eschew all worldly interests and devote themselves to religion. In practice they often took an active part in politics: they were one principal cause of the hostility to British rule in Burma, and in Ceylon a decade ago they helped to bring about the electoral defeat of the Kotelawala government. A wise ruler would have conciliated and used them as U Nu did in Burma. This course of action was extremely advisable for Ngo Dinh Diem and his family since they were Roman Catholics and one of the brothers was an archbishop. The monks were predisposed to be hostile, and when open conflict developed their object was to strengthen their position and bring about the downfall of the Ngo family. Confronted by this threat the Ngos behaved with a stupidity which bordered on the incredible. Just at the moment when the independence of the country from Communist control was balanced on a knife edge the morale of the soldiers and the peasants was attacked by the knowledge that monks and nuns whom they regarded as holy were burning themselves to death. The sole policy of the government was brutal suppression and arrests, and Madame Ngo Dinh Nhu's gibe at "barbecued monks." The last straw was Ngo Dinh Diem's incurable distrust of his subordinates which led him to remove one general after another from his command. Not one of them could feel secure, and in the end the generals whom he still trusted appear to have joined those who had become his enemies in overthrowing his dictatorship and putting him and one of his brothers to death. The end of the whole matter was the dictatorship of a group of generals who were united by their determination to destroy the power of the Ngo family. Their assurance that they intended to set up a democratic government did not need to be taken very seriously. If the history of military dictatorships in other Asian states could be taken as a criterion, the victors would divide into cliques struggling for power. In 1964 General Nguyen Khanh seized power and imprisoned his predecessors.

The Communist Guerilla War

During the Vietnamese revolt against France the principal field of military operations was in the north, but guerilla bands were also active in what is today South Viet Nam from 1947 onwards. Many of the secret camps in the jungle and the caches of arms and supplies which are being used at the present time were prepared then. These hiding places now exist all over the countryside. The Geneva Agreement of 1954 stipulated that all guerillas must be withdrawn to North Viet Nam. Many were removed, but others were left behind as the nucleus of a fifth column. During the first years of his rule Ngo Dinh Diem weakened the Viet Cong, the Vietnamese name for the Communist guerillas. In 1959 Ho Chi Minh decided to intensify his campaign. Additional guerillas were sent to South Viet Nam, nearly all being southerners who had been withdrawn in 1954. It is believed that some came by sea while others crossed over from their bases in Laos, which borders on South Viet Nam. They gained many recruits from among the South Vietnamese peasants by a mixture of persuasion and terrorism, and it has been estimated that their number increased from a few hundred to perhaps twenty-five thousand in 1962, most being South Vietnamese. In addition there were many thousands of sympathizers, part-time guerillas, and political and propaganda agents. The forces at the disposal of the government were an army of a hundred and fifty thousand and a civil guard of forty-seven thousand intended to protect the villages and the provincial governments from Communist attacks. The army was too small to close a frontier of twelve hundred miles, much of which ran across sparsely inhabited jungles and mountains. The swampy rice lands in the delta of the Mekong river south of Saigon have been another center of activity, and bands of guerillas varying in number from fifty to two hundred were scattered throughout the

91

country in the rural areas. By 1962 they dominated about eighty per cent of the countryside.

The object of the Viet Cong has been to bring about the collapse of authority in the rural areas, and to nullify the attempts to improve the living conditions of the peasants. Adroit use was made of their grievances, such as abuses of power and exactions by officials. The armed forces were also disliked, because they were poorly paid and given to looting. Then again the peasants' huts were burnt when the soldiers were trying to clear a district of the Viet Cong. The consequence was that they refused to help by giving information about guerilla movements. The Philippine army created the same non-cooperative attitude among the peasants until Magsaysay made it into a disciplined force. Terrorism has also been used by the Communists: provincial officials, village headmen, and peasants who were loyal to the government were assassinated. In 1961 the authorities estimated that something like four hundred peasants and officials were killed each month, as compared with about thirty a month in 1960. Medical-aid stations and bridges were destroyed, village health officers and anti-malaria teams were assassinated, teachers were intimidated into abandoning their schools, taxes were levied, peasants were punished for accepting government crop loans, and occasionally a village was burnt. The Viet Cong made it clear that in the areas where they operated the government was unable to give security to the peasants. Ngo Dinh Diem had given some of them farms by eliminating the landowners, but he was unable to protect them from being murdered. The result was that their support for him declined. The situation deteriorated rapidly from 1960 onwards, and was similar to that which confronted the French during the war in North Viet Nam. The government held the towns, but in Viet Cong areas control of the countryside was more or less shared. By day strong forces could move almost anywhere, though small detachments were always likely to be attacked. After nightfall the countryside belonged to the guerillas.[30]

The Viet Cong used the same hit-and-run tactics as in North Viet Nam and Malaya. They made no attempt to hold towns or villages, and they never attacked regular soldiers unless they had an overwhelming superiority. If they entered a village they only stayed long enough to levy taxes, obtain recruits, and perhaps carry out an assassination or two. Long before the troops could be informed of the attack and arrive on the scene the guerillas had vanished. There were so many villages which might be attacked that it was impossible to spare enough soldiers to protect all of them. In the absence of definite information as to which village was target for tonight, all the army could do was to come to the rescue as fast as possible, and usually too late. The vice-president of South Viet Nam stated that "our main difficulty in finding the Communists [is] we lack sharp information." In other words, the government had a poor intelligence service, the same handicap which confronted the French in their war against Ho Chi Minh and the British during the earlier years of their fighting against the Chinese guerillas in Malaya. The Viet Cong, on the other hand, had a good intelligence service, and were helped everywhere by their underground village organization. This was similar to the Min Yuen which the Communists in Malaya created during their revolt. Another similarity was that the peasants supplied the Viet Cong with food.[31] In addition to these handicaps the army had been trained and equipped by the French to fight a conventional war, and its tactics were of little use in a jungle war against guerillas. Until 1962 the American military mission did little to alter this situation. The reason in part at least was that American military advisers operated only at divisional level, and had no contact with the battalions and smaller units which carried on the actual fighting. Senior Vietnamese officers were often unwilling to discard the tactics they had learned from the French.

At the beginning of 1962 the Communists were clearly in the ascendant. They were better trained, better armed, and better led than in the past, and they seemed to have little trouble making up their losses through local recruitment and infiltration from North Viet Nam. By the end of the year their advance had been slowed down and there were grounds for a cautious optimism. The amount of American military aid was very considerably enlarged, and by 1963 expenditure was running at the rate of $1,000,000 a day. The size of the government's armed forces increased by two thirds, the army rising to 200,000, and the civil guard and the self-defense corps to 165,000. The American military mission grew from 865 in November 1961 to 11,000 a year later. The majority were specialists in guerilla warfare, and they accompanied the battalions and smaller units which were actually fighting the Viet Cong as advisers instead of being attached only to the senior officers of the Vietnamese army. They also took part in transport and air support missions. Their losses in 1962 were thirty-four killed and eighty-five wounded. A British mission was brought in from Malaya, made up of officers who had taken part in the suppression of the Communist revolt there, and much was learned from their experience. The Vietnamese soldiers were taught more effective tactics. Intelligence was improved to the point where it was sometimes possible to anticipate Viet Cong movements. Better communications reduced the time needed to learn of Viet Cong activities, and the mobility of the Vietnamese army was increased by using helicopters.[32]

Part of the credit for improvement in the situation belonged to the strategic village program. Between 1959 and 1961 the government tried to give the peasants security by resettling them in agrovilles. These were fortified towns built by forced labor where the inhabitants were provided with amenities such as electricity, schools, and clinics. The strategic village is a more modest successor of the agrovilles. It is a fortified village with an armed guard, and peasants living outside are compelled to move into it. There are about sixteen thousand villages, and the government intends to fortify two thirds of them. Over four thousand were fortified in 1962 and 500,000 peasants were brought under government control. The British in Malaya found that the only way to break up the guerillas' intelligence network and cut off the supply of food, recruits, and money was forcibly to uproot 500,000 scattered Chinese peasants and rehouse them in five hundred fifty villages built for the occasion, where they could be protected — and prevented from helping the Communists. The task in South Viet Nam is on a much larger scale, since virtually the entire peasant population of a country of 14,000,000 must be protected.

The position in 1963 was better than it had been a year earlier, but this could be reversed if mistakes were made. The war will be long, bitter, and expensive, and there are certain to be local defeats and more American casualties. Further improvement in the army's tactics and the completion of the strategic village program are not the whole answer. The Viet Cong will still retain the important advantage that the war is fed from outside. They receive some recruits and equipment from North Viet Nam, although most of their arms appear to have been taken from the government's forces. To capture them is a principal reason for the attacks on the Vietnamese army. Moreover, the Viet Cong have bases in Laos and North Viet Nam which can only be attacked at the risk of bringing about Chinese intervention. One reason for the French defeat in Algeria was that the guerillas could always take temporary refuge in Tunisia and Morocco when hard pressed. The analogy is not exact, because the Algerian guerillas also received much of their equipment via these same countries. Nevertheless secure base of operations is not a negligible factor. Ngo Dinh Diem's attack on the Buddhists weakened the army's morale and the Viet Cong gained strength. The military dictatorship which succeeded him failed to recover the lost ground.

Thailand

The nationalist revolt in Thailand was carried out by the same small, Western-educated middle class as elsewhere. It differed from the others in that the old order which was overthrown was not a Western colonial government, but a god-king whose absolute rule was sanctified by immemorial custom. Ironically, too, the monarchy created the group which destroyed it. Thailand had had a succession of reforming kings who changed an Asian monarchy of the traditional type into a twentieth-century state. They modernized the armed forces, built roads and railways, and introduced social services. To do this assistants were needed, and the cleverest boys from the schools were sent to Europe or the United States at royal expense to receive further training. On their return almost all entered the king's service. In this way the monarchy created a small middle class which had not existed before, and it was this group which carried out the bloodless *coup d'état* of 1932.

The revolutionary clique numbered a hundred fifteen, of whom sixty-four were civilians, the majority civil servants, who provided the ideas. Their leader was Pridi Banomyong, a professor of international law at Chulalongkorn University. They were joined by thirty-three army and eighteen naval officers, varying in rank from captain to colonel, who supplied the force. Thai privates and sailors follow the junior officers whom they know personally and not the generals and admirals with whom they have no personal contact. On this occasion the relatives of the king who held the supreme command suddenly

95

discovered that the armed forces had gone over to the side of the revolution, and that resistance was impracticable. The leaders of the *coup d'état* called themselves the People's Party, but the peasants who formed the majority of the population had no part in the revolt which was made in their name.[33] Like all the later coups, this one was carried out by a small group in Bangkok.

The Constitution

The king was retained as a constitutional figurehead, and his power was transferred to the revolutionary clique. The constitution was of the parliamentary democracy type, the premier and cabinet being responsible to a single-chamber legislature known as the House of the People's Representatives. Half the members were elected and half appointed by the clique who had seized power. The reason given for this arrangement was the perfectly correct one that the people did not understand democracy, and must be educated before their full rights were conferred upon them. The appointment of half the legislators was to continue until half the Thais were literate or for ten years at most. This arrangement made certain that the clique which was entrenched in the executive would also control the legislature, so long as it did not itself split into factions. It could count on the votes of the appointed members, and some of those who were elected could always be won over by bribes or threats. The legislature could only exercise real authority if the ruling oligarchy became hopelessly divided against itself. Thirty years later the appointed element still remained, although the proportion of elected members was now about two thirds. This was brought about by a decision of the Supreme Court, which overruled the government's attempt to retain the fifty-fifty division.[34]

After a few years the revolutionary clique began to divide into factions, although the gulf between them did not become unbridgeable until the period of Japanese rule. Various causes brought about the separation. Once the absolute monarchy had been overthrown the clique as a whole had no agreed upon policy for the future. The only approach to it was Pridi's plan for a form of utopian socialism which was wrongly condemned as Communism by the more conservative members. So after the successful *coup d'état* the only aim of the group was to maintain itself in office, and this was not strong enough to counteract the tendency to divide into rival factions. Personal rivalry developed between Pridi, who led the civilian element, and Captain Phibun Songgram, who had the support of the army and naval officers and therefore of the armed forces. If the king had been supported by a strong party the bond of common danger might have held the revolutionary group together. The royalists were so weak, however, that Pridi and Phibun felt that they could safely work against one another for the control of the state. The underlying reason for the breakdown of unity was that the *coup d'état* had destroyed the constitutional basis of authority, and the only justification left for the revolutionary government was force. Therefore whichever faction was the stronger had the right to seize power.

The Basis of Authority and the *Coup d'État*

Every government must have a basis of authority, a reason why the people support it. As long as they believed in the divine right of kings they hesitated to disobey God's order by rebelling against the ruler whom He had chosen. In a genuine democracy it is considered that the government which has been elected by the majority must only be opposed by constitutional methods. In Soviet Russia no one imagines that God has any responsibility for the rise of Stalin or Khrushchev. And in a country where every election gives the dictator a 99.7 per cent majority, no one can believe that he owes his position to the free vote of the people. The only reason for it is that he destroyed all his opponents because he had more power than they did. From this it follows that any rival who can win control of a still stronger force has justification for his seizure of power.

In Thailand the authority of the god-king rested on veneration and custom. The Thai had always obeyed a king, and a custom which has lasted for centuries tends to continue from force of habit. The revolutionary clique shattered the traditional basis of authority. They tried to substitute popular sovereignty, but the vast majority of the Thai neither understood nor wanted it. They believed in government from above by an autocrat and they gave their loyalty to an individual and not to the rights of the people. This point of view was expressed by the peasant who said he voted for Phibun Songgram because "He is

97

like our Master. He has been very good and kind to us." [35] When the struggle developed between Phibun's and Pridi's factions neither could win any peasant support by the claim that it was the representative of democratic sovereignty. So the sole right to govern was the possession of superior force. The internal history of Thailand since 1932 has been largely a struggle between cliques to decide which possessed this justification for seizing power.

The authors of an unsuccessful coup have usually been punished leniently and rarely executed. The Thai had a mild disposition and shared the Buddhist dislike of taking life. Politics have been contests between personalities and not principles, and political leaders have regarded a coup as one of the gambles of the political game. It is resorted to by a faction which cannot win power by peaceful means but is confident it can do so by force. Once in office the faction deals with its opponents by exile or imprisonment and seriously tries to observe the constitutional proprieties. It buys supporters by an elaborate system of bribery. It may well hold an election to legitimize its position, confident that it can obtain a majority in the legislature. The ins and the outs understand one another. Each knows that the other will make a new attempt to return to power but will not try to eliminate the opposition physically. The losers live and quite possibly regain power.

The Transition to Army Rule

The government was controlled by civilians until 1938, and again from 1944 to 1947. They cooperated in Phibun's first government from 1938 to 1944 though the military faction was the dominant group. The period of Japanese control completed the irreparable division of the revolutionary clique because Phibun's followers worked with the Japanese while those of Pridi formed the underground which supported the Western Allies. In doing this they had the help of the police. In 1944 Phibun resigned the premiership, and the government came under the control of Pridi and his civilian faction. In order to win a majority in the legislature Pridi formed an alliance with some of the political parties which had arisen among the elected members of the legislature. For part of the time he himself was premier and at others he substituted a reliable seat warmer. His control of the government was precarious because he was unable to compose the jealousies and conflicting ambitions of some of the groups which supported him. He was also opposed by Phibun's faction and by many of the elected members of the legislature. In 1947 a clique of army officers organized a conspiracy in which Phibun was involved, to seize power. This was a more serious threat to Pridi's position than the instability of his parliamentary majority, for the army was by far the strongest organized force in Thailand. A government which had its support could easily obtain the necessary majority in the legislature, while one which had merely a parliamentary majority held power on sufferance. Pridi was also weakened by his failure to end the corruption among his supporters, and by the widespread belief, quite possibly unfounded, that he had engineered the killing of King Ananda.

The *Coup d'État* of 1947

In November 1947 another bloodless *coup d'état* put most of the principal members of the government in prison, except for Pridi and a few others who evaded arrest. Temporarily the army did not openly take over control, but installed Aphaiwong as premier. He was a moderate conservative and a royalist, and was well thought of in Thailand and abroad. He had a majority in the legislature, but he resigned in April 1948 to make way for Phibun because the army ordered him to do so. This was another illustration that force was the real power in Thailand. Phibun's resumption of the premiership did not mean that he had regained the authority which he had held from 1938 to 1944. It also marked the passing of the original revolutionary clique, one or the other faction of which had controlled the government since 1932. A new clique of younger army officers had arisen, and they were the power behind the throne.

The leaders of the *coup d'état* of 1947 numbered sixty-five of whom fifty-seven had the rank of colonel or below. Only three of them had been members of the revolutionary clique of 1932. A high percentage of the 1932 group had been educated abroad, while very few of the 1947 clique had gone further than secondary school, followed by training in the army. They were junior officers who resented their poor pay and the control of the government by the old guard. Among their number were two colonels, Phao Sriyanon and Sarit Thanarat, who had leading roles in the coup of 1957. The 1947 clique realized that they were unknown men who had no knowledge of how to conduct do-mestic or foreign affairs, and they had no ideas beyond the seizure of power. Phibun could supply their deficiencies, and he was a master of the arts of intrigue and manipulation which were essential to politi-cal success in Thailand. He had the further recommendation that he could not oust them from power, since they and not he controlled the army. When he had gained control of the government in 1938 he had promoted himself to the rank of field marshal. This might have been no more than a proper recognition of his merits, but so far as the army was concerned it raised him to the stratosphere and he lost con-tact with the rank and file. They transferred their allegiance to the junior officers whom they knew personally, the leaders of the 1947 coup. Phibun could only retain the premiership so long as they sup-ported him, and at the same time they were conscious that they needed his superior knowledge and political acumen. As Hitler used to say, there was ground for fruitful collaboration.

Pridi's Abortive Coups

Pridi had not given up his ambition to return to power, and in 1949 and more seriously in 1951 attempts were made to overthrow Phibun and the 1947 clique. The navy supported Pridi on both occasions, and the reason for his failures was that the army was the stronger branch of the services. The victories of the 1947 clique enabled them to carry out a purge of their opponents which greatly weakened them. Incidentally Pridi's resort to force was a confession that he agreed with Phibun that armed strength and not an election was the way to win power in Thailand. The abortive coup of 1951 was quite spectacu-lar. In June 1951 a few junior naval officers concocted a plot of which their admirals were seemingly as ignorant as the generals of the army. The opening move was a resounding success. The United States had presented a dredger to Phibun's government, and to mark the solemnity of the occasion a reception was held on board so that the American ambassador could hand over the vessel. While the ceremony was in progress a handful of sailors came up in a launch, snatched premier Field Marshal Phibun from the midst of the rank and fashion of Bangkok, and imprisoned him on a warship. The navy was anchored in the river which runs through the city, while the army was quartered on both banks. Several hours of confusion followed, after which three days of heavy fighting took place between the army and the police on the one side and the navy on the other. The outcome was in doubt until the air force which had usually followed a policy of neutrality intervened and sank three warships, including the one on which Phibun was imprisoned. He managed to escape, and the navy surrendered. The 1947 clique took advantage of its victory to put its own nominees in command of the navy, and the air force had committed itself by its intervention. The 1947 group now controlled all the armed forces. There was also a suspicion that it had come to look upon Phibun as expendable, since it had allowed the air force to sink the ship on which he was imprisoned. The two men who emerged from the coup as dominant figures in the state were Generals Phao Sriyanon, chief of police, and Sarit Thanarat, commander of the Bangkok army. They had been colonels when they plotted the 1947 *coup d'état*. From then onwards Phibun to retain his position must trim his sails between the two.

Five months later the 1947 clique still further strengthened its position by changing the constitution. In 1949 a constitution had been adopted by which the selection of the legislature was completely free from direct control by the government. In November 1951 the 1947 group restored the constitution of 1932 under which the executive appointed half the members. The change eliminated the power of the political parties which had opposed it, and gave it control of the legislature. The opposition was forbidden to form political parties. Phibun's position was weakened, but he was still needed to win the support of some of the elected half of the members. There was only one threat to the 1947 clique's control of the state: the growing rivalry between its leading members threatened to make it go the way of its predecessor and divide into hostile factions.

The 1957 *Coup d'État*

As the unity of the 1947 group weakened, Generals Phao Sriyanon and Sarit Thanarat emerged as the leaders of rival cliques, and Phibun walked delicately between them. The government was made up of Phibun's faction of personal followers: General Sarit's faction which controlled the army and had strong influence over the navy and air force: and General Phao's faction which controlled the police and the government's majority of elected members of the legislature. Sarit controlled the majority of the appointed fifty per cent of the members. Phao's police were armed with tanks and artillery to assist them in their war on crime. In 1955 Phibun permitted free public discussion of politics and the registration of political parties. Twenty-five took advantage of the permission, of which the most impressive was that of the government, the Seri Manangkhasila. More accurately it was the party of General Phao and Phibun. Freedom of discussion produced widespread criticisms of Phibun's government, its membership in the South East Asia Treaty Organization, and of American policy.

An election was held in February 1957, and Phibun and General Phao spent money very lavishly and compelled the civil service to act as their party machine. Even so their Seri Manangkhasila won only a bare majority. The press and intelligentsia of Bangkok took such full advantage of Phibun's concession of free public discussion that he declared a state of national emergency and appointed General Sarit commander-in-chief of the army. The latter greatly increased his popularity by vigorously condemning the corruption of the election. By an adroit combination of military and student demonstrations and parliamentary maneuvers he drove Phibun and General Phao into exile in September. Sarit held a new election in December 1957 which was a model of good order. No party won a majority but this was immaterial since Sarit's army clique was in control. Sarit formed a coalition government composed of his elected supporters in the Unionist party which he had formed in May 1957 together with the bloc of half the members whom he appointed. They were combined in the National Socialist party, and Sarit's faithful supporter, General Thanom Kitikachorn, was installed as premier. A series of minor crises followed which weakened his position. In October 1958 Field Marshal Sarit carried out another bloodless *coup d'état* and established himself as military dictator.[36]

Sarit Thanarat revealed himself more autocratic than Phibun Songgram, and more intolerant of criticism from the politicians. He believed that benevolent despotism was the best form of government for Thailand. The initiative must lie with the government in promoting welfare and security, while the duty of the people is to obey. At the same time Sarit

102

recognized the need of popular support, even though his main reliance was on the army. He thought that Western democracy had shown itself unsuitable for Thailand, and that the various constitutions drawn up since 1932 made a mistake in imitating Western political institutions and paying so little attention to Thai ideas of government. A new constitution must be drafted which would be more in keeping with the needs of the people. In October 1958 he abolished the existing constitution. He also dissolved the legislature, arrested many of its members and others who had opposed him, forbade all political parties, declared martial law, and established a new Revolutionary party which was controlled by the army.

Sarit drew up a provisional constitution in 1959. In accordance with its provisions he appointed all the members of the legislature, the majority being senior officers of the army of whose loyalty he felt assured. In addition to functioning as a parliament they were to draft the new constitution. Sarit himself became premier, and he and his cabinet were no longer responsible to the legislature. Furthermore, he could rule independently whenever he decided that law and order were in jeopardy. It would appear that the principal duty of the provisional legislature is to endorse the proposals of the executive and act as a camouflage for Sarit's benevolent despotism. He seemed to be popular with all except the small urban educated class.[37] After his death in 1963 he was succeeded by General Thanom Kitikachorn.

The Politically Effective Class

The politically effective class is perhaps one or two per cent of the total population, and the majority live in the capital city of Bangkok. Practically all the leaders of importance have been prominent members of one or other of the three principal coup d'état groups of 1932, 1947, and 1957. The majority have been army officers, since each coup depended for its success on military support. The politically effective class can be divided into three sections, according to the amount of power which they wield. At the summit are ten or fifteen men who dominate Thailand because they control the armed forces and the police, and have great prestige and influence because of their record as members of a coup group or in political life. Subordinate to them but at the same time possessing considerable powers of their own are a group of about a thousand. Among them are generals and colonels, senior civil servants, prominent members of the legislature, a few princes, and perhaps a few leading business men. This last category is very small: most business men are Chinese, in spite of a quarter of a century of government efforts to eliminate them in favor of Thai. Finally, there is the politically conscious and vocal public, most of whom are graduates of a university, a secondary school, or a military academy. The majority are civil servants, and the group includes professional men, journalists, office workers, and students.[38]

Nationalism pervades every stratum of society, although it is strongest in the ruling class. It is not chauvinistic and xenophobic like that of Indonesia. The Thai are proud of their independence and mean to maintain it, and they want to be let alone, free from foreign interference. Their only antipathy is to the Chinese, whom one of their writers described as the Jews of Asia. In spite of the important part which the government plays in economic life, socialism and radical movements generally seem to be much weaker in Thailand than in Indonesia or Burma. Western private enterprise is encouraged, and so far as Communism exists it appears to be very largely confined to the Chinese. The bulk of the politically effective class are government officials, civil or military, with an established position and a vested interest in the existing order of society. They have no wish to see it overturned and are conservative in outlook. Another factor working to the same end is that until very recently at least there has been no intellectual proletariat. This is the army of educated unemployed who have passed all the school examinations and have no assured position because the supply of white-collar jobs is too small to give employment to the large number of students who spent years in training for positions which did not exist. In Thailand most of the educated group have found employment in the government services.[39]

The Peasants

The peasants have not understood or wanted democracy. They have acquiesced in the government's decisions and have been indifferent to national politics. They have known vaguely of the *coups d'état* and the rise and fall of Bangkok politicians, but they have not been greatly concerned with changes which had little or no effect on them. Their interest has been in their crops and village affairs, and national policies were felt to be the concern of the government. In spite of the revolution of 1932 the king was still venerated, and many peasants looked upon government officials as his agents. Newspapers were few and readers limited. In the provinces knowledge of political affairs was confined to officials, a few well-to-do families and some of the principal Chinese business men. The tenets of Buddhism made for acquiescence in government orders. The monks used their great influence over the peasants to this end, while the government gave the church its benign support. Moreover, the peasants were frugally prosperous and content. The majority owned their own land, the burden of the money lender seems to have been lighter than in most parts of Asia, and law and order were usually good. The government compulsorily bought the peasant's rice and resold it abroad at as high a profit as possible. It had the wisdom, however, to pay him a reasonably good price which satisfied him. His desire for democracy can be gauged by his attitude toward voting in elections. "It is the custom of the country: when we are told to go and vote we have to do so." Elections were another incomprehensible invention of that mysterious body the government. The peasant was told that it was for his benefit but he could not see that it made any practical difference. So the majority did not vote unless their village headmen specifically ordered them to do so.[40]

Political Parties

Political parties in the Western sense do not exist. When they have been allowed they have been ephemeral factions supporting one or another of the rival contestants for power among the small governing group. Their party platforms have been unimportant, and the reason for their existence has been to promote the interests of the leader and his followers. Personal friendships and enmities have had much influence in determining allegiance. A member has frequently moved rapidly from one faction to another if it offered him better hopes of advancement. Since the government has been in a better position to provide these inducements than any other clique, this has been one secret of the success with which it has controlled the legislature. Factions have dissolved and new ones formed as the political situation changed. There has been a constant struggle for power within the governing group. Because appeals for popular support had little effect, a faction which aspired to office was compelled to ally itself with some organization which really possessed power. Under existing conditions this could only be the armed forces or the police.[41]

No faction had anything but the most rudimentary organization. Each candidate had to create his own campaign machinery by enlisting the aid of his family and friends. It was a great advantage if he could gain the support of the village headmen since they had much influence over the votes of the peasants. The government clique was no better organized than its rivals, but since it controlled the treasury it was able to pay the campaign expenses of its candidates. This was a real handicap to the opposition factions, whose party funds were much smaller. The government could also send instructions through the provincial administrations to the village headmen to tell the peasants whom to support. This was quite effective: they were accustomed to obey government orders, and were, moreover, indifferent to the election. On the whole, crude pressure on the voters and fraudulent counting of votes were unusual. Bribery was rare because few candidates could afford it. When they were in a position to do so, bribery had a decisive influence on how the votes were cast. In most post-war elections a majority of the elected members belonged to the clique which supported the government.

The Significance of Elections

Elections perform a real function in Thailand, even though it is not the one which is normally ascribed to them. They do not choose the government, for that is done by the clique in power in Bangkok. It is true that the politically conscious minority in Bangkok does have a growing realization that through elections it can exert some influence on the leaders. It is a force of some consequence, but it is unable to control the government owing to its limited numbers and the political immaturity of the peasant majority. In the *coup d'état* of 1957 General Sarit Thanarat received very vociferous support from the educated class in Bangkok, but the decisive factor in his victory was his army and not student demonstrations and a press campaign. Sarit in power did not believe it was necessary to democratize his dictatorship and was more overtly autocratic than his predecessor. Under the conditions which existed in Thailand after the overthrow of the absolute monarchy it was almost inevitable that a dictatorship would be established by the army, which was the only organized and disciplined group in the country. The real significance of the election is that it gives a hallmark of legitimacy to the clique which has already gained control of the government. Many of the Thai feel that their rulers should have a lawful claim to power, and that this should be made manifest by some form of ceremony. This attitude is a survival from the period of the absolute monarchy when elaborate ceremonies were a symbol of the king's right to rule. The election takes the place of the former ceremonial observances as an affirmation that the king's democratic successors are legally entitled to their authority.[42]

As long as the ruling clique controls the bulk of the armed forces and has enough money to win loyal followers and retain them it need have little fear of losing the necessary legislative support. Lack of either of the above prerequisites means a good deal of opposition in the legislature. Thailand in the days of the absolute monarchy believed that officials had a right to the perquisites of office. The principle survived the revolution of 1932 and is an essential part of the operation of democracy in Thailand. The majority of the legislators have had a shrewd eye to their own advancement and are prepared to modify their political principles if suitable arguments are advanced. These can take the form of patronage, pork barrel, grant of government contracts or export licenses, and bribes. On occasion persuasion or threats are effective, and in addition the government has the power itself to appoint members. The result is that with rare exceptions it controls a dependable majority. Provided that the executive includes a politician like Phibun who has a flair for manipulating the political factions, it has little to fear from the legislature. Still other reasons for the latter's weakness are that it is a recent institution which the peasants do not understand or value, and the political factions have little support in the country at large.[43]

Perquisites of office have not been confined to members of the legislature: they have been enjoyed by all who had an official position from cabinet ministers downwards. In the days of the absolute monarchy they were on the whole moderate. There was some nepotism in appointments and promotions and "presents" were expected in re-

107

turn for favors. After 1932 the leaders of the revolution practiced nepotism on a much more extensive scale, and also ensured the loyalty of their principal supporters by appointing them to lucrative positions. Following World War II there was a very grave deterioration in honesty in the civil service from top to bottom. A principal reason was that salaries were very inadequate, and the cost of living had risen to such an extent that bribes were essential to maintain a decent standard of living. A contributory factor was that the high price of rice on the world market made it immensely profitable to evade the government monopoly of its foreign sale by smuggling it out of the country. Those who were engaged in the trade bribed customs officials to turn a blind eye to their activities. This established the habit of bribery, and additional openings for the practice were soon found. By 1951 positions in the civil service were no longer worth taking except for the social position they conferred and the opportunities afforded for receiving bribes.[44] Another reason for the growth of dishonesty was the series of *coups d'état* and especially that of 1947. It was essential to reward the army officers who had put the leaders of the coup in power and ensure their future loyalty. When to this was added the necessity of buying the support of a majority in the legislature, it became necessary to devise an extensive system of legalized squeeze.

The government engaged in banking and many types of business, and every company needed well paid directors. Other directorships were provided by the government monopolies of rice, tobacco, liquors, opium, and other commodities. A Chinese business man who wished to buy immunity from the laws restricting his operations found it expedient to bring an influential member of the faction in power into his company. The leaders of the coup group held a remarkably wide range of positions. In addition to their army posts they were cabinet ministers as well as being directors of banks, government monopolies, and private corporations. The potentialities of companies holding government contracts were not overlooked. Lesser men were rewarded with opportunities commensurate with their value to the leaders, and rackets and corruption were rampant. The junior officers were not forgotten, for the leaders remembered that the privates followed their immediate superiors. As Colonels Phao and Sarit and their peers rose in rank and lost close contact with the troops it became essential to retain the support of the captains and colonels. So they displayed a remarkable versatility of talents if one could judge by the positions which they held in the civil service and in business.

The government of Thailand might be described as a dictatorship with democratic camouflage. The basis of its power has been the army, and great pains have been taken to retain its support. Leaving the peasants enough to keep them in what an English liberal once described as a state of pathetic contentment has also been part of the ABC of successful rule. The innovation has been in the policy adopted toward the politically conscious minority which has been influenced by Western ideas. They have not been dragooned into sullen submission: at times they have been allowed to express freely their condemnation of dictatorship, and as a rule there has been no interference with freedom of voting. So long as the peasants continued to be indifferent to elections the protests of the politically conscious in Bangkok had only a limited effect. The government had merely to buy the support of enough of the elected representatives to ensure a democratic majority in the legislature. Sarit's nominated legislature was not likely to modify the system: his appointees knew their value and saw that they got it.

IV

The Chinese

China's trade with Southeast Asia has gone on for two thousand years or more. There were groups of merchants in the principal seaports, but the Chinese did not settle abroad in large numbers until the establishment of European rule had created stable conditions. From the nineteenth century onwards the majority of the immigrants were manual laborers and peasants, but they were unwilling to follow their former occupations when they reached Southeast Asia, preferring more lucrative forms of employment. Moreover, in some countries local laws prevented them from being rice farmers. They were exclusively interested in making a living and saving enough to return home as soon as possible; and they took very little interest in local politics. It has been said that the Westerners colonized the tropics by exporting capital and establishing estates, mines, and commercial enterprises, while Chinese colonization relied on brains and brawn. The typical Chinese immigrant was a penniless laborer who worked with concentrated energy until he had saved enough to forsake manual labor for some form of business. Gradually he rose in the economic scale, and he might end as a wealthy merchant, estate-, mine-, or ship-owner, or banker. If Horatio Alger had chosen to place his success stories among Chinese rather than Americans, he could have found a plethora of examples for his favorite theme of poor boy from the farm makes good in the big cities. The prosperity of Southeast Asia at the end of the colonial era was the combined result of Western government and capital and Chinese enterprise and industry.[1]

110

Dislike of the Chinese

The Chinese were disliked in all the countries of Southeast Asia with the exception of Burma where they were regarded as kinsmen. Here they were few in number and hostility was concentrated against the Indians. The essential role of the Chinese was as shopkeepers, produce buyers, and money lenders. The native peoples were by custom and choice farmers or fishermen, and were not attracted to business. They were also unsophisticated in economic affairs, and had no money sense. The Chinese were infinitely more astute and had a consuming urge to get on in the world and return to China with their savings. They realized that the way to affluence lay through business and not farming. They were ready to work up to eighteen hours a day and continue this indefinitely until they succeeded, while the Southeast Asian peasant spent half the year in leisure. To the Chinese the native of Southeast Asia was the answer to prayer. Moreover, his aversion to business left an economic vacuum, and the Chinese filled it. Someone must be the village general storekeeper, selling the peasants what they did not produce themselves. Someone must buy their small crop of rubber, rice, or copra and sell it to a bigger dealer. Someone must lend them the money they demanded for necessities or more often extravagant outlay. Since the people of the country were unwilling to perform these functions the Chinese did so. Often all three roles were filled by the same individual, and he built up a triple economic stranglehold over the peasants in his district. Price rings were formed by neighborhood merchants which eliminated competition, so that peasants were charged more than the market price for what they bought and paid less than the current price for their produce. The rates of interest on loans were usurious, and once a farmer was heavily in debt he was compelled to sell his produce on the buyer's terms to lessen his obligation, irrespective of the market price. The peasant was caught three ways at once through his own economic weaknesses, and resentment at his exploitation was the basic reason for his hostility to the Chinese. The Western rulers of Southeast Asia on the whole did not favor them, but looked upon them as a detrimental influence upon the local peoples whose prosperity they were trying to advance. At the same time they felt that the Chinese were indispensable, since someone must be shopkeeper, produce buyer and provider of credit, and there was no one else

111

to fill these positions. So they were protected from native hostility as regrettable necessities. The only explanation of their success was that they had a superior aptitude and worked much harder than the local population.

Another reason for their unpopularity was that besides being too successful they were alien in race, color, and culture, and had a genius for cooperation against outsiders. In every Southeast Asian country the Chinese were a compact and alien community. They drew the hostility which such a group always attracts when it is felt that it has acquired too large a share of the national wealth. This was a basic reason for the hostility toward the Jews in Central and Eastern Europe, and for the Armenian massacres in Turkey. Particularly in the twentieth century it became increasingly more impossible to assimilate the races by intermarriage. In the Buddhist countries such as Thailand inter-marriage had been frequent until about 1910. Prior to that date the emi-grants had been predominantly men, and they married women of the country. In two or three generations their descendants were absorbed into the general body of the population. From about 1910 onwards Chinese women emigrated in increasing numbers and the sex ratio became more nearly equal. Intermarriage steadily declined because the men preferred to marry women of their own race. In twentieth-century Indonesia and Malaya the unwillingness of the Chinese to marry women of the country was reinforced by religious antagonism: a Muslim could not marry an idolater. So the Chinese became an unas-similated lump in the body politic.

They were also unpopular for political reasons. Unlike the Euro-peans who came to the United States, they had no intention of settling permanently abroad and assimilating themselves with the people among whom they lived. They looked upon their new home as a place of exile to which they had been driven by poverty. Its sole attraction was that they could make far more money there, and they intended to return to China as soon as they could afford it. Eventually the majority did so and were replaced by newcomers. They were migrants and not perma-nent settlers, and the new arrivals particularly felt no loyalty to their adopted country. Gradually a minority became permanent residents in Southeast Asia, although some of the Chinese born there ultimately went back to China. Birth abroad gave no certainty that they had accepted their country of domicile as their permanent home. The Chinese had a superiority complex, and looked upon their own culture as infinitely superior to those of Southeast Asia. In Malaya many still object to learning Malay and studying Malay subjects on the ground that the civilization of the country is not worth bothering about. There were of course exceptions, but broadly speaking the loyalty of the Chinese was reserved for China.

This attitude was greatly accentuated by the development of Chinese nationalism which began about 1910. The emigrants to Southeast Asia were deeply interested in the politics of China, and gave generous financial help to the revolutionary party which overthrew the Manchu dynasty in 1911. The government of Chiang Kai-shek appreciated this financial support, and did everything in its power to foster the growth of Chinese nationalism and counteract any tendency of the emigrants to identify themselves with the country where they lived. Agencies used for this purpose included the consulates and branches of the Kuomintang party which were set up in Southeast Asia. During the interwar period the majority of the Chinese supported Chiang Kai-shek. His government also insisted in accordance with the nationality law of 1909 that all Chinese born abroad were Chinese nationals according to *jus sanguinis*, provided the father was a Chinese national. This policy caused much friction with the local governments. It denied the claim of *jus soli*, that nationality was determined by the country of birth, and it also refused to recognize that a different nationality could be acquired by naturalization.

A particular cause of trouble was the Chinese private schools. In all the countries of Southeast Asia the government schools taught the national language, history, and culture. The Chinese insisted that their children must study the Chinese language and culture, and for this reason they established their own private schools. The text books and often the teachers were brought from China. As a rule they were ardent nationalists and they reinforced the patriotic bias of the text books. At a later date some of the teachers were Communists and taught their pupils Marxism as well as loyalty to China. The lesson was inculcated that a child born in, say, Thailand must never backslide into Thai patriotism but must always remember that it was a loyal citizen of China living in temporary exile abroad. Besides being factories for the manufacture

113

of Chinese patriots the schools also helped to perpetuate the cultural gulf between them and the people of the country. They did much to create the strong feeling of Chinese nationalism which exists among the overseas Chinese at the present time. A report made in 1951 on the schools in Malaya described a situation which was common to other countries of Southeast Asia. It stated that they were "China-conscious to a degree . . . that limits their consciousness of being a part of Malaya."[2] During the interwar period the governments tried to prevent the schools from being used for nationalist propaganda, but were not very successful. The teachers were ingenious in evading regulations, and the inspectors of education were too few and often too overburdened with work effectively to supervise.

Nationalism developed in the countries of Southeast Asia about the same time that it appeared among the Chinese. This increased the popular dislike of them. The feeling was latent with the majority, but the Western-educated elite were consciously and actively hostile. They resented exploitation and were determined to lessen the economic power of the Chinese. The latter were too few to be a political threat except in Malaya, where they outnumbered the Malays and were the largest single minority. The Malay leaders were afraid that the Chinese would gain political control of the country in addition to the economic power which they already possessed. In the Western dependencies the colonial governments prevented the enactment of discriminatory legislation against them. In the independent state of Thailand this protection was lacking, and the measures adopted there from 1919 onwards were a forewarning of what was going to happen in the other countries when they gained their independence. Beginning in 1919 the Thai monarchy began to bring the private schools under increasing control to compel them to reduce the time given to Chinese studies and pay more attention to the Thai language and culture. Restrictions on immigration were imposed from 1927 onwards. Anti-Chinese measures were intensified after the revolution of 1932, and reached their climax during the first premiership of Phibun Songgram from 1938 to 1944. In 1939 the amount of time which could be given to teaching Chinese was reduced to only two hours a week, and almost all the private schools were closed because of their persistent efforts to evade the regulations. Drastic attempts were made to dislodge the Chinese

114

from their domination of commercial and industrial life, and to replace them by Thai. They were forbidden to engage in various occupations, and were expelled from some parts of Thailand.[3] Phibun expected that by creating an economic vacuum it would be automatically filled by Thai who had shown no previous interest in a business career, but this hope was not fulfilled.

The Chinese in Transition

The post-war emergence of strongly nationalist states and Mao Tse-tung's victory had profound effects upon the position of the Chinese. These factors are still working themselves out, and it is not possible to foresee what will be the outcome. Nor can one predict what attitude the Chinese themselves will finally adopt. For obvious reasons of expediency they are not talking. It is not possible to generalize about the unexpressed ideas of eight to nine million people who run the gamut from millionaires to penniless laborers, and from the English-speaking and partially anglicized Queen's Chinese of Penang and Malacca through conservative supporters of Chiang Kai-shek to Communist agitators. Still another complication is that the treatment and future prospects of the Chinese are different in every country, so that each must be considered separately. The probability is that they do not know what is the wisest course for them to follow. In most parts of Southeast Asia the assured position which they held before the war has changed very much for the worse, and every course of action has as many uncertainties and disadvantages as it has possible benefits. The likelihood is that their minds are confused and that they cope as best they can with each emergency as it arises without trying to forecast the future or devise a plan of action for years ahead. They seem to be driven by the tide and to follow a policy of one step enough for me. It is unlikely that they are considering whether they can make a bargain with Mao Tse-tung by which they will become his fifth column and in return he will be their protector and promise to respect their economic interests. It is also improbable that they have consciously decided that they will not irrevocably commit themselves to either side in the cold war, but will remain sitting on the fence with a leg on each side until it becomes clear which is going to win. Doubtless they intend to be on the winning side, but to write in these terms is to oversimplify. It is much more likely that they do not see any necessity to choose between West and East. Of course much will depend on how rigorous the anti-Chinese measures are that each government adopts. They might be pushed so far that they are driven over to the side of Mao Tse-tung.

The end of colonial rule deprived the Chinese of their Western protectors. In Thailand and South Viet Nam the governments set up a monopoly of the rice trade which they had largely controlled. Their commercial position was attacked in Indonesia, Cambodia, and Burma by reserving the bulk of the licenses for importing and exporting to nationals. In the Philippines and Indonesia they were partially excluded from retail trade. The Chinese showed their usual acumen and ingenuity in evading many of these laws, and so increased the hostility of the new governments. They profited from the incompetence of the new Southeast Asian importers and exporters, they evaded controls by smuggling, and they used their traditional weapon of bribing officials. Almost every government passed regulations to curtail the freedom of the private schools, and sometimes closed them. The unwillingness to give up Chinese citizenship was overridden, and limits on immigration were imposed which sharply reduced the number of entrants.[4] The only exception was Malaya, where the Chinese were too numerous to be attacked, and Tengku Abdul Rahman was able to control the Malays and prevent any unjust discrimination. Elsewhere the Chinese were made to realize that they were an unpopular minority, and that they were not strong enough openly to oppose the new governments. They badly needed a protector and the only possibility was the Communist government at Peking. Its failure, however, to halt the drastic measures taken by Sukarno against their retail trade in 1959 must have made them realize that they could not rely on its help. There were probably two reasons why Peking did not go beyond protests. It did not have the power to compel Sukarno to change his policy. Furthermore, it has been trying hard to cultivate friendly relations with the neutralist states, and success would have been endangered by too vigorous a championing of the Chinese in Indonesia.

Within limits Peking was willing to help, since it wanted the overseas Chinese to contribute liberally to the party funds and repatriate their money for investment in China. In addition they could be a very useful fifth column. A special government department, the Commission of Overseas Chinese Affairs, was set up in 1949 to protect the interests of Chinese abroad, foster close ties between them and China, and persuade them to send home money on a generous scale. Their pride and affection for China were appealed to, and they were exhorted to help the reconstruction of their fatherland. Copying an old practice of the Kuomintang, intimidation was used to reinforce patriotic appeals. Most of the Chinese emigrants had relatives in China, and they were threatened with reprisals unless handsome remittances were made. An energetic campaign was carried on to persuade Chinese students to come to China for their education, and they were promised scholarships and subsequent employment. The Communist teachers in the private schools acted as recruiting agents. Hundreds of boys and girls accepted deck passages to China provided by the local consul, despite the tears and protests of their parents. They departed "singing and chanting Communist songs and looked for all the world as if they were destined for a New Jerusalem." The governments of Indonesia and the Federation of Malaya passed laws forbidding them ever to return.[5] Propaganda was carried on by radio, books, and newspapers. In the electoral law of 1953 provision was made for the overseas Chinese to elect thirty deputies to the All-China People's Congress. Imitating Chiang Kai-shek, the government insisted that nationality was determined by racial descent, and that once a Chinese always a Chinese. Whenever diplomatic relations were established with one of the new states, the embassy and consulates were used to control the Chinese and support the local branch of the Communist party. As a result of the victory of Mao Tse-tung the Chinese Communist party acquired an overwhelmingly dominant influence over Asian Communism. An elaborate organization was developed with its headquarters in Peking and branches overseas by which the government was able to coordinate and control the branches of the party in Southeast Asia.[6]

The overseas Chinese regarded Peking's mingling of blandishment and threats with confused and contradictory feelings. They realized that they needed protection and that this could come only from Peking. Their leaders at least knew that the outcome of the cold war was uncertain, and they wanted to safeguard themselves against reprisals if Communist dictatorships were set up in Southeast Asia. This was the reason why some wealthy Chinese in Malaya subsidized the Chinese Communist revolt and for some years did little to oppose it, although their own interests were bound up with the success of the British government. The majority were not Communists, and they would suffer economically if the party brought Southeast Asia under its control. It was true that only a minority were wealthy, but even the manual laborers had the ambition to become rich and respected, as many had done before them. The Chinese were well aware of conditions in China, and by 1951 they were beginning to be disillusioned. Their relatives had written them of how the government had seized the remittances which they had sent, and some had been deprived of their land. In 1955 Peking belatedly tried to repair the damage by ordering that families should not be robbed of funds sent them from abroad, and that greater facilities should be given for the investment of money from overseas. The Chinese in Southeast Asia knew of the liquidations and concentration camps in China, the treatment of private business, and the collectivization of the peasants. Their conclusion was that they did not want Communist rule in Southeast Asia but that this was unlikely to take place, at any rate in their lifetime.[7]

Chinese Nationalism

Another factor which has very greatly influenced the Chinese has been the growth of Chinese nationalism since World War II. This appears to be general throughout Southeast Asia. The term "nationalism" is not strictly accurate, for apart from the Communist minority they do not want annexation. Perhaps a more accurate description would be that they are determined to preserve their distinctive Chinese characteristics and particularly their language and culture which separate them from the people among whom they live. The majority are unwilling to abandon their Chinese nationality. Along with this goes great sympathy and approval of the Peking government. This attitude is most pronounced among the students and the younger Chinese, but it also affects the older generation including the wealthy business men. It is strongest among the Chinese-speaking, but is gaining ground among those who know a Western language much better than their own. One symptom of it is that a stigma attaches to a Chinese who cannot speak his own vernacular, and some who find themselves in

118

this predicament have belatedly begun to study it. The pro-Peking attitude is compounded of traditional loyalty and affection for China, attachment to Chinese culture, and pride in the much more important position that China has won in the world under Mao Tse-tung. For over a century the Chinese felt bitterly humiliated that they, the world's most civilized people, had been defeated and ordered about by despised Western barbarians. They hoped for a time that Chiang Kai-shek would make the West accept China as a first-class power. His failure in this was one main reason for his loss of support. It is dangerous to generalize because in countries where the government is anti-Communist, as in the Philippines and Thailand, it would be very inexpedient for the local Chinese to show any preference for Mao Tse-tung. The guess might be hazarded however that on the whole Chiang Kai-shek has been written off as a failure.

Mao Tse-tung succeeded where Chiang Kai-shek did not. As the Chinese see it he fought the United States, the strongest of the Western powers, to a standstill, and prevented it from conquering North Korea. With his help Ho Chi Minh defeated the French. Mao Tse-tung made China feared and respected by the West. A government that could accomplish this deserved the sympathy of all Chinese, even though they might not want to come under its control. This point of view is not due to conversion to Communism: it arises from Chinese nationalism. It explains why wealthy business men in Singapore who were not Communists gave dinner parties to celebrate the defeat of General Mac-Arthur at the Yalu river.

By standing up to the foreign powers in the way it did, and by the speed and energy with which it set about carrying out its plans, the new regime quickly made it clear that it was totally different from anything that had been seen in China for well over a century. Here at last was a strong central government, seemingly efficient and free from corruption, which knew its own mind and was prepared not only to enforce its will on its own people, but to ensure that the New China and its people received from other powers the treatment and respect due to equals. No longer would China tolerate any treatment short of equality . . . either in her own ports or in foreign lands.[8]

This pro-Peking attitude was one reason why Tengku Abdul Rahman declared in 1961 that if Communist intervention in Laos led to war with the West, he would not allow the British to use their military and air-force bases in the Federation of Malaya to assist the government of Prince Boun Oum. His power was based on the alliance between U.M.N.O. and M.C.A., and he could not afford to alienate his Chinese supporters.

Another influence which seems to be affecting the Chinese is that apparently they are abandoning the hope of returning to China, and are coming to look upon their country of domicile as their permanent home. Movement to and from China has been interrupted for a quarter of a century, first by the Japanese invasion, then by World War II, and after that by Mao Tse-tung's victory. Moreover, the Chinese know that from the economic point of view a return to Communist China would be a change for the worse. A large number have married and established homes in Southeast Asia, and a generation is growing up which was born and brought up overseas. It is likely that they toy with the idea of going home, as a city clerk may talk of becoming a farmer when he retires, but that this is a vague dream and not a real intention. Probably their chief desire is to be let alone so that they can make money without interference, and preserve their own nationality and culture. On the whole they seem to have no political ambitions, and are content to let someone else govern the country so long as they are left in peace. The extent to which they approve of a government depends on how far it protects their special interests. The mass of the Chinese continue to believe that "governments exist to be placated, to be evaded or to be bought when they are oppressive: to be patiently obeyed at other times." China was not a democracy, and emigration did not give them democratic ideas.

The Chinese in Indonesia

Prior to 1941 the Chinese triple monopoly of retail shopkeeping, produce-buying, and money-lending had aroused a latent resentment among the peasantry which could flare into violence when stimulated by local Indonesian leaders. The small middle class was consciously hostile, and one purpose of Sarekat Islam, a political party which was founded about 1910, was to liberate the Indonesians from economic dependence on the Chinese. Nationalism and support of the Kuomintang party were strong among the large majority of the Peranakans (Chinese born in the East Indies) as well as newcomers from China.

120

The Chinese private schools which were established in large numbers from about 1900 onwards were strongly nationalist in their teachings. There was the same deadlock as elsewhere over dual nationality, the Dutch government claiming under *jus soli* that all Chinese born in the Indies were Dutch subjects, while China insisted under *jus sanguinis* that they were Chinese citizens.[9]

The Chinese suffered severely in life and property during the Japanese occupation and the ensuing revolt against Dutch rule. In many parts of Java they were robbed and killed by peasants or guerillas of Sukarno's army. The peasants repudiated their debts to the money lenders, who incurred heavy financial losses. The attitude of the Chinese community during the revolt increased the illwill of the Indonesians. A minority profited greatly, some by supplying the Dutch armies and others by running the Dutch blockade and bringing much needed goods to Sukarno's soldiers. The majority tried to remain neutral and carry on business as usual, following their traditional policy of taking no part in politics. They did not especially like the Dutch, but they tended to feel that a return of colonial rule was the best guarantee of a restoration of the pre-war security of life and property. Very few were active and loyal supporters of the Indonesian Republic, and after the war was over the gulf between the Indonesians and the Chinese was perhaps wider than it had been in 1941.[10]

The government of the republic wished to solve the problem of dual nationality, and in 1949 Chinese who had been born in Indonesia were automatically given Indonesian citizenship unless within two years they rejected it and declared themselves citizens of China. This offer encountered two obstacles. China still insisted on citizenship by *jus sanguinis*, and the Chinese in Indonesia were unwilling to give up their Chinese nationality. Even when they accepted Indonesian citizenship there was reason to suspect that they did so only from motives of expediency. In 1954 Chou En-lai announced that China was willing to settle the question of dual nationality, and a treaty was negotiated which was signed at the Bandung Conference of Afro-Asian states in 1955 and ratified in 1960. It did not apply to Chinese who had rejected Indonesian citizenship, nor to those born in China who were never naturalized as Dutch subjects. These groups were recognized as Chinese citizens, and were given no further choice in the matter. The agreement was confined to those of Chinese descent born in Indonesia who had accepted Indonesian citizenship. Within two years they were required again to choose whether they wished to be Chinese or Indonesian citizens. Those who failed to do so would automatically acquire the nationality of their forefathers. They would become Indonesian citizens "when his or her father's side is of Indonesian descent," and Chinese when the father's side of the family was Chinese. In future all children born in Indonesia of alien Chinese parents would have Chinese citizenship. The treaty did not provide for voluntary naturalization, either of immigrants or of their children born in Indonesia. However, for the first time China abandoned her traditional claim that all persons of Chinese descent remained Chinese citizens even when they acquired another citizenship. In 1958 Indonesia passed a law which provided that aliens who were over twenty-one, who had lived there for five years, and who could speak the language, could apply for citizenship. It was estimated that the number of Chinese in Indonesia was around 2,100,000, of whom about 1,500,000 had been born there and 600,000 were immigrants. The majority were merchants, small manufacturers or rubber-estate owners, and only a minority were laborers. It was believed that something like forty to forty-five per cent of the total number were Chinese citizens.[11]

Chinese private schools numbered about a thousand and were believed to have between 250,000 and 300,000 pupils. Most of the teachers were alien Chinese, and the emphasis was on Chinese studies although the Indonesian language was taught. Communist influence was strong, and more young Chinese from Indonesia went to China to complete their education than from any other part of Southeast Asia. The government looked upon the schools with disfavor and made some attempts to control the curriculum. The teachers evaded them as far as they could, and some schools were closed.[12]

Economic discrimination of increasing severity was enforced against the aliens and also those who had accepted Indonesian citizenship. Apart from the long-standing dislike of them the government wished to create a class of Indonesian business men and oust the Chinese. It used its control of import licenses and the allocation of bank loans and foreign exchange to reduce the Chinese share of foreign trade. An ordinance was issued that the only way in which a Chinese firm could avoid the discrimination was by forming a partnership with native Indonesian business men and turning over fifty per cent of the capital and profits to them. The regulation applied whether the owners were aliens or Indonesian citizens. Some firms complied with the order, some accepted Indonesian partners at least in name, and a good many got their import licenses and foreign exchange by bribery. Chinese were also prevented to a large extent from establishing new industries which required imports of foreign machinery.[13]

In 1959 Sukarno forbade Chinese retail trade in rural areas and ordered that the businesses be closed and the owners moved to the towns by January 1, 1960. The decree seems to have been pretty generally enforced in Java at any rate. The protests of the Peking government were rejected, and the Chinese were given an object lesson of its failure to protect them. Sukarno's attempt to replace them by Indonesian cooperatives did not succeed, and the result was chaos and confusion in the rural retail trade. A large number especially of the younger men left Indonesia, many going to China. They discovered that government restrictions forbade them to take with them the proceeds from the sale of their property.

The Chinese have a growing sense of insecurity and alarm. They feel that accepting Indonesian citizenship has been no safeguard against discrimination, and they know that many Indonesians including officials look upon all Chinese as undesirable aliens. There seems to be little wholehearted loyalty to the government of Indonesia, and most of those who became Indonesian citizens did so from motives of self-interest. The majority would like to avoid taking part in politics and attend to their own business affairs, but they realize increasingly that their economic prospects are precarious. As to the attitude toward China, a large part of the Chinese are nationalist though not Communist and therefore sympathetic toward the Peking government and proud of its successes. There are conflicting opinions as to whether the Indonesian Communist party is financed by the Chinese community or the Soviet and Chinese embassies. A dwindling minority still adhere to Chiang Kai-shek, and a much larger number of those who are interested in politics support Mao Tse-tung.[14] Chinese Communist propaganda has been carried on vigorously, and the discriminatory policy of the Indonesian government has intensified the effect of nationalism in making many of the Chinese look toward Peking. If Sukarno continues to antagonize the Chinese the number responding favorably to Communist propaganda will grow, with the qualification that they realize that Peking cannot protect them at present.

The Philippines

No reliable statistics exist of the number of Chinese. The one certain fact is that far more than the legal annual quota of fifty enter by giving bribes or being smuggled in from Borneo. The average Filipino estimate of the total number which tends to magnify the "menace" is over 600,000, while the Chinese, who prefer to minimize it, give a figure of under 350,000. The Chinese have been strongly entrenched in the retail trade as well as in importing and exporting, wholesaling, manufacturing, and money-lending. Discriminatory legislation has wholly or partly excluded them from various fields of business such as foreign trade, but even here their share was still 13.2 per cent in 1957. In retail trade they accounted for 46 per cent of the sales in 1951, or in other words less than two per cent of the population handled nearly half the retail business. There is a strong suspicion that the published figures are most likely a gross understatement. Chinese ownership is often concealed by using a Filipino man of straw as the nominal owner, by transferring assets to a Filipino wife, or by obtaining Filipino citizenship. For a Chinese to become naturalized, however, is very expensive and difficult even when he has been born in the Philippines.[15]

The Chinese are strongly disliked as alien exploiters, and there is a long history of legislation against them. The earliest was the Bookkeeping Act which required Chinese businesses to translate their accounts into English, Spanish, or Tagalog (the official national language). The result was a dual set of books — an official statement for the Bureau of Internal Revenue and a private record of actual business. When the Philippine Commonwealth was established, the constitution excluded Chinese from owning land, developing natural resources, or operating public utilities. Many Chinese dealt with these restrictions by the methods mentioned in the preceding paragraph. The government tried to force the Chinese out of the rice trade by setting up a corporation to buy, sell, and refine rice, and thus break the large measure of control which the Chinese had over the industry. Other laws

124

imposed restrictions such as forbidding aliens (principally Chinese) from entering certain occupations.

The public demand for laws limiting Chinese economic rights was widespread and persistent, and politicians found it profitable in two ways. To advocate further restrictions was sure to be popular, and it was equally certain that the proposer would be well paid by the Chinese to abandon his proposals. The threat to introduce anti-Chinese legislation in order to be bribed to abandon it is a widespread and lucrative method of raising funds. The necessity of giving bribes has become a normal operating expense of Chinese business men, and according to Professor Appleton almost amounts to "unofficial and unregistered taxation." They also contribute to political parties so liberally that they are the chief source of funds for both sides.

The heaviest blow suffered by the Chinese was the Retail Trade Nationalization Act of 1954. It provided that no person who was not a citizen of the Philippines, and no partnership or corporation the capital of which was not wholly owned by Philippine citizens might take part in retail trade after May 15, 1954. Aliens engaged in retail business prior to this date might continue until their death or retirement, but their heirs must close it down within six months. Corporations and partnerships must liquidate within ten years of the passage of the law. The majority of the Chinese merchants were aliens owing to the expense and difficulty of becoming naturalized. They controlled 46 per cent at least of the retail trade, and the purpose of the law was to eliminate them, although in a less confiscatory fashion than Sukarno's decree of 1959.

Professor Appleton investigated the manner in which the bill became law, and his account was illuminating. It

was passed by the Philippine Senate in the closing hours of its 1954 session, under unusual circumstances. Leading representatives of the Chinese community appealed to influential Congressmen who had received substantial Chinese financial aid in their campaigns and were assured that the bill would not pass. Due to "politics," however, including an attempt by a Congressman to extort money from Chinese leaders in return for a promise to block its enactment, the bill was brought to a vote and passed, because many Congressmen feared that opposing it would not only be unpopular but might lead to charges that they had accepted bribes . . . Many of the Chinese interviewed expressed resentment against Magsaysay's "betrayal" after the generous financial backing Chinese had given his campaign.[16]

Some abandoned retail trade for other occupations, while others transferred their capital through the black market to Hong Kong. A large number made Filipino dummies or their common-law wives the nominal owners, while many fell back on their traditional solution of bribery. The law apparently failed to break the Chinese "economic stranglehold" of retail trade. Professor Appleton concluded that, faced by the public insistence on anti-Chinese legislation

only a very courageous (or very well bribed) Filipino politician would venture to introduce significant modifications in favor of the Chinese. . . . For the fact of the matter is that "the Chinese Issue" is being used by demagogic Philippine politicians . . . to divert public attention from more fundamental economic issues, such as the polarization of wealth, mass unemployment, official corruption and retarded industrial development.[17]

So far the government's attempts to create a class of Filipino business men which can compete successfully with the Chinese have been only moderately successful.

There are about a hundred and fifty Chinese elementary and secondary schools with around fifty thousand pupils. Until 1957 the curriculum was dictated by Chiang Kai-shek's Department of Education, and the subjects and text books were substantially the same as those on Formosa. In 1957 control was taken over by the Philippine Department of Education, but there seems to be a lack of Chinese-speaking inspectors for adequate supervision. The curriculum includes Philippine as well as Chinese subjects, but there is a subtle differentiation. "Our" country is China and "foreign" is Philippine history. The schools help to maintain the community's Chinese cultural identity to a remarkable degree. For the most part they staunchly support Chiang Kai-shek, but there is evidence that some of the teachers are sympathetic to Communism. Many Filipinos would like to close the schools, although their right to exist is guaranteed in the treaty negotiated between the governments of Chiang Kai-shek and the Philippines.

The Chinese community insists that it is loyal to Chiang Kai-shek, and it is impossible to determine how much support there is for the Peking government. The Huk revolt made the Philippine government uncompromisingly hostile to Communism, and the party was declared illegal in 1957. If in addition a Communist were a Chinese the offense would be aggravated, and he would be immediately deported. The community realizes that it dare not give its Filipino enemies an opportunity to attack it, and all the leading institutions such as the Federation of Chinese Chambers of Commerce and the schools seem to be solidly pro-Kuomintang. The government has diplomatic relations with Chiang Kai-shek but none with Peking. Trade with China is forbidden, although some commodities from there are smuggled in. The Philippine intelligence service estimated in 1958 that there were about two thousand Chinese and nine thousand Filipino members of the Communist party, and at least thirty thousand Chinese who were potential Communist supporters. Professor Appleton came to the conclusion that it was impossible to discover how far the community genuinely supported Chiang Kai-shek. On the whole it had a strong sense of the superiority of Chinese culture and wanted to preserve its separate identity and not be assimilated, although there was some intermarriage. Most Philippine Chinese including those who were naturalized were Chinese first and Filipino second, and their attitude was strengthened by the government's hostile policy. As a protector Chiang Kai-shek had been a failure, for he had not been able to prevent the passage of the Retail Trade Act. As business men the Chinese did not favor Communism and some at least were genuinely loyal to Chiang Kai-shek. But if Mao Tse-tung were able to prove himself a more effective protector, it was widely believed that this would be the determining factor with most of the Chinese in deciding their political alignment.

Thailand

The Chinese in 1955 were estimated to be 11.3 per cent of the total population of 20,480,000, or 2,315,000. Of these 1,619,000 were born in Thailand and 696,000 were immigrants. Probably half at least of the latter group emigrated from China between 1918 and 1931. The hostile policy which Phibun Songgram followed during his first premiership in 1938 to 1944 was almost completely reversed during 1944 to 1947 when Pridi controlled the government. Diplomatic relations were established with Chiang Kai-shek's National Government, and his embassy did everything in its power to strengthen Chinese nationalism and encourage the private schools to persist in their system of education. By the end of 1947 the schools had increased to over four hundred and flouted the regulations of the Department of Education. Immigration was almost unrestricted and about 170,000 Chinese entered the country. Phibun Songgram's return to power in 1947 was followed by the revival of his earlier policies which lasted until 1955. He was hostile to both Chiang Kai-shek's and Mao Tse-tung's governments, since each of them encouraged the Chinese to disobey his orders. Chiang's embassy was forced to curtail its activities. A large number of journalists and leaders of trade unions and other Chinese associations were arrested on charges of Communist activities, and were usually deported without trial. Decrees reserving certain occupations for Thai were revived. Immigration was closely restricted to a yearly quota of two hundred, and the annual alien registration fee was raised from slightly less than one dollar to nineteen dollars. Only well-to-do business men could afford this amount and the entrance of laborers was prevented. The Chinese community was no longer reinforced by annual contingents from the homeland. Many teachers were arrested, some schools were closed, the text books were rewritten and the hours allotted to Chinese studies were sharply decreased while those given to Thai subjects were increased. Special attention was paid to the elimination of Communist teachings. Chinese secondary schools were closed throughout the country, and the elementary schools were brought under strict control by unremitting pressure. Many of them closed for lack of funds, since the Chinese were unwilling to support them when they were Chinese in little more than name. Over half the schools went out of existence, and between 1948 and 1956 the number of students fell from 175,000 to 50,000. At the present time every school has more Thai than Chinese teachers, and only a fraction of the pupils achieve a real ability to read and speak Chinese, or learn much about Chinese culture. On the whole they read and write Thai far better, and a growing number attend government schools. Chinese education is moribund, and one of the principal causes of the growth of Chinese nationalism is disappearing.[18]

From 1955 onwards a rather more liberal policy was adopted. It was made easier for Chinese born in Thailand to become naturalized, and they were officially encouraged to do so. The alien registration fee was halved, but the annual immigration quota continued to be negligible. The decrees discriminating against citizens of Chinese descent in the acquisition of land were rescinded. Unceasing pressure was maintained on the schools, and if this policy should be continued there seems reason to hope that by the third generation the descendants of the immigrants will have become Thai. The government's purpose seems to be to encourage the assimilation of the races by firm but moderate pressure. It is reinforced by the alliance which has been growing up between Chinese merchants and the Thai governing group.[19]

Thirty years ago the Chinese controlled retail trade, rice-milling, transport, and the export of rice and rubber. They also had an important share of tin-mining and lumbering, and supplied most of the labor for the tin mines and rubber estates, the rice and the saw mills. In his relations with the peasant the Chinese merchant was shopkeeper, money lender, and the buyer of his crop. As a rice trader his custom was to make an advance payment against the future crop, and this was accepted because of lack of money. The price which the peasant finally received was dictated by the buyer and was to the disadvantage of the seller. It was estimated that the Chinese made up eighty-five per cent of the commercial class and controlled ninety per cent of the trade.[20] The policy of the Thai governments was to transfer the control of business to nationals by ousting the Chinese. They met the same difficulty as in other Southeast Asian countries, that most of the population preferred to be peasants, and those who went into business did not have the money to finance their operations or the aptitude for it. The government weakened the hold of the Chinese money lender and rice trader over the peasant by encouraging the formation of credit and marketing cooperative societies. It built and operated factories, and excluded Chinese from a number of occupations. After World War II it created corporations which had a monopoly of the sale of rice, liquors, and other commodities. In many ways the peasants benefited, though the major share of the profits did not go to them but to the members of the governing clique who were directors of the corporations.

The most important effect of the policy was that it led in the end to an alliance between the Chinese merchants and the Thai ruling group. Militant economic nationalism did not lead to the defeat of the Chinese enemy but to cooperation between the antagonists. The Chinese supply the money and the business experience and their Thai associates provide the necessary protection from government interference, official contracts, and influence in high circles. Most of the important government corporations established since 1951 include Chinese on their boards of directors and often have Chinese managers. This is also true of the quasi-official corporations such as banks; insurance, import-export, and shipping companies; factories; and rice-milling syndicates. Chinese companies are careful to include an influential Thai among their directors. As for the rice trade, the government ended its monopoly in 1954 and substituted a heavy tax on private exporters. The Chinese still control the milling and export of rice, but a large share of the profits is taken by the Thai soldier, police official, or politician who is a member of the board of directors. The majority of the principal Chinese and the members of the Thai governing clique have lucrative and reciprocally beneficial connections with one another. A study made of the leaders of the Chinese community in Bangkok in 1955 showed that almost all of them were wealthy and successful business men. Three quarters of them came from China, usually from families of the lower class, and almost all had made their fortunes in Thailand. Of the hundred most influential leaders sixty had business connections with the Thai governing clique, and this included all ten of the most outstanding Chinese. The relations between the two groups were social as well as economic, and the Chinese were anxious to acquire the prestige which came to them from being on intimate terms with the ruling group. They sent their children to Thai or mission schools more often than to Chinese schools, and intermarriages between the two ruling groups were becoming increasingly frequent.[21]

The wealthy Chinese have assured their own position and have no intention of doggedly opposing the government and endangering what they have secured for the sake of their poorer compatriots. Their influence benefits the rank and file of their community, who on occasion need protection from the authorities. They now have an interest in the continued power of the Thai ruling group, and are beginning once more to be assimilated with them. Up to fifty years ago the policy of the kings of Thailand was to encourage the assimilation of the Chinese settlers. Their leaders often became royal officials and received titles of nobility. Their descendants of mixed blood are among the leading Thai

130

families today. The kings succeeded in skimming off the cream of the Chinese elite. With the mass defection of its leaders the cohesiveness of Chinese society and the resistance to assimilation on the part of the Chinese masses were greatly weakened. Up to the twentieth century some children and practically all grandchildren of Chinese immigrants became completely absorbed into the Thai. After half a century of estrangement and struggle the assimilation policy has been resumed. The arrival of fresh drafts of newcomers has almost ended with the virtual cessation of immigration, and the shortage of females compared with males will compel many of the settlers to marry Thai. The Chinese schools are no longer allowed to intensify the division between the two races. Assuming that the Peking government is not able greatly to increase its influence among the Chinese and that the present Thai policy is not reversed again, the rate of assimilation may be expected to remain moderately high in the foreseeable future.

The influence of Chinese Communism grew steadily in the later 'forties owing to the victories of Mao Tse-tung and the failure of Chiang Kai-shek. The party which had been at work half underground and partly in the open since 1946 became a major political force among the Chinese. It is believed that the actual members never exceeded about five thousand, and in addition it was estimated that there were thirty thousand sympathizers. The Communists gained control of the Chinese trade unions, and many of the teachers in the private schools indoctrinated the students. The Chinese press became increasingly friendly to the Peking government and the Kuomintang newspaper collapsed. Support for Chiang Kai-shek fell very sharply, and the Chamber of Commerce and other Chinese associations became first neutral and then favorable to Mao Tse-tung. In 1952 30 per cent of the Chinese were believed to favor the Communist regime, while only 7 per cent continued to support Chiang Kai-shek and the rest adopted a wait-and-see policy. Out of 135 of the principal Chinese leaders, most of them wealthy business men, 13 per cent strongly supported Chiang Kai-shek, 31 per cent leant in that direction, and 56 per cent refused to commit themselves or supported the Peking government.[22]

Communist influence declined from the early 'fifties onwards for several reasons. Many Chinese were disillusioned by the news which reached them of the actions of the Peking government. American policy in Eastern Asia and the alliance with Thailand assured them that China would not be allowed to dominate the country. They were also impressed by the firm measures which Phibun Songgram was taking to break up the Communist party. Most of the politically conscious Chinese changed from an uncritical endorsement of the Peking government to neutrality. Support for Chiang Kai-shek increased somewhat, but few believed he would ever reconquer China or had any sincere enthusiasm for him. He was, however, the only enemy of Communism around whom its Chinese opponents could rally. They were outnumbered by those who were Communists or who favored the Peking government, but these groups either went underground or felt it was expedient to be neutral. It would have been unwise to follow any other course in view of the anti-Communist policy of the government. This makes it difficult to assess the real opinion of the Chinese, but it seems doubtful whether their support for Chiang Kai-shek has really grown in the past decade.[23]

South Viet Nam

Eighty-five per cent of the Chinese in French Indochina were in Cochinchina (now part of South Viet Nam) and Cambodia. There was a considerable amount of intermarriage with women of the country because male immigrants outnumbered female. Neither the French government nor the peoples of Indochina welcomed the Chinese. Immigration was restricted, and heavy taxes were imposed on them. They were predominantly engaged in retail trade and produce-buying which they combined with usury. They took advantage of the improvidence and indolence of the peasants, who were chronically in need of money, and were disliked for their exploitation and at the same time admired for their superior ability. They controlled the purchase, milling, and export of rice, and owned saw mills and most of the sugar refineries.[24]

After the French defeat in 1954 most of the Chinese in North Viet Nam fled to the south. They were estimated to number over 950,000, and to control eighty per cent of the retail and particularly the rice trade. Ngo Dinh Diem was determined to bring them under his authority, since he was afraid that they would support the Peking government and become a dangerous fifth column. In 1956 he issued a decree that all Chinese born in the country were Vietnamese citizens, and those born in China could be naturalized. Another ordinance required their private schools to conform with the regulations of the Department of Education. This meant that Vietnamese must be the language of instruction and the schools must be controlled by Vietnamese and not Chinese teachers. The president forbade alien Chinese to be retail shopkeepers or engage in the rice trade. These decrees struck at two of their most cherished possessions, their separate Chinese identity and their principal source of livelihood. The Chinese retaliated with a boycott, and the inexperience of the Vietnamese who tried to replace them in trade brought about a condition approaching economic paralysis. Chinese merchants in Hong Kong and Singapore helped by boycotting the trade of South Viet Nam. In 1959 both sides agreed to compromise: Chinese in increasing numbers took out Vietnamese citizenship, and alien traders resumed possession of their businesses but transferred fifty-one per cent of the shares to their sons who had been born in Viet Nam and were technically Vietnamese citizens. The quarrel over the schools was settled, at least for the time being, by the Chinese agreement to add the Vietnamese language to the curriculum. It would not be surprising if eventually South Viet Nam adopted the same educational policy as Thailand. The Peking government does not appear to have much influence, and there is a cultural link between the two peoples which encourages the hope that eventually their antagonism may be ended by assimilation.

Cambodia has some two hundred fifty thousand Chinese and trade is largely in their hands. The government is trying to break their monopoly of the rice trade and has debarred them from some occupations. They are believed to favor the Peking government, and Cambodia has forbidden them to engage in political action.

The Federation of Malaya

The policy adopted by the government of the Federation might best be described as incorporation. The size of the Chinese community makes impossible the discrimination practiced in Indonesia and the Philippines, and it is also alien to the tolerance and shrewd farsightedness that have distinguished Tengku Abdul Rahman. The result of discrimination would be civil war and the destruction of Malaya's prosperity. Assimilation is equally impossible, given the refusal of Malays and Chinese to consider intermarriage. The only hope for the future is that the two communities preserve their separate identity yet at the same time develop a realization that both are Malayans and that they must work together harmoniously. To help bring this about the leaders of the Alliance government agreed that the Malays and Chinese should have substantially equal rights, with some minor reservations that favored the former. There were no restrictions on the economic rights of the Chinese, but the Malays were given preferential quotas for licenses to operate certain businesses such as road haulage. A special government department was set up to carry out rural development projects and assist Malays in establishing small businesses. The requirements for citizenship were made so liberal that the bulk of the alien Chinese living in the Federation could become naturalized. The requirement that applicants must have some knowledge of Malay was waived for one year in order to accommodate the large number who had never troubled to learn the language. The Malays insisted that all aliens who became naturalized must swear allegiance to the Federation and renounce all other loyalties. This rejected the demand of some of the Chinese that they be allowed to retain their Chinese citizenship and have dual nationality. All those born in the Federation after its establishment in 1957 would be citizens by right of birth, thus satisfying the Chinese demand for *jus soli*. The government refused to give Chinese equal status with Malay and English as official languages. Malays retained their existing preferential quota of four to one in appointments to the administrative service.

The Chinese kept their private schools, and continued to teach their own language and culture. The reasonable requirement was laid down that they must also use Malay or English as the principal medium of instruction and emphasize the Malayan aspects of their curriculum, so that their pupils would no longer be "China-conscious to a degree . . . that limits their consciousness of being a part of Malaya." In return the schools were offered the important inducement that grants at uniform rates would be paid to all of them which conformed to the government's education policy. Those which did not would be refused assistance. The plan was a reasonable compromise, but part of the

134

teachers condemned it as an attack on Chinese culture. They demanded the grant but insisted on teaching whatever they liked. The government's policy was condemned by extreme nationalists of both races, and the complexity of the Federation's problem makes prediction impossible. At bottom the Malays are afraid of political and economic domination by the Chinese, while many of the latter are unwilling to make concessions to a people whom they regard as inferiors.

V

Communism

Communist Aims in the Dependencies

The tropical dependencies were given a significant role in the Communist plans for world revolution. They were an important element of strength to the capitalist countries because of their value as markets, sources of raw materials, and income from investments. If they could carry out a successful revolt the colonial powers would be seriously weakened, and the task of bringing about a Communist revolution in the West would become easier. The subject peoples were hostile to those they considered their capitalist imperialist exploiters and were struggling to gain their freedom. Their immediate aim was thus the same as that of Soviet Russia, and the two could collaborate. The population of the dependencies must be convinced that Soviet Russia was their disinterested friend and ally, and must be won over to her support. It would be necessary to recruit from amongst them a large number of professional revolutionaries and propagandists. The most promising should be given a thorough training in the universities established for this purpose in Russia, such as the University of the Toilers of the East. After graduation they should be sent home to continue the struggle. The most valuable agent who was obtained in this manner from Southeast Asia was Ho Chi Minh, the dictator of North Viet Nam.

Communist parties must be established in the dependencies and build up and control followings drawn from the peasants as well as the workmen. Since they were overwhelmingly peasant countries with

136

little manufacturing there was only a small urban proletariat, the most hopeful ground for recruits. The existing nationalist parties had as their aim political independence but not a Communist dictatorship, and were led by the urban Western-educated middle class. In the long run they and the Communists would conflict, but for the near future their object was the same. As early as 1928 at the sixth congress of the Comintern Moscow instructed the Communist party in each dependency to cooperate with the nationalists and any other parties which were anti-imperialist. The immediate aim was to overthrow colonial rule and then confiscate all foreign investments, in order to weaken capitalism at its source. Conservative elements such as native landowners must be destroyed and their property divided among the peasants to secure their support for the Communists. After the defeat of the colonial power there should be a transitional stage, during which the Communist party would promote the establishment of rural co-operative societies and state industries. The latter would create an urban, industrial proletariat who could be converted into reliable Communists. The alliance with the middle-class nationalists was strictly temporary, and the ultimate aim was the destruction of all non-Communist parties and the establishment of a soviet state under the dictatorship of the Communist party. During the interwar period the Soviet government was unable to make any serious effort to foster colonial revolts. It was fully occupied with grave problems inside Russia and later with Nazi Germany. The opportunity came after the end of World War II.

Following World War II Moscow tried to disguise its control of the world revolutionary movement by greater use of seemingly harmless bodies such as the World Federation of Trade Unions which was affiliated with the United Nations, the World Federation of Democratic Youth, and the International Union of Students. Ostensibly non-Communist, they were actually Communist-front organizations, and Communists held the key positions in them. Branches were set up in Asian countries, and the Communists in control guided their unsuspecting and non-Communist members in the direction in which Moscow intended them to move. In 1949 a World Federation of Trade Unions Liaison Bureau for Asia and Australia was established in Peking to coordinate Communist activities in the trade unions. Its purpose was not to help the members of the unions get better working conditions but to use them as tools for weakening the power of colonial governments or of independent Asian governments which opposed Communism. In 1952 a Peace Liaison Committee and Secretariat were also established in Peking to coordinate the activities of the Communist-front World Peace Council for Asia and Australia.[1]

Moscow's orders were sometimes conveyed to Asian Communist parties at meetings of these seemingly innocuous organizations. They provided admirable camouflage for interviews between agents sent from Moscow and members of Asian Communist parties. Communist embassies were also used as a liaison between the local parties and headquarters.

Chinese-Communist Imperialism

The influence of the Peking government has greatly increased of recent years in directing the strategy and tactics of the Communist movements of Southeast Asia. Too little is known of the inner forces at work in the Moscow-Peking Axis to allow one to hazard a guess whether Khrushchev has delegated authority to Mao or whether he cannot prevent this development. One inclines toward the latter, for China is very far from being a mere satellite. The motives of the Peking government are equally conjectural. It has a crusading zeal to enlarge the territory under Communist control which is reminiscent of the Russian Communists of a generation ago. There is also a chauvinist ambition to extend China's empire, which is fortified by the traditional claim that, for example, Viet Nam and Burma are dependencies. The success of the party in establishing its power over China itself, in bringing to a halt the American attempt to overthrow the Communist regime in North Korea, and in assisting Ho Chi Minh to win his war in North Viet Nam must have strengthened its confidence in its ability to impose its will on its weak neighbors. The reluctance of the United States, France, and the United Kingdom to become involved in war over Laos in 1961 was certainly not overlooked in Peking. Probably, too, China believes that it would increase its security by creating an outer ring of satellite states on its southern border, as Russia did in eastern Europe. It has particularly strong objections to any of these states coming within the American sphere of influence. This was plainly

138

shown in 1961 at the Geneva Conference on Laos. China refused to allow the pro-American government of Prince Boun Oum to continue, and did not want even an independent and neutral state. It joined Russia in spinning out negotiations for months, so that the Communist-controlled Pathet Lao should be given time to bring as much of the country as possible under their control. Another factor which must carry weight with Peking is the strategic importance of Southeast Asia, and its value as a source of raw materials and rice. Burma, Thailand, and South Viet Nam among them produce a large part of the world's exportable surplus of rice. Apart from its use to China herself in supplementing her own supply, control of these states would give Peking a powerful weapon in negotiations with the rice-deficit countries of Asia.[2]

The Technique of the Inside Job

The method used to establish Communist control in Southeast Asia has not been open invasion but what has been called the technique of the inside job. The imperialist government of the old school sent its army into the territory it intended to annex, and everyone both at home and abroad was immediately aware of the facts of the situation. Patriotic citizens of the victim offered what resistance they could, and foreign governments were faced with the clear-cut problem of whether they would acquiesce in the aggression or oppose it. Russia's attack on Finland in 1939 and Hitler's invasion of Holland were examples of old-fashioned imperialism. The technique of the inside job was used with great success by Soviet Russia in establishing her control over Czechoslovakia, and is far more difficult to combat. The local Communist party builds up a fifth column inside the country, and when it feels strong enough it seizes control of the state. This action is labeled a rising of the freedom-loving people to regain their democratic rights. No foreign army crosses the frontier and most of the fifth columnists are natives of the country. The rules of the game allow the Communist powers to send in equipment and enough trained revolutionaries and soldiers to organize and lead the fifth column, as in South Viet Nam. It can prove exceedingly hard to obtain legal proof of the participation of foreign personnel. Effective intervention by the Western powers is far more difficult when there is no clear-cut foreign invasion. Ever since the days of the Holy Alliance the democratic states have been very hesitant to intervene in a domestic uprising which calls itself a popular revolt. The indications are that the new method of conquest from within will continue to be the favored form of Communist imperialism.

The Communist Revolts of 1948

Zhdanov made a speech at a conference in October 1947 which was a veiled order to the Communists of Southeast Asia to revolt. In an article which appeared the same year in *Bolshevik*, an official Soviet publication, Zhukov declared that revolts should be engineered not only against the colonial powers but also against the governments of former colonies which had won their independence. They were denounced as "lackeys of imperialism" and enemies of the revolutionary proletariat and peasants. This marked the abandonment of the pre-war policy of cooperation with the nationalist middle-class parties against the colonial governments. The new policy was discussed at the Communist-sponsored Youth Conference of South and Southeast Asia which was held at Calcutta in February 1948. Shortly afterwards there were Communist revolts in Malaya, Indonesia, and Burma. Malaya was still under British rule, but Burma was an independent republic under U Nu's A.F.P.F.L. government, and in Indonesia Sukarno was fighting the Dutch. The Indian Communists began to oppose Nehru as a British agent, and in Japan the Communists started a campaign for "racial independence" to save the country from American capitalist domination.[3] There is no clear evidence that these events occurred because of orders from Moscow. But though once is nothing and twice may be a coincidence, five times cannot be an accident. That is too many coincidences to be a coincidence.

The Indonesian revolt was crushed within two months and the party temporarily discredited. By about 1952 it was clear that the rebels in Burma and Malaya had been beaten. The reason for the failure in the first two countries was that the Communists were running counter to nationalist feeling. Sukarno was looked upon as the incarnation of Indonesian nationalism, and the A.F.P.F.L. government of Burma had

140

won independence from the United Kingdom. So the attempt to represent them as tools of the imperialists fell flat. In Malaya almost all the Communists were Chinese, and this was enough to make the Malays hostile. Only in Viet Nam were the Communists able to identify themselves with nationalism so successfully that in the end they were able to make the northern part of the country a Soviet dictatorship. This revolt, which began in 1945, was not a result of the tactics laid down by Moscow in 1947 and was not helped by shipments of military equipment until 1950. Even after that date the principal support seems to have come from China rather than Russia. The Vietnamese Communists owed a good deal of their success to the government of France. It refused concessions until they were forced from it and then gave too little, so that it played into the hands of Ho Chi Minh. The climax came when in 1948–1949 Bao Dai, who was a nationalist after his fashion, consented to help the French and become the Chief of State, in return for the promise that his government should be given independence. France agreed in principle, but authority was transferred so slowly and in such niggardly measure that it was the best proof of Ho Chi Minh's argument that France could not be trusted, and that the only way to win freedom was to continue the war under his leadership. So the French hope failed that the nationalist allies of Ho Chi Minh would be won over to the side of Bao Dai.[4]

Until Ho Chi Minh was sure of victory he emphasized nationalism and kept his Communism in the background. The Communist party was nominally dissolved from 1945 to 1951 to reassure the Vietnamese nationalists who wanted independence but not a Soviet dictatorship. Communists, however, gradually gained complete mastery over the Viet Minh party, the government, and the army. Nationalists who opposed Ho Chi Minh were assassinated or imprisoned, and terror was used to break down opposition. The control over the government was camouflaged by appointing to innocuous cabinet positions some representatives of the other parties. The Communist organization was extended into the villages where party cells were established. The support of the peasants was obtained by a mixture of terrorism and of promoting their interests within limits. Their debt to the money lender was lessened, and the land belonging to Frenchmen and supporters of Bao Dai was confiscated and divided among them.[5]

141

The Policy of Peaceful Coexistence

A change of policy was adopted in 1952. The governments of the new Asian states were no longer attacked as imperialist puppets, and no further attempt was made to overthrow them by revolts. The new tactics did not require them to be Communist: it sufficed if they were neutralist, hostile to the West, and sympathetically inclined toward Russia and China. Friendly relations with them were cultivated, and the local Communist parties were instructed to adopt national front tactics. They were to cooperate with any parties which were trying to improve the condition of the peasants and workmen, and direct their hostility against privileged minorities such as large landowners. Soviet Russia and China were presented as peace-loving and the supporters of freedom for all oppressed peoples. The prevalent suspicion and hostility toward the former colonial powers and the United States were exploited in order to stigmatize them as enemies of free Asia and warmongers. S.E.A.T.O., which most Asian governments strongly condemned, was denounced as proving that the United States was trying to re-establish control of Asia under the guise of a defensive alliance. Chou En-lai charmed many of the Asian and African delegates at the Bandung Conference in 1955 with the irreproachable generalities of his five principles of peaceful coexistence. Burma, Thailand, Laos, and Cambodia were assured that China had no designs upon their independence and would not carry on subversive action against them. No help was given to the Communist rebels in Burma, since they had now become an obstacle to the policy of winning the friendship of Asian states. They were advised to negotiate a peaceful settlement with U Nu. A treaty with Indonesia settled the dispute over the citizenship of the Chinese. In 1957 Radio Peking advised the Chinese in Southeast Asia to obey the laws of their country of domicile and acquire its culture. It was made clear that China would not support them if they quarreled with their government.[6] Economic and technical aid, loans, and trade agreements were offered to Indonesia, Burma, and Cambodia, as described in another chapter.

The policy had a fair measure of success, for instance in Cambodia. If one has to live near a Chinese dragon who is suspected of carnivorous tendencies, and the creature begins to purr or make whatever friendly noises a dragon makes, there is a temptation to take the overtures at

142

their face value. Burma was not altogether convinced by the assurances of non-aggression, respect for territorial integrity and sovereignty, and the rest of the five principles. The government hoped that China had abandoned its traditional claim that Burma was a dependency, but was not altogether certain of it. China's subsequent aggression against India in Ladakh and on the Himalayan frontier have aroused misgivings as to the validity of the five principles.

The Communist rebels in Burma and Malaya tried to bring their revolts to an end on their own terms. The past must be forgiven and forgotten, all their democratic rights must be restored, and they must be allowed to operate as political parties without restraint. Revolt having failed, they wished to revert to political activity and be free to enlarge their membership. They intended to infiltrate the trade unions and student organizations, and regain control of them. They wished, too, to form a national front with left-wing political parties and influence their policies. Sometimes infiltration was so successful that a party was in part at least Communist-controlled, like the Burma Workers' and Peasants' party and P.A.P. in Singapore. In Southeast Asia generally the Communist parties stressed nationalism and likewise socialism. The confiscation of Western investments was demanded to free the people from exploitation and concealed imperialism. Western economic aid was denounced as a mask that concealed a plot to destroy Asian freedom, while Soviet and Chinese aid were praised as disinterested. In foreign policy the Communists supported neutralism and preached hostility to S.E.A.T.O. and American imperialism. The policy was most successful in Indonesia where, thanks to the favor of the Nationalist party and Sukarno, the Communists in the end became an essential support of guided democracy.

Communist Arguments in Southeast Asia

Communism knows how to be all things to all men, and skillfully varies its appeal to suit the individual or the group. The party members are carefully trained, and promising neophytes are gradually informed of its dogmas. For the generality, however, the Communists rarely preach the complete tenets of their creed. To the nationalist it is presented as nationalism: none have supported Sukarno's claims to New Guinea and his opposition to including British Borneo in the Federation of Malaysia more stoutly than they. From this it is an easy step to appeal to the suspicion of the West and the fears of Western imperialism. To the ambitious and those who are discontented with their position in society, Communism is commended as the road to power. Many are attracted because they have been persuaded that it is the winning side, the wave of the future. For those who want to equal the West's material prosperity, it is the short cut to industrialization and a high standard of living. For vague idealists who wish to help and uplift the masses it is the formula for utopia. To the workman it is presented as the only certain way of achieving better pay and working conditions with less labor, and to the peasant it promises land of his own and freedom from financial burdens. Communism as a rule plays upon existing grievances and hopes. In the Philippines it concentrated upon the abuses of tenancy and debt slavery: in Viet Nam on the desire for independence from French rule: and in Java upon xenophobia and the failure of the democratic politicians to redeem their promise that political independence meant greater material prosperity.

The best recruiting ground for Communism seems to be among the students and what for want of a better term may be called the lower middle class. By this is meant the group who have had a partial education, sometimes Western and at other times in an Asian language, and whose pay and prospects seem to them altogether incommensurate with their deserts. Some of them only went part way through the schools, others attended an inferior school where the diploma they received was worth little, and still others completed their education. All of them want a white-collar job because this carries infinitely more social prestige than an occupation which involves physical labor. In this category come office workers and school teachers. Teaching has sometimes been described as the last desperate refuge of the educated unemployed. Since they look upon themselves as educated men and have a high opinion of their own ability, they consider that they are entitled to a good salary. Unfortunately there has been overproduction of men of this type, and with the expansion of education the output continues to increase. There are not enough sedentary positions to go around, and since supply exceeds demand the pay is low and the prospects poor. By comparison with the mass of the population the white-collar workers are well off, but what they have is so much less than what they think they ought to have that they are bitterly disappointed and discontented. The oversupply of secondary-school and university graduates with a literary education was already a serious problem prior to World War II, and it became much worse after the former dependencies obtained their freedom. A widespread public demand for education arose all over southern Asia. Just as before the war, most of the students wanted it to be literary and not scientific or technical, to qualify themselves for white-collar jobs which did not exist. The governments established a very large number of new schools and universities. In some countries the lessons were given twice a day, with part of the students attending classes in the morning and the rest in the afternoon. Quality was sacrificed to quantity. The number of trained teachers was inadequate, and in the secondary schools they were swamped by the influx of students. Standards were lowered all along the line. Far too many half-educated students were graduated, and the entrance requirements for the universities were made easier in order to admit them. A great part were unfit for university work, and once again the standards were lowered so that they could get their B.A. degree. The consequence has been far too many poorly trained B.A.'s competing for far too few vacancies. Many of them are not qualified to become competent civil servants or business executives. For those who secure an appointment pay and prospects are poor. A formidable army of what used to be called the intellectual proletariat, or in other words the educated unemployed, has come into being, with nothing to hope for from the present order of society. Any change will be for the better. They are what a Dutch official once described as the army of the revolution. A generation ago they worked for the overthrow of colonial rule, but today their hostility is apt to be directed against the independent governments of Asia. They are very susceptible to Communist propaganda, and the leaders and hard core of all the Asian Communist parties are drawn largely from this class.[7]

Communism's appeal is enhanced by the reflection that one has joined a world-wide movement which gravely troubles even Washington, London, and Paris. Desire for power and position are potent attractions, because the party members will be the rulers when the dictatorship of the proletariat is established. Professor Pye's study of Chinese Communist terrorists who had been captured during the revolt in

145

Malaya emphasized the importance of personal ambition as their reason for joining the party. He found that they had attended the primary
and occasionally the secondary Chinese private schools, and later on
discovered that because of their inferior education the employment
they could get was vastly inferior to what they believed they were
entitled to. A particularly bitter blow was that illiterate laborers sometimes received as much pay as they did. They craved material success
and positions of authority and influence and doubted their ability to
attain them if they followed their parents' code of conduct which they
held in contempt. They felt that they lived in an age of transition
when revolutionary methods were necessary. They admired opportunism and shrewd unscrupulousness, and had no desire to help the
toiling masses they despised. Professor Pye described them as rootless
in a changing age. He suggested that Communism was likely to attract
any rootless Asians at the present time.[8] M. N. Roy, an Indian ex-
Communist, emphasized that the middle class was the mainspring of
Communism, and personal ambition a dominant motive. To this he
added xenophobia and hostility to imperialism, together with a vague
idealistic wish to improve the condition of the masses. The admiration
for Soviet Russia was "rather an admiration for the powerful and
successful than an intelligent understanding and appreciation of Communism," along with the belief that Russia was hostile to imperialism
and capitalism.[9] Roy believed that the peasants were not the driving
force behind Communism, but rather its pawns. Their revolt against
poverty was not spontaneous but was engineered by members of the
middle class, some of whom were Communists.[10]

Support of nationalism has been heavily relied upon. The educated
middle class were consciously nationalist, while the peasants were
discontented with foreign rule before World War II and since then
have supported government by their own people. By working for independence, the Communists were able to form a political alliance
with the middle-class nationalist parties, and to persuade them that
they themselves were merely patriots who were agrarian reformers.
During World War II the Communists took a prominent part in the
underground resistance movements against the Japanese in Burma,
Malaya, Indonesia, Viet Nam, and the Philippines. They worked with
the nationalists, and after the war they fought alongside them in the

146

struggle for independence in Burma, Indonesia, and Viet Nam. The revolts of 1948 were a temporary aberration brought about by Moscow's tactical blunder of 1947.

Asian suspicion of Western imperialism has been another of the most useful Communist weapons. The rehabilitation of the party in Indonesia after its revolt in 1948 was a good example. One way in which it regained its respectability was that "recognising that xenophobic nationalism was the most effective slogan to rally the masses, they decided to pose as its principal champions" by urging measures such as the immediate nationalization of all foreign investments without compensation. This went a long way toward reassuring the public about the party's impeccable nationalism.[11] The effectiveness of the method was heightened because the contact which Southeast Asia had had with the West had been with their former colonial rulers and the United States but at no time with Russia. Never having experienced Soviet imperialism they discounted heavily anything they were told about it as Western propaganda. The same attitude prevails in the Middle East, where the Arab states look upon Russia as the liberator of oppressed colonial peoples. The only countries which regard her with suspicion and hostility are Turkey and Iran, which have seen her conquer one province after another of their territories. Presumably the explanation is that human beings seldom learn from the experience of others, and refuse to be convinced until the same thing has happened to them.

Good use has been made of the policy of neutralism and the desire of Asian states not to commit themselves to either side in the cold war. They have been afraid that if another world war should take place they would be drawn into it, in spite of their efforts to stay out. Their suspicion of the West makes them very susceptible to the propaganda of Communist-front organizations like the World Peace Council that Soviet Russia and China are the champions of peace and disarmament, and that the danger comes from the Western warmongers, particularly the United States. The chronic suspicion of Western motives is skillfully used to intensify hostility to alliances such as S.E.A.T.O. or the Bagdad Pact involving Turkey and Iran as evidences of Western imperialism and a threat to world peace. At the Bandung Conference Chou En-lai cleverly combined this theme with his parade of his five principles as the lodestar of Peking's foreign policy, and convinced many of the delegations of China's sweet reasonableness.[12]

In the economic sphere the countries of Southeast Asia expect to revolutionize economic life without going through the century of evolution during which the United States changed from an agricultural to an industrialized state. The desire to attain the goal quickly gives the Communist powers a competitive advantage over the Western states. Soviet Russia compressed the transformation into a generation, and does not mention that the foundations of her industrialization were laid during the last thirty odd years of the Tsardom. Propaganda and directed tours in Russia have spread the knowledge of her achievements widely in Asia. China has embarked on the same course, and her accomplishments have lost nothing in the telling.

Moscow and Peking claim that the reason for their rapid success is that they have established authoritarian states which enforce the Communist way of life. This argument has a strong attraction for Asians for several reasons. The tradition of government is despotic and power is feared and respected. There is not the strong belief in democracy and the rights of the individual which has been growing in the West since the Renaissance and the Reformation, and derives its ultimate origins from classical Greece and Rome and the tenets of Christianity. In Western Europe, the United States, and the older British Dominions such as Australia this Western way of life is strongly supported by the middle class, the workmen, and a great part of the intellectuals. In Southeast Asia it is a twentieth-century foreign import which has influenced the small minority of the Western-educated, but has not basically affected the traditional attitude of the mass of the population. There is not a large and powerful middle class which in the West has been a chief support of democracy. In the West Communism has been opposed by the majority, but in Asia the resistance to it is inevitably weak because there is no democratic tradition to defend, and those who have accepted it as a way of life are few. Moreover, the so-called democratic governments established in Southeast Asia have usually been inefficient and corrupt, and their record has not been of a sort to arouse the allegiance and respect of their peoples.[13]

Most Asians are more concerned with lessening the poverty which they have known than with defending the democratic freedom which has hardly touched them. So the Communist promise to give them greater prosperity quickly has much effect. The theory is on the whole correct that poverty breeds Communism and that economic aid tends to counteract it. It is not, however, universally true, for Communism has made its greatest headway among the comparatively prosperous lower middle class and not among the peasants. Another reason why Asians are attracted is that they know little of the cost in human suffering of material progress, Communist style. When the facts about it cannot be concealed they are justified as necessary measures to protect the state against enemies and agents of foreign powers. Furthermore, human life has a lower value in Asia, and people are less repelled by actions which the West looks upon as completely uncivilized.

Communism and the Peasants

The peasants of Southeast Asia do not follow Communism, but some follow leaders who are Communists. On the whole they are attracted to those whose personalities appeal to them, who seem to take an interest in their welfare, and who promise to fulfill their wants. What the peasant appears to desire most is ownership of his own farm and freedom from debt to the money lender. The Communists promise him these things, and are very careful not to disclose their ultimate aims. A man who wants to own his own farm is not attracted to a party the final object of which is to nationalize the land, and make him a landless laborer on a state farm. Far from preaching Marxism, the agitator expounds a creed of rugged individualism. The landlord and the money lender must consider it altogether too rugged. "Kill the landlord and own your own farm." "Kill the money lender and be rid of the mortgage on your land." Or if it is inexpedient for the time being to go to such extreme lengths, rents and debt payments may be sharply reduced. The later stages of liquidation of landowners and money lenders and nationalization of the land are postponed until the Communists are firmly in power.

The agrarian policy of the Indonesian Communist party illustrates the methods employed. Before 1953 it had to a large extent ignored the peasants, but it then decided that it was necessary to secure their support in order to have a mass following. A program was drawn up

149

in 1959. It warned that as a class they had a "bourgeois" addiction to private property. The leaders must therefore see to it that the party did not become contaminated by a capitalist mentality, and that the working class retained control. The rich peasants — the word "rich" had about the same technical meaning as Stalin's use of the term *kulak* — were particularly dubious associates because they were able to lend money and rent part of their land. Reliable allies could be found among the middle or moderately prosperous and above all the poor peasants. The latter owned little or no land and made a living as tenants or sharecroppers. The landless farm laborers were equally dependable. Since all of them were land-hungry, confiscation without compensation would be advocated only for estates held by foreign companies, or by Indonesian landowners who had supported the rebel government in Sumatra. The confiscated land would be given to the poor peasants and landless laborers. At this stage in its growth the party wanted to antagonize as few as possible, and patriotic Indonesian landlords who had opposed imperialism would be allowed to keep their land. Their rent, however, must be limited to at most forty per cent of the tenants' crops, which should align the latter on the side of the Communists.[14] Squatters who had seized parts of the estates of foreign companies must be confirmed in possession of their holdings. Debts to money lenders must be abolished, and as most of them were Chinese the policy would be popular. There must be larger government loans to peasants, more cooperative societies, and higher wages for farm laborers. Many party members must live in the villages and do all they could to further the peasants' interests to gain their allegiance.[15] The large number of Javanese peasants who voted for the Communists showed the success of the policy. Its calculated moderation is reminiscent of that of Ho Chi Minh during the years when the issue of the war was uncertain and the support of the population was vital. In both cases the Communists posed as agrarian reformers whose only desire was to help the peasant. Even the native exploiters were treated with some tenderness so that they would be quiet lest worse befall them.

The Hukbalahaps

The peasants' grievances in the Philippines were land tenures and debt slavery. The storm center was the fertile and overpopulated plain

150

of Luzon. From the time the Communist party was first established in the nineteen twenties it worked among the peasants and laborers. And when the Japanese invaded, the Communists and Socialists raised in Luzon the force of guerillas known as the Hukbalahaps or Huks, thus showing themselves to be good nationalists. The Huks fought continuously and successfully against the Japanese from 1942 to 1945. At the same time they carried on a civil war against landlords and *caciques*, the ruling class which had controlled the pre-war government and in many cases worked with the Japanese. The Huks took over the estates of collaborators and abolished the abuses of landlord-tenant relations. They ended the power of the *cacique* in the territory which they controlled, and set up their own administration. It appointed officials, held courts, operated schools, and collected taxes. The Huks made the claim that they killed five thousand Japanese and twenty thousand Filipino "obstructionists in the class war." [16] A typical case was the assassination of a man who was the largest landowner in his province, and also its governor and an important member of the pre-war Nationalist party.

Some of the leaders of the Huks were Communists but the majority of the guerillas were land-hungry peasants. They were the spiritual descendants of the Sakdals of 1935 who came from the same part of Luzon. There had been earlier agrarian revolts in 1931 and 1923, and indeed from the nineteenth century onwards. All the Communists had done was to fasten on a promising local grievance and make the most of it. The earlier rebels had been raw peasants whose arms were farcically inadequate and who were easily crushed by the semi-military Philippine constabulary. The Huks were a far more serious threat. They were well armed, and three years of fighting the Japanese turned them into seasoned guerillas. So at the end of the war they refused to hand in their arms and once again become law-abiding sharecroppers. President Roxas contended that it was unnecessary to pass laws embodying the agrarian reforms they demanded since this had already been done. He omitted to add that they were very badly enforced, and he ordered the army to give the rebels neither rest nor quarter.[17] The revolt continued, and the rebels were now able to give their undivided attention to attacks on the governing class. Roxas played into the hands of the Communists, just as French policy in Viet Nam helped Ho Chi Minh. Gradually the Communists established complete con-

151

trol over the Huks, and carried out a program of systematic indoctrination in Marxism.

After the death of Roxas, President Quirino made an attempt in 1948 to negotiate a settlement. He failed because the Communist leaders felt confident of success and did not want to make peace. They kept widening their demands, and in addition to agrarian reforms of so sweeping a character that the government had neither the power nor the money to grant them, they required the abrogation of the American-Filipino Trade Treaty. The scandals of the election of 1949 increased popular support, and the revolt spread to the Visayan Islands and Mindanao. The majority of the peasants had not joined the rebels who were estimated to number ten thousand, but many sympathized because they had the same grievances. Terrorism was used to intimidate the unwilling into supporting the rebellion, as it was in the guerilla revolts in Viet Nam and Malaya. The Filipino army was inefficient and its morale low, and the peasants were antagonized by looting and other acts of oppression. The combined result was that the peasants refused all information, although some of them were undoubtedly aware of the Huks' location and plans.[18] The experience in all the guerilla wars has been that without this information soldiers have been unable to track down and defeat the rebels. The murder in 1949 of Mrs. Quezon, the widow of the pre-war president, was a typical example of the wall of silence which cut off the government from knowledge of what was being planned. She with her daughters and sons-in-law and some of her military escort were ambushed and shot while driving to attend a civic celebration. Investigation showed that the Huks had been waiting in ambush for their victims for a couple of days, and that many peasants must have been aware of this. Yet not a single one informed the authorities.

During 1949 and 1950 Huk guerilla attacks became more frequent and were on a larger scale. Their headquarters were in Manila itself, they were the real government in many areas of central Luzon, and they had underground cells scattered throughout the islands. The revolt was financed by levying taxes, the proceeds of raids and robberies, and large gifts from a few Chinese. The Bell Economic Mission stated:

The present Hukbalahap movement is clearly an organized effort to disrupt the economy of the country and to destroy confidence in the

Government . . . it would be a mistake to under-estimate the extent
to which failure to deal boldly with the problems of economic poverty
and the lack of economic opportunity has increased the feeling of
desperation among the people and provided a breeding ground for
agitation and disorder.[19]

The Huks hoped that in 1951 they would be able to seize control of
the Philippines.

Magsaysay was appointed Secretary of Defense by President Quirino
in 1950. He made the army more efficient, and also gained the goodwill
of the peasants by summarily punishing all who were convicted of
misconduct against them. Gradually they began to give information.
Informers were given generous rewards and protected from reprisals;
Huk leaders were bribed to betray one another. An intelligence service
was created which penetrated the enemy's organization. The Huks
began to find that it was they who were being ambushed and suffering heavy losses. Magsaysay's policy was to kill the irreconcilables,
but regain the loyalty of the non-Communist majority by offering them
a pardon and land of their own. He established agricultural colonies
in Mindanao and gave free farms of from fifteen to twenty-five acres
to those who surrendered. The government helped to clear the land
and built roads, wells, houses, hospitals, and schools. The settlers were
given farm tools and enough food to last them until the first harvest.
Thereafter the loan had to be repaid in instalments. About eighteen
per cent of the members of each farm colony were a "stabilizer group"
of loyal ex-soldiers and civilians who were included to counterbalance
the former rebels. The wisdom of Magsaysay's policy was vindicated
because the majority of the former Huks lost all interest in Communism. Those who remained in arms were increasingly discouraged by
their losses and the growing number of surrenders. By 1956 a few hundred Huks, most of them irreconcilable Communists, still held out, and
the peasants no longer helped them. The Huk revolt had ended.[20]

Communism in Thailand

The Communists have had an uphill struggle in Thailand and have
made little headway. It was pointed out in the account of its government that most of the educated class which control the country have
employment and an assured position in the administration. They have

a vested interest in upholding the present regime and Communism makes no appeal. The urban working class is very small, and since most are employed in small family businesses they do not feel that they are a downtrodden proletariat. The peasant majority have a frugal prosperity. Eighty-five per cent own their own farms: tenants usually pay a fixed rent and are not sharecroppers: there is ample vacant land for all: and the debt to the money lender is not heavy. The peasants would probably agree with Mr. Harold Macmillan that they have never had it so good, and the Communists have been unable to find any of those agrarian grievances which were so useful to them in the Philippines, Indonesia, and Burma. Nationalism is no use to them, for Thailand has been independent for centuries. There appear to be some small Thai Communist groups, but the state of public opinion is so unfavorable and the government so hostile that they lurk in obscurity. Apart from them the only sign of leftist politics among the Thai seems to be various tiny parties which profess a vague socialism, condemn the military dictatorship, and demand democracy. In foreign policy they advocate neutralism and oppose the American influence in Thailand and its alliance with the dictatorship.[21]

What Communism exists is almost completely confined to the Chinese and the Vietnamese minority who live in Thailand. The government arrested and deported the Chinese Communists whom it was able to discover, and those who escaped the purge went underground. For this reason it is not possible to estimate their number, and their ability to win converts is lessened by the dislike of the Chinese. The Thai will not accept Chinese leadership in ideology. In all the countries of Southeast Asia where Communism has made headway the leaders were natives of the country and not unpopular aliens.

Communism in Malaya

Communism in the Federation of Malaya has been greatly handicapped because it was a Chinese import and therefore automatically repugnant to the Malays. The Kuomintang party in its early years included Communists and conservatives, and agents of both factions were sent to Malaya to establish branches there. The expulsion of the Communists from the Kuomintang in China and the resultant civil war caused a similar break in Malaya. Henceforth the two parties opposed one another, although they continued their anti-British propaganda. Both won a footing in the Chinese private schools, and the Communists gained a following among the laborers, particularly the Chinese. They brought about a series of strikes from 1937 to 1941, but ceased to instigate them when the Germans invaded Russia. They took an active part in the defense of Singapore in 1942, and after the fall of Malaya they built up a Chinese guerilla force of between six and seven thousand men, known as the Malayan People's Anti-Japanese Army. It played a useful part in harassing the enemy and received valuable training in guerilla tactics. The jungle camps were highly disciplined centers for Communist indoctrination. After the British return large quantities of arms were concealed in the jungle for later use. The party kept in touch with ex-guerillas by organizing them in an old comrades' association.[22]

After the war the aim of the Communists was to overthrow the British government and set up a Soviet state. Infiltration into the Chinese private schools was carried out on a much larger scale than before 1941, and they became an important source of recruits. The Communists cooperated with the conservative Chinese, the Indians, and a few small, left-wing Malay parties in opposing the constitution drawn up for the Federation of Malaya by the British and U.M.N.O. Their principal weapon was the strike: they organized Chinese and to some extent Indian labor in a federation of trade unions under their control. By 1948 it was estimated that they controlled over sixty per cent of the unions. There was an epidemic of strikes, and two abortive general strikes, many of them accompanied by acts of violence and lawlessness. It was not difficult to persuade the men to demand higher wages because of the scarcity and high price of rice and other necessities in the immediate post-war years. A Workers' Protection Corps was organized of thirty-five hundred professional intimidators, partly recruited from former guerillas. They were used to coerce the workmen, whenever they showed reluctance to do so, into obeying their Communist leaders' orders to strike. The real purpose of the strikes was to prevent the economic recovery of Malaya, and gradually to undermine and bring down the British government. The policy of the government was to foster the development of trade unions as a means of promoting the interests of the laborers. It opposed political strikes, and it wished to break the control of the Communist party over the workmen. An experienced trade-union official from Great Britain was added to the government service to help them organize effectively, and assist in setting up industrial courts for the arbitration of labor disputes. Some of the more notorious agitators who were aliens were deported to China. Gradually the Communist grip on the unions was loosened, and the process was completed when the party was declared illegal after it revolted in 1948.

The Communists' plan was to instigate a mass uprising accompanied by guerilla warfare. In the second phase of the rebellion they hoped to establish "liberated areas" which they had brought under their control. In the third phase they intended to create a "liberation army" which would link the "liberated areas" and conquer Malaya. An important part of the plan was to paralyze the rubber and tin industries, which provided the livelihood of about half the population as well as a large part of the revenue. The Communists were encouraged to expect success by the weakness of the police and the limited number of soldiers in the country. In 1948 the terrorists were believed to be between four and five thousand, and they reached their maximum of eight thousand in 1951. They included the former guerillas, professional criminals, and many teenage recruits of both sexes from the Chinese private schools. All but a small minority were Chinese, and a large part of them were immigrants from China. In addition to the terrorists in the jungle the Communists had an effective network of secret agents scattered through the towns and villages. Known as the Min Yuen, its functions were to collect food, money, and information for the guerillas, and distribute propaganda.

In the Federation of Malaya, though, Communism was unable to appeal to nationalism because there was no Malayan people but instead three antagonistic communities, each with its own exclusive nationalism. From its first appearance in the 'twenties the Communists were almost entirely Chinese. By June 1957, 6,341 terrorists had been killed of whom 5,893 were Chinese.[23] The revolt was in no sense a national uprising against colonial rule, in spite of the efforts to make it so. The Malays firmly supported the British, and enlisted by thousands in the Malay Regiment and the armed police. The Tamils and Telugus, mostly laborers on the rubber estates and railways and in the towns, stuck to their jobs in spite of the terrorism used to make them panic. Few joined the armed forces, for they were not fighting races and no one expected this of them. The bulk of the Chinese remained neutral and for some years gave very little help or information to the government. Many both rich and poor alike were terrorized into helping the guerillas with food, money, and information. Gradually they gave more and more help to the government when they saw that it was winning and equally important was able to protect them.

To the Malays Communism was an alien ideology whose followers were Chinese. Since they looked upon them as heathen exploiters, and would have liked the government to deport them to China, they were happy to be provided with rifles and good pay and to know that it was open season on any whom they might encounter in the jungle. Moreover, most of them were easygoing peasants with one of the highest standards of living in Asia. They did not suffer from the poverty that gave the Communists so many peasant followers in Java, or the sharecropping and debt slavery which drove them to join the Huks in the Philippines. The Indians were mostly laborers, but they had migrated to Malaya and very often settled there permanently because they could make more money than in India. So far as they were interested in politics most of them supported Nehru's Congress Party and Indian independence. The Chinese Communists had to fall back upon their own community for support.

The revolt ran true to the type of guerilla wars — hit-and-run attacks, ambushes, far too few soldiers to cope with them, and for some years a paralyzing lack of information as to the location and plans of the guerillas, while the Min Yuen kept them well informed about troop movements. There was even a Communist cell in the official residence of the British High Commissioner, Sir Henry Gurney. This was probably the explanation of the accurate information which enabled the terrorists to set an ambush which lay in wait for him for forty-eight hours and murdered him in 1951. This was the nadir of the revolt, and by 1954 its ultimate failure was assured. There were never more than 8,000 terrorists, and to deal with them required 42,500 soldiers — European British, Gurkhas, Fijians, King's African Rifles, seven battalions of the Malay Regiment, and Dayaks from Borneo whose forte was tracking game in the jungle. There were also 73,000 armed police, mostly Malays. The Min Yuen was disrupted by compulsorily moving some 500,000 squatters (85 per cent Chinese) who cultivated plots of ground to which they had no title on the outskirts of the jungle. They were resettled in five hundred fifty new villages provided with schools, community centers, electric light, short courses in civics, and other amenities — and a barbed wire fence with armed guards who allowed no one to enter or leave between sunset and sunrise. The squatters were also given an assured livelihood such as a thirty-year lease of a farm with a secure title, unlike the squatters' holdings which they had held on sufferance. Gradually the Chinese, who alone had accurate knowledge, volunteered information about the terrorists.

By 1956 they were reduced to about twenty-five hundred, who had retreated to the heart of the almost impenetrable jungle which covers three quarters of Malaya. Their high command had removed itself to the safe asylum of southern Thailand where the British could not follow them, and the Thai had too few troops to cope with them. They have remained there ever since and grow food, levy taxes, and maintain rest camps for tired terrorists. From 1955 onwards the Communist leaders made overtures for peace, but on their own terms. They realized that their revolt had failed, and they wished to return to the methods of infiltration and agitation which they had used down to 1948. They insisted that the Communist party be legalized and allowed to carry on political activity without restraint. It must also be permitted to retain its arms, and the leader, Chin Peng, admitted that its ultimate aim was to impose a Communist dictatorship. Tengku Abdul Rahman rejected the proposals and continued military operations until July 31, 1960, when he officially announced that the rebellion was over. At the present time the Communists are believed to number about six hundred, of whom some five hundred fifty are in southern Thailand. There is evidence that they have had some success in worming their way into Chinese private schools and trade unions. The government watches them closely and does not hesitate to use its extensive powers of arrest and imprisonment.

Apart from occasional political murders and riots there was no violence in Singapore during the Communist revolt. A small island with very little jungle required different tactics than the Federation. The number of Communists and fellow travelers was estimated to be about three thousand. They used Singapore as a supply base from which they smuggled men, arms, money, and food across the narrow straits to Johore, a principal center of terrorist activity. As narrated elsewhere, they gained control of a powerful group of trade unions and some of the Chinese private schools. They instigated many strikes, some of which ended in riots in which several were killed. The Communists had a very strong influence in the P.A.P., although the more moderate leftists managed to remain in control of the party and the government. The formation of a separate party by the Communists in 1961 threatened to give Singapore a Communist government. Since the population is predominantly Chinese the Communists have been able to appeal to Chinese nationalism with much success. Whether the P.A.P. government will succeed in its attempt to substitute a Malayan nationalism is problematical. Unless, too, the problem can be solved of finding employment for the rapidly growing population, the Communists will have an excellent opening for their activities.

VI

International Relations

The Economic Value of Southeast Asia

Southeast Asia is of great economic importance, and the loss would be serious if it came under Communist control. It provides 59 per cent of the world's tin and 90 per cent of its natural rubber. The development of synthetic rubber has made the natural product less essential but has not replaced it. A few years ago the calculation was made that American manufacturers used natural rubber for 27 per cent of their products and synthetic for 38 per cent. For the remaining 35 per cent the choice depended almost entirely on relative price. This analysis is only partially applicable outside the United States, but can be used as a rough guide.[1] Two thirds of the world's coconut products and a third of its palm oil come from Southeast Asia, though other vegetable oils are available as substitutes. The estates of cinchona trees on the volcanic mountain slopes of western Java are the main source of quinine. Among the minor but valuable products are *abaca* or Manila hemp: most of the kapok: much of the pepper: a tenth of the chromium (Philippines): and down to 1941 more than 17 per cent of the tungsten (Burma). The oilfields of Indonesia and British Borneo produce less than 3 per cent of the world's oil, but are an important source of supply for Southeast Asia, Japan, and Australia. Before World War II, Burma, Thailand, and Indochina provided more than two thirds of the rice in world trade. At the present time the percentage is less owing to the fall in production in Burma and Indochina and its growth elsewhere, but Southeast Asia is still the principal source of supply for the rice-deficit countries. The Straits of Malacca between Malaya and Sumatra are used by the global shipping lines of all nations, and are one of the great ocean trade routes of the world. The Straits are of vital importance to Europe in particular, since they are its principal sea link with the Pacific and the Far East. All the round-the-world airlines must use Southeast Asia, since they are not allowed to fly over Russian or Chinese territory. Whoever controls Southeast Asia can grant or withhold passage over the global air routes and sea lanes.

Strategic Importance

In addition to its economic value, Southeast Asia is of strategic importance to several of the leading powers. From the American point of view the mainland cannot be separated from the naval and air bases in the islands of the Western Pacific. The whole area, continental and insular, is an interconnected strategic unit. The Philippines are only about a thousand miles from the port of Saigon in South Viet Nam. The port of Davao in the Philippines was the advanced base from which the Japanese sent one of the expeditions which attacked the Dutch East Indies. The East Indies in turn could be used as a base for attacking Australia. This is of as much concern to the United States as to Great Britain since Australia is at one end of the chain of island outposts which begins in the Aleutians. The most direct route from the United Kingdom to Australia and New Zealand is from Aden diagonally across the Indian Ocean, far to the south of Southeast Asia. An alternative route passes down the Straits of Malacca and then through the center of the East Indian Archipelago. The passage through the Straits of Malacca is likewise of the utmost importance to Great Britain because of her trade with the Far East. For Japan this is the most direct route to India, the oil of the Middle East and Europe. The security of the Straits of Malacca is therefore of the greatest importance to these countries, though less so to Australia and New Zealand because of the Indian Ocean route. Singapore commands the passages from the Pacific into the Bay of Bengal and the Indian Ocean, both through the Straits of Malacca and the Straits of Sunda between Java and Sumatra. Singapore cannot be held if the mainland of the Malay Peninsula is in enemy hands. To ensure safe communications through the East Indian Archipelago it is essential that Indonesia be friendly or at least neutral.

The strategic importance of Indochina was shown by what happened in 1941–1942. By May 1941 it had been brought under the control of the Japanese, and the port of Saigon was made their advanced base. This brought them within 627 miles of Singapore, as compared with 3,000 miles if their attack had had to start from Japan. In December 1941 two Japanese expeditionary forces sailed from Saigon. One of them conquered Thailand and the other landed on the eastern side of the Malay Peninsula, fighting its way down the railway towards Singapore. Thailand itself became the base for the main Japanese attack on Malaya and the conquest of Burma, and from there in turn India was attacked. Substitute the Chinese for the Japanese, and there is the possibility that history might repeat itself. China is primarily a land power, and there are good communications by road and rail from Indochina to Singapore. Chinese coastal shipping is extensive, and could be used for sea transport. North Viet Nam is a Chinese satellite, and none of the states of Southeast Asia is capable without help of offering much resistance to an invasion.

India is intimately concerned with Southeast Asia, since it is her first line of defense against attack from the east, as Japan showed in World War II. Within ten days after the fall of Singapore Japanese warships were as far west as southern India and Ceylon. Burma was the base from which Japan attempted to invade India by land. The Burma Road, which led from Burma to China, has not been kept up and apparently is not usable by a large army. There is however a practicable road of invasion from southern China to Viet Nam and Thailand by road and railway and from there into Burma. What Japan accomplished by sea would be possible for China by land and coastal shipping.

Southeast Asia is worth taking and is incapable of defending itself without outside help. Even if all the states could be persuaded to combine their strength it would not materially improve their position. None of them has enough coal and iron to develop a large steel industry, and the bulk of their materiel must be imported. In any event an alliance is not practical politics. Apart from the division into neutralists and Western allies, the new states are strongly attached to

162

their independence and unwilling to risk lessening it by coming together either militarily or politically. The Philippine republic made abortive attempts to form an anti-Communist league, but all that came out of the conferences was an agreement for cultural cooperation. In the immediate post-war years there was some expectation that the states might move closer together, since all of them were Asians who had been recently emancipated from Western control. Before long it became clear that nationalism was a dividing force, and that the vague sentiment of Asian solidarity would not prevail against it.

In the economic field too there is nothing to bring them together, since they are competitive much more than they are complementary. Their principal exports are rubber, vegetable oils, tin, and rice. To encourage industrialization, trade barriers have been erected to preserve home markets for domestic manufactures. The governments have shown little interest in proposals that they should diversify production in order to lessen competition and expand sales to one another. There is no common language or racial descent. The Burmans, Thai, and most of the peoples of Indochina are of Mongolian origin. The Indonesians, Malays, and Filipinos are Malaysians. Most of the countries include minorities who differ from the dominant race in origin, language, and customs. In religion the Burmans, Thai, and the peoples of Indochina are on the whole Buddhists. The Indonesians and Malays are Muslims, and almost all the Filipinos are Christians. The Burmans, Indonesians, Malays, Thai, and Cambodians received their religion and much of their culture from India. The Vietnamese civilization was deeply influenced by China, which ruled the country for a thousand years. The culture of the Filipinos was strongly affected by nearly four hundred years of Spanish and American rule. History too makes for disunity. Unlike China and India, Southeast Asia never produced a great empire which ruled over the whole area. Instead there were separate states which conquered the weaker peoples on their frontiers and sometimes fought one another. There is no memory of a united and prosperous past to which advocates of unity can appeal. In some cases the legacy of history makes for continued division in the present. The Cambodians remember the attempts of Viet Nam and Thailand to conquer them. Almost the only common interests of the peoples of Southeast Asia are that they live in the same part of the continent and that they all

163

want to be independent. There are more factors that make for disunity than for cooperation. The disappearance of the pre-war colonial regimes has left Southeast Asia a zone of weakness in the East-West struggle.

Australia

Australia is more intimately concerned than any other Western state that Southeast Asia shall remain in friendly hands.[2] World War II convinced her that the key to her security lay here, since it was the base of operations for enemies who wished to imperil her lines of communication or invade her. If Communist control could be prevented, defense in depth is possible, precluding any direct threat to her security. One aim of her foreign policy has been to win the goodwill of the states of Southeast Asia and strengthen their resistance to Communism by helping them to raise their standard of living. For this reason Australia was the first to suggest the Colombo Plan, and she has contributed liberally to it, so far as her means have allowed. Since it was realized that economic help was not the whole answer, the security of Malaya became an essential part of the policy of warding off Communism. In 1950 several squadrons of the air force were sent there for service against the Chinese Communist terrorists. In 1955 the prime minister, Menzies, announced that a battalion of infantry and supporting units would be sent to Malaya together with three squadrons of aircraft and several warships. They were to serve two purposes, the immediate one being to take part in the operations against the Communist rebels. In the long run the primary reason for their presence was to form part of a British Commonwealth strategic reserve for the defense of Malaya and Singapore, and for action wherever else they were needed.

When the Federation of Malaya became independent it negotiated an Anglo-Malayan treaty of mutual defense. Although Australia and New Zealand were not direct parties to the agreement they later acceded to it. The signatories agreed to cooperate in the defense of Malaya against a foreign attack and in operations against the Chinese terrorists. A British Commonwealth strategic reserve was to be maintained in the Federation, and could operate from there to protect Singapore, the British dependencies in Borneo, and Hong Kong. It

164

could not use its Malayan bases for operations in support of the South East Asia Treaty Organization, of which the Federation was not a member. In 1961 Tengku Abdul Rahman declared that if war broke out in Laos the Commonwealth reserve could not use its bases in the Federation in order to take part in it. So long as the United Kingdom retained its control of the defense and foreign policy of Singapore the difficulty could be surmounted by transferring the troops there. After Singapore became part of the Federation of Malaysia this would only be possible with the consent of the federal government. In 1962 the British government decided that the small amphibious joint-service squadron based on Singapore would be enlarged by the addition of two aircraft carriers and other warships. Its field of operations would cover the Persian Gulf, Aden and the Indian Ocean.[3] The long-range purpose of Australia in contributing to the strategic reserve was that the troops could be used wherever they were needed to carry out her obligations under S.E.A.T.O. The attitude of the Alliance government makes it uncertain whether this could be done. The policy of using Malaya as its first line of defense rests upon insecure foundations.

The United States

American interest in Southeast Asia was slight until after the defeat of Chiang Kai-shek by Mao Tse-tung.[4] The decision was then made that Japan should replace China as the principal American ally in the Far East, and that military equipment and economic aid would be given to France and the governments of Indochina. In the same year it was announced that economic and military aid would be furnished to the other states of Southeast Asia, and that the economic help would be coordinated with the Colombo Plan which had recently been established.

The purpose of the United States was to build a protective bulwark against external Communist attack. This involved deterrence of aggression: collective security: economic and technical aid: and support of the French and Bao Dai's government. On the first point Dulles enunciated the policy that since local defense by itself could not "contain the mighty landpower of the communist world" it "must be reinforced by the further deterrent of massive retaliatory power." The best means of resisting Communist aggression was "to depend primarily upon a

165

great capacity to retaliate, instantly, by means and at places of our choosing." He emphasized that retaliation could include the use of nuclear weapons, and that their employment would not necessarily be confined to the place where the aggression occurred. The forces of the state attacked would be assisted by American material aid and perhaps naval and air support.[5] Collective security was sought by a series of military alliances which included Japan, the Philippines, the Anzus Pact with Australia and New Zealand, and S.E.A.T.O. Under the pressure of the Korean and Indochinese wars the grant of economic and technical assistance soon took second place to military aid and collective security. By 1951 American programs of foreign help came to be regarded primarily as a means of relieving weak economies of some of the burden of building military forces for mutual defense. Foreign-aid budgets were seventy-five to eighty per cent military in nature. Statements of policy emphasized the need to resist Communism through military preparedness much more than by helping Southeast Asians to carry out their aspirations for economic betterment. In the later years of the Eisenhower administration greater emphasis was placed on the need to increase the amount of economic as opposed to military aid, and this trend was accentuated under President Kennedy.

The South East Asia Treaty Organization

The coping stone of the American system of alliances was S.E.A.T.O., which was concluded in 1954, soon after the final defeat of France in the war in Viet Nam. One weakness of the treaty was that it was a predominantly Western alliance, the only Asian members being Pakistan, the Philippines, and Thailand. The Philippines were dismissed as an American satellite, and Thailand as a minor state already aligned with the West. Nehru expressed the general Asian attitude when he described the agreement as diplomacy by threats and an unwarranted intrusion into Asian affairs. S.E.A.T.O., moreover, unlike N.A.T.O. did not have a standing military force, but would depend on the contingents which the members decided individually to contribute. A council was set up to consider matters arising from the treaty; but on the military side it consisted of little more than a series of meetings, exchanges of plans and ideas and occasional naval maneuvers.

Doubt exists how much help the Western governments would be

prepared to give in the event of a Communist attack on a large scale, for only limited forces could be expected from the Asian allies. The armed forces of the Philippines and Thailand are small, and ever since 1948 the greater part of the Pakistani and Indian armies have immobilized one another owing to the undeclared war over Kashmir. It is most improbable that France would send more than a token contingent because her interests in eastern Asia are now so slight. The British armed forces have been drastically reduced in size, and the principal preoccupation is the defense of Western Europe which involves the security of the United Kingdom itself. British interests in Asia end at Singapore, since Hong Kong is an indefensible outpost. The situation in Europe would determine whether substantial reinforcements could be sent to Southeast Asia. The armed forces of Australia and New Zealand are not large. In the past American policy has apparently been that the principal contribution would be the air force and the Seventh Fleet, while other allies provided the bulk of the ground troops. The decision whether to send a large army or not would probably depend upon American public opinion. Dulles when Secretary of State laid down the doctrine of massive retaliation. Air action would not necessarily be confined to the area of hostilities but might be extended to places of America's own choosing, and the use of nuclear weapons was not excluded. Put into plain English this meant that if the Peking government sent in its own army as in Korea or supplied equipment and personnel as in the war against France in Viet Nam, the American air force might carry out a nuclear bombing of China.

The efficacy of this policy was doubtful even at the date of its promulgation, and is much more open to question now. Long-range strategic bombing would be of very little use in Southeast Asia and have limited effect in China owing to the paucity of targets such as manufacturing cities and railway and air centers. The war effort of an underdeveloped and predominantly peasant country cannot be paralyzed like that of a developed and highly industrialized nation by selective bombing. Moreover, the Sino-Soviet alliance would probably bring in Russia, and since Dulles laid down his policy its strength in guided missiles has grown immensely. Whatever the value of massive retaliation in the middle 'fifties it is most unlikely to be employed today to counter the attack of a Communist army in Southeast Asia.

The defense must depend upon determined and well-led ground troops and not upon long-range bombing of the hinterland. The effectiveness of American air force and naval assistance to a defending army would depend upon the location of the fighting. It could give very valuable support to a distance of three or four hundred miles inland if the country attacked were contiguous to the ocean. This would not be possible if direct access were prevented by an intervening neutral state which would not allow American aircraft to fly over it. The air force would make possible the fast transport of troops and supplies, and could give support to the military operations of ground troops. This is being shown in South Viet Nam at the present time. A hostile army advancing on Malaya could be subjected to a heavy air and naval attack in close support of the ground troops, but this is not possible in Laos owing to its geographic position. Navy and air force alone could not have a decisive effect: there must also be a strong and determined army, as was shown in Korea. There is no inexpensive or easy defense in Southeast Asia against an invasion on a large scale. In view of the uncertainty already expressed as to the size of the army which the members of S.E.A.T.O. might provide, the alliance does not give a reassuring degree of security against an invasion in force.[6] This impression was not changed by the American, French, and British decision in 1961 to try to salvage Laos by negotiations and not engage in military operations. Finally, S.E.A.T.O. has been concerned chiefly with countering the threat of armed aggression; but the most probable form of attack is by internal subversion, strengthened at times by a limited infiltration of Communist guerillas as in Laos and South Viet Nam.

The Formation of Foreign Policy

The average Asian has little knowledge of international affairs or interest in them.[7] Since there is no articulate public opinion the formation of foreign policy is largely in the hands of a few in the capital cities who are national leaders or prominent members of political parties. Most of them led the movements for independence, and their opinions tend to be determined by memories of the recent past. Sukarno is a case in point. To some extent their behavior is affected by a feeling of inferiority to the West, and as a result they are extremely sensitive to any suggestion of foreign pressure. In general they are predominantly concerned with domestic problems. Their knowledge of world affairs is not extensive and they handle each question as it arises on a day-to-day basis, without having any profound or far-reaching plans. They do not have to concern themselves with public opinion to the same extent as Western foreign ministers, and have wide latitude in determining policy.

Speaking generally, their thinking is influenced by a number of factors which in varying degrees are prevalent throughout Southeast Asia. The strongest of these is nationalism. It shows itself in pride in national sovereignty, in the demand for absolute equality with the West, and in rabid opposition to the slightest suspicion of foreign interference. To many, nationalism is almost synonymous with hostility to imperialism. It also contains elements of racialism, though this is not yet a major force. Part of the influence of China in Asia is because it is an Asian power which has put the West in its place. Nationalism is a principal reason why all the attempts to bring about political collaboration between the states of Southeast Asia have failed. Each state is too much attached to its recently acquired independence to be willing to lessen its freedom of action by binding itself to any form of regional cooperation.

Dislike of imperialism is very much alive, and there is a refusal to recognize that the former colonial powers have abandoned it. The greater part of Southeast Asia considers that the basic conflict today is between nationalism and imperialism and not between Communism and freedom. Many leaders do not regard imperialism as confined to Western political control. They look upon almost any activity, such as investments, S.E.A.T.O. or American bases in Japan, as a manifestation of it. Apparently it is only a mature and self-confident nation like France or Great Britain which does not regard American bases as a foreign servitude that besmirches independence. The most curious point about much Asian hostility toward imperialism is that it is confined to the Western powers and is not applied to Soviet Russia and China. This attitude is typical of the neutralist states, but not of those which have allied themselves with the West. At the Bandung Conference the latter stigmatized Communism as the new imperialism and successfully opposed a resolution which condemned it when practiced by the Western but not by the Communist states. The conflict

SOUTHEAST ASIA

between Holland and Indonesia over the control of western New Guinea was considered by most Asians to be a colonial problem.

The governments are interested in the United Nations as a means of promoting the aims of their foreign policies. They belong to the Afro-Asian bloc which contains about half the members of the Assembly. Most of the Afro-Asian countries are very minor states, and their voting strength is out of all proportion to their economic and military power. It has been American and British policy to defer to them lest a contrary attitude cause them to move closer to Russia. The Afro-Asian bloc falls roughly into three groups, those who are allied with the West or consistently anti-Communist like the Federation of Malaya, the Philippines, and Thailand, the neutralists to which Indonesia and Burma belong, and those like Cambodia which may vote either way. The bloc vote is often divided in spite of the intensive lobbying carried on to create a united front. On most colonial issues group solidarity is attained, and also on economic aid to the underdeveloped countries. Here the aim of the Afro-Asian bloc is to secure an increase in the amount and ensure that as high a proportion as possible is distributed through the United Nations rather than the International Bank or the donor countries themselves.

Neutralism is the policy of Indonesia, Burma, Cambodia, and Laos. All of them have urgent domestic problems and peace is a necessity if they are to solve them. The Western powers are believed to have imperialistic aims, so any proposals they make for joining a defensive alliance are suspect. Soviet Russia and China are not regarded as imperialistic, though Burma has some uneasy reservations about the latter. Burma, Cambodia, and Laos, however, are on the mainland, uncomfortably close to China, and they realize that any defense they could offer would be futile. So they have looked upon the Five Principles as a better basis for international relations than alliances with the West. Their reliance upon them was somewhat shaken by China's invasion of India in 1962, but they did not support Nehru's denunciations of Chinese aggression. The only action taken was an attempt to arrange a peaceful settlement between India and China. Perhaps this was not surprising, because even Nehru continued to be as wedded to neutralism as ever, despite his verbal attacks upon China and his prompt appeals to the United States and Great Britain for military

170

equipment. The policy of Russia and China has been to encourage neutralism and play a waiting game. After all it benefits them: the governments which practice it are not adding to the strength of the West. Although India is the leading neutralist state, it would be an oversimplification to believe that the foreign policies of Burma and Indonesia are directed from there. They are too wedded to independence to accept outside direction. Whatever influence Nehru has is due rather to the personal relations between him and U Nu and Sukarno. It might be more accurate to write that India, Burma, and Indonesia follow somewhat parallel courses of action.

The Philippines

The leading principle of Philippine foreign policy is the maintenance of close and friendly relations with the United States. This is essential because the republic relies upon America for its defense, as a market for its exports, and as the principal source of economic aid. In 1947 an agreement was signed by which the United States acquired for ninety-nine years the right to use air, naval, and army bases. Other agreements provided for the supply of American equipment and the establishment of a military mission to train the Filipino army. By these measures the Philippines became a part of the chain of bases in the western Pacific. In 1951 the two states signed a treaty of mutual defense of indefinite duration. To add to its security the Philippine government had long advocated a more extensive defensive alliance which would include the countries of Southeast Asia. It therefore welcomed the creation of S.E.A.T.O. in 1954, of which it became a member.

The government is strongly opposed to Communism both at home and abroad. This is not surprising in view of its experience with the Huk revolt. In 1957 a law was passed which outlawed the Communist party. No diplomatic relations are maintained with any Communist state, and ambassadors have been exchanged with the Nationalist government of Chiang Kai-shek. The Philippines considers Formosa its first line of defense, and would be most reluctant to see it fall into the hands of the Peking government. The measures taken to restrict the economic activities of the Chinese in the Philippines have at times strained relations between the two republics. Chiang Kai-shek protested strongly against the retail trade act of 1954. During the Korean

171

war the Philippines fully supported American policy, and sent five thousand soldiers to join the allied army in Korea. This action was strongly approved by public opinion.

Relations with Japan are correct but not cordial. In addition to the hostility created by World War II and the fear of a recurrence of Japanese aggression, there was the dispute over reparations. The Philippine government demanded $8,000,000,000, and had high hopes that deliveries of machinery and so on would be of great help in carrying out the program of industrialization. Japan wanted to pay as little as possible, pleading poverty. In this it was supported by the United States, after the policy of strengthening the country as an American ally had been adopted. Abortive negotiations were carried on for some years, and a compromise was arranged in 1956. The Philippines abated its claims, and Japan realized that unless it gave some satisfaction it would be unable to expand its trade. Japan promised to provide $550,000,000 in capital goods and services over twenty years, and to expedite from private industrial sources $250,000,000 credits for capital goods which would be available to Filipino private enterprise.[8] Japan hopes and the Philippines fear that this will lead to partnerships between Japanese and Filipino firms which will enlarge its economic holdings in the republic.

Philippine relations with the other states of Southeast Asia have been friendly but much less intimate than with the United States. This has been strongly criticized by a section of the Nationalist party, the principal spokesman of which was Senator Claro Recto. The government was accused of being too pro-American, and of failing to cultivate closer ties with other Asian states. The argument was that since the Filipinos were Asians and not Westerners their destiny was inseparable from that of the peoples of their continent. This attitude has been linked with an undercurrent of anti-American feeling, though so far this school of thought has not been able materially to influence government policy. It is not likely to decrease, and it is quite possible that in the long run greater stress will be laid on Asian solidarity.

Thailand

Thailand has been independent for centuries, and of all the countries of Southeast Asia it was the only one which preserved this status during the late nineteenth-century period of imperialism. The government followed a policy of impartiality and friendliness toward all, and adroitly played off the British and French against one another. The result is that while Thailand is strongly nationalist and firmly attached to its independence, it does not have the fear and suspicion of the West that are found in Indonesia. It is opposed to colonial rule, but it does not consider that this is a monopoly of the West. At the Bandung Conference it insisted that Soviet imperialism was equally real and dangerous.

Apprehension of China is a major consideration in foreign policy, and it is intensified by fear of Communism. For centuries China looked upon Thailand as a vassal state. The distrust of its powerful neighbor was heightened by the presence in the kingdom of the large Chinese minority the loyalty of which was given to its country of origin. Thailand was separated from China only by Laos and Burma, and their weakness made them a feeble protection. On January 31, 1953, China announced the establishment of a Thai Autonomous People's Government in the province of Yunnan. This was the original home of the Thai, and it was from there that they migrated seven centuries ago to settle in North Viet Nam, Laos, the Shan States of Burma, and Thailand. Fewer than two hundred thousand were left in their original home, and to elevate them to the position of a separate government unit under Peking's tutelage looked suspiciously like the opening move in a campaign of aggression against the Thai of Southeast Asia. The threat to the security of Thailand was increased by Ho Chi Minh's victory over France and his successful creation of a fifth column, the Pathet Lao, which by 1954 controlled two provinces of Laos. Another disquieting occurrence was that in 1954 Pridi, the exiled rival of Phibun Songgram, broadcast from Peking appeals for a revolt in Thailand. The government has also been much concerned about the fifty thousand or so refugees from Viet Nam who live on the Thai side of the Mekong river across from Laos. Many of them are supporters of Ho Chi Minh and the part of the country in which they live is only weakly held by Thai soldiers. Thailand refused to establish diplomatic relations with the Communist People's Republic, lest the embassy in Bangkok became a center of seditious activity among the Chinese

173

minority. Diplomatic relations exist with Chiang Kai-shek's government but are cool.

The traditional policy of Thailand was neutrality, but in 1950 Phibun aligned his country with the United States. British was largely replaced by American influence at Bangkok. Phibun became convinced that Communist China was a threat, and could best be met by an American alliance. The United States for its part had reversed its earlier policy and had decided to intervene in Southeast Asian affairs. Thailand was looked upon as vitally important in the security policy of the United States. In 1950 agreements were signed which provided for American military, technical, and economic assistance. Equipment was provided for the Thai army, and also a military training mission. When the Korean war broke out Phibun sent a contingent and supported American policy in the United Nations. He strongly approved of the formation of S.E.A.T.O., and would have preferred a more explicit declaration in the treaty that any Communist aggression would be answered by war. What he would have liked was an automatic guarantee of armed help, instead of the promise that the allies would regard an armed attack as a threat to their own security and would act to meet the common danger in accordance with their constitutional processes. In 1961 when the Pathet Lao conquered a large part of Laos with help from North Viet Nam and the Soviet bloc, Sarit Thanarat was very far from satisfied when the United States and the other S.E.A.T.O. allies decided to negotiate a settlement instead of armed intervention. He had little faith in the plan to which the United States agreed that the war should be ended by setting up a government of Communists, anti-Communists, and neutrals. Sarit feared that the end would be control by the Communists, and that they would then try to overthrow his own government. The refusal to intervene in Laos by force made him afraid that there would be equal reluctance to go to war to support his own government. He demanded a firm promise of American help if the need arose. Reassurances were necessary, for despite his hostility to Communism it could not be taken for granted that he would offer unyielding opposition to an invasion in force unless very substantial American armed assistance were sent. In March 1962 the United States promised to defend Thailand against direct Communist aggression without waiting for prior agreement by S.E.A.T.O. The government regarded its obligation as "individual as well as collective," and not dependent upon the outcome of discussions with all the other members of the alliance.[9]

The States of Indochina

When the Geneva Agreements established South Viet Nam as an independent state in 1954 the belief was widespread that it would not last long. There seemed to be a strong probability that it would become part of Communist North Viet Nam. The success with which it was able to maintain its independence was due to President Ngo Dinh Diem and the help received from the United States. As narrated elsewhere he fought against the attempts of Ho Chi Minh to strengthen his fifth column and overthrow the government by the technique of the inside job. French influence was eliminated from the administration and the army, and by 1955 the United States was already playing a major part in its training. In 1957 the French military mission was withdrawn. Viet Nam ceased to send representatives to the High Court of the French Union. Much of the foreign trade of the country was diverted from France to the United States, and the Vietnamese piastre was linked with the dollar instead of the franc. The Geneva Agreements forbade Viet Nam as well as Cambodia and Laos to form any military alliance, and they were thus precluded from joining S.E.A.T.O. The protection of the alliance was extended to them in the event of overt aggression. No action could be taken without the consent of the government concerned.

Cambodia is a weak little state of 4,500,000 inhabitants. Ho Chi Minh tried to make it a Communist satellite. He invaded it in 1954, and built up a fifth column in the Khmer Issarak movement. The Geneva Agreements laid it down that the kingdom was to be independent and the fifth column must be disbanded. Cambodia must not join any military alliance as long as its security was not threatened. Prince Norodom Sihanouk has developed a foreign policy, the aim of which is to preserve the country's independence in the event that the rest of Indochina should come under Communist control. The state is anti-Communist in domestic affairs and the Khmer Issarak movement was eliminated after the end of the war in 1954. Since that date there has been little Communist activity. In foreign policy Cambodia is neutral and does not wish to join any alliance. In 1956 it rejected the protection given by S.E.A.T.O. The Peking government strongly encouraged the policy of neutrality, and at the Bandung Conference Chou En-lai went out of his way to assure Prince Sihanouk of his country's peaceful intentions, and of its determination to adhere to the five principles of peaceful coexistence in its relations with Cambodia. Prince Sihanouk regards the assurances as sincere, and believes that Mao Tse-tung would restrain Ho Chi Minh if he attempted to invade Cambodia.[10] The prince took American military aid, but insisted that he would not grant any bases or accept any military instructors.

In the economic field the policy has been to obtain aid from both sides. The United States and to a lesser extent France have given economic assistance, and some help has come from the British Commonwealth under the Colombo Plan. One of the principal results of American and French aid was the building of a seaport, Kompong Som, on the Gulf of Siam, and a road which connected it with Phnom Penh. Provision of a direct outlet for foreign trade lessened the need to use the port of Saigon, and helped the Cambodian policy of minimizing economic dependence upon South Viet Nam. A visit to Peking by Prince Sihanouk in 1956 resulted in an agreement for economic aid in carrying out a program of industrialization. Similar agreements were made with Soviet Russia, Poland, and Czechoslovakia. Relations with France improved after Cambodia obtained complete independence in 1953 and severed its connection with the French Union. French citizens ceased to leave Cambodia, where they own large rubber plantations, and cultural influence continues to be strong. A French military mission has been training the Cambodian army. Relations with Thailand and South Viet Nam have often been strained. Cambodia remembers several centuries of wars in the course of which both Thailand and Viet Nam annexed much of the state. Historical memories are strengthened by contemporary quarrels. There are territorial disputes with South Viet Nam and Thailand. There are four hundred thousand Cambodians in South Viet Nam and three hundred thousand Vietnamese in Cambodia, and each government accuses the other of discriminatory treatment of the minority. Cambodia gave asylum to a pilot of the Vietnamese air force who bombed Ngo Dinh Diem's palace, and Cambodia is incensed because Thailand has allowed a political opponent of Prince Sihanouk to live there and continue his plots. Both the Thai and the South Vietnamese governments condemn Cambodia's policy of neutralism and its friendship with China and Russia. All three governments cherish their grievances against one another and have no intention of replacing them with friendship and cooperation.[11]

Laos is about the size of France, and is mainly mountains and jungle. It has no railways and few roads. It is bordered by China on the north, Burma and Thailand on the west, Cambodia on the south, and North and South Viet Nam on the east. The population is about one million five hundred thousand, and the dominant race is the Lao. They are akin to the Thai and are about half the population. The remainder are a heterogeneous collection of on the whole primitive tribes at varying stages of civilization. Technically Laos is a constitutional monarchy with universal suffrage, a cabinet, and all the other democratic accompaniments. Actually it is an oligarchy of a few hundred Lao, many of royal descent and with a French education. They cabal against one another for power. One of them, Prince Souvanna Vong, had the original ideas of turning Communist and recruiting a following from among the primitive tribes who had been left outside the exclusive circles of Lao politics. The pro-American clique tried vainly to crush the Communists and opposed the neutralist faction headed by Prince Souvanna Phouma which worked for an alliance of all three groups. The United States equipped, trained, and paid the army of twenty-five thousand at a rate that far exceeded the cash income of the average inhabitant. Its only military shortcoming turned out to be a reluctance to do much serious fighting against Prince Souvanna Vong's Communist guerillas. Laos is not an organized state with a national patriotism but a geographic expression. The government has so little control, owing to completely inadequate communications, that about half the population are practically autonomous tribes who rarely see an official.

During the war with France Ho Chi Minh invaded Laos in 1953, and created a Communist fifth column, the Pathet Lao, of several thousand guerillas, which controlled the two northern provinces of Phong Saly and Sam Neua. They were headed by Prince Souvanna Vong, and the organizers were Communist Vietnamese, while the rank and file appear to have been recruited from the local tribes. The Geneva Agreements established the independence of Laos, and forbade it to join any alliance, so long as its security was not threatened. The government of Laos was to administer the provinces of Phong Saly and Sam Neua, but until this was arranged the Pathet Lao was to occupy them. There followed several years of abortive negotiations varied by desultory fighting, which ended with the Pathet Lao still in occupation of the two provinces while the king controlled the rest of Laos.

The Peking government gave assurances that it would respect the independence of Laos in accordance with the five principles. There was strong suspicion although no legal proof that the Pathet Lao continued to receive foreign Communist assistance. The United States strongly supported the government of Laos. Officially it followed a policy of neutrality, but in practice a pro-American faction was usually in power for several years. American economic aid was given on a fantastically lavish scale, but the benefits from it seem very largely to have been restricted to the few hundred Lao who made up the governing class. In 1961 the Pathet Lao allied with the neutralists and openly supplied with Russian equipment began an offensive which overran a good half of the kingdom. The royal army retreated again and again, and the Western powers were unwilling to intervene forcibly. Endless negotiations were carried on at Geneva between the Western powers and Soviet Russia, and a plan was evolved to end the fighting by setting up a coalition government of Communists, anti-Communists, and neutralists. The most hopeful forecast was that what was left of Laos might perhaps be allowed by the Communists to continue to exist as a neutralist state. The renewed attack in 1963 by the Pathet Lao against their ally the neutralist faction made even this qualified optimism seem excessive. If a Communist dictatorship won control of Laos Thailand would consider this a threat to its own security. Its adjacent provinces are only separated from Laos by the Mekong river and are weakly defended. They also contain thousands of Vietnamese who took refuge there during the war against France, and who are supporters of Ho Chi Minh. The United States would be involved as it was in 1962 because of its treaty obligations to Thailand.

Malaya

The foreign policy of Malaya has been largely covered in the discussion of Australian and United Kingdom interests. So long as Tengku

Abdul Rahman's government remains in power it will support the alliance with the British Commonwealth. It will not join S.E.A.T.O. for domestic political reasons. The Chinese in the Federation are sympathetic to the Peking government and would oppose a policy which made Malaya a S.E.A.T.O. base from which China could be held in check. Nor are they interested in preserving the sea and air communications of the British Commonwealth. Some of the Malay and Chinese leaders urge that the Federation should adopt a neutralist policy. Both the Pan Malayan Islamic party and the Socialist Front advocated abrogation of the existing defense treaty in the election of 1959. There have been the usual accusations that the presence of British soldiers is a foreign servitude, that it estranges the Federation from neutralist Asia, and that the defensive alliance is "a device to bind us indirectly to support colonial expansion." Tengku Abdul Rahman feels that he has gone as far as is expedient in negotiating the present alliance. Its continuance depends upon his retention of power. Lee Kuan-yew, the P.A.P. premier of Singapore, is much less friendly to the British alliance. Now that Singapore has become part of the Federation of Malaysia he will try to persuade the government to abrogate it and demand that the Commonwealth give up its base at Singapore.[12]

Burma

Burma is a weak state bordering upon China, and for a century it was a British colony. These have been the most important factors in shaping foreign policy. The government of China has claimed Burma as a dependency ever since the temporary conquest of the thirteenth century. Burma could not defend itself against an invasion, and pretexts for an attack have not been lacking. The mountain frontier was delimited during the period of British rule by joint Anglo-Chinese boundary commissions, but the agreements were never ratified by the Chinese government. During the nineteen thirties it claimed sovereignty over territory which had been part of Burma for several centuries. Chinese maps, both Nationalist and Communist, showed large areas in the Kachin, Wa, and Shan states as belonging to China, and in 1956 Chinese soldiers occupied a portion of the territory. After abortive attempts to settle the dispute in 1956 and 1957, agreement over the boundary was finally reached in 1960, and a treaty of friendship and

179

non-aggression was signed. Burma made several small territorial cessions while China abandoned her earlier claims, and with minor modifications accepted the boundary negotiated by the British government.[13] In 1950 soldiers of Chiang Kai-shek's army crossed the border into the Shan States. They refused to leave or surrender their arms. In 1951 they raided the Chinese province of Yunnan and again retreated to Burma. They numbered about twelve thousand, and arms were flown in to them by airplanes. The Burmese army failed to dislodge them, and the government was seriously concerned. If China were thinking of moving into Burma it would never find a better excuse. In 1953 Burma asked the United Nations to intervene, and after protracted negotiations some seven thousand were evacuated to Formosa by 1954. About three thousand refused to leave, and on several occasions the Burmese army carried on operations against them. An additional cause of concern has been the increasing support for the Peking government which has developed among the three hundred fifty thousand Chinese in Burma.

The government would never admit it but the chief consideration in molding the country's foreign policy has been apprehension over the intentions of its Chinese neighbor. Officially the establishment of S.E.A.T.O. was condemned, but there was not the marked hostility to the treaty that there was in Indonesia. In certain Burmese circles it was welcomed as a counterweight to the growing power of Communist China.[14] Since resistance would be impracticable, the government has made neutrality the core of its foreign policy. It has refused to take sides in the cold war and has tried to be friendly with both power blocs without committing itself to either. Burma was the first non-Communist state to recognize the People's Republic of Mao Tse-tung, and ambassadors were exchanged in 1950. In 1954 Chou En-lai and U Nu issued a communiqué in which they stated that the relations between the two countries would be conducted in accordance with the five principles. The same year a trade agreement was negotiated.

A legacy from British rule is that hostility to imperialism has been a basic principle of foreign policy. Nevertheless relations between the two countries have been friendly. Burma has strongly opposed imperialism in the United Nations; it has condemned Soviet as well as Western imperialism. Burma has also pressed strongly for foreign assistance to the underdeveloped countries. The policy has been to accept it from both sides. Burma has received economic assistance from the United States and also from the British Commonwealth under the Colombo Plan. In 1955 agreements were made for the exchange of Burmese rice and agricultural products for Soviet industrial goods. Similar arrangements were made with Czechoslovakia and other Soviet satellites.

The foreign policy of India has had strong influence upon that of Burma, though it would be incorrect to write that it was directed from New Delhi. The point of view of the two countries has been similar in many respects, and there were close personal relations between Nehru and U Nu. The foreign outlook of India, as defined by Nehru, met a sympathetic response in Burma. Realizing that Burman nationalism was very sensitive to outside interference Nehru carefully avoided any action which might seem to savor of dictation. It is very much an Indian interest that Burma should be in friendly hands since it could be used as a base from which to mount an invasion. Nehru's firm support was of considerable help to U Nu's government during the years when it was in danger of being overthrown by the rebels.

A number of issues exist which could easily impair relations between the two countries, but owing to the friendship between U Nu and Nehru they were not allowed to cause any trouble. Prior to the war the Indians in Burma filled much the same role as the Chinese in the other countries of Southeast Asia, and were regarded with the same hostility. Since the war immigration restrictions have prevented an influx of Indians, and it is estimated that they number about eight hundred thousand at the present time. Nehru's policy has been that Indians living abroad should either keep their Indian citizenship and have the status of foreigners in their country of residence, or else seek the citizenship of the country where they live and identify themselves with it. In the first case India would try to secure the same treatment as that of the most favored aliens; and in the second they should be given full rights of citizenship. Burmese qualifications for citizenship have excluded many Indians who were entitled to it in Nehru's opinion, but he has not made an issue of the matter. The *chettyars* have protested strongly at the nationalization of their lands in Burma and the inadequacy of the compensation offered them. Nehru has refused to demand the return of their property and has limited himself to urging adequate compensation under the prevailing economic conditions.

Indonesia

Indonesia has the comfortable feeling that since it is an island republic, further away from China than any other part of Southeast Asia,
any threat to its independence from the Communist bloc neither exists
nor is possible. Owing to the intense nationalism and anti-Westernism
which dominate its foreign policy, the republic tends to sympathize
with any Asian or African state that opposes the West as Communist
China has done. As regards subversion from within, Sukarno favored
the growth of the power of the Indonesian Communist party, and relies
upon it as one of the principal supports of his dictatorship. The abolition of Western control over the dependent peoples of the world is
looked upon as the most fundamental issue in contemporary world
politics. The cold war is thought to be merely another conflict between
rival great powers, in which Indonesia's only vital concern is to avoid
being drawn in. So the government practices neutralism with a bias
in favor of the Communist powers. It has been anxious to gain prestige
as one of the leaders of Asia, though it has been careful not to challenge
the position of India. On colonial, economic, and cold-war issues the
two countries very often vote alike in the United Nations. As regards
foreign economic aid the government believes that by playing off the
United States against Russia it can obtain increased assistance from
both.

Dutch New Guinea (West Irian)

The only real connection between New Guinea and Indonesia was
that for reasons of administrative convenience Holland put both under
the control of the Dutch Governor General of the East Indies. The
Papuans of New Guinea were completely different from the Indonesians
in race, language, religion, and type of civilization. It was in no way an
Indonesia irredenta. The historical argument advanced by the Indonesian government was very tenuous. Three centuries ago the Sultan of
Tidore had established control over some of the seaports on the coast
of western New Guinea. When he was compelled to make his submission to the Dutch East India Company, he was allowed to retain his
possessions there. In the second half of the nineteenth century the
Dutch government removed the territory from the Sultan's control,
and extended its rule from the coast into the interior. After Indonesia

182

obtained its independence it took over the government of the Sultan's remaining territory. On this ground it claimed that it had a historical right to New Guinea, which the Sultan's ancestor had been compelled to transfer to the Dutch over two generations earlier. The real ground on which Indonesia demanded New Guinea was that it was administratively part of the Dutch East Indies and therefore should have been transferred with the rest of the empire. When Indonesia achieved its independence at the Hague Conference in 1949 the negotiators were unable to agree on the status of Dutch New Guinea, and the question was postponed to a future meeting. When this was held the Dutch government refused to hand it over. What Sukarno was really declaring was that he had the right to govern all the territory formerly held by the Dutch, whether the inhabitants were Indonesians or not. He took the same attitude as the governments of other newly independent countries such as Ghana and the Congo. The European powers in Africa imposed their rule on a large number of tribes, some of whom were traditionally hostile to one another. The grant of freedom was followed by the revival of tribal hostilities, and the threatened collapse of the artificial unity which had been created. The new negro rulers refused to allow tribes like those in Ashanti and Katanga to revert to their former independence.

The colony of New Guinea was a financial burden to Holland, and promised to remain so indefinitely. The annual cost of administration was nearly twice the revenue, and the deficit of $30,000,000 was paid by Holland. The principal products were limited amounts of oil and copra, and the prospect for any great increase was not encouraging. The Papuans were one of the most primitive peoples in the world, and the Dutch were trying to bring them from the stone age to the twentieth century as rapidly as possible. Not long ago a large number of the villages were independent tiny states which periodically went to war with their neighbors. This facilitated the national habits of head-hunting and cannibalism. The aim of Holland was to civilize the Papuans and train them for democratic self-government. In 1961 all Papuans over twenty-one were given the vote, and a legislature was set up where sixteen of the twenty-eight members were elected. A ten-year plan for political and economic development was inaugurated, which it was hoped would prepare New Guinea for independence.[15]

The record of the Dutch was admirable, though there was some ground for fear that they were moving too fast toward independence.

Nothing in the history of the relations between the Indonesian government and its fellow countrymen in the Outer Islands gave one any confidence that it would be more successful than the Dutch in handling a people which was totally divorced from it in race, language, and stage of civilization. The ruling power in New Guinea must pay large annual deficits or starve the social services. Holland had the money and spent it generously. Indonesia, with its chronic deficits met by printing more paper money, had not. In the third place the officials in charge must speak the language and understand the customs of the people. Here again Holland had a well-trained and competent civil service, while Indonesia had not. So far as it was possible to ascertain the views of the Papuans themselves the large majority seemed to oppose annexation to Indonesia and to believe that the Dutch plan gave them the best chance of soon governing their own country.[16]

Anger at the refusal to surrender New Guinea led the Indonesian government in 1954 to abrogate the loose union of Holland and Indonesia which had been arranged at the Hague Conference in 1949. It repudiated the portion of the government debt which it had taken over, confiscated Dutch assets, and severed diplomatic relations. From 1954 to 1957 Indonesia annually brought the dispute before the United Nations Assembly, but was unable to obtain the necessary two-thirds majority. Developments from 1961 onwards aroused the suspicion that Sukarno was preparing to attack West New Guinea, or else was bluffing in the hope that Holland would hand it over without a fight. In 1961 General Nasution, the minister for National Security, visited Moscow and arranged for the purchase of a large quantity of additional materiel, which was to be delivered before the end of the year. It was believed that the cost of the Soviet equipment bought between 1960 and 1962 was nearly $1,000,000,000.[17] Included in it were a squadron of long-range bombers, an aircraft carrier, a Sverdlov-class light cruiser, destroyers, landing craft, submarines, and eight batteries of guided ground-to-air missiles for offensive purposes. Speeches by Nasution, other leading generals, and civilian officials hinted at the intention to take West New Guinea by force unless Holland gave way. Subandrio, the foreign minister, insisted that the only acceptable settlement was annexation.

184

He referred to self-determination — the Dutch policy for New Guinea — as "old-fashioned," an enlightening comment since this was the ground on which the Indonesians demanded freedom from Holland. Subandrio also said that it was pointless to take the New Guinea question to the United Nations Assembly again, since it was doubtful whether Indonesia could obtain a two-thirds majority.[18] As the year advanced Sukarno became increasingly bellicose in his threats of war.

Sukarno's reason for buying the destroyers and landing craft might have been to strengthen his control over the Outer Islands, for the causes which brought about the rebellion of 1958 still existed. This did not apply to the cruiser and aircraft carrier. Soviet Russia had never yet built an aircraft carrier, and the delivery date was decidedly problematical. Assuming that it should finally arrive, the strength of the Dutch and Indonesian fleets would have been roughly equal on paper. The Indonesian sailors, however, would require at least several years of training before they could hope to operate a cruiser or aircraft carrier effectively, while the Dutch navy though small was very efficient. A warning of what would happen was given in January 1962, when a very few Dutch ships drove off a numerically large Indonesian force encountered in New Guinea's territorial waters. For this reason Sukarno's threats that war was imminent needed to be taken with a grain of salt. There was the suspicion that the aircraft carrier was an example of getting ahead of the Joneses: its possession would make Indonesia the only state in Asia apart from India which had a warship of this type. Only five Western states had aircraft carriers, and Russia had none. Sukarno would also have an atomic reactor and the largest sports stadium in Asia, and even Nehru himself could not equal that combination.

The Dutch government was under heavy pressure to rid itself of New Guinea. Leftist parties in Holland demanded that it pull out as quickly as possible, and influential business groups urged it to come to terms with Sukarno. Other arguments advanced were that financially the colony was a dead loss, and that there was no hope of compensating for this by economic development. There were indications that public opinion would oppose sending soldiers to defend the Papuans against an attack. The Dutch government complained that Australia refused to give help if war broke out. The Australian government did not want Indonesia to replace Holland in West New Guinea, since it suspected

185

that Sukarno would soon demand the liberation of the rest of New Guinea from its trusteeship. The Australians had vivid memories of how Japan used New Guinea as a base for attacking them in 1942, and they did not want Indonesia as a near neighbor. On the other hand, Holland intended to be quit of New Guinea in a few years at most, while Australia would still be on Asia's doorstep and under the necessity of cultivating friendly relations with her neighbors. So the Australian government announced in January 1962 that it would not go to war over West New Guinea except in concert with the United Kingdom and the United States, an unlikely conjuncture.[19] The former gave Holland no support, and the Dutch say that the American government exerted pressure in 1962 to make them give way to Sukarno and avoid a "colonial" war. Apparently the United States was afraid that a war would increase Sukarno's dependence upon Soviet Russia.[20]

Holland offered in September 1961 to terminate her sovereignty, and place the administration and economic development "under the active supervision of the United Nations." She offered to continue her annual subsidy of $30,000,000, and to urge her twenty-eight hundred officials to remain if the United Nations wanted them. The only stipulation was a resolution of the United Nations Assembly "which clearly guarantees the right of self determination of the population." Holland also proposed the appointment of a United Nations commission of inquiry to investigate the situation and the wishes of the Papuans, and decide whether the territory should be placed under the control of a United Nations international development authority. Indonesia opposed the Dutch offer, insisting on annexation, and was supported by the Soviet and the majority of the Afro-Asian blocs, led by India. They rejected the proposal that "the destiny of a non-self governing territory must be based on the principle of self determination." [21] Sukarno redoubled his threats of war and insisted that he would not consider any settlement except annexation. In January 1962 the Dutch government abandoned the condition on which it had previously insisted that it would negotiate only if Indonesia recognized beforehand the right of the Papuans to self-determination. It now announced that it would negotiate without any prior conditions whatsoever. The United States intervened to bring about negotiations which took place between March 20 and 23, when they were broken off by Sukarno. Mr. Bunker, a former

American ambassador, drafted a plan for a settlement which the State Department commended to U Thant. He accepted it and negotiations were resumed under United Nations auspices in May 1962. During these months Sukarno had been attacking New Guinea by periodically dropping small groups of paratroopers. Bunker proposed that the administration of West New Guinea be transferred from Holland to the United Nations. In two years at the latest the United Nations would hand over control to Indonesia, Sukarno promising that at some unspecified future date he would allow the Papuans to exercise their right of self-determination. The agreement which was signed by the Dutch and Indonesian representatives on August 15, 1962, was even more favorable to Indonesia than Bunker's proposals. The period of United Nations trusteeship was reduced to seven months and ended on May 1, 1963: the Indonesian paratroopers infiltrated to conquer New Guinea were to be used as part of the United Nations neutral force brought in to maintain law and order: and if the United Nations were unable to find enough officials to administer the country it would "employ personnel provided by Indonesia." The United Nations soon discovered that very few of its officials were willing to serve in New Guinea. Finally it was agreed that the Papuans would be allowed to vote on whether they wished to be independent or annexed to Indonesia in seven years. Two days after the agreement was signed, on August 17, 1962, Sukarno said that he interpreted the promise of a free vote as meaning that the Papuans would have only internal self-determination and not external self-determination "which we reject." Three months later a widespread campaign was started in Indonesia to rescind the promise of a free vote after seven years.[22] It is pretty clear that the Papuans would be wise to build no hopes on being allowed genuine self-determination, or on receiving help from the United Nations or any other outside power.

$\stackrel{\textstyle\downarrow}{\textstyle\curlywedge}$

VII

The Economic Effects of Colonial Rule

A Peasant Economy

The nine states of Southeast Asia all have the same general characteristics which they share with the other underdeveloped countries of the world. Agriculture is by far the principal occupation, and 70 to 90 per cent of the population are engaged in it. In Japan the proportion is 35.5 per cent. Although fairly large estates worked by tenants or sharecroppers sometimes exist, e.g., the Philippines, the typical cultivator is a freeholder whose main object is to produce enough to support himself and his family. Surplus production is limited, and is sold to pay the taxes, meet debt payments, and buy necessities such as salt or cloth which the peasant cannot produce himself. Cattle-farming is of minor importance, the prevalent crops being cereals, particularly rice, and tubers such as yam and cassava. The average farm is about five acres, or roughly the area which can be managed by one family. During the past half century a growing number have planted all or part of their holdings with a cash crop such as rubber, but despite this qualification the predominant characteristic of peasant agriculture is production for subsistence and not for the market.

Farming methods and tools are antiquated, and the peasant does not receive a return commensurate with his labor. The binding force of custom is a very great handicap, and the cultivator is slow to change habits that are sanctified by immemorial tradition. The yield of rice per acre in Southeast Asia is less than half what it is in Japan, where the

188

peasantry has adopted Western methods. Production per hectare (2.47 acres) is anywhere from 2,464 pounds in Indochina to 3,652 pounds in Indonesia, while it is 7,942 pounds in Japan. The yield in Japan doubled between 1880 and 1920 because such innovations as artificial fertilizers and higher-yielding seeds were adopted. The contrast between Japanese and average Asian production is the difference between an agriculture which has been transformed by the impact of Western science and one which continues unchanged in the old peasant ways. A revolution in farming methods would remove a principal cause of the low standard of living of the Asian peasants. The widespread custom of dividing the farm equally among male heirs is also a handicap. Its frequent result is that the farm consists of several separate plots a considerable distance apart, a thoroughly uneconomic practice. Fragmentation has increased as the population has grown, with the result that farms are smaller as well as subdivided. The inadequacy of irrigation works is sometimes a cause of poverty. Fields solely dependent upon rain produce one rice crop a year, whereas irrigated fields often grow two. Yet another characteristic of Asian agriculture is that the farmer is idle for five or six months of the year. He approves of this because he attaches high value to leisure, and has little enthusiasm for an occupation where, as on a Western rubber estate, he is expected to work a fixed number of hours a day throughout his term of employment. It is unfair to describe this as laziness, as Westerners often do. Asian farming means periods of exceedingly hard work with primitive tools, alternating with months of idleness. This enables him to attain a level of existence which has satisfied him until recently, but inevitably the standard of living is low. Peasant self-sufficiency at its best gives everybody something, but it gives nobody very much.

An underdeveloped economy is predominantly one of small-scale agriculture, apart from the mainly Western estates which have been established during the past hundred years. Mining, usually carried on by foreign private enterprise or the local government, is often extensive, but manufacturing is in its infancy. There is an acute shortage of skilled labor, technicians of all kinds, and experienced business executives. Southeast Asia has another characteristic which is in marked contrast to, for instance, India. This is that business operations are very largely controlled by Westerners and Chinese, and to a minor extent Indians.

Import and export firms; banks; insurance, shipping, mining, and oil companies; and most of the factories are owned by Europeans or Americans, though the Chinese share has been growing. The Chinese also dominate retail trade and produce-buying from the peasant, and provide him with the bulk of his credit at very heavy rates of interest, though they seem to be less usurious than native money lenders.

European vs. Asian Living Standards

The disparity between Asian and Western standards of living appears to be comparatively recent. Two or three hundred years ago they seem to have been roughly similar. Definitive proof of this statement is impossible, but apparently this was the impression of European travelers in Asia during the seventeenth and eighteenth centuries. Their writings were concerned chiefly with the wealth and power of the Asian monarchs, and they did not greatly concern themselves with peasants and workmen. The general impression conveyed, however, was that they saw no great difference between their standard of living and that of the corresponding classes in Europe. Thereafter the West suddenly began to forge ahead. The productivity of agriculture rose, and fortunes were created through manufacturing which far exceeded any that had existed previously. A general rise in prosperity occurred, and a gap opened between the standard of living of Asia and the West which is still widening at the present time.

The immediate reasons for the advance of the West were scientific discoveries and inventions. The beginning of the change dated from the early seventeenth century when a radically different attitude from that of the earlier period appeared. It asserted that conditions of life were not everlasting or dictated by supernatural causes. On the contrary, they were the result of natural causes which could be discovered by observation and experiment, and the knowledge gained by these could be used to bring about changes. Gradually this theory of progress was applied in every walk of life and changed the comparatively static existence of the middle ages into the dynamic life of the twentieth century. In the eighteenth century experiments considerably increased the yield from agriculture. Machines replaced hand labor, factory production took the place of handicrafts, and transportation was revolutionized. From the nineteenth century onwards the transformation went on faster and faster, and the divergence between material conditions in Asia and the West became increasingly wide.

The difference between the two is not explained by saying that the scientific spirit of inquiry appeared in the West and not in Asia. This merely pushes back the inquiry one stage further and poses the question why the scientific attitude arose in the one and not in the other. No certain answer is possible, and one passes into the realm of speculation. Before life in Asia began seriously to be affected by Western influences in the later nineteenth century it had many resemblances to that of medieval Europe. The economy of Europe in the middle ages was predominantly one of landowners and subsistence peasants, farming methods were primitive and not very productive, and wealth was limited. The revenue of the English government in the fifteenth century was about £100,000. Material conditions of life were accepted as inevitable and ordained by God, and changes came about very slowly. Yet suddenly a new point of view appeared in this static European society which transformed it, but it did not show itself in Asia.

Maurice Zinkin attempted to explain it in his *Asia and the West*. He pointed out that one of the most important developments of the middle ages in Europe was the growing power of the towns. They became independent of the barons and to a considerable extent the kings to a vastly greater extent than the towns of Asia. They were the strongholds of the middle class of merchants, master craftsmen, and artisans. They were marked by an attitude of independence and adventure, a spirit of inquiry, and a willingness to take risks, whereas the peasants on the whole showed conformity to traditional and unchanging ways of life. Zinkin's belief was that change came from the townsman and not the peasant, and that in the end this produced the scientific spirit. He argued that in Asia the town never attained the importance and independence that it did in Europe. In Southeast Asia foreign trade was monopolized by the rulers and their ministers. Some of them owned their own ships and exported their produce, or else sold it to the Arab, Indian, and Chinese merchants who visited their ports for centuries before the arrival of the Europeans. The emergence of a native commercial middle class was prevented. The towns were overshadowed by the power of the rulers and were dependent upon the royal courts for their prosperity. Instead of independence and a willingness to make

191

innovations there was conformity with established custom. In this intellectual climate the scientific attitude could not arise.

European Imperialism

The beginnings of European control in Southeast Asia date from the early sixteenth century, but it was not extended over the greater part of the area until well into the nineteenth century.[1] The empires of the West were generally restricted to a number of coastal towns, forts, and trading posts. Only the Spaniards in the Philippines and the Dutch in Java and the Moluccas acquired more extensive territory at an early date. Elsewhere the Europeans were the employees of trading companies who wanted dividends and not territory. Imperialism was expensive: it entailed wars of conquest, and forts and soldiers to hold the conquered territory against revolts from within and attacks from without. The patriotic gratification of extending the power of one's state was no compensation for the heavy cost. The policy of the commercial companies was to carry on operations as economically as possible in order to increase profits. The character of the trade made this possible, since the object was to buy Asian products such as spices, textiles, and tin which could be sold at a high profit. The cheapest way was to obtain them from their producers by making contracts for the delivery of specified quantities with Asian rulers. Territorial control was established only where this method proved ineffective as in Java and the Moluccas, or where, as in the Philippines, the principal object was the conversion of the natives to the Roman Catholic religion. Here it was felt that the exhortations of the missionaries would be strengthened if the objects of their ministrations were brought firmly under the control of the Spanish government. Elsewhere the population was usually left under the rule of native princes who acknowledged the suzerainty of the foreigner. As a result Western rule was limited to the regulation of trade and the maintenance of peace, and interfered little with the traditional way of life. A deep and direct penetration of Western culture was absent both in intention and in fact until well on in the nineteenth century.

The extension of European control over the whole of Southeast Asia except Thailand was the result of several causes. One effect of the Industrial Revolution was greatly to increase the importance of colonies as markets for exports. Machine-made goods were cheaper than Asian handmade articles, and dependent peoples acquired a new value as consumers of surplus production. Territorial expansion became an aim in itself since it meant expansion of controlled markets. Furthermore, the growing demand for raw materials could no longer be satisfied from the earlier sources of supply, and additional areas had to be sought overseas. As the century advanced industry began to demand far larger amounts of tropical raw materials. Rubber was one of the most striking examples. Previously little use had been found for it save for making erasers and rainproofing the coats of the ingenious Mr. MacIntosh. The invention of the automobile made it a necessity of life. The millions of acres under rubber, palm oil, and the like in Southeast Asia dated from the end of the nineteenth century. Occasionally annexation was brought about by the inability of an Asian government to maintain law and order. When a highly developed and a less advanced state came in contact with one another, sooner or later there would be incidents which the more advanced state regarded as intolerable. One reason for British intervention in the Malay States was the adverse effect on the trade of the Straits Settlements of Malay piracy and the wars between the Chinese in the Perak tinfields. At times territory was taken because of domestic politics in a European state as in the annexation of Cochinchina by Napoleon III, or in order to forestall another European government, as when the United Kingdom conquered Upper Burma to keep out France. For one reason or another European control was extended over the whole of Southeast Asia with the exception of Thailand.

The Duties of Government

The character of colonial rule was radically altered from about the middle of the nineteenth century onwards, owing to a revolutionary change in the idea of the duties of government. The earlier conception was much what it had been for several thousand years. If Hammurabi, the Emperor Augustus, Elizabeth I, and Akbar the Great could have exchanged views with any early nineteenth-century governor general of the East Indies, they would have found themselves in substantial agreement. The government must deal justly with its subjects, avoid excessive taxes, protect them from foreign invasions and civil wars,

193

maintain law and order, and safeguard the rights of all through the operation of the courts of law. Beyond this little was expected, though local authorities might sometimes provide pure drinking water. Such matters as education and curing the sick were left largely to private benevolence. So long as a government confined itself to this restricted list of duties, it interfered little with the traditional way of life of its subjects. The change began when the European powers started to introduce social services into their Asian colonies.

Few of the present social services in Western countries are more than a hundred years old, and many are much more recent. The beginnings of public health measures go back to the early nineteenth century, and state education began about the same time. The social services were first evolved in the wealthy, industrialized nations of Western Europe. After a variable time each new service was introduced into the overseas colonies, and a new department of government was created to administer it. Many of the innovations were not appreciated by the peoples upon whom they were firmly bestowed. There was truth in the story of the Ceylonese villagers who built a model latrine under pressure from a health officer, put a sign bearing the word "Welcome" over the door, and never used it. The poorer Chinese of Hong Kong did their best to evade the fumigations and disinfections of a health inspector when anyone in the house died of an infectious disease, and no one could understand why he disapproved of taking drinking water from a toilet bowl. So often the work of a social-service department was to persuade, cajole, and at times compel the people to accept benefits they did not want. Much has been written about European exploitation in the tropics, and the disruptive consequence of Western economic forces upon the traditional way of life. Probably the impact upon it of Western standards had an equally great effect.

Economic Changes

The economic character of the countries of Southeast Asia was profoundly altered during the nineteenth and twentieth centuries. To an important extent handmade articles were replaced by less expensive machine-made goods, initially from Great Britain and the other industrialized nations of Western Europe. During the period between the two world wars Japanese and to a minor extent Indian manufactures partly replaced those of Europe because they were cheaper. Looked at from the point of view of the Asian consumer this was a gain. Very large numbers of handicraft workers however lost their traditional livelihood, and upon them the effect was calamitous. The same thing had happened in Europe during the early stages of the Industrial Revolution. There however the handicraftsmen migrated to the new factory towns and found employment. In Asia this was impossible since very few factories were built. Displaced workmen were forced to remain in their villages and earn their living as farm laborers. This increased pressure on the land, and the effect was intensified by the growth of population caused by the introduction of Western medical and health services. In countries where there was ample vacant land the problem could be handled by expanding the cultivated area. Where the supply of land was limited, however, and notably in the small island of Java, a large surplus of agricultural laborers was produced. Too many laborers competed for too little work, with the result that they held down the level of wages.

It is difficult to see how this situation could have been avoided. A revolutionary change in methods of production inevitably causes hardship, and Asian consumers benefited to the extent that they paid less for their manufactures. All the colonial powers insisted on free entrance for their manufactures into their dependencies. In the Philippines and Indochina the Americans and French gave themselves a preferred position in their colonial markets. The Dutch and the British, the two leading colonial powers in Southeast Asia, followed an open-door policy until the 1930's. None of them considered for a moment erecting tariff barriers against the free entrance of their own commodities, and yet such protection was necessary if manufacturing were to be encouraged. As it was there were virtually no industries to protect, and no demand for them.

The overwhelming majority of the peoples of Southeast Asia continued to be peasants as they had always been. They had neither the capital nor the training to become business men, and, more important, they preferred to continue their traditional way of life. There was a growing demand for a Western education, but the object was to qualify for sedentary employment as government officials, lawyers, office workers, etc. The only exceptions were the Chinese and to a lesser

SOUTHEAST ASIA

extent the Indians, who were as much foreigners in Southeast Asia as the Europeans. The story of the Chinese is particularly significant. In China most of them had been peasants or laborers, and when they arrived as penniless emigrants they were compelled to work as coolies. They looked upon this as a stopgap, and their ambition was to embark upon the more lucrative career of business. In this many were successful, and a considerable part of the economic development of all the southeastern Asian countries except Burma was due to their enterprise and acumen. They received no special favors from the colonial governments, which tended to regard them as an undesirable but regrettably essential element in the economy. Their success was due solely to themselves. Contrasting them with the failure of the local Asians to change their mode of life, one is forced to the conclusion they lacked an aptitude for business which the Chinese possessed. Furthermore, the Chinese worked much harder and were willing to risk their capital in strange and unaccustomed enterprises which held out the hope of profit. In view of these facts, it is hard to see how the governments of Southeast Asia can be blamed for failing to create a native business class.

Lack of Industrialization
The only way in which industries could have been established was by Western capital. None of the governments could have done so, for all of them subscribed to the doctrine of free private enterprise. It was true that they owned and operated railways, hydroelectric works, and, in the Dutch East Indies, tin mines, but they considered that to begin manufacturing was altogether too socialistic. This was emphatically in the field of private business, and the governments had no right or power to influence the decisions of private corporations, which were free to build factories if they chose, since it was only in Indochina that their establishment was discouraged in the interests of manufacturers in France. On the whole, Western companies decided that it was more profitable to manufacture in Europe or the United States and export their products to Southeast Asia. The principal exceptions were the semi-manufacture of local raw materials. There were, for instance, tin smelters in Malaya, oil refineries in the Dutch East Indies, and sugar and coconut oil refineries in the Philippines. They were too

few to provide much alternative employment to agriculture. It is sometimes alleged that the failure to build factories was the result of a determination on the part of private enterprise to prevent the colonies from competing and keep them as markets. The truth was that individual firms considered the alternatives from the point of view of profit and loss, and decided that it would pay them better to export their products to Southeast Asia and not establish factories there. The post-1945 attitude has been similar. Western investment was principally for the production of raw materials and foodstuffs for which there was a market overseas. Typical examples were estates for rubber, palm oil, coconuts, tea, sugar, tobacco, and cinchona; oilfields; and mines of tin, iron, coal, manganese, chrome, tungsten, gold. Shipping, banking, insurance, and export and import trade were largely controlled by Europeans, and to a lesser extent by Chinese and Japanese. The Chinese had almost a monopoly of retail trade and produce-buying from the peasants as well as of money-lending. In Burma Indians filled the same position as the Chinese. Native capitalists so far as they existed were chiefly landowners and money lenders.

Effects of Western Imperialism

Colonial rule and Western capital built an astounding edifice of order, wealth, and social services in Southeast Asia. The purpose was not pure altruism: a healthy population made more efficient workmen than a diseased one, and prosperous peasants would be better customers. Yet along with self-interest there was a genuine desire on the part of the governments to improve the position of their subjects. Asians were given a period of law and order, equality before the law, and freedom from war which they had never before experienced. In the late nineteenth century scientific research discovered the cause and cure of tropical diseases, health measures were introduced, malarial swamps drained, pure water supplies installed, medical services established, hospitals built, and quarantine regulations issued. Agricultural research evolved higher-yielding seeds and varieties more resistant to disease, acclimatized new cultures like rubber, and made improvements in farming methods. Great efforts were made to persuade the peasants to adopt the results of the discoveries. Millions of acres

197

were cleared of jungle and brought under cultivation. Large irrigation projects were carried out, and food production was progressively increased. An attempt was made with not overmuch success to provide the peasant with loans at a reasonable rate of interest, and liberate him from the money lender. Here the Dutch were less unsuccessful than the other colonial powers. The country was opened up by roads and railways, and these benefited the peasants as well as the foreign estates and mines. Previously the lack of roads had meant that every small district was isolated and largely self-sufficient. When cheap transport was lacking it did not pay to carry for any distance bulky products like rice, the sale price of which was low. The cost of freight soon ate up the profits. So each district had to provide itself with most of the necessities of life. It was useless to produce a surplus when every peasant in the district was growing the same crop. The building of roads and railways linked the peasant with a market in the towns and overseas. The importance of roads was illustrated by an incident which occurred about 1948. Shanghai imported wheat from the United States because this was cheaper than to bring it by road from a province of China some seven hundred miles away. The population multiplied increasingly, since the natural checks of war, famine, and disease were largely abolished. To a noticeable extent, indeed, the growth of population canceled the efforts of the social services to raise the standard of living. The most startling instance was Java, where an estimated population of 4,500,000 in 1815 had risen to 48,000,000 in 1940. Other causes were also at work, but it could be said with a good deal of truth that the medical and health services combined with the other social services enabled several Asians to exist at about the same low standard of living where formerly there had been one.

In earlier centuries Southeast Asia had been of minor importance in world trade apart from its production of spices. By 1941 it supplied 95 per cent of the world's natural rubber, 70 per cent of the tin, 65 per cent of the copra, and 40 per cent of the palm oil. Burma, Thailand, and French Indochina among them provided the bulk of the world exports of rice. The area also produced large quantities of sugar, tobacco, and tea and was the principal source of vegetable fibers (manila hemp and sisal) and pepper (85 per cent), as well as 90 per cent of the cinchona or quinine and 70 per cent of the kapok.

THE ECONOMIC EFFECTS OF COLONIAL RULE

The Plural Society

In economics as well as government the European colonies were plural societies. Europeans held the controlling positions in government and, along with a growing minority of Chinese, in the economic field. The Chinese together with some Indians made up the bulk of the middle class, especially in business. The Western-educated people of the country were chiefly professional men, government officials in the middle ranks, journalists, and school teachers. The lower class was composed of the native peasantry, skilled craftsmen, and manual laborers, and in some countries a number of Chinese and Indians. The Europeans and most of the foreign Asians were temporary residents who eventually returned to their own countries. Their object was to make money, and their primary concern was with whatever promoted this aim rather than with the ultimate interests of their country of temporary residence. There was little social intercourse or community of interests between the races. They were in economic competition with one another, and almost the only thing they had in common was that they all lived in the same country. A plural society was at the opposite pole from a homogeneous society such as that of the United States or Great Britain.

The Village in Transition

Colonial rule profoundly affected the traditional village community, both for good and ill. It changed more from the later nineteenth century onwards than it had for uncounted centuries. It is now in a stage of transition, a mixture of new and old, and the transformation is still in progress. The traditional village was an almost self-contained economic unit which supplied most of its own necessities. The villagers rarely traveled far from their homes and had little contact with the outside world. Life was regulated by immemorial custom which ensured that there was no break with the past. The guiding principle in everything was as it was in the beginning, is now and ever shall be. The duty of the peasant was to till the fields, manage village affairs, and obey the orders of his ruler. The ills of life such as occasional epidemics or famines and extortionate taxes were accepted as inevitable. The peasant was content with his lot and had no desire for change

199

or a higher standard of living. As long as this attitude continued no economic advance was possible.

The traditional village economy began to disintegrate as a result of colonial rule. The government built roads and railways the purpose of which as far as the peasants were concerned was to raise the standard of living by giving them access to a larger market. The opening of the Suez Canal lessened the cost of ocean freight to an extent that made it profitable to sell Burmese rice in Europe. This led the British government to encourage Burmans to take up land in the lower valley of the Irrawaddy river, and convert millions of acres of almost uninhabited jungle into fertile rice fields. The British and Dutch governments took a great deal of trouble to induce Malays and Indonesians to plant crops such as rubber for which there was a good market overseas, and thus give them a cash income. The French did the same thing in Indochina by encouraging the growing of rice for export in the delta of the Mekong river. The American method was to give Philippine exports free entrance to the United States, so that the Filipinos concentrated upon producing products such as sugar which brought the best returns, thereby creating a colonial economy which depended for its prosperity upon free access to the American market. The result everywhere was to destroy the economic isolation of the village and link it with the currents of world trade. Previously it had been insulated from the booms and slumps of the business cycle, but this immunity was now destroyed. When world demand increased prices rose and the peasant received more money than before. When demand and prices fell his income declined. Linking the villages with the seaports was a prime reason for the decay of handicrafts. Roads and railways facilitated the sale of machine-made goods to the villages of the interior. The result was that very large numbers of the village handicraftsmen lost their livelihood, and in the old army phrase became useless mouths. Java was a particularly bad example owing to its very dense population and the unwillingness of the Javanese to emigrate to the other underpopulated islands. In 1954 it was estimated that between a quarter and a third of the agricultural laborers were not needed to carry on the work of the farms. In 1957 another estimate was made that about 10,000,000 out of the existing laboring population of 27,000,000 were superfluous. The introduction of a money economy caused further changes. Formerly the peasant had carried on all transactions by barter, but from the nineteenth century on he found that money was needed for business transactions and paying his taxes. He did not understand the new medium of exchange, and the result was to increase his debt to the money lender. Frequently the freeholder lost his land through foreclosure of his mortgage and became a tenant or a landless laborer. The social services contributed another element of change. Previously it had been taken for granted that the son would labor as his father did: the new system of education opened up the possibility that he might become a government official or an office worker. Beyond this the cult of individualism which is a part of all the Western systems of education had its effect on some of the students who came in contact with it. This had a corrosive influence on the doctrine that custom was sacrosanct and that the wishes of the individual must always be subordinated to the will of the village community.

All these changes developed slowly, and until the present century the peasant was content with his position in life. He accepted his sparse livelihood with its periodical vicissitudes as unavoidable, and he valued its compensations highly. He was able to follow his accustomed way of life in the village where he was born, and he could attain a standard of living which satisfied him by working for only part of the year. He was not indifferent to money, but unlike the Westerner he placed a much higher value upon leisure. For this reason he was usually unwilling to take employment with a European estate or mine, since this entailed working a set number of hours every day as well as leaving his village. The attitude of the peasant has altered, and this has become increasingly evident since World War II. He does not have a detailed program of his aims. It would be nearer the truth to write that he is somewhat confused as to exactly what he wants and still more about how he is to obtain it. He does not realize that one principal reason for his poverty is reluctance to break with custom and change his traditional methods of farming, and that another is his continuing to have a large family. On one point however he knows his own mind: he wants to improve his material condition, and he no longer accepts the burdens of debt and rent as inevitable evils.

Various influences contributed to undermine the "pathetic contentment" of the peasants, to quote a phrase coined some forty years ago to describe the Indian raiyats. Poverty alone does not produce dangerous discontent, so long as the poor do not know that others who have the same occupation are far more prosperous than they are. As long as the villager knew nothing of the world beyond his own district he was resigned to his lot, because almost everyone was as poor as he was. He knew of course that a very few were wealthy, the government officials, the landowners and the money lenders. But this group had always been there, and in a world ruled by custom their position was accepted as inevitable. The peasant rarely rebelled against them. The position changed when he acquired a standard of comparison, and learned that people like himself in foreign countries were far more prosperous than he was. When that happened he began to ask himself why he could not live as well as they did. The knowledge of the higher living standards of the West percolated slowly but effectively. Films, especially American films, and the radio had great influence. The growing number of Asians who traveled to Western countries had their effect. During World War I, for instance, Vietnamese served in France as soldiers or in labor battalions, and brought home with them stories of the incredibly luxurious way of life of the French peasants. Another cause was the tactics used by nationalist leaders to enlist the support of the cultivators in their struggle to win independence from the colonial powers. Prior to World War II they were not consciously nationalist and still less were they democratic, so that it was no use appealing to them on these grounds. Perhaps their state of mind could best be described as one of vague discontent caused by the changes which were taking place in their customary way of life. They did not clearly know what they wanted, but they connected the unpleasant period of transition in which they lived with their foreign rulers. Life had never been like this in the good old days before they came under European control. The Asian leaders persuaded the peasants that their poverty was the result of imperialist, capitalist exploitation, and that political independence would give them a higher material standard of living. They were led to expect that freedom from colonial rule would of itself bring about a miraculous change in their condition. In the Philippines this was the principal argument by which the Nacionalista party, the political organization of the land-owning governing class, secured the support of the peasants in their struggle to rid themselves of American control. Incidentally, leaders like Sukarno who held out this inducement are now suffering from the pressure of rising expectations. The peasants were taught to expect a rapid improvement in their position, and the failure of their new rulers to work miracles exposes them to the danger that they may be replaced by more radical leaders.

VIII

Financial Problems
of the Underdeveloped Countries

Peasant Agriculture

A Southeast Asian government which wishes to preserve itself from Communism must rest on the solid base of a contented peasantry. They can only be kept contented if they are enabled to own their own land, if they are freed from dependence on the money lender, and if their farming is made more profitable. The landowner caused dangerous agrarian discontent in the Philippines, South Viet Nam, and Burma, and in the first-named his position is substantially unaltered. In South Viet Nam and Burma he was eliminated after World War II, and his estates divided among his former tenants. Redistribution of the land is not enough, for before long much of it will be controlled by the money lender. The peasant has always had a very small reserve of capital, and any emergency forced him to borrow from the money lender, whose rates of interest were extremely high. Moreover, the cultivator was improvident and lacked thrift and foresight. He spent extravagantly on such occasions as the birth of a son, when custom decreed a lavish celebration. He has been known to borrow as much as three years' income from his land for such a reason, and thus incur a debt which it would take years to repay. It has been calculated that a high percentage of the peasants of Southeast Asia were in debt, and that the greater part of it was incurred for unproductive purposes. Laws fixing the rate of interest proved to be ineffective since they could easily be circumvented, and the only remedy was for the governments to pro-

vide an alternative source of credit. None of them have adopted adequate measures to this end, in considerable degree because of lack
of sufficient financial resources.

Experience has shown that the third point of the program, to increase the productivity of the peasant, is also expensive. A large staff
of agricultural agents must be employed to persuade him to modernize
his methods by using higher-yielding seed, fertilizer, and better tools.
Probably the government would have to provide them at cost or below
it, since the peasant had so little to spend. Where overpopulation existed or the rainfall was uncertain, the cultivated area might be extended
by irrigation works. Sometimes flood-control works were necessary to
prevent the rivers overflowing their banks. In districts which were
already densely settled it might be necessary to move the surplus population to vacant land further afield. It would not be enough, however,
to present the peasant with a title deed and an axe, and exhort him
to hew his farm out of a jungle. The government must roughly clear
the land, survey it, and lay it out in small holdings. Anti-malarial works
must be carried out, roads built, and the settlers and their families
supported until they had established themselves on their new farms.
Altogether the cost of agricultural betterment will continue to tax
the financial resources of the new governments.

In the long run the program would have the great advantage that
by raising the peasant's income it would increase his purchasing power
as a consumer of local manufactures. Asian factories will have to depend principally on the domestic market, and the peasants will be about
four fifths of their customers. The more their ability to buy is increased,
the more industrialization can expand and employ part of the surplus
farm population. As to sales abroad, Western governments are sympathetic and to some extent admit Asian manufactures even when this
is to the detriment of their own industries. If, however, the competition
should become too widespread and serious it would be a very unusual
government which would withstand heavy pressure from shareholders
and trade unions for protection.

Manufacturing and Raw Materials

Southeast Asia as a whole has a considerable range of minerals, but
they are so widely scattered that by and large mining for export seems

205

more probable than use by local industries. Coal is usually of inferior quality and unsuitable for heavy industry, though water-power resources are large and widely distributed. Deposits of iron ore are extensive, but only the coal of North Viet Nam can be used for smelting. The Philippines, to give a typical example, have large deposits of iron, chromite, copper, and manganese but no coal: Malaya has tin, iron, and some bauxite but little coal, and that of poor quality. There was sound economic common sense in the Japanese plan to conquer the whole of Southeast Asia and exploit its minerals to supply some of Japan's deficiencies. Unless coal is imported factories must rely principally on hydroelectric power or oil. This last is found in Indonesia, Brunei, and Burma. The principal vegetable raw materials are rubber, copra, coconut oil, and palm oil. Generally speaking light industry seems to be the type best adapted to local resources. The manufacture of textiles would be a natural development, although for the time being most of the raw material would have to be imported. The cost of freight would be only a small fraction of the value of the finished article. Home production would remove the necessity for finding the foreign exchange to pay for the heavy annual import of cloth which is one of the principal articles of trade. Another natural industry is the manufacture of tires and other rubber products. The possibilities for developing manufacturing are somewhat limited, and the principal occupation will continue to be agriculture. Before extensive development of manufacturing is possible there must first of all be a great expansion of hydroelectric power, roads, and railways and the training of skilled workmen. The program means heavy expenditure with little immediate return.

Industrialization is not a magic panacea for raising the standard of living. The emphasis should be placed upon increasing the present low productivity of agriculture, both in food and raw materials. This would not only make the peasants a better market but would relieve the food-deficit countries such as Indonesia from the heavy cost which they can ill afford of importing rice. It would also increase the amount available for export and add to the earnings of foreign exchange with which the underdeveloped countries must pay for the bulk of the imports needed to carry out their development programs. The greater part of the necessary foreign exchange will almost certainly come from the profits of the export trade in raw materials or food, and not from financial aid given by Western governments. The importance of industrialization is that to some extent it will relieve the pressure of population on the land, and also that by supplying the domestic market it will lessen the volume of imports which must be paid for out of the scarce foreign exchange. The improvement of agriculture is the quickest and surest way of obtaining the capital necessary to finance economic development.

During the period since 1945 the governments of the new states have often adopted spectacular and costly schemes for industrialization which were beyond their financial resources and supply of skilled personnel. Frequently the object has been to enhance national prestige or increase national power. One of the strongest motives in the new states is the desire for an international position equal to that of the Western powers. Industrialization is regarded as a symbol of status. There has also been the reassuring thought that the political leaders who made the decisions were not risking their own money. Typical examples have been the creation of a national air or shipping line or both. They are expensive to establish and keep up, and divert sorely needed funds from more essential purposes. In a world which is pretty well supplied with means of communication, the chief justification is that they increase the national prestige. The culmination of prestige spending is reached when a steel mill is built. Burma is a good example: it built one although it had only low-grade coal and virtually no iron. Since most countries of Southeast Asia do not have both coal and iron one or the other must be imported, and the freight charges make the costs of production considerably higher than those of countries which have both. Heavy industry to be efficient must be on a large scale, and the cost of operation is too great unless it is producing to full capacity. The demand is limited in a backward agricultural market, and much of the product must be sold abroad. Here it has to compete with the output of established producers in the industrialized nations, and it cannot match them in price unless it receives a subsidy which the government can ill afford. The principal argument advanced for ambitious plans for industrialization has been that it brought about the high standard of living in Western Europe and the United States, and that to do likewise on a large scale will quickly produce the same result. The Asian governments ignored the important point that the growth of manufacturing and the rise in living standards took place gradually over several generations, and that this occurred because there was already a large domestic market with high purchasing power. The first essential is to expand the consuming capacity of the local market, and this means improving the productivity of agriculture. This is likely to be a slow process owing to the influence of custom, and the reluctance of the peasants to break with it. The new governments are trying to telescope into a few decades economic progress that took a far longer period in the West.

The Example of Japan

The underdeveloped countries could study with advantage the example of Japan during the earlier stages of its evolution from an underdeveloped to an industrialized state. Between 1880 and 1920 great emphasis was placed upon the improvement of agriculture, and its productivity was doubled at comparatively moderate cost. A rise in the standard of living of the peasants was deliberately retarded by the government, which took much of their increased wealth by raising the taxes. It was, however, well aware of the parable of the donkey and the carrot and it allowed them to keep enough of their increased production to give them an incentive to improve their output still further. Until about 1890 taxes on agriculture provided the greater part of the funds needed to finance the program of industrialization. Since at this period Japanese business men were unwilling to risk their capital in unfamiliar enterprises, the factories were often built and operated by the government until their profitability had been clearly shown. Sometimes it subsidized private business to induce it to undertake a new venture. Agricultural exports paid for almost all imports, and foreign loans were eschewed. At first enterprises were avoided which required heavy imports of machinery or the help of large numbers of foreign technicians. These were postponed till a later date when they could be better afforded. The government knew that its capital was limited, and it spent shrewdly and to the best advantage. It is regrettable that the underdeveloped countries pay great attention to the economic success of Soviet Russia and China, and ignore the less advertised but impressive achievements of Japan.

Socialism and Private Enterprise

Most of the new governments of Asia are in varying degrees socialistic, and have no intention of permitting a regime of free private enterprise on the American model. To a considerable degree their attitude is a legacy from the period of colonial rule. The pre-war nationalist elite saw that their foreign rulers controlled economic as well as political life. They realized that political self-government was only a half measure. Every Burman, Indonesian, Malay, Vietnamese, and Filipino who rose above the mass of the population found himself in a corridor of which the exit was blocked by a European or American superior, and knew that he would always have to obey an alien command. He decided that his country would not be truly independent until it controlled its economic as well as its political life. Very often, too, foreign business men were regarded with suspicious hostility as imperialist exploiters. There was no native business class which had the wealth and the trained experience to replace them. The government alone had the power to do so, and it alone could mobilize the capital necessary to develop the resources of the country.

Very few of the nationalist leaders who controlled the governments had any experience of business or knowledge of economics. They did not belong to the business class but were lawyers, intellectuals, teachers, students, and civil servants. Many of them ignored and condemned the motive of private profit, especially if it were made by a foreigner. This explained why a politician who realized the need for foreign private investment and tried to attract it was often thwarted by other leaders who could not see the necessity of what he was trying to do. The same attitude of mind explained the mania for government regulations and controls over private business, native as well as foreign, of which Indonesia has been an outstanding example. Often the merits of a scheme were not judged by asking whether it were the one which would increase the national income the most at a given cost. The decision was frequently based on the desire for national prestige and power or the general principle that any form of manufacturing increased the national wealth. So uneconomic industries were created and bolstered by protective tariffs.

The money needed for economic development comes from one of four sources. The first is domestic capital, the sums collected by an

Asian government by taxation and loans, and the savings of individuals which are used for productive purposes. The greatest part of the funds must come from this source. In the second place there is the foreign exchange obtained by the sale of exports. Thirdly come the investments of private foreign capital. In the fourth place are the funds received from Western governments and international organizations like the United Nations and the International Bank for Reconstruction and Development.

Domestic Capital

Asian domestic capital exists in considerable amounts, but it is difficult to direct it into productive channels. There are very few reliable statistics on incomes in Southeast Asia, and so far as the peasant is concerned figures are deceptive. His farm provides most of the basic necessities for himself and his family. The cash value of these is not included in the usual estimate that the average annual income per head of population is $60 to $75. It is clear however that between his low productivity and his debt to the money lender there is not much margin for taxes or saving, and that his reserves of capital are small. What little he does possess is hoarded and not invested in government bonds or industrial securities.

The traditional custom of converting savings into cash and hoarding instead of investing them is still widespread, and is found among the wealthy as well as the peasantry. The practice originated in pre-colonial times when any display of wealth invited spoliation by the royal tax collectors. Hoarding was one phase of the Asian tradition that government was a dangerous and capricious power. No one would lend money to it or for that matter to business men, since they had a reputation for dishonesty which was frequently deserved. The tradition was also established that the best forms of investment were to own land or lend money on the security of land mortgages. Land gave prestige and an assurance of stability, and lending at high rates of interest was lucrative and also the first step toward becoming a land-owner. These traditions were so ingrained that they survived the period of colonial rule.

In several of the countries of southeastern Asia they have been strengthened by the instability of the governments and the lack of law

210

and order. As a rule the native capitalist in southeastern Asia is the owner of an estate or residential property, a money lender, a merchant, or a nobleman who hoards gold and jewelry. To lend money to government or private business is a new and untried departure, and there is widespread reluctance to embark upon such a revolutionary course of action. Despite its poverty Asia could raise considerably larger amounts from domestic savings if the traditional deterrents to investment could be removed.

Export Trade

The exports of Southeast Asia are almost entirely raw materials or foodstuffs, and usually there are only one or two staples. In the 1950's rice provided 75 per cent of Burma's and 55 per cent of Thailand's total exports by value: rubber and tin accounted for 80 per cent of Malaya's exports: rubber, tin, and petroleum were 75 per cent of Indonesia's exports: and copra, sugar, and hemp provided 75 per cent of the Philippines' exports. The price fluctuated widely and sharply in accordance with world demand, to the great detriment of the exporting countries. The governments' plans for economic improvement required heavy purchases abroad of everything which could not be produced locally, such as machinery. Payment was made largely with the foreign exchange obtained by the sale of exports. Sometimes as in Indonesia private firms were required to transfer to the government the proceeds of their foreign sales. The fluctuations in price meant that the government could not estimate in advance what amount of foreign currencies it could count on for carrying out its economic plans.

The price of rubber in 1951 was three times what it had been in 1949 owing to very heavy buying particularly in the United States as the result of the Korean war. The governments of Indonesia and Malaya received a very welcome windfall, but in 1952 the average price was less than three fifths what it had been the year before. Burma and Thailand had a similar experience with rice. For some years after World War II there was an acute shortage of it, and the two governments profited prodigiously. By 1953 several of the rice-deficit countries had considerably increased their production and reduced their imports. In addition the United States had expanded the acreage under rice and become a major competitor of Burma and Thailand for the markets of Japan and Korea. The result was that both countries accumulated stocks which they could not sell, in spite of a considerable lowering of the price. This seriously threatened the Burmese government's plans to build a welfare state and led to the negotiation of agreements with Russia and China by which rice was bartered for manufactures. The results were not altogether satisfactory, for Burman connoisseurs complained of the flavor of Czech whisky and Chinese toothpaste. Moreover, the government had not bargained for mountains of cement which filled the warehouses and overflowed on the wharves where it was deluged by the heavy rain.

There have been years when the fall in the value of exports owing to a decline in price exceeded the amount received in grants and loans from Western governments. The governments of Southeast Asia have pointed out the serious harm that this did to their economic policies, and they urged that the world price of their exports should be stabilized, but so far their representations have had little effect.

Foreign Capital

If the underdeveloped countries were to depend entirely upon domestic savings and export trade, economic progress would be very slow. In the United States, Canada, and Western Europe from 16 to 17 per cent of the gross national income has been invested each year in economic development. In Indonesia, potentially the wealthiest country of Southeast Asia, the net investment was estimated at 5 per cent of the national income annually. The current rate of population growth has been 1.7 per cent a year, and since additional income must be created to give it a livelihood, the real annual investment in economic betterment was only about 3.3 per cent.[1] Indonesia's rate of investment has only been sufficient to keep national income growing a little faster than population. In some of the smaller countries such as the Philippines rates of investment are believed to have been higher, and the prospects for a satisfactory advance in economic betterment are more favorable. So slow an improvement is not enough to satisfy Asian demands, and the Communists are quick to point out that they do these things much better in Soviet Russia and China. One cannot be positive about the percentage of the national income invested in China, but the rough estimate of 15 per cent has been made. Whatever the true percentage may be it is much larger than in the non-Communist countries. A dictatorship can force a higher rate of investment than a less arbitrary form of government because it does not hesitate to use unlimited coercion and can to a very considerable extent ignore popular demands for greater consumption. It is a cogent argument for cooperation when everyone knows that objectors will be withdrawn indefinitely from circulation.

The only way to hasten economic progress is if the underdeveloped countries receive considerable imports of foreign capital. There is the further consideration that one powerful appeal of Communism in these countries is that it promises a short cut which will in a few years lead a backward, agricultural state to a Western standard of living. The Five-Year Plans did this for Russia, and China has begun to move in the same direction. The very large majority of Asians know nothing of the human misery which went to the making of Soviet Russia and is now achieving the same result in China: they are impressed by the short space of time in which the results were accomplished. The argument that the price of material betterment is the loss of democratic freedom has little weight with people who live near the borderline of existence and are weary of it. Moreover, most Asians never have been democrats and are not democrats today. One does not miss what one has not known or appreciated. Of recent years Soviet Russia has begun to compete with the West in giving economic aid to the underdeveloped countries, and there is every indication that this will increase. The uneasy global balance of power would be upset if the underdeveloped countries moved to the Soviet side, and it is to the interest of the West to assist them to achieve their economic aspirations so far as this is possible.

After World War II it was taken for granted that Western private capital would provide the bulk of the funds. Heavy investments had been made in Southeast Asia prior to the war, mostly for the production of raw materials. The social services were financed largely by the taxes which they paid. It was assumed that this situation would continue and that the Western governments would find only a minor although substantial part of the needed capital. They would concentrate particularly upon basic forms of development such as irrigation and hydroelectric works, railways, roads, and harbor installations. These were essential for further progress, but the return from them was not large enough to appeal to the private investor. Private capital, it was believed, would continue to invest on a large scale in enterprises where the profit was larger or more immediate.

IX

Private Investment Abroad since 1945

Statistics on the investment of private capital abroad since the end of World War II are incomplete and sometimes inaccurate, particularly as regards the underdeveloped areas. This is especially true if one tries to ascertain the amount invested in any one country. The general picture, however, is clear. With some notable exceptions such as the oil companies private capital has fought shy of the newly independent states of Asia and Africa.

The United Nations came to this conclusion after a series of inquiries into the international flow of private capital since 1955[1] which showed that the bulk of the investment was in the advanced industrial nations such as the United States, or in those which were already fairly well industrialized and were expanding rapidly. Examples of this second group were Canada, Australia, South Africa, and Mexico. A very large part of the investment in the underdeveloped countries was in those which had oilfields or deposits of non-ferrous metals, the Middle East and Latin America being the favorites. Investment was small in the underdeveloped countries of Asia and Africa which had neither important natural resources nor large domestic markets. The Philippine Republic was one of the few states which appeared to have attracted a moderately large amount of private capital, chiefly American, investment in 1956–1958 being estimated at $99,000,000. During the same period investment in Indonesia was $38,000,000, mostly in oil. About $1,770,000 was invested in Burma, mostly from the United Kingdom, in 1956–1958. Approximately $13,500,000 of French capital were repatriated from South Viet Nam in 1955–1957, but thereafter withdrawals fell off sharply.[2]

The principal investors in Southeast Asia were the United Kingdom and the United States. Far and away the greater part of French investments were in the franc area. Nearly three fifths of the investments of the Federal Republic of Germany during the 1950's were in developed Western countries, and most of the remainder in Latin America. Only about 4.5 per cent was invested in the whole of Asia, particularly in India where there were some large industrial undertakings. Dutch foreign investment seems to have gone largely to Western Europe and to some extent Latin America. Japanese investment of $20,000,000 in Southeast Asia was rather more than a fifth of the total investment abroad.

American Foreign Investment

The total amount of American direct foreign investment in 1959 was approximately $29,700,000,000. Of this about 34.3 per cent was in Canada, 30.3 per cent in Latin America, 17.8 per cent in Western Europe, 4 per cent in the Middle East, and only 13.6 per cent in the rest of the world. Out of this last amount the total investment in South, Southeast, and East Asia was $1,028,000,000, or 3.4 per cent. Nearly two fifths was in Japan, India, Pakistan, and Hong Kong, and the remainder, $607,000,000, was in Southeast Asia. The Philippines came first with $385,000,000, Indonesia next with $163,000,000, followed by Malaya with $45,000,000, and Thailand with $14,000,000. By comparison, $210,000,000 was invested in Japan and $136,000,000 in India.[3] Most of the investment in the underdeveloped countries was in oil, mines, and raw materials such as rubber. This was very similar to the pre-war position. Only a limited amount was invested in manufacturing. This ran counter to the policies of the governments of the new states, which were much more interested in industrialization than the production of raw materials. American companies, however, had found that the profits from a factory in an underdeveloped country were no higher than in the United States and possibly lower. Furthermore, the political and economic uncertainties involved made it difficult to estimate profits, and as a rule a manufacturer preferred to export his product to the underdeveloped market. When a factory was built the usual reason was to avoid the loss of the market through the erection of trade barriers. Where possible the building was financed from the local profits earned by previous sales, and not from new capital sent from the United States.

The announced policy of primary reliance on private investment must be regarded more as the expression of a hope than as an operating policy. Yet government officials follow as a matter of ritual the pronouncement of this policy whenever the subject of foreign economic assistance is discussed, and continue to have faith that some one will discover the magic formula which will release a large flow of American private investment to the capital-hungry areas of the world.[4]

President Kennedy's message to Congress on his foreign aid on April 2, 1963, was a typical example. He said that "The primary new initiative in this year's program relates to our increased efforts to encourage the investment of private capital in underdeveloped countries." He went on to list the inducements held out to business companies. Several of them, such as investment guarantees, were of long standing and had not produced notable results. British political leaders have been as prone as American to make similar statements.[5]

United Kingdom Foreign Investments

The total amount of United Kingdom private direct investment overseas was estimated to be £4,000,000,000 ($11,200,000,000) in 1958. Total capital exports from 1948 to 1958 were not less than £2,500,000,000 ($7,000,000,000), and of these exports approximately £2,000,000,000 ($5,600,000,000) went to the sterling area. The remainder was invested in the oil-producing countries, the United States, and Canada.[6] To a considerable extent the small amount invested outside the sterling area was due to the exchange control. It permitted investment only if the investor intended to play an active part in the business and it promised to lead to increased United Kingdom exports, the development of sources of raw materials, or the use of British technical knowledge. Portfolio investment (i.e., the buying of a diversified list of government bonds, debentures, or stocks) in the nonsterling area was thus completely ruled out. The exchange control also restricted direct investment (e.g., building or enlarging a factory).

A United Kingdom company could not without official permission transfer profits from its home operations or transmit a loan from a United Kingdom bank to expand its operations in a non-sterling country. So far as the sterling Commonwealth was concerned, funds could be freely transferred, although there were restrictions which have of late been progressively relaxed on the raising of new money on the London market. Until recently it was likely to be allowed only if the government were satisfied that the purpose was urgent and that it would "maintain or increase the production of goods or services for essential purposes, with particular regard to the production of exports, the saving of imports and the earning of foreign exchange" or would "contribute materially to strengthening the Sterling Area's balance of payments with the non-sterling world." The United Kingdom investor was restricted to investment within the British Commonwealth to a much greater extent than prior to World War II. At the present time exchange control is gradually being abolished.

Examination of the destination of private capital exports shows that the greater part did not go to underdeveloped countries but to those which were already partially developed. The favorites were South Africa and Northern and Southern Rhodesia, which received between them about a third of the total capital exported. In 1962 the National Association of British Manufacturers estimated that British industry had about $2,800,000,000 invested in South Africa. A large part was invested in the gold and copper mines, and most of the rest in manufacturing, trade, and finance. About a fifth of the exports went to Australia, the greater part being invested in manufacturing. United Kingdom investments in New Zealand increased substantially. India was less attractive than before 1939, and in 1956 United Kingdom private investments were $864,043,000 compared with $1,750,000,000 before the war. This was about 80 per cent of the foreign private business investments in India. Most of it was in manufacturing and commerce, and particularly in the oil industry. In 1958 the private investment in both India and Pakistan was estimated to be $1,120,000,000.

United Kingdom post-war private investment in the dependencies cannot be given in detail or computed with any claim to accuracy. Up to 1958 the amount would appear to have been $1,680,000,000, or $2,100,000,000 if colonial government loans floated in London were added. This was about 37.5 per cent of the total post-war investment in the sterling area. It was impossible to find out how much was new capital and what amount was profits ploughed back by pre-war companies. It was roughly estimated that in 1958 United Kingdom investment had risen to $2,380,000,000 from a total of $1,500,000,000 in 1938. In addition to the private capital listed above the dependencies received $980,000,000 in grants and loans from the United Kingdom government and investments by government companies such as the Colonial Development Corporation.[7] It is impossible to ascertain how much private capital was invested in each colony, but the greatest part seems to have gone to East and West Africa and the West Indies. Among the principal items of investment were oil in Trinidad and Nigeria, $140,000,000 in an oil refinery in Aden, bauxite in Jamaica, and (until the recent development of racial tension) manufacturing in Kenya. Malaya, a favorite with British investors before the Great Depression, received little private capital after 1945, apart from the reinvestment of profits by existing companies.

Comparison between American and British foreign private investments shows a basic similarity. Both had a preference for countries which were already partly developed, Canada in the case of the United States and Australia and South Africa in that of the United Kingdom. Only a minor part of their investment was in the underdeveloped countries, and its purpose was the production of raw materials for export much more than manufacturing. The American and British oil companies were responsible for an important part of the investment. The export of private capital was on a much smaller scale than the American and British governments had anticipated. Their exhortations and the mediocre incentives they held out had little effect.

There was naturally no single cause. A manufacturer sometimes considered that the market for his product was so small that it would not pay to build a factory. Firms were deterred by a requirement that the controlling interest must be held by natives of the country. Some decided against investing because of poor means of communication or uncertainty whether an adequate supply of labor could be obtained. The most important deterrent, however, has been the fear that conditions in the underdeveloped country might render it impossible to make a profit. The reasons for this attitude are to be found in the profound changes which have taken place in the former Asian and African dependencies since 1945.

Pre-War Incentives for Tropical Investment

The heyday of Western investment in the tropics was the century which ended with the Great Depression of 1929. The cost and the danger of loss were greater than in the native country of the investor, but they were outweighed by the hope of profit. The cause and cure of most tropical diseases were not discovered until between two to three generations ago, and malaria, to cite one example, wrecked more than one enterprise. There were also heavy expenses peculiar to the tropics. Planters on estates in Malaya and the Dutch East Indies were required to provide their laborers with living accommodation, pure drinking water, and adequate sanitary arrangements. They must also furnish them with medical and hospital care and carry out anti-malarial work. All this was done at the expense of the employer, whereas in the West none of the cost would have fallen upon him. At times it was difficult or impossible to obtain labor. The science of tropical agriculture hardly existed until the present century, and even now there are important gaps in knowledge. The rubber industry was a good example. An unfamiliar tree which had grown wild in the jungles of Brazil had to be acclimatized in Southeast Asia. The planter must discover by trial and error the best methods of cultivation, how to deal with the tree's diseases, and how to increase the yield of latex. The chances of failure were often great, and while some companies were very successful others went bankrupt and lost everything.

There is little accurate information; but Lord Hailey came to the conclusion that when a balance was struck over a fifty-year period between companies which failed and those that succeeded, the investors who put their money in African enterprises would have done about as well if they had bought government bonds. Dividends of rubber companies varied between an occasional 40 per cent to 60 per cent during a boom and zero during depressions. During World War II an analysis was made of the annual reports of some two hundred Malayan rubber companies with an issued capital of $170,000,000. Their average dividend over their whole life was 7 per cent. Frequently capital was written down after heavy losses; shares were issued in prosperous times at a premium; and often profits were ploughed back into the business. As a result the assets of the companies were much greater than the issued capital, and on this basis the return to the investors was roughly only 4.5 per cent.

Apart from what might be called the normal commercial risks of tropical investment, the dangers of loss were minimal. With the exception of Thailand the whole of Southeast Asia was made up of colonies of the leading powers. The governments were stable and efficient, and there was no danger that they would be overthrown by civil war or foreign invasion. The code of law was similar to that of the ruling power and familiar to its investors, and justice in the courts could be taken for granted. Debts could not be repudiated or assets confiscated, and the colonial currency was linked with that of the ruling power. Profits could be freely transferred abroad with no risk that they would be frozen in the colony. Taxes and costs of labor were low, and strikes were few. Altogether, the incentives for investment were quite large, and were sufficient to counterbalance the risks and attract a considerable amount of capital.

Post-War Deterrents to Investment

When an Asian or African colony becomes independent, capital is frankly hesitant to place itself within the power of an unknown and inexperienced government. This generalization applies particularly to businesses which have not operated previously in the country. It is much less true of those established there prior to World War II. They were already committed, and though some sold their holdings and withdrew their capital the majority decided to carry on. Very often this meant that they had to increase their investment. Where possible this was done by ploughing back profits made locally and not by exporting new capital from the Western state where the firm had its head office. When the projected expenditure was too heavy to be paid for out of profits, such as the building of an oil refinery, new capital would be exported. It is impossible to be categorical, but the rough estimate has been hazarded that half or perhaps more than half of the Western capital invested since 1945 in Asia has been profits ploughed back by pre-war companies and not new capital. This hesitancy to invest is not because capital is imperialistic by nature and opposed to colonial freedom. The

221

form of government is immaterial; what capital is concerned about is the risk involved in placing itself under the control of an unknown quantity. It remembers the many heavy losses caused by the policies of the new Asian and African governments since 1945, and it is always apprehensive of possible unfavorable political and economic developments. So it becomes wary and tends strongly to adopt a wait-and-see policy until it is sure that investment in the new state is a good business risk.

This was the point emphasized by Lord Chandos, formerly Secretary of State for the Colonies in the United Kingdom and subsequently the chairman of a large electrical firm. He was thinking particularly of Africa, but his remarks applied equally to Asia.

Most African politicians, like most other politicians, depend in the long term for their offices, or for the support given to their parties, on their ability to raise the standard of life of the African. And in 1959 this can only be done by persuading capital from abroad to risk itself in these territories. The equally insistent demand of the people, as I have said, is evidence that self-government is on the way. So that here is the dilemma for African politicians, and this is a very real one, believe me; for every step that they take, or urge over-quickly in constitutional advance, they tend to take a step back in economic development. Well, to-day at an early stage in the development of sound administration, when ministers are inexperienced, when there are difficulties of working modern constitutions, a large part of the population being illiterate, all these tend to frighten that young lady, capital, and make her turn her back upon those countries and give her favours more readily to those countries administered by experienced civil servants, presided over by experienced ministers and finally, those countries whose currencies have at least a good chance of maintaining their stability.[8]

The hostility shown toward Western private capital in many of the newly independent states of Asia and Africa has been a primary cause of the hesitancy to invest in them. The pre-war commercial risks remain, and every former incentive has been changed into a deterrent. Furthermore, capital invested in a trustworthy Western country can earn a return as large or sometimes larger than it would earn in one of the new states. Asian and African nationalism has a strong element of suspicion and hostility toward the West. In some countries this element is an undercurrent which does not control the government, as in the Philippines and the Federation of Malaya. In others as in Indonesia the government itself incarnates the attitude and fosters it among the mass of the population. Despite the freeing of the former dependencies many nationalists believe that the ex-colonial powers still have designs upon their independence. They are living in the past and refuse to see that Western imperialism is in full retreat. Western private enterprise is often regarded as a survival of colonial control, and a potential threat to freedom. The United States is not placed in a different category from the former European colonial powers. It is suspected of developing a new form of economic imperialism under the guise of economic and military aid. As the strongest and wealthiest of the Western nations it is considered more dangerous than Britain or France.

The reasons for this attitude toward Western capital go back to the period of colonial rule. Its dominant position was looked upon as the economic counterpart of foreign political control. It was widely believed that the capitalist deliberately kept the country in colonial status in order to keep it as a market or expand the production of raw materials for export instead of building factories to raise the standard of living. Another grievance was the withdrawal of a considerable part of the annual profits, known as the drain.

There was no realization that colonial status was not confined to dependencies but also existed between underdeveloped Western states and the industrialized nations. In some respects Canada was and still is in colonial status toward the United States, just as the United States was toward Europe in the nineteenth century. A country which does not have the native capital to exploit its own resources must either resign itself to a very slow development, or else take a short cut by borrowing from abroad. In the latter event the foreign capitalist will dictate the terms. He will decide what kinds of enterprise he will invest in, and he will insist on draining away part of the annual profits. For many years foreign capital in Canada went principally into the production of such raw materials as lumber and minerals. This is still true of a considerable part of American investment, e.g., in the oilfields of Alberta and the iron ore of Labrador. The building of factories was delayed until American companies decided that this would be profitable because of the growing market in Canada, and also in the British Commonwealth after the introduction of Imperial Preference. This was the rate of import duty, lower than that levied on competing foreign commodities, charged by the British Dominions and the dependencies on "products of the British Empire." Colonial status is the consequence of an early stage of capitalist development and not the result of imperialist exploitation. The difference between the two is political rather than economic. The Canadians by their own choice invited the entry of American capital, whereas with the colonial peoples the decision was made for them by their governments. Moreover, the dependencies urgently needed the social services their governments were setting up; but they lacked the revenue to support them owing to the very low tax-paying capacity of the population. The only way to pay for them was to encourage Western enterprises and then collect from them the bulk of the taxes. In Malaya tin and rubber provided the bulk of the revenue through income tax, export and import duties, and land rent. It was estimated that in Java before the Great Depression forty per cent of the revenue came from Western corporations, forty per cent from the Javanese, and the balance from government industries.

Few of the leaders of the new states have any understanding of economics, or realize their need for foreign private capital if they are to carry out their ambitious plans. They have no intention of adopting the system of free private enterprise, and in varying degrees they believe in government ownership or regulation. They exaggerate the eagerness of capital to invest, and many of them think that it is the duty of the West to provide the necessary funds as atonement for the sins of imperialism. The foreign investor is considered to be a capitalist imperialist exploiter. There is also the personal factor that many Western-educated nationalists with no training in business can only get the well-paid positions they seek if the government nationalizes foreign industries and places them under its own control. In Southeast Asia the attitude is most pronounced in Burma and particularly Indonesia, where President Sukarno has declared that he does not want private investment but merely large and continuing grants from Western governments.

Concrete Grievances of Western Capital

Uncertainty about government policy on nationalization has been one of the chief deterrents to investment during the past ten to fifteen years. Not only may assets be nationalized, but this may be done with inadequate compensation or with none at all. Security of private property in Asia and Africa was one of the casualties of freeing the colonies. The outstanding cases were the nationalization of the Anglo-Iranian Oil Company's holdings in Iran; Nasser's seizure of the Suez Canal and of the property of British, French, and Belgian citizens in Egypt; Sukarno's confiscation of Dutch assets in Indonesia; and Castro's confiscation of American property in Cuba. In the first two instances inadequate compensation was finally paid, and in the others none at all. Burma nationalized several British companies with partial compensation. The failure of the British, American, and other governments to obtain justice for their nationals taught the investor that it was useless to rely on them for protection. The International Court of Justice also proved to be a broken reed. The Anglo-Iranian Oil Company's contract contained the clause that if it and the government were unable to agree the dispute would be referred to arbitration. Yet when the case was placed before the Court it decided that it had no jurisdiction for want of Iranian consent. The United Nations Council was equally futile when Iran's action and Nasser's seizure of the Suez Canal were brought before it. The United Nations Assembly has become an organ of anti-colonialism, and has consistently refused to condemn breaches of international agreements when the colonial issue was involved. Robbery does not cease to be such because it is the property of foreigners that is seized in the name of nationalization. There is no reason to suppose that so lucrative a practice will end for lack of imitators when it has been shown that there is no need to be afraid of national governments or of the international authority.

Nothing came of the proposal of a German banker that the Western nations should refuse to supply funds to a state which broke its agreements. The same lack of success followed the suggestion of Tengku Abdul Rahman, the Prime Minister of the Federation of Malaya, that the governments of the underdeveloped countries should pledge themselves to behave honestly and justly in their dealings with foreign capital. The result is that the investor is afraid to risk his capital in an underdeveloped area until he has satisfied himself that it is safe to do so. One of the most recent examples has been Kenya, which had become rather a favorite with United Kingdom investors. The approach of independence and the threats to confiscate European property by Mboya

225

and other African leaders resulted from about 1960 onwards in the cessation of investment and the withdrawal of capital estimated at $92,000,000. The only reason why more was not removed was the inability to find buyers.

Another deterrent is the weakness and instability of many of the new governments, and the risk that they might be overthrown. Some of them have failed to suppress revolts or maintain law and order. At times the administration is inefficient and corrupt, and there are irritating and expensive delays in carrying on business. Taxes are high, and some states discriminate against the foreigner. Many have broken the link between the national currency and that of the colonial power to which it was formerly attached. The result has been fluctuations in value, and at times a considerable variation between the official rate of exchange and the black-market rate. Even if the government is well disposed it may not have enough foreign exchange to allow the free withdrawal of profits, and it is not always well disposed. So profits may be frozen, or part only may be allowed to be transferred abroad after long delays.

Wages are much higher than before 1939 although productivity continues to be low. There is a shortage of skilled workmen. Strong pressure is exerted to employ Asians instead of Westerners in responsible positions as quickly as possible. To do this is the policy of Western companies, but they insist that the Asians appointed must be well qualified. Often the governments ignore this stipulation, and refuse or delay for a long time the grant of entrance visas for trained Europeans who are needed to fill positions for which suitable Asians cannot be found. Sometimes a manufacturer is deterred by uncertainty about the supply of electric power, by inadequate roads and railways, or by the low purchasing power of his prospective customers. All that any country of southeastern Asia can guarantee is its domestic market, and with the exception of Indonesia this is limited to a few million people. Most of the new states are trying to industrialize, and they have raised tariff barriers against one another to such an extent that trade is seriously hampered. There is no reason to expect any lessening of this economic nationalism, and the effect upon many manufacturers is to make them doubtful whether so small a market can repay the cost of building a factory. Sometimes, too, the type of product, e.g., industrial chemicals, is too advanced to have much sale in a predominantly peasant economy, and the corporation decides that it is more profitable to manufacture in the West than to build a local factory.

A final factor which must not be overlooked is the effect of heavy taxation in the United States and the United Kingdom. It has engendered a cautious attitude which is in contrast to that of fifty years ago when taxes were low and took a much smaller share of the profits. Today an individual or a company is less willing to take risks and tends to play safe. If a firm has to choose between a moderate profit with little risk and the chance of a much larger profit with commensurate danger of loss, very often the first alternative is chosen. If the more enterprising course fails, the firm will lose, while if it succeeds the treasury will take most of the profits. This prospect arouses a notable lack of enthusiasm. The consideration applies with added force to investment in a newly independent country where in addition to the normal commercial risks there are all the additional disadvantages already set forth. It was absurd to exhort the English to inaugurate a new Elizabethan age in foreign trade and investment because a second Queen Elizabeth had ascended the throne. This ignored the incentive of free private enterprise which was one cause of the outburst of creative activity of the Elizabethans of the sixteenth century. The Spaniards thought it much too free, when Drake brought the *Golden Hind* home to England crammed to the hatches with loot which was estimated by one of the queen's officials to be a million and a half sterling, or between a quarter and a half of the whole annual produce of Spain's American mines. There is great dispute about the contemporary purchasing power of this amount, but one estimate puts it at $126,000,000. It is no use to penalize with progressive taxation and then call for the results of free enterprise and low taxes.

India vs. Southeast Asia

No Western country is investing heavily in Southeast Asia or is likely to in the foreseeable future. Americans never have done so to any marked degree, and their attitude today is not essentially different from what it was before 1939. The British are still the principal investors, but their interest is less than it was thirty years ago, for the reasons already mentioned. Pakistan and especially India have attracted more

Western capital than Southeast Asia. About eighty per cent has been British, although recently the small American share has been growing. The principal reason has been that the government of India has had a good record and foreign companies have felt that they can trust it. Its policy has been socialistic, but in practice it has confined its activities to basic industries like steel and has not encroached on the large field left to private enterprise. Taxes have been high but foreign investors have been treated reasonably and allowed to transfer profits abroad. Capital also decided that India and Pakistan had and still have stable governments which were not threatened by revolt or foreign conquest. British rule bequeathed a corps of trained civil servants and an efficient administration, and law and order have been well maintained. The Indian market was more than twice as large as that of the whole of Southeast Asia. There has been a numerous and experienced business class with command of Indian capital with which British firms could continue to form partnerships as they had begun to do before World War II. A United Kingdom firm did not have to depend for financing its operations on its local profits or on funds brought in from abroad. This important advantage did not exist in most of Southeast Asia. Moreover, British firms and banks had been active in India for two centuries and continued their activities in a field with which they were well acquainted. This combination of reasons political, economic, and historical explains why the majority of the United Kingdom companies and banks interested in Asia concern themselves primarily with India.

X

Western Investment in Southeast Asia

Investment in 1941

No reliable statistics exist for Western investment prior to World War II. The following figures should be regarded as an estimate which probably contains a considerable margin of error.[1] They cover only capital invested in business enterprises, since it was impossible to determine the nationality of ownership of government bonds. The total amount of foreign investment (excluding Chinese) was $2,715,000,000, and of this the largest single holding was that of the Dutch in the East Indies. Callis in his detailed study put it at $900,000,000, though other writers estimated it at anything up to $2,000,000,000. The Dutch also owned the bulk of the bonds of the East Indian government, the amount of the debt being estimated at $853,000,000. The British came next with a pre-war business investment of about $775,000,000. American interests were believed to be about $285,000,000, some two thirds of which were in the Philippines and most of the rest in the Dutch East Indies. The bulk of the French capital was in Indochina, and was believed to be some $290,000,000. Japanese investment was believed to be $60,000,000.

The greater part of the foreign investment in each dependency belonged to nationals of the ruling power. The East Indies were the only important colony of Holland, and for two generations a considerable part of the national savings had been invested there. The annual income drawn from them was an important factor in the Dutch standard of living. Over half the investment of the British was in Malaya and Burma, but they also had interests all over Southeast Asia except Indochina, where France discouraged all investment except her own. The bulk of the Western investment in Thailand was British, and was believed to be about $67,000,000. British holdings in the Philippines were about $35,000,000. Great Britain was the principal source of foreign capital for Southeast Asia as a whole. The small amount of American capital reflected the national lack of interest in this part of Asia. Business investments in the Philippines were only about 2.2 per cent of American foreign investments.

Most of the Western enterprises were engaged in the production of raw materials or foodstuffs. In the Philippines the principal American interests were mines of gold, manganese, and chromium: telephone, electricity, and radio companies: sugar and coconut-oil refineries: and lumber companies. In the Dutch East Indies subsidiaries of American oil companies controlled 40 per cent of the industry. The Goodyear Tire and Rubber Company, Firestone, and the United States Rubber Company had large rubber estates, and Goodyear operated a tire factory. There were American factories for soap and margarine. The principal British interests in Malaya were rubber and tin, and in the Dutch East Indies rubber and oil and to a lesser extent sugar, coffee, and tea. In Burma the British controlled the production of oil; the mining of lead, silver, zinc, tin, and tungsten; teak-lumbering; and the refining and exporting of rice. In Thailand the British owned tin mines and teak lumber companies. The principal Dutch assets in the East Indies were estates for the production of rubber, sugar, palm oil, tea, and tobacco; oil companies; and public utilities. The French in Indochina were interested chiefly in rubber, coal, and tin. Western companies also controlled shipping, both ocean-going and local, banks, insurance, importing, and exporting. Chinese economic interests were similar to Western, though on a much smaller scale. In addition they were the indispensable link between the large Western import·export firms and the peasants, because they had the monopoly of retail trading and produce-buying from the native growers. They had also a monopoly of money-lending, apart from the competition of local rivals and, sometimes, Indians.

Official statistics on Western investment in Southeast Asia since the end of World War II are very incomplete and frequently of doubtful validity. Quite often a figure is given for the whole of southern Asia, and sometimes the underdeveloped part of Africa is added for good measure. It is impossible to ascertain the amount invested by individual companies in the different countries, owing to the marked disinclination to disclose this information. It is not possible to state the amount of Western capital invested at the present time, nor the contemporary value of the assets owned by foreign companies.

The Philippines

The policy of the Philippine Republic has been to encourage industrialization by both Filipinos and foreigners, in order to provide employment for the rapidly growing population and raise the standard of living. The government itself carried on a wide range of activities. This policy was adopted in 1916, and was especially marked after 1935 when the Philippine Commonwealth was established and given control of domestic affairs. One reason for the policy was that wealthy Filipinos were often hesitant to engage in manufacturing and preferred traditional forms of investment such as the ownership of land. Under these circumstances the government itself took the initiative in starting new industries. The official policy was that the government firms would give the initial stimulus in fields where private capital was incapable of venturing or unwilling or hesitant to do so, but that they were not intended to compete with private companies. This policy was not followed in practice and sometimes the existence of government firms deterred private business from competing. By the early 1950's the government operated banks and insurance companies; railways; hotels; coal mines; hydroelectric, gas, and water works; and controlled a large part of the rice trade. It manufactured cement, steel, textiles, and paper, and owned shipyards and engineering shops. It had substantial investments in airline and shipping companies and other enterprises. There was, however, no suggestion that private businesses be nationalized as in Burma. Investigation showed that the government corporations were often inefficient and run at a heavy loss owing to political influence and nepotism. Magsaysay transferred many of them to private ownership, and since then the policy has been to limit governmental

231

activity to public utilities, land settlement, marketing, and the regulation of prices.[2]

Americans have been given a preference over other foreign investors, and Filipinos have been preferred to both. An amendment to the constitution was adopted in 1946 on the insistence of the United States which gave Americans the same rights as Filipinos in the development of all natural resources and the operation of public utilities. The Laurel-Langley trade agreement of 1954 made the arrangement reciprocal, and Filipinos were given the same economic rights in the United States as American citizens. Apart from Americans, the development of natural resources and public utilities has been reserved to Philippine citizens or to corporations sixty per cent of the capital of which was owned by Filipinos. Government policy on the remittance of profits abroad has been relatively liberal, but Philippine nationalism has strongly preferred development by Filipinos, and has been opposed to the investment of foreign capital on a large scale. There has also been resentment at the role of American interests in the Philippine economy. Philippine nationalists have been restrained, however, by the realization that the country is dependent on the United States for a market and for financial help, and that discrimination could provoke retaliation. Filipino firms have been favored by tax concessions and the allocation of permits to obtain foreign exchange. Foreign exchange controls were imposed in 1949 and were not removed until 1962. The government could reduce the amount allowed to a company to pay for imports. Restrictions were also placed on the remittance of profits abroad. The discrimination affected American investment only to a minor extent, owing to its special rights. Investors from other Western states have been much more affected. President Macapagal was unable to persuade the legislature in 1962 to pass a law which would make the Philippines more attractive to foreign investors. The principal sufferers have been the unpopular Chinese. Many American and other foreign firms already established in the Philippines formed a partnership with Filipino interests in order to strengthen their position. Spaniards still have extensive holdings, and some of the leading Spanish families became naturalized so that they secured the rights of Philippine citizens. One result of the preference shown to Filipinos has been that only a very limited amount of new foreign capital has been brought in. When factories have been built the tendency has been to cover the cost from the profits of existing firms or by loans from Philippine banks. European companies have shown little interest in the development of natural resources, and some which had been debating whether to invest decided against it.[3]

The government's Filipino first policy was justified by President Garcia in 1959 on the ground that "The ugly but incontrovertible fact about our economy to-day is its dominance by aliens . . . As long as this condition exists we shall remain in many ways a colonial country." "To allow the operation of a completely free enterprise to-day will also mean in effect the preservation of the very condition which we wish to correct, namely alien economic domination." A study made in 1958 concluded that "foreign firms which continue to show an interest in the Philippine market have been limited to those possessing pre-war relationships and which are mostly concerned with protecting established markets rather than opening up new ones. There has been a marked scarcity of new foreign firms seeking entry in the Philippines for the first time." The study said that the best hope of success for a foreign firm lay in forming a joint venture with Filipino business interests. This would assure it of foreign exchange for the import of machinery and raw materials and the remittance of profits, since the policy of the government was to give preferential treatment to Filipino business men. In 1960 it was "rumoured that a number of long established American and other foreign owned firms are, by sales of stock and otherwise, converting their organizations into the joint venture form, while still hoping to maintain the control which is so necessary."[4] In January 1962 President Macapagal abolished exchange controls, and authorized banks to sell the foreign exchange needed to pay for imports at the current free market rate. He also brought the value of the peso more in line with reality by substituting for the official rate of two pesos to the dollar the free market rate, then 3.4 pesos to the dollar.

The major part of the foreign capital in the Philippines is American, followed by Spanish and then British. The Chinese also have a considerable holding. There has been some increase in Western investment since 1945, and it was estimated that the average annual inflow in 1952–1957 was $25,000,000. Conflicting estimates were made of the value of American assets both before and after World War II. Callis estimated that American direct investments in 1935 were $163,500,000 and that an additional $36,000,000 were invested in government bonds. Miss Jenkins put the total investment at $258,000,000.[5] In order of magnitude the American holdings were in mines, public utilities, sugar and coconut-oil refineries, plantations of coconuts, hemp, and rubber, and trade. In sugar, the staple export, Americans controlled about a third of the refineries while Filipinos owned most of the sugar estates. An unofficial estimate placed American investment in the middle 1950's at $350,000,000, whereas the figure given by the United States Department of Commerce was $188,000,000. In 1959 the Department of Commerce estimated American direct private investment to be $385,000,000, or more than 1 per cent of the total American foreign investments.[6] This was about half the percentage of the pre-war period. The types of investment were similar to those of the pre-war period, the principal differences being that manufacturing was now 22 per cent of the total instead of 8 per cent and the investment in sugar had decreased. Most of the factories produced consumer goods, and three oil companies — Caltex, Stanvac, and Shell — had built or intended to build refineries.

The entry of American capital into the Philippines was not large, and a considerable part of it was used to repair war damage. To some extent new capital was counterbalanced by the withdrawal of earlier investments, for example, from the sugar industry. This conformed to the general picture of the very mild interest of American private capital in the underdeveloped countries. It was deterred by the disturbed conditions in the Far East, and the undercurrent of anti-American feeling in the Philippines. Hostility to the West was very much less pronounced than in some other Asian countries and every government has supported close relations with the United States, but there was an uneasy feeling that it might become stronger. There was hesitation because of uncertainty as to how extensively the government might eventually engage in business. Then too the domestic market was small, there was a shortage of electric power and inadequate communications, and Filipino capitalists were hesitant about investing in industry. American firms preferred a partnership in order to share the risk.

Indonesia

Indonesia with its ninety million people is by far the most populous as well as the largest state of Southeast Asia, and has the most extensive range of natural resources. Its potentialities for development are greater than those of any other country of Southeast Asia. The Dutch built a good system of roads and railways, especially in Java, and inter-island transport was well developed by the Dutch K.P.M. line. In 1941 more Western capital was invested in Indonesia than anywhere else, and economic development was correspondingly more extensive. Much destruction was wrought during the Japanese invasion and by the post-war revolt against Holland, but it does not seem to have been as severe as in the Philippines and Burma. The foreign owners wished to restore their properties and frequently did so. Holland made grants for reconstruction in the immediate post-war years and showed every. intention of continuing this policy. There were clear indications that Western capital was interested in making additional investments. A decade after the establishment of the republic the general opinion is that Indonesia is the worst risk in Southeast Asia. New capital has been pretty well confined to what was sent in by the oil companies, and special circumstances explain why their policy has differed from that of other corporations.

The government had ambitious plans for increasing general pros-perity, and there was no reason why they should not gradually succeed with Western help. Since the amount of capital required far exceeded the assistance given by the American and other governments foreign private investment was essential. Professor Higgins, who was for some years economic adviser to the government, estimated in 1957 that there was a gap of at least $400,000,000 a year between the available domestic capital and the amount needed to raise the per capita income by 2 per cent per annum. The deficit could only be covered by foreign aid, either from Western governments or private investment.[7] Professor Higgins pointed out that "the influx of foreign [government] loans and grants falls far short of what is needed," and that failure to obtain the sum he mentioned might make the "difference between economic progress and further retrogression." He went on to reiterate that Indonesia's re-sources were sufficient to warrant a substantial degree of industrializa-tion, but that success depended upon attracting foreign capital and experts. They would not be forthcoming unless there were a radical change in the policy of the government and the political parties.

There was in Indonesia nothing corresponding to the conservative party found in the industrialized states which supported the capitalist system. The business men who were one of the most important elements of a typical Western conservative party were in Indonesia for the most part unpopular Western and Chinese foreigners. The members of Indonesian political parties did not come from the business class but were the sons of school teachers, government officials, and professional men who had no connection with business or understanding of its character and requirements. In varying degrees they all believed in socialism and government control of economic life, and none of them had any intention of setting up a Western-style capitalist system in Indonesia. All of them were hostile to foreign corporations in varying degrees.

Some parties, like the Masjumi, believed that the development of Indonesia required Western investment, and were willing to make concessions in order to attract it. "Since national capital is still not sufficient to finance industrialization plans, opportunity should be created for foreign capital to build new industries . . . on conditions profitable both to Indonesia and to the foreign enterprise." Many parties, however, were thoroughly hostile and believed it to be of the first importance to complete the revolution. By this was meant the elimination of the influence over Indonesian national life which aliens might possess through their economic interests. Dutch political domination had gone, and foreign economic control must follow it into oblivion. Parties with this policy opposed the concessions which must be made if Western capital were to be attracted. The two conflicting groups were never able to come to a compromise on the terms to be offered to alien investors. Moreover, all politicians were very conscious that popular opinion regarded foreigners with suspicion and hostility, and that any concessions could easily be twisted by opponents into betrayal of the national interests. The government periodically put forth statements in general terms that it welcomed Western investment when it was in the national interest. Little was done to make these generalities concrete and sometimes new measures were devised to harass the foreigner still further. The Foreign Investment Act which was passed in 1958 offered concessions too meager to attract foreign capital.

An account was given in the preceding chapter of the reasons for the limited investment in most of the independent underdeveloped countries since World War II. Indonesia could be given as an example of virtually every one of these deterrents. The treatment meted out is accurately summarized in the following description. Foreigners

are now regarded at best as instruments of economic administration to be dispensed with as soon as native agencies are competent to take their place — or even earlier if, as is not unlikely, policy should continue to yield to the pressure of extreme nationalism. They have been compelled to submit to arbitrary and unpredictable measures of economic control which discriminate in favour of Indonesian nationals. These measures cover import licences, taxation, leases of land, the remittance of profits overseas, and visas for European staff. Even where there is no deliberate discrimination, Western enterprise suffers from bureaucratic incompetence inseparable from a regime which seeks to discharge complicated tasks of administration without a trained civil service. In some parts of the country the collapse of public order has obliged firms to abandon their properties, while inflation has had its usually corrosive influence on the economy as a whole. Many instances have been given of long established firms which are now seeking in other lands opportunities denied to them in Indonesia, and this process is likely to continue. Recently the amount of new direct investment has been very small. Nevertheless Western enterprise is unlikely to lose its still predominant position in the course of a few years. Firms with heavy fixed investments and with established trading connections cannot quickly withdraw from the country without heavy losses, and Indonesian-controlled enterprise is not yet ready to play more than a minor part . . . so far as Western entrepreneurship is concerned the next decade will see a steady contraction. In particular, it is improbable that Western firms will continue to pioneer new types of production and trade. Such ventures are not undertaken unless the risks are matched by the prospect of lavish reward.[8]

Part of the capital invested before 1941 was withdrawn, and in addition some properties were abandoned by their owners. Estimates of how much has been lost or withdrawn are vague, but it appears to be considerable. There is an equal dearth of accurate information regarding imports of capital since 1945, but the evidence points to the conclusion that most of the post-war investment came from profits ploughed back, and not new capital exported from the United States or the United Kingdom. A high percentage of these profits were frozen, and the owners had the alternative of leaving them in an Indonesian bank or investing them in the business. New capital was brought in

237

when the cost of repairing wartime damage or expanding the enterprise was so heavy that it could not be paid for out of profits earned locally. The only important instance of this was apparently the oil companies.

Attempts have been made to estimate the present value of Western investments. The very rough estimates range widely, and accurate information is impossible to obtain. The United States Department of Commerce believed that the total contemporary value was "considerably less" than before the war owing to the extensive wartime destruction of property and the "sizable" repatriation of Dutch capital. As to what this value might be the Department tacitly admitted that it was baffled, and stated without comment that it lay somewhere between the Indonesian figures of $316,000,000 or perhaps $561,000,000 and the Dutch statement of $1,800,000,000, of which Holland's share was seventy per cent or $1,260,000,000. The pre-war estimates of total foreign investments ranged all the way from $1,250,000,000 to $3,500,000,000 and admittedly involved a great amount of guesswork. Professor Vandenbosch, a careful and reliable authority, put the total amount at $2,000,000,000. If his figure is accepted, the Dutch post-war total of $1,800,000,000 makes too little allowance for the fall in value referred to by the Department of Commerce. The Indonesian figures are undoubtedly too low in view of the estimates of American and British investments given below.[9]

The Department of Commerce estimated that the value of American direct investment in 1954 was $66,000,000, the three principal items being oil, rubber, and manufacturing. It then went on to state that the true value was perhaps twice as large. It put the value in 1957 at $150,000,000, attributing most of the increase to additional investment by the oil companies.[10] This greatly underestimated the oil investment. Professor Higgins estimated in 1957 that the Standard-Vacuum (Stanvac) and the Caltex Pacific Oil Companies together had spent on reconstruction and modernization over $200,000,000 since 1945, and were planning to spend an additional $100,000,000.[11] In 1960 the two companies gave the value of their assets as $328,000,000, one of them stating that this was "probably a substantial understatement." The Indonesian Association which represents United Kingdom firms in Indonesia roughly estimated the value of United Kingdom investments as $420,000,000, but qualified this with the proviso that it might be

$70,000,000 too much or too little, since the value of the Anglo-Dutch Shell Oil Company's property was uncertain. An estimate put the value of the latter at $110,000,000 including projected expenditures in the Balikpapan oilfield in Borneo.

Estate Agriculture

The output of estate agriculture is well below the pre-war level. Rubber, coffee, and tobacco have fallen by a quarter, and tea, sugar, and palm oil by fifty per cent. Sugar, which was formerly exported, is now insufficient to supply the domestic demand. All estates except rubber are unsuited to peasant agriculture, because they require a command of technical resources and capital which the smallholder does not possess. This explains why the total production of rubber alone is greater than before the war. Its preparation is simple and inexpensive, and the peasants have increased their output. The reason for the fall in production of the estates has been the treatment of their owners. Taking rubber, a typical instance: Western estate managers were not allowed to have arms to protect themselves, and some properties had to be abandoned owing to the government's failure to maintain law and order. There were heavy losses of latex through theft, and large tracts were taken over by peasants who turned them into smallholdings. In the Medan area of eastern Sumatra where estate exports earned over half of Indonesia's foreign exchange, it was estimated in 1957 that 500,000 squatters had seized 285,000 acres. There were organized mass invasions and the number of squatters was steadily growing. There was no lack of vacant land, but the estates had the advantages that they were already cleared of jungle, well drained, and easily accessible. The squatters were organized in peasant unions which were linked with the Communist, Nationalist, and Masjumi parties and were politically powerful. The estate owners appealed to the government and offered to surrender part of their lands if the squatters were removed from the remainder. The government was inclined to agree but finally refused to intervene because it would be politically most unwise to restrain Indonesian citizens from an illegal action in order to benefit unpopular foreigners. In addition there was serious trouble with the estate laborers, who had been assured by the nationalist leaders that political independence would in itself bring better living conditions

SOUTHEAST ASIA

They translated this into less work and more pay. They were organized into unions under Communist control, and there were frequent strikes which the government usually supported. Wages were raised and the government reduced the hours of labor to seven a day and forty a week, while the output per laborer fell to considerably less than it had been before the war owing to absenteeism, strikes, and slackness generally. The strikers sometimes made other demands which could not be granted unless the estate were to run at a loss. There were not enough technically trained Indonesians to manage the estates, but the government often refused permission to bring in competent Westerners.

Another deterrent was the government's tax policy and exchange controls. Income tax on a sliding scale took from 40 per cent to 52.5 per cent of a company's profits, after which 40 per cent of the balance had to be paid into an account with the Bank of Indonesia. This money could only be used for items of capital expenditure which would improve the estate. The remainder was then subject to an exchange surcharge of 40 per cent. Permission was given to remit abroad what was left, after negotiations had been carried on for two years or longer. Out of every $100 of profits the amount eventually transferred abroad was $17 to $22. Owing to the continuous fall in the foreign-exchange rate of the rupiah, when the profits were eventually received their value had considerably decreased and might be too small to pay more than a microscopic dividend. Very often a company had to dip into its reserves to meet its expenses and pay a sufficient dividend to keep its shareholders more or less contented. The reserves have been steadily falling, and there is a real danger that the shareholders may insist that the company be wound up and whatever assets are left be divided between them so that they may recover part of their investment. The Indonesian government would take over the abandoned estates, and the inefficiency and corruption which has marked its management of the confiscated Dutch properties would presumably lead to a still further loss of foreign exchange from falling exports. Another semi-official expense incurred by all foreign enterprises as well as estates was the frequent necessity of bribing government officials. A typical reason was to obtain the release from the customs of machinery or raw materials for a factory.

The periodical threats to nationalize foreign enterprises kept investment to a minimum. There was also uncertainty about the renewal of the leases on estates. The Dutch government had granted the land on seventy-five-year leases, and many of them would expire within ten years. The government could not make up its mind whether to renew the leases and if so for how long, since it was afraid to run counter to the prevalent xenophobia. Estate owners could not be expected to incur heavy expense for the maintenance and improvement of their properties unless they were sure they would be allowed to keep them long enough to recover their outlay. The uncertainty had special urgency for rubber, the leading export and the principal source of foreign exchange. The economic life of a rubber tree is about thirty-five years, and by the late 'fifties a considerable proportion of the Indonesian trees were over thirty years old, so that there was urgent need to replant. A very important additional reason was that if natural were to compete successfully against the cheaper synthetic rubber, the unselected seedling rubber on the estates must be replaced by high-yielding rubber. This would give a yield of from two and a half to three times as much per acre, and sometimes even more. Replanting was not cheap and the normal practice was to carry it out at the rate of 3 per cent per annum of the estate area. A newly planted tree yielded no rubber until it was six or seven years old, so that it took forty years to replant a whole estate. The government vaguely suggested a renewal of leases for thirty years, which was too short a period for an estate to replant its whole area or recoup its expenditure. The combined effect of all the factors affecting the rubber industry was that the British companies did little replanting until the government required the deposit of part of the profits in an Indonesian bank. Previously they withdrew more of their profits for the payment of dividends than the American companies. The latter were not troubled with the problem of keeping their shareholders content, since their function was to produce rubber for the parent companies' factories in the United States. During the immediate post-war years they did more replanting with high-yielding rubber than the British companies. At the present time all the companies are doing only a limited amount of replanting.

The best way of presenting the results of the government's policy towards estate agriculture is by a recital of statistics: they speak for themselves. In 1941 the rubber estates were estimated to be about

241

1,500,000 acres and in 1960 1,250,000 acres. Of this about 750,000 acres were the confiscated Dutch estates. British companies held 265,000 acres, American firms 150,000 acres, and there were also some French and Belgian companies. The principal American companies were subsidiaries of the United States Rubber Company and the Goodyear Tire and Rubber Company. In 1941 the area replanted with high-yielding rubber was about 300,000 acres, and between 1945 and the end of 1959 an additional 175,000 acres were replanted. The average annual rate of replanting was only two per cent. During the same period the estates in the Federation of Malaya planted 786,000 acres with high-yielding rubber. Adding the area planted with high-yielding rubber prior to 1940 about 52.5 per cent of the acreage of the Malayan estates had been replanted. In Indonesia the area replanted was only about 38 per cent. The gravity of this situation is clear. Rubber is the principal source of the foreign exchange on which Indonesia depends for carrying out its plans for economic improvement, and a growing percentage of the estate acreage is becoming worthless. Meanwhile the Malayan estates are increasing their output, and Malaya is beginning to replace Indonesia as the world's largest producer of natural rubber. A director of one of the American companies wrote that if the present situation continues Indonesia "will become a very poor second to Malaya as a world rubber producer by 1970." The position is even more startling when it is remembered that down to 1941 the Indonesian estates had done more replanting than those in Malaya.

The reason is the very different attitude of the two governments. Planters in Malaya know that their properties will not be nationalized and the government pays a subsidy which covers part of the heavy cost of replanting. The Indonesian government does everything in its power to penalize and discourage the estates. The result is that they use for replanting only the portion of their profits which is frozen in Indonesia. A director of one of the largest companies wrote that "we would not send new capital to Indonesia even if additional cash were required for replanting." The estates which produce other agricultural products follow the same policy in the upkeep and improvement of their properties. One observer summed up the situation with the remark that "there appears little doubt that the profit squeeze has left very little return if any for estate investment."

Manufacturing and Trade

During the nineteen thirties the Dutch government stimulated the growth of manufacturing both by Indonesians and foreigners. It made a promising start especially in Java, and most of the Western factories which still exist were established during this period. Unilever and Procter and Gamble built factories for soap, margarine, and cooking oil, Goodyear had a tire factory, and the British American Tobacco Company had three cigarette factories. After the war conditions were as adverse for Western manufacturing as for other types of foreign enterprise. Profits were moderate at best and largely frozen. The owners financed operations out of local profits and avoided sending in new capital unless it were unavoidable, e.g., to rebuild a factory destroyed during the war. Few new Western-owned factories have been built since 1945 or are likely to be, as long as present conditions continue. To carry out its ambitious plans for industrialization the government will have to depend on factories built by Indonesian private enterprise or by the state. Accomplishments to date have been mediocre.[12]

Prior to the war the import and export trade was largely controlled by European and especially Dutch firms, with the Chinese holding a minor share. Virtually no Indonesians were engaged in it. The policy of the Indonesian government was to transfer foreign trade as far as possible to Indonesians. They were given preferential treatment in the grant of import licenses and the government established the Bank Negara to provide them with lavish credit. In 1954 the Minister of Economic Affairs declared that "the government's prosperity programme requires that all enterprises shall be owned or at least managed by Indonesian citizens. Holders of import agencies must therefore voluntarily transfer them to national enterprises." The intention was that 70 per cent of the importing should be done by Indonesian firms, 15 per cent by Indonesian citizens of non-Indonesian (e.g., Chinese) origin, and the rest by foreigners, and foreign exchange was allocated on this basis.

The new Indonesian firms discovered that generous bank loans did not compensate for a comprehensive ignorance of even the ABC of foreign commerce. Some of them sold their allotments of foreign exchange to European firms, charging a commission of 15 to 35 per cent. Others went into partnership with Chinese who took over the management of the business while the Indonesian contributed the camouflage of nominal national ownership and all the special privileges which this conferred. The typical Indonesian business man was described without much exaggeration as one who had influential official connections through which he obtained unsecured bank loans and import licenses. His guiding principle was that the bank absorbed the losses and he took the profits. When the government itself went into business it entrusted the management to these same business men or else to inexperienced civil servants and army officers. The cost of imports and retail prices rose sharply, and officials found another lucrative source of squeeze in the payments they collected to allow the government regulations to be circumvented. The result to date has been that great damage was done to foreign merchants, the urban Chinese strengthened their commercial position, some Indonesians made a handsome profit, and the government failed to transfer foreign trade to national control.[13] A widespread smuggling trade developed in imports and exports, with the result that the government lost much foreign exchange and its revenue fell owing to the lower yield from import duties and corporation taxes.

Oil

There are three large oil companies, two American and one Anglo-Dutch. The American companies are Stanvac, a subsidiary of Standard Oil of New Jersey and Socony Vacuum, and Caltex, a subsidiary of Standard Oil of California and the Texas Company. The ownership of the Royal Dutch Shell Company is forty per cent British and sixty per cent Dutch. There are also two small Indonesian companies, one of which was formerly a partnership between Shell and the Dutch government. The other, operated by the Indonesian army, has fields in northern Sumatra which were formerly the property of Royal Dutch Shell. The government did not nationalize them but took them over without compensation, and claims a production of six hundred thousand tons a year. Recently it has been negotiating with Japanese interests to assume the management and enlarge the output. The oilfields and refineries of both American companies are in Sumatra, and Shell has fields and refineries in southern Sumatra and Balikpapan in eastern Borneo. Of recent years Caltex has become the largest producer since its wells did not come into production until after World War II, while the other two companies began operations earlier and their reserves of oil are more depleted. In 1960 Caltex produced 46 per cent of the oil, Shell 27 per cent, and Stanvac 23 per cent. By arrangement with the government Shell supplies 70 per cent and the two American companies 30 per cent of Indonesian consumption, exporting the remainder. Oil for domestic use is sold below cost and the government has refused to sanction higher prices in spite of the protests of Stanvac and Shell. The oil reserves of Indonesia are limited, and since 1945 domestic demand has grown by 700 per cent while supply has only doubled.[14]

The principal competitor of Indonesian oil in foreign markets is Middle Eastern oil. The Middle East has far larger reserves, costs are lower, production has increased immensely since World War II, and the Asian demand is much larger. The yield from some of the older wells in Indonesia has declined, and the government has refused to allow the companies to acquire additional fields. The market for Indonesian oil at the present day is, roughly speaking, Southeast Asia, Japan, Australia, and New Zealand. Here it has the advantage of propinquity and lower cost in freight. Middle Eastern oil supplies India and Pakistan, but it is also sold in Japan and Australia, and there is no sharp demarcation between the markets. In 1938 60 per cent of the oil used in this area came from Indonesia, but by 1955 it met only 36 per cent of a much larger demand, and much of the oil sold by Caltex, Shell, and Stanvac came from fields outside Indonesia. The oil they obtained from Indonesia was not indispensable, and if their concessions were nationalized they could obtain supplies from elsewhere.[15]

The post-1945 investment of the oil companies far exceeded that of other Western firms, and most of the new capital which was sent to Indonesia came from them. The explanation is that the expenditure of an oil company is much greater than that of other corporations. The cost of exploring for oil, proving and developing a new field or building a refinery is exceedingly heavy. For this reason an oil company is less able to pay for its expenditure out of local profits than other corporations. During the war very great damage was done to the refineries and oilfields, and the cost of reconstruction was so extensive that new capital had to be brought in to pay for it. Subsequent expenditure was paid for as far as possible from profits earned from the sale of Indo-

245

nesian oil, but especially heavy costs such as the construction of a refinery or the Shell's Tand-Jung pipeline, the capital cost of which was $56,000,000, were met by bringing in new capital. Needless to say, the expenditure would not have been incurred unless the companies had believed that Indonesia's dependence on them to sell its oil abroad would restrain its hostility enough to allow them to make a satisfactory profit.

The Indonesian government's policy wavered between its usual hostility to foreign investors and its realization that the companies were indispensable. They had training programs for their Indonesian employees, but there were not enough of them to replace the Americans and British in the oilfields and refineries. The objection to bringing in Russian or Rumanian technicians has been that this would make Sukarno more dependent on Russia than he wished to be. This objection would not apply to Japanese, and they could be substituted for the Americans and British without injury to the production of oil. The reason that the companies are indispensable is that they own most of the oil tankers of the world and control the sales organization in foreign markets. If the government seized their concessions it could work the fields but would have very great difficulty in selling the oil abroad. It has also been influenced by the consideration that next to rubber oil was the principal export and provided about ten per cent of the total revenue, including a substantial amount of the badly needed foreign exchange.

The Five-Year Plan which was drawn up in 1956 recognized that Indonesia did not have enough domestic capital and trained personnel to carry it out. Major responsibility was assigned to foreign companies for developing industries such as oil which required a large amount of money and technical skill. The government made an agreement with the companies by which unlike other foreign firms they were allowed to retain for a number of years the foreign exchange earned by the sale of their exports abroad. These profits were not frozen in Indonesia like most of those of the other companies, but could be transferred abroad as dividends after taxes and costs of operation in Indonesia had been met. Owing to this agreement the parent companies were able gradually to reimburse themselves for the new capital which they had exported to Indonesia for capital investment.[16]

Though the oil companies were in a favored position they did not find everything was plain sailing. They encountered labor troubles as did other foreign employers, and the usual official reluctance to grant visas to foreign staff needed in positions for which there were no suitable Indonesians. For the time being the position of the companies was reasonably good, but their future prospects were not so encouraging. The government refused to give permission to prospect for new fields, even though production from some of the older ones was beginning to fall. A resolution passed by the legislature in 1951 forbade the grant of additional concessions to non-Indonesian companies pending the passage of a new mining and petroleum law. A draft of the new law was not introduced until 1960, and further delays were caused by Sukarno's dissolution of the legislature. A spokesman for one of the companies described its terms as "far from ideal." The gist of it was that existing companies might continue to operate their concessions for twenty years, after which they might be nationalized. Meanwhile, they must exploit them to the utmost regardless of losses incurred elsewhere, and must refine all oil in Indonesia instead of exporting part of it in the form of crude oil as at present.

In November 1960 President Sukarno signed a bill by which "it will be impossible for foreign companies to get mining concessions in Indonesia any longer." Present rights of the Western companies which ranged from one to nearly thirty years would remain valid for the "shortest possible period." Exploration for new fields, production, refining, and sale must be conducted by government firms. The law then went on to admit that Indonesia did not have the capital and technical skill to carry out this program. For this reason the companies would be given first priority to act as contractors for the government firms which were unable to do the work themselves. This law was part of the Eight-Year Plan for development launched by Sukarno in 1961. It proposed that the oil companies should form a partnership with the government to double production, and for this purpose invest an additional $1,500,000,000. The Plan estimated that this would provide the government with $1,180,000,000 in foreign exchange.[17] The law did not nationalize the properties of the companies but declared that their ownership would revert to the state. The companies could continue to operate them on a contractual basis. In future no concessions would be granted on traditional lines, and any new areas assigned to oil companies would also be developed on a contractual basis. Clearly, the government was still torn between its hostility toward Western "exploitation" and its realization that for the time being it needed the foreign companies. Early in 1962 developments occurred which appeared to show that the hostility was in the ascendant as far as the Shell and Unilever companies were concerned. Unilever has had the largest soap and margarine factory in Indonesia since 1933. In both companies control is shared by British and Dutch interests, but their branches in Indonesia have been under full British control since the confiscation of the Dutch investments in 1957. The Indonesian claim to New Guinea provided the occasion for a left-wing demand for action against the companies. It was accentuated after an Indonesian gunboat was sunk by Dutch destroyers off the coast of New Guinea on January 15, 1962. In February, Abdulgani, one of Sukarno's principal advisers, revealed that the president was considering the confiscation of Shell and Unilever on the ground that both contained Dutch as well as British capital. Abdulgani went on to claim that the death of the Indonesians who were killed in the naval action not only gave the government "the legitimate right to confiscate other Dutch capital, but makes it their duty to do so." [18] The oil companies negotiated with the government for modifications of the law, and a final settlement was not reached until June, 1963. The decisive factor in breaking the deadlock seems to have been the strong pressure exerted upon Sukarno by President Kennedy. Sukarno threatened serious but unspecified sanctions against the three oil companies unless they accepted his terms. Officials considered that some of the demands came close to being confiscatory, and the oil companies believed that they were being forced to work under conditions and under threats that made long term operations impossible. President Kennedy was afraid that if the companies were nationalized Congress might interpret this as an act of expropriation and insist that no more American aid be given to Indonesia. He therefore sent a personal representative to Sukarno to warn him of the serious risk he was running, and as the result an agreement which the companies accepted was signed on June 1. Indonesia's demand was granted that it was the owner of the oil, and in consequence the status of the companies was changed from that of

248

owners to contractors. They also agreed to give Indonesia sixty per cent instead of fifty per cent of the profits. On the other hand Sukarno promised that the companies would continue to produce and export Indonesia's oil for the next twenty years, after which the contract would be renegotiated. The companies by paying a bonus would also be given the right to explore and exploit new oil deposits. In five years the government would take over domestic distribution facilities. Payment would be made in hard currency, though the amount was not stated. The companies' refineries might also be taken over in ten to fifteen years. The Anglo-Dutch Shell Company benefited by President Kennedy's intervention and received the same terms as the American companies.

The reprieve was only temporary, so far as one could judge from what happened in the last months of 1963. An account was given in a preceding chapter of how Sukarno allowed the British embassy in Djakarta to be burnt by an Indonesian mob, as an expression of their disapproval of the United Kingdom's support of the Federation of Malaysia. At the same time the trade unions controlled by Sukarno's Communist supporters seized the property of the Shell Oil Company and other British corporations in different parts of Indonesia. The next stage was that Sukarno ordered the civil and military authorities to oust the trade unions in order to "safeguard" the operations of the British companies. According to the reports of employees who were evacuated to Singapore, the word control would have been more accurate than safeguard. British executives were not restored to their former positions but were required to obey the orders of the Indonesians whom Sukarno had put in charge. The British government asked in September when the properties would be returned to their owners. The reply of the Indonesian government evaded the question and was described as equivocal and ambiguous. A director of the Shell Oil Company was sent from London to Djakarta in an attempt to persuade Sukarno to honor the oil agreement which he had made. Oil company executives and diplomatists in Singapore and Bangkok were privately sceptical of his chances of success. One of them, an American, expressed the opinion of the rest when he said that "I expect the Indonesians have thrown it [the agreement] in the waste basket." The general belief was that Sukarno intended to nationalize the Shell Oil Company's holdings in a matter of weeks. In the past its chief safeguard had been that if it were nationalized it would refuse to sell Indonesian oil abroad, and that Sukarno did not have the oil tankers and the marketing organization to do this for himself. In October, however, he announced that at least one member of his oil commission would be included in a trade mission which he was sending to China. This led oil company executives to fear that Sukarno hoped to free himself from his dependence on the oil companies by arranging an oil barter deal with China. What he intended to do with the other British investments was known only to himself. They would be unlikely to escape if he seized the Shell Oil Company's concessions, the most valuable of them all and the one which was in the strongest position to bargain with him. Perhaps an indication of his policy was given in a decree which he issued in November 1963. He ordered the seizure of all rubber-milling companies in East Sumatra which were owned by citizens of the Federation of Malaysia. The lame excuse was made that his order forbidding trade with Malaysia might be circumvented by smuggling rubber from Sumatra to Singapore. The usual method of countering smuggling is to tighten control by customs officials and coastal patrol boats, and not to seize foreign property before an offense has been committed.

Marked similarity exists between the tactics used when Sukarno seized the Dutch assets in 1957 and those which are being employed against the British investments in 1963. The first stage was a succession of inflammatory speeches which were intended to excite the Indonesians to a state of hysterical patriotism by arousing their xenophobia and their suspicion that the West was scheming to destroy their independence. In 1957 this was done by harping on the inalienable right of Indonesia to Dutch New Guinea. In 1963 it was British neo-colonialism in Borneo and the preposterous accusation that Malaysia with its small army and less than 10,000,000 inhabitants was a threat to Indonesia with a population of 90,000,000 and the largest armed forces in Southeast Asia. On each occasion the refusal of the United Nations to support Indonesia was brushed aside, a revealing indication that Sukarno's devotion to what has been called the voice of world moral opinion could be depended on only as long as it supported him. The next stage was the seizure of the Dutch and British assets by the Communist-controlled trade unions. Sukarno then intervened as the champion of law and order to oust the trade unions and bring the investments under his own control. The parallel is so exact that no one will be surprised if the British like the Dutch are stripped of their property. The sole deterrent would be if he became convinced that he would lose more than he would gain; and so discouraging a prospect seems unlikely. The only pressure which the United Kingdom is likely to employ is the cancellation of its technical aid, and the government announced in November 1963 that this was being suspended. The amount was so small — $140,000 for 1963–1964 — that the loss is immaterial to a government which needs hundreds of millions. The principal source of Western foreign aid has been the United States, and while President Kennedy expressed his disapproval of the sacking of the British embassy and of Sukarno's hostility toward the Federation of Malaysia he gave no sign of intending to apply financial pressure. He continued to give economic aid on a moderate scale, and his policy was considerably to increase it if only Sukarno would concentrate on carrying out his program of economic stabilization, as is pointed out in Chapter XI. At a press interview a week before his assassination he vehemently condemned the movement in Congress to forbid aid to Indonesia because of its hostility toward the Federation of Malaysia. The State Department also authorized the export of $28,000,000 worth of spare parts for troop transport planes which the British were convinced were used for dropping soldiers and equipment along the border area of British Borneo. Spare parts for bombers were also sent to Indonesia. Unless President Johnson should reverse his predecessor's policy Sukarno is not likely to be deterred by the American attitude.

Dutch Investments

The agreements made in 1949 at The Hague which ended the Indonesian revolt against Holland guaranteed the security of the Dutch investments. They were to be returned to their owners, and reasonable compensation was to be paid if they were nationalized. The Indonesians regarded them with even more hostility than other Western investments, and it was a very popular argument that the revolution would not be complete until Western and particularly Dutch economic domination of Indonesia was destroyed. In 1956 the Indonesian government abrogated the loose political union with Holland, and at the same time repudiated the debt it had assumed in the Hague Agreements. This debt, an obligation of the former Dutch government of the East Indies, was said to have amounted to $1,046,000,000.[19] In December 1957 the whole of the Dutch assets were taken over and most of the sixty thousand Dutch in Indonesia were forced to leave the country, except the technical experts who were indispensable. The immediate occasion of the move was the continued refusal of Holland to surrender Dutch New Guinea, and the defeat of a resolution in the United Nations Assembly demanding that she do so. Before the debate President Sukarno had threatened that if the United Nations failed to support him he would resort to measures that would startle the world. He carried on a propaganda campaign which aroused the latent anti-Dutch feeling of the population. When the failure of the United Nations to give its support became known, the Communist trade unions began to seize Dutch enterprises. The military and civil authorities then took over their control and the premier, Dr. Djuanda, threatened that unless the Dutch handed over New Guinea their investments in Indonesia would be eliminated. If they did so a decision would be taken later on what should be returned to them. Holland refused to give way, and in October 1958 Dutch property was nationalized. Compensation would be fixed by a committee appointed by the government, and the Dutch owners might appeal its decision to the Indonesian Supreme Court, which was also controlled by the government.[20] No compensation would be paid until Holland surrendered New Guinea.

There was no means of redress, for previous experiences had shown the futility of appeals to the International Court and the United Nations. Three leading authorities on international law, Lord McNair, formerly President of the International Court, Professor Henri Rolin of Brussels and Professor Doctor Alfred Verdross of Vienna, gave the unanimous opinion that the action of the Indonesian government was flagrantly illegal. The rights of the Dutch investors were guaranteed by the Hague Agreements of 1949, and the single-handed repudiation of these treaties by Indonesia was itself illegal. A government had the right to nationalize property for "some *bona fide* social or economic purpose," e.g., for the construction of a railway. In this case, however, the official statements showed that the motive was to exert pressure on Holland to transfer sovereignty over New Guinea, and by no stretch of the imagination could this be described as a *bona fide* social or economic purpose. International law also required that nationalization must apply to all properties in a similar situation and not be confined to any particular group of aliens. Indonesia's action avowedly singled out the Dutch alone for discriminatory treatment. Furthermore, nationalization must be accompanied by the prompt payment of adequate compensation. The statements of the Indonesian government made it clear that payment would be withheld until it had obtained possession of New Guinea at some indefinite future date. There was also strong reason to believe that whatever compensation might be paid would be less than the value of the property.[21] The Indonesian government naturally was not impressed by the accusation that it was guilty of a flagrant act of confiscation.

One of the first effects of the seizure was to disrupt sea communication in Indonesia. Most of the inter-island services were provided very efficiently by a Dutch company, the K.P.M. It was essential for the viability of the economy and for maintaining Indonesia's rather precarious political and administrative unity. National pride was outraged at this dependence upon a foreign enterprise, and for some years the government had given financial encouragement to small Indonesian companies to compete with it. They were totally inadequate to replace the K.P.M.; and the government failed in its attempt to compel it to continue to operate after the seizure of its property in 1957. The K.P.M. was able to remove its vessels to Singapore, and freight and passenger traffic between the islands were partially paralyzed. The government secured some ships abroad by making inroads into its scarce foreign exchange, but there is every indication that inter-island transport will be inadequate for a long time.

The government placed 542 Dutch estates, three quarters of the total number in Indonesia, retail stores, and other assorted enterprises under the management of Indonesians, usually inexperienced. The new regime was marked by inefficiency and a good deal of corruption. The output of the estates declined, with a consequent fall in exports and earnings of foreign exchange.[22] Apart from the psychological satisfaction of eliminating the Dutch, it is hard to discover any gain that the confiscation of their property has brought to Indonesia.

In addition to the loss suffered by investors in Holland, the country had to provide for thousands of refugees, many of them penniless. A corporation was formed with government financial support to assist the companies expelled from Indonesia in making a fresh start. They showed a distinct preference for Latin America and Africa as against Asia. There was some investment in Dutch New Guinea, but not so much as the government would have liked. Dutch investments in the other countries of Southeast Asia were not very extensive, and consisted chiefly of import-export firms, banks, offices of the Dutch airline and shipping firms, and three small factories. One of them in the Philippines was owned by the Philips electrical company, and the other two in the Philippines and Burma were branches of the Anglo-Dutch firm of Unilever. One final effect of Sukarno's action may be noted. It would be politically impossible for a government of Holland to give any help toward raising the standard of living in Indonesia except perhaps in return for restitution to the Dutch investors.

Burma

Western business investments in Burma before World War II had an estimated value of $236,000,000, ninety per cent being British. Asian investment was almost entirely Indian, and was estimated at $290,000,000. Far and away the largest item was the loans advanced to the Burman peasants by the *chettyars*, a caste of Indian money lenders, and the rice lands on which they had foreclosed their mortgages. Most of the rest was made up of retail trade and rice mills. British investments were drastically lessened by wartime destruction and nationalization by the government of the Burmese republic. Figures given for their post-war value did not attain even the quasi-accuracy of a rough estimate and their authors themselves described them as guesses. The amount of $56,000,000 or less was tentatively suggested, the greater part being the holdings of the Burmah Oil Company. The property of the *chettyars* was taken over by the Burmese government with a promise of future compensation which the owners considered very inadequate. The British assets belonged almost entirely to companies which were in Burma before the war. Post-war investment was principally local profits ploughed back though some new capital had to be sent in for the reconstruction of wartime damage or building a factory. Very few new firms entered the field. All the indications were that British like Indian private capital would continue to avoid Burma, in spite of the spasmodic attempts of the government to attract it.[23]

Lack of law and order and uncertainty about the political future of the republic were deterrents although less important than formerly. In the late 'forties it seemed problematical whether the government could survive the attacks upon it by the Karens, the Communists, and other rebels. By the middle 'fifties they were no longer a threat to the existence of the state but they survived as bandits and in many districts life and property were insecure. There was factional strife within the A.F.P.F.L. government, and it has again been replaced by another military dictatorship. There was some doubt whether China would always respect Burma's independence and territorial integrity. Communications have been poor, though improving both by rail and river steamer, and the wrecking of trains by rebels continues to occur. Postwar labor has been largely Burman and no longer predominantly Indian as it was until 1941. The Burman still prefers to work when the spirit moves him, and employers have complained that he is apt to vanish without warning. His attitude has been anti-Western and his demands for higher wages and shorter hours have had the government's sympathy, although strikes have not been so frequent as in Indonesia. There has been the usual difficulty in getting entrance visas for essential European employees, and insistence on the appointment of Burmans irrespective of their qualifications.

The principal reason for the unwillingness to invest in Burma has been the unfriendly attitude of the government. The A.F.P.F.L. which controlled the government until 1962 was socialist and hostile to foreign interests, and until recently it had the delusion that the Western capitalist was most anxious to invest in Burma. The constitution of 1947 laid it down that the state had power to nationalize the land, and that public utilities and the exploitation of natural resources should be carried on by the government or by Burmese cooperative societies. Private companies might be allowed to operate if sixty per cent of the capital were owned by the government or by citizens of Burma. This percentage might be varied when the public interest so required. Under this clause joint undertakings in which foreigners held more than forty per cent of the stock were declared legal by the Supreme Court. In 1948 the government nationalized lumber concessions, saw mills, and the Irrawaddy Flotilla Company which owned the river steamers. Subsequently other British enterprises — mines, factories, and a cement works — were nationalized. The compensation paid was inadequate. The government itself assumed the monopoly of rice-milling and the foreign sale of rice, the principal export. Licenses for imports were progressively restricted to Burmans. Foreign-owned factories were not allowed to import their raw materials and machinery directly, but had to do so through a licensed Burman agent.

The government had ambitious plans for the establishment of a welfare state. Its understanding of economics was very sketchy, and it completely failed to realize the handicaps presented by the lack of native capital and of Burmans with business training. By 1949 the situation had become so serious that attempts were made to attract foreign capital, but without success. In 1955 the government announced that new enterprises would not be nationalized for at least ten years, and that the same guarantee might be extended to existing companies if they invested additional money. At last, satisfactory arrangements were sanctioned by which companies could transfer their profits abroad after the payment of taxes. These inducements had little effect in attracting new capital.[24] The principal exceptions were two joint undertakings arranged between the government and British companies. One of them, the building of a factory for the manufacture of drugs by the Evans Medical Company, was not a success. The other was a small factory built by Unilever in 1960. Of the companies which were not expropriated, some sold out and withdrew. The remainder continued operations on a smaller scale: one firm which employed two hundred Europeans in 1941 had five in 1960 and compensated for its shrunken activities in Burma by acquiring interests in western Canada. Investors felt that the government regarded them as a necessary but strictly temporary evil, and that it would get rid of them as soon as it could safely do so. One informant summed up the attitude by saying that the government's chief success did not lie in its attempts to establish a welfare state but in its suppressing much private enterprise and putting nothing in its place.

The A.F.P.F.L. government was hostile to firms which were entirely owned and controlled by foreigners, and strongly preferred joint ventures where it and the firm each provided part of the capital and control was shared between them. It was doubtful whether this arrangement was intended to be permanent, since the prime minister, U Nu, stated that they would be nationalized as soon as there were enough trained Burmans to operate them.[25] Most of these joint undertakings were with companies that had been long established in Burma. Among them were the Burma Corporation for the exploitation of the Bawdwin lead and silver mine: the Anglo-Burman Tin Company for tin and tungsten mining: and the Burmah Oil Company. The last was formed in 1954 by a union of the three pre-war companies. An agreement was made with the government by which it acquired a one-third interest in return for a payment of $14,000,000, half of which was lent it by the British government for the purpose. The Burmese government was to appoint two of the five directors, and had the right to increase its percentage to any limit whenever it desired. In 1960 the government proposed to buy 51 per cent of the shares in order to get control of the company as soon as it could find the money. The following year an agreement was made by which the government promised not to acquire any further shares for fifteen years, in return for the company's providing 49 per cent of the capital required to enlarge the refinery at Syriam. When General Ne Win became dictator in 1962 he asked the Burmah Oil Company to revise this agreement, and the upshot was that he bought all the remaining shares for $13,125,000. The attitude of the company was that if an agreement drawn up to last for fifteen years were going to be upset within a year, business operations in Burma would be "one headache after another." So the sale was arranged amicably, the Ne Win dictatorship obtained complete control of the oil industry, and the Burmah Oil Company ended an association with Burma which had lasted over seventy-five years.[26] The refineries, pipeline, and other installations had been systematically destroyed in 1942 to deny them to the Japanese. A new refinery was built at Chauk in Upper Burma in 1954, and the pre-war refinery at Syriam near Rangoon was restored in 1957 at a cost of $2,800,000. The combined output is less than before the war, but is enough to make Burma self-sufficient in her major oil requirements. The pipeline was never rebuilt, partly because of the lack of law and order, and also for the reason that the company found it satisfactory to transport crude oil to the refinery by river barges. The above costs were met by the import of new capital, whereas the funds for subsequent expenditure came mainly from the depreciation charged against annual profits.

The company's operations after 1945 were on a smaller scale than before 1941, and Burma is no longer an exporter of oil as it was then. The principal reason is that the output has been falling since before the war, and attempts to find fresh fields have not been successful. Exploration has been restricted by lack of security, and by long delays in the issue of prospecting licenses. Even before 1941 the company got less than half its oil from Burma. It held shares in the Anglo-Iranian Oil Company and obtained oil from Assam and from what today is Pakistan. Since 1945 important discoveries have been made there, and the Burmah Oil Company's most important fields are now in Pakistan. Subsidiary companies are operating in the United States, Canada, and South America.

General Ne Win is a more extreme socialist than U Nu. He has made it clear that private foreign investments will not be allowed in Burma. The remaining lumber companies and the twenty-four foreign and Burmese banks were nationalized, and most of the other foreign-owned businesses were taken over. The army intends to nationalize every large and medium-size enterprise in the near future. Small businesses are not to be nationalized for at least five or ten years. Both commerce and industry will be carried on by the government Burma Economic Development Corporation which was established in 1958. It owns or controls banks, hotels, department stores, export-import companies, and shipping lines, and will soon take over the marketing of petroleum. The Ford and the Asia Foundations, which had spent $10,200,000 in aid to Burma, were ordered to close down in 1962. U Nu's attempts to establish a socialist state came to grief from lack of funds, technical experts, and officials who knew how to manage businesses competently. General Ne Win intends to attain this same goal as quickly as possible. For funds he apparently relies on the proceeds from the government sale of rice and other exports, deficit financing, and foreign aid from the free world and the Communist bloc. In the past, American and British government aid has averaged about $8,300,000 a year, but the American government has been proposing to spend an additional $30,000,000 and possibly more. Ne Win's decision to follow an uncompromisingly socialist policy was linked with the dismissal or enforced resignation of Brigadier General Aung Gyi, who had been deputy chief of staff and Minister of Commerce. Although a socialist he had advised allowing scope for private enterprise and a less hasty advance toward the goal. His fall seems to have been caused at least as much by a conflict of personalities as by differences in policy. His position had been systematically undermined by Brigadier General Tin Pe, who had been third man in the military hierarchy. Aung Gyi had also collided with Ne Win personally, possibly because of his growing popularity. The exceptional measures taken for the protection of Ne Win since the banishment of Aung Gyi to a remote village show that his action is widely resented among the officers of the army. It is to be hoped that the factiousness which has characterized civilian politics will not spread to the army.[27]

The Federation of Malaya

Western private investments in Malaya prior to the war were variously estimated at $394,000,000 and $372,000,000 of which at least seventy per cent was British and the rest American, Dutch, French, and Japanese. Rubber estates comprised nearly seventy per cent of the total, tin-dredging companies eighteen per cent, and the remainder consisted of tin smelters (the largest in the world was at Singapore), hydroelectric works, a solitary coal mine, and a few small factories. In addition, Chinese investments were believed to amount to $200,000,000.[28] As usual only rough estimates are available of the contemporary value of investments. The members of the Rubber Growers' Association, which includes most but not all of those engaged in rubber production, have an issued capital of between $140,000,000 and $154,000,000. This, however, is only the par value of the shares when they were originally sold thirty to sixty years ago, and does not allow for the enhanced value from profits ploughed back. The extent to which this was done varies greatly. Some estates are worth two and a half times as much as the original issued capital. Others, particularly many of the small estates, have done little or nothing to increase their value since the Great Depression. So it is only a very rough estimate to put the present value of the rubber estates between $350,000,000 and $386,000,000.

Accurately to estimate the value of the tin mines is even more impossible. It varies widely from mine to mine and even in different parts of the same mine according to the richness of the ore and the character of the rock underlying the alluvial deposits. There may be a smooth surface, or the deposit may lie in pockets between limestone pinnacles and be difficult or impossible to scoop out. Even with borings it is impossible to discover how many pinnacles are buried beneath the mixture of tin ore and sand brought down by the rivers in past geologic ages. At the present time forty per cent of the tin comes from Chinese and sixty per cent from some fifty-five European-controlled mines, all of which use the bucket dredge. "Like Noah's Arks of corrugated iron they float in their mud holes with a chain of buckets running through their metal intestines and scooping out ore and mud from the alluvial deposits." "European-controlled" means that the control is European although an unknown percentage of the stock may be owned by Chinese. One of the mines is owned in the United States and four or five in Australia, while all the rest are owned in the United Kingdom. The companies are conservative in estimating the amount of unmined ore. They also make heavy depreciation allowances for their dredges because they cost over $2,800,000 and may be impossible to move when the deposits are exhausted. The Malayan Chamber of Mines gave the estimated value of the European-controlled mines as $154,000,000, with a margin of error of perhaps as much as forty per cent either way. As to the factories, oil refineries, and other Western holdings, the owners guard the secret of their value — to quote the Pathan proverb — like the strings of their wives' pajamas.

The Federation of Malaya is one country where the Western investor is not plagued with fears of nationalization, frozen profits and bureaucratic red tape, endless procrastination, and squeeze. Law and order are good, administration is honest and reasonably efficient, and though there is some petty corruption among minor officials it is severely punished when it is discovered. This unusual situation is due to the care with which the Alliance Government have maintained the standards of the former British regime. They are a combination of Malay aristocrats and wealthy Chinese business men. Convinced nationalists, they nevertheless have a sane commonsense in their attitude toward Western private investment which is noticeably lacking in some other countries. They are opposed by parties which appeal to narrow Malay or Chinese nationalism or to socialism and condemn Western business

260

as imperialist exploitation, but so far the Alliance has won a majority of the votes. It has an ambitious program of extending the social services and raising the standard of living, which is already one of the highest in Asia. It realizes that without the help of foreign capital it cannot find the funds to carry out its expensive proposals. An official summed up the government's attitude in the remark that "unless we allow foreigners to make a profit we cannot expect them to invest." Strong emphasis is placed upon industrialization, but it is not regarded as a panacea. Large amounts are being spent on rural development to increase the prosperity of the peasants, most of whom are Malays. A severe handicap is that Malaya is poorly endowed with natural resources; it has only two staple products, rubber and tin, and its principal industry is the production of babies.

The government does not own or operate factories and relies upon private enterprise. To encourage investment it has been carrying out an extensive program of increasing the production of hydroelectric power, improving the harbors, and extending the already very good system of roads. Guarantees were given that there would be no nationalization of private firms or discriminatory legislation. In 1958 a law was passed which gave pioneer status to new industries which were officially approved. Both Malayan and Western firms were offered complete relief from income tax for two to five years depending on the amount invested. They were assured of protective tariffs, the waiver of import duties on essential imports, and the free transfer of profits abroad. The government would provide adequate electric power and transport and assist in housing developments. Preference would be given to a pioneer industry which was financed wholly by local capital. Companies with entirely foreign capital would be given these privileges only if similar proposals were not received from local investors either by themselves or in partnership with outside capital. Members of the legislature who opposed the proposals were warned that the "Federation needs foreign capital far more than foreign capital needs the Federation. The failure of our policy will mean that the number of unemployed will be increased by 200,000 every year." [29] "The country needs both local and foreign capital which will only go where there is a stable government which provides a satisfactory climate for investment and where there are safeguards for the remittance of dividends and the repatriation of capital. It is simple to drive capital away but very hard to encourage its inflow." The Malayan dollar continued to be linked with the pound sterling so that the exchange value remained stable. Realizing that the local market was small, the Prime Minister, Tengku Abdul Rahman, tried, so far without success, to persuade neighboring states to work out a program of complementary production accompanied by low tariffs. Instead of all manufacturing the same commodities and each protecting its domestic market by high tariffs, they should allocate the manufacture of different products to avoid competition.

The result of the Federation's policy has been that a growing number of foreign corporations have decided that it would be profitable to invest a minor part of their capital there. They as well as Malayan firms have built small and medium sized factories for light manufacturing which employed from a few dozen to a few hundred workmen. Most of the capital came from the United Kingdom, and the remainder from Hong Kong, Japan, and the United States.

Between 1958 and 1962 about ninety firms with a nominal capital of $100,000,000, half of which had been raised in Malaya, took advantage of the pioneer status plan. About eighty factories were built at Petaling Jaya in Selangor, the factory townsite laid out by the government. Not much room remains for more factories, and the government intends to lay out another townsite and increase the supply of hydroelectric power. Other towns are preparing factory sites, and in some of them factories have been built. The Shell Oil Company has built a refinery at Port Dickson, and Esso (a subsidiary of Standard Oil) has decided to imitate it. The cost of building a factory was met by exporting new capital, but if possible subsequent expansion was financed from local profits. The following instances seem to be typical of the moderate expenditure on the factories. The Unilever factory which was built at Kuala Lumpur in 1948 employs about 450, and makes soap, margarine, and cooking fats and oils for the Malayan market. The cost of the factory and of housing for the employees was about $3,400,000, and in 1960 Unilever decided to spend an additional $500,000 for making detergents, and $2,800,000 on its palm oil plantation. The Dunlop Company which has 90,000 acres of rubber estates has a factory for making foam rubber. It has been negotiating with the government for permission to build a tire factory at a cost which is believed to be some $8,000,000.

Estate Rubber

The planted area of the foreign-owned rubber estates is 1,325,000 acres, of which approximately 1,250,000 acres are British and most of the rest American and French. Malayan nationals, principally Chinese and Indians, own about 700,000 acres of rubber estates. The small-holders, largely Malays, are estimated to own about 1,600,000 acres. A decade ago the need for replanting with high-yielding rubber was more urgent than in Indonesia since on the whole the trees were even older. In 1954 the Mudie committee, which was appointed to investigate the condition of the industry, reported that more than half of the mature seedling rubber trees (the unselected descendants of the original trees brought from Brazil) were over thirty years old, and that less than three per cent had been planted since 1942. The bulk of the replanting had been on the larger estates, mostly European-owned. Less had been done on the smaller estates, the majority of which were Asian-owned, and least of all on the smallholdings. A good half of the estate acreage and most of that of the smallholders were heading toward collapse. The principal reason for the failure of the estates to replant was the heavy taxation in Malaya and the United Kingdom, and the Mudie committee considered that probably the majority could not afford to replant regularly after they had paid their taxes and costs of operation.

The economic life of the rubber tree is on the average about thirty-five years, and the Mudie committee drew the conclusion that "If the present state of affairs is allowed to continue . . . the end of the rubber industry in Malaya as we know it is inevitable within the next fifteen or twenty years." The committee also pointed out that altogether apart from the age of the trees the best hope that natural could compete successfully with the cheaper synthetic rubber was by replanting with high-yielding rubber. The latter gave a yield of around twelve hundred pounds per acre, while old seedling rubber gave four hundred pounds or less. There was the further point that the Federation's income tax and export duty were heavy. In 1961 they took 52.5 per cent of the gross profits, and over the previous thirteen years even a very efficient estate like Sua Betong had paid an average net dividend of less than 7 per cent on the capital invested. Costs of production on an estate planted largely or wholly with seedling rubber were a much greater burden than on one with high-yielding rubber. The former could only meet its expenses, pay dividends, and replant when the price of rubber was high. When it was very low such an estate might be unable even to cover costs, with no margin for replanting. This combination of causes largely explained the considerable number of estates where replanting was irregular and inadequate or non-existent.

The Federation refused to lower taxes; in fact it raised them on the ground that it needed the revenue to pay for the expansion of the social services. In 1955, however, it adopted the policy of giving assistance to estates for all replanting with high-yielding rubber carried out between 1953 and 1961 inclusive. Each application must be for not less than 3 per cent of the property, and help could be obtained up to a maximum of 21 per cent of the planted acreage. The average cost of replanting was $268 an acre and the financial assistance $133, less income tax. The replanting subsidy to smallholders was $167 an acre. The United Kingdom also helped in 1957 by reducing its taxes on corporations registered there but carrying on all their operations abroad, such as rubber and tin companies.[30] Government assistance stimulated replanting, even though to a very large extent the industry subsidized itself. In addition to income tax of 40 per cent on profits there was a duty on a graduated scale on all rubber exported. When the government decided to help in 1955 it sharply raised the rates of export duty when the price rose above twenty-seven cents a pound. Up to the end of 1959 the government had received $38,300,000 in increased duty and paid $43,300,000 in financial assistance. The probability is that the enhanced rates of duty will be continued indefinitely on the ground that the revenue is needed. On the other hand, the government is considering the extension of the scheme for a further period of five years and of the acreage by fifteen per cent.

Temporarily the scheme has accelerated replanting and new planting by about 50 per cent.[31] The average rate rose from 55,000 acres a year to 82,360 acres in 1955–1959. It was estimated that the amount reinvested from profits by the British companies during the period 1953–1959 on their acreage of 1,250,000 was between $182,000,000 and $189,000,000. The corresponding estimate for the British and other foreign companies on their acreage of 1,325,000 was between $203,000,000 and $210,000,000. The amount of replanting and new planting on estates from 1948 to 1959 inclusive was about 786,000 acres. Adding the area planted with high-yielding rubber at an earlier date, there were in 1959 1,044,562 acres of high-yielding rubber on the estates owned by foreigners and Malayan nationals, or 52.5 per cent of their total area. This is a striking contrast to the position of the Indonesian estates where in 1959 the area replanted with high-yielding rubber was only 475,000 acres. With more high-yielding trees each year reaching the age when they can be tapped, it is easy to see why Malaya's output has grown as Indonesia's has fallen, until it has become the world's leading producer. Closer examination shows a disquieting portent for the future. It had been known for a long time that most of the replanting was on the larger and more efficient estates which were usually owned by Europeans. Many of the smaller estates had done little or no replanting. The government subsidy does not seem to have brought about any material change. The bulk of the replanting and new planting is still on the larger and more efficient European-owned estates. The danger continues that a substantial part of the acreage will eventually become derelict.

Tin

The tin mines face the situation that the rich ores have largely been exhausted, and it is necessary to work the large deposits of low-grade ores. The steady improvement in mining machinery makes it possible to extract the tin from deposits which formerly were unworkable. The dredge can go down to a depth of a hundred and thirty feet compared with thirty feet sixty years ago. No substantial increase is possible in output, but existing production can be maintained. It is very important, however, to prospect for new deposits. A serious hindrance to this is the conflict between the interests of mining and agriculture. The unavoidable result of alluvial mining is that the topsoil is stripped off and replaced by sand and gravel, so that the land cannot be used for farming. The state governments control the disposal of land, and their primary interest is to expand the cultivated area. Many of them have been unwilling to issue permits for prospecting or mining.

Singapore

Singapore's importance as a trade entrepôt arose from its excellent harbor and its position as a focal point of trade. It lay on the sea route through the Straits of Malacca, and was the natural center for the trade of Malaya, Sumatra, Western Borneo, and to some extent countries further afield such as Thailand. Ocean-going steamships unloaded their cargoes of manufactures from overseas at Singapore for distribution throughout its trading area by local steamers. On their return voyages they brought back raw materials and foodstuffs which were sent on to their ultimate destinations in Europe, the United States, and Japan. Western interests in Singapore were chiefly concerned with the entrepôt trade such as import and export firms, steamship offices, banks, and insurance companies. Manufacturing was of minor importance.

Singapore has a high birth rate and owing to the excellence of its medical and health services a falling death rate. The infant mortality rate has fallen from 140 per 1,000 in 1940 to 41.4 in 1957. The result is that the rate of population growth is 3.9 per cent, one of the highest in the world. The population, 1,634,000 in 1960, is expected on a conservative estimate to rise to 3,295,000 by 1980.[32] Already there is unemployment, and the most pressing problem of government is to promote economic development so that the creation of new jobs will keep pace with the growth of population. The entrepôt trade is more likely to fall than to expand, owing to the increase of economic nationalism, particularly in Indonesia. Its government is jealous of Singapore's position as a major center of trade through which passes a large share of Indonesia's imports and exports, and talks of establishing a rival free port. Singapore does not take this very seriously since it believes Sukarno's government is incapable of creating anything which would be free from official incompetence, endless procrastination, and corruption. In the future, however, as in the past there is likely to be interference with the part of Indonesia's foreign trade that passes through Singapore.

The government believes that the solution is to encourage the development of manufacturing, and here it is a question whether the provision of increased employment "can move ahead of or even keep up with the pace at which the population and the labor force are growing."[33] The local market is inadequate and it is improbable that foreign Asian countries will admit manufactures which compete with their own. The success of Hong Kong, likewise a trade entrepôt, in developing industry to the point where manufactures now make up a third of the exports is not so encouraging as it might seem at first sight. The factories in Hong Kong were built partly by wealthy Chinese in the colony, and in part by funds transferred there by Chinese in Southeast Asia. Wages are higher in Singapore, and so far Hong Kong and Western companies have been wary of investing there, owing to the political developments of the last few years.

The establishment of democracy in Singapore was accompanied by growing Communist influence, violent strikes, and turbulence which did not commend it to investors. The People's Action Party (P.A.P.), established in 1954, was made up partly of left-wing Socialists, and in part of Communists and fellow travelers. The leader, Lee Kuan-yew, a lawyer, was a very adroit and ambitious politician. He denied that he was a Communist, but said that no man who wanted to win the Chinese vote could afford to be anti-Communist because of the sympathy for China. The Communists in P.A.P. controlled a powerful group of trade unions and the teenage students of the Chinese high schools. With their help they engineered the violent strikes and bloody riots of 1955 and 1956. P.A.P. gained control of the government of Singapore Municipality in 1957. Its record fulfilled the worst forebodings of those who feared it would win a victory in the elections for the government of the colony. An American observer commented that "parliamentary privileges were flagrantly breached, personal invective was indiscriminately employed, and periodically all business was suspended in favor of attack upon personal and political enemies." P.A.P. was the only party which had an effective organization, and as anticipated it won the election in 1959.

P.A.P. made its appeal to the voters as the enemy of private business, and above all of European colonial exploiters. Its record and electoral promises were well calculated to lead to a flight of private capital, and they produced exactly that result. It was feared that P.A.P. would be dominated by its Communist wing, and a number of Singapore firms transferred to Kuala Lumpur, the capital of the Federation. Companies which had been debating whether to establish branches in Singapore decided against it, including some Chinese business men from Hong Kong. They inspected Singapore with the idea of building a factory, but departed with the announcement that they preferred the peace and tranquillity of Hong Kong. An indefensible island half a mile off the coast of Communist China does not automatically suggest a cloistered calm, so their opinion was enlightening.

Once Lee Kuan-yew became prime minister he was studiously moderate in his policy, and for about a year kept the Communists under control. His twin aims were to reassure private capital and persuade the Alliance government to allow Singapore to enter the Federation. He saw no future in becoming a Communist outpost of Peking, and apparently realized that the help of private enterprise was necessary if the problem of unemployment were to be solved by industrialization. It was easier to lose the confidence of capital than to regain it. Fear of what the P.A.P. government might do was allayed to the extent that the flight of capital ended, but new firms showed no eagerness to come in. There was talk of a five-year plan to promote manufacturing and expand the social services, the greater part of the necessary $330,000,000 to be provided by British and American loans. Both governments had so many calls upon them that financial aid on such a scale was improbable.

The Communist wing of P.A.P. broke away to form a rival party, and Lee Kuan-yew lost a couple of by-elections. This left him with a precarious majority of one in the Legislative Assembly. Communist control seemed imminent, and once more there was a withdrawal of capital. The gravity of the situation was the reason why Tengku Abdul Rahman reversed his previous policy and agreed in 1961 to Singapore's joining the Federation. How far this will reassure investors depends upon the success of the federal government in controlling Communism in Singapore. The problem of providing employment will be eased by the access to the market of the Federation.

Thailand and Indochina

Foreign investments in Thailand are less than they were before World War II. In 1954 the Bank of Thailand placed their value at $40,000,000, the bulk invested in trade or the production of raw materials and not in manufacturing. The principal types of industry were rice and saw mills, sugar refineries, weaving mills and printing establishments. The most important investor was the Danish East Asiatic Company. A shipping and trading firm, it also owned a teak concession, a saw mill, and a rice mill. Several British firms had substantial interests in teak, tin, and rubber, and in trade and banking; Unilever had a soap factory. Caltex, Stanvac, and Shell had oil storage tanks and marketing organizations. American firms were engaged in the import and export trade, banking, and to a very limited extent manufacturing. Among the lesser causes of the lack of interest in this last were the small domestic market, the scarcity of skilled labor and the inadequate supply of hydroelectric power. The most important reason was the attitude of the government and its economic policy. Hostility to foreign enterprise first appeared in the 1930's: nationalists attacked it for exploiting the natural resources of the nation and sending a large part of their profits out of the country. The government nationalized some foreign holdings and subsidized competing Thai firms. After the end of the war it set up a large number of firms which were in competition with established foreign enterprises. The International Bank reported in 1959 that the government was "involved directly or indirectly in a large number of commercial and other industrial enterprises." In addition to its monopolies of tobacco and alcoholic liquors it dominated several important industries such as timber and sugar: it had extensive interests in the manufacture of cement, glass, drugs, tin, and textiles: and it operated a large number of small factories. Very frequently the Thai who controlled these establishments lacked business experience but had secured special privileges because of their political influence. All the state industries except the monopolies were unprofitable, but they had had an adverse effect upon private foreign and domestic investment. Apart from direct competition with established firms, there was no assurance that the government might not invade other fields of private enterprise. Ministers often gave assurances that they wished to attract foreign investment, but their actions ran counter to their professions. The result was that Western capital held aloof.

The International Bank advised that the government should close some of its more unprofitable ventures and should not create new ones. Encouragement should also be given to private businesses. If this were done the Bank believed that there was scope for development, particularly in light engineering, assembly plants and textiles. The chances were "remote" that basic heavy industries could successfully face international competition. The Bank urged a further development of hydroelectric power, since the supply available was much less than the demand although the potential was large. Sarit Thanarat modified his economic policy in accordance with the Bank's advice. The government gave a guarantee that it would not nationalize foreign businesses or compete with them. Participation of Thai capital was not required, and no limit was placed upon the transfer abroad of profits or capital. The result was that from 1958 onwards there was a marked increase in foreign investment.[34]

Little Western capital has been invested in the countries of Indochina since the war. The pre-war investment was almost all French, and some of it was repatriated after the grant of independence. The government of South Viet Nam has discriminated against French companies. Cambodia has been more friendly, and there does not appear to have been the same withdrawal of French capital as in South Viet Nam. Communist North Viet Nam offers no attraction, and uncertainty whether the other states will retain their independence has been a deterrent. The government of South Viet Nam has been somewhat hostile to private business in general. It is regarded with fear and suspicion, and this is one reason why not much foreign capital has been invested. Plans for industrialization were drawn up which emphasized state ownership and operation, and President Ngo Dinh Diem tried unsuccessfully to persuade the American government to finance them. The latter urged that they be left to private enterprise. American firms have shown only a limited interest in South Viet Nam. Various light industries have been set up which are wholly or partly owned by government. Industrialization has made limited progress since the government does not have enough capital and its civil service is "conspicuously inefficient and inexperienced."[35]

Western Investment in Southeast Asia, A Summary

American investment in Southeast Asia is made up principally of the holdings in the Philippines and Indonesia, with minor interests only in the other countries. British investment is much more widespread though with emphasis upon Malaya, Indonesia, and Burma. With the confiscation of the Dutch assets in Indonesia it is the largest Western investment in this part of Asia. Any marked increase in British and American holdings is improbable, and the conclusion seems inescapable that private business cannot be expected to play the major role in providing outside capital for the economic development of Southeast Asia as a whole. Moreover, it is concerned mainly with the production of raw materials, though the interest in manufacturing is somewhat greater than before the war.

Until about thirty years ago the individual small investor in the United Kingdom more than in the United States furnished a large part of the capital. The funds of the British rubber and tin companies in Malaya and the rubber companies in the pre-war Dutch East Indies came largely from this source. Since World War II, however, the majority invest in companies which carry on business in the investor's own country, or alternatively in those which operate principally in the Western world. Investment trusts have become increasingly popular both in the United States and the United Kingdom. Southeast Asia is not regarded as a good risk. The investor has a somewhat vague recollection of sharp fluctuations in dividends and the years when there were none at all — during, e.g., the Japanese occupation. He has heard of the danger that the Communists may gain control, and the idea is firmly fixed in his mind that independent Asian governments are quite likely to celebrate their freedom by confiscating Western assets. He feels that what the tax collector has left him is safer if invested in a settled Western country. His financial advisers strongly support this attitude. One London banker who was interviewed said that he told his clients that if they already had a good collection of government bonds and reliable industrial securities and still had funds with which they wished to speculate, they might as well buy stock in one of the better rubber or tin companies as bet on the horse races. Exactly the same lack of interest is shown toward loans floated by Asian governments. The attitude of Dutch investors appears to be similar. The government of the United Kingdom tacitly recognized this attitude in 1958 by the announcement that it would make loans to independent Commonwealth countries which were unable to float them on the London money market. Since then loans have been given to Asian and

African governments. Previously the official attitude had been that bond issues would be sold to the investing public.

The directors of the British companies which operate entirely in Southeast Asia do not believe that new capital could be obtained from the public. This opinion is shared by bankers and stockbrokers. The only exception is that a fairly large number of existing companies seem to have sold additional shares to their stockholders. They appear to have used the argument that the best way they could safeguard their original investment was to subscribe additional funds. The result is that companies which operate entirely in Southeast Asia have to depend for funds on profits ploughed back into their enterprises.

Some of the companies operating on almost a world-wide scale take a minor interest in Southeast Asia. Among them are Unilever, the British American Tobacco Company, and the oil companies. Most of their capital is in the more settled countries of the world, and only a small part with which they can afford to take risks is allotted to Southeast Asia. So the individual investor has no hesitation in buying their shares. Unilever, for instance, had a volume of sales in 1958 of $4,838,400,000. Of this 60 per cent was in Europe, 13 per cent in North and South America, 22 per cent in Africa, the Middle East, and Australasia, and only 5 per cent, $227,000,000 in the whole of southern, southeastern, and eastern Asia. The capital employed was $1,472,800,000, of which only 3.6 per cent or $53,000,000 was invested from India around to the Philippines. Of this amount $23,800,000 was invested in India and only $21,000,000 in the whole of Southeast Asia. This was the amount actually invested, and not the cost of replacing the company's assets or the price which could be got for them if they were sold. Unilever's factories in Indonesia, Thailand, and the Philippines date from the interwar period. Two have been built since the war, one at Kuala Lumpur in 1948, and a small one in Burma in 1960 in partnership with the government, which owns about a quarter of the stock. Another large corporation, the British American Tobacco Company, had three cigarette factories in Indonesia before World War II. Since 1945 three more have been built in the Federation of Malaya, in Singapore, and, in partnership with French companies, for South Viet Nam and Cambodia. The oil companies in Indonesia are subsidiaries of the principal oil companies, and Southeast Asia is only of minor importance as a source of oil and a market. Stanvac, for instance, obtains less than a third of its oil from Indonesia. Only one of its six refineries is there, and it has interests in Africa, Asia, and Australasia. It would not pay to build a refinery in each Asian country because of the smallness of the market. Occasionally a refinery might be built as a concession to economic nationalism, if the alternative were that a rival company would do so in return for a tariff preference which would give it a competitive advantage. Shell's policy is to build a refinery at a few strategic points, and have storage tanks and a sales organization in the other countries. It has two refineries in Indonesia, one in the Federation of Malaya, and a fourth which is to be built in the Philippines. Another might be built at Singapore, but much would depend on the policy of the government.

Initially the large corporations carried on their manufacturing in a Western country and exported their products to Asia. Many of their factories in Southeast Asia were built before World War II, when colonial rule gave assurance of security. In the post-war period a factory was not built unless stringent examination showed that this was the most likely way to enhance profits. A typical presentation of the corporations' point of view was given by Lord Heyworth, the chairman of Unilever, at the annual general meeting on April 26, 1960.

Is the population going up? Is the general standard of living rising? Have any strong competitors dug themselves in before us? Can we get materials to build a factory, labour to work in it, transport to carry our goods away? Can we get materials to make products to our standard of quality? Is the government fairly stable? What kind of a view does it take of foreign investors? Shall we be able to get our profits out if we want to (often we prefer to leave them there for the development of the business)? [36]

Every corporation placed Indonesia at the bottom of its list as a very bad risk, and Burma was not regarded as too safe.

The decision to build was sometimes made in order to surmount a tariff barrier. The great increase in ocean freights after 1945 was another factor. Occasionally a small factory was built as a concession to Asian nationalism, in order to disarm the accusation that by selling some necessary product which was manufactured abroad the corporation was draining the country of its wealth and was not helping to carry out the local program of industrialization. Expenditure has been on a moderate scale. The factories are much smaller than those built in a Western country, and the number employed is limited. So far as information is obtainable about their cost it seems to be anywhere from about $2,000,000 to $6,000,000. An oil refinery is far more expensive, but is much smaller than those built in the West owing to the limited size of the market. For many of them the cost runs between $17,000,000 and $20,000,000, whereas those built in Europe cost up to three times as much. Some corporations, such as those manufacturing chemicals, took the attitude that most of their products were so unsuited to underdeveloped agricultural societies that manufacturing locally was justified only occasionally as in India where there was a very large domestic market. All the corporations had a policy of training Asians and promoting them to responsible positions when they were qualified. Such men were assets because of their knowledge of the market and their local connections, but the companies resisted government pressure to appoint unsuitable men to important posts.

$$\stackrel{\textstyle\downarrow}{\text{人}}$$

XI

Economic Progress and Problems

The Philippines

The Philippines have made better progress than several other Southeast Asian countries in industrialization. There is hydroelectric power, the raw materials are available for light industries which manufacture consumer goods, and institutions such as the Development Bank provide long-term loans to industry and agriculture. Government enterprise is now limited to projects vital to the economy but unattractive to, or beyond the financial capacity of private investors. Several plans were drawn up by American experts for the development of manufacturing, mining, agriculture, and electricity. Experience showed that the earlier planning was too ambitious and had to be modified. Distinct progress has been made in the expansion of manufacturing, Filipino as well as foreign.

Agriculture is the staple industry and will always remain so. One of the most serious problems is to modify the colonial economy which resulted from the establishment of reciprocal free trade between the Philippines and the United States half a century ago. The result was that production for export concentrated upon a few commodities such as coconut products and sugar, for the sale of which free entry into the American market was essential. Before the war eighty per cent of the exports went to the United States, and since the Philippines was a high-cost producer most of them were unsalable anywhere else. Their free entry was strongly opposed by American interests, particularly the producers of sugar, cotton seed oil, and dairy butter. After

275

World War II it was urgently necessary to restore the Philippine economy, which had suffered very great damage. It was argued that this would be impossible unless free access to the American market were continued. This position was supported by American manufacturers who profited from the free entry of their products into the Philippines, and by companies which had invested there before the war. They were opposed by the same American farm interests as before. The result was a compromise, the Bell Trade Act of 1946. It provided that Philippine sugar, cordage, rice, tobacco, and coconut oil up to limits fixed by quotas should enter the United States free of duty until July 4, 1954. From then onwards the American market would gradually contract until by 1973 none of the above commodities would enter duty-free. This would be done for sugar, cordage, and rice by leaving their absolute quotas intact but subjecting them to a graduated tariff. On July 4, 1954, this would be 5 per cent of the American customs duty, in 1955 10 per cent, and thereafter rising by 5 per cent a year until they were subject to the full rate of duty in 1973. For the other commodities such as coconut oil the duty-free quotas would be decreased by 5 per cent a year from 1954 on until they were extinguished. Products of the United States would enter the Philippines duty-free from 1946 to July 4, 1954. Thereafter they would be subject to a graduated import duty rising from 5 per cent of the Philippine Tariff in 1954 to 100 per cent in 1973. This act, with subsequent modifications, continues to govern trade relations between the two countries. The Philippines benefited by the temporary continuation of the American free market, followed by a period during which it could gradually adjust itself to the loss. The American sugar and coconut-oil companies which had operated in the Philippines before the war received a similar benefit, while the American farm interests could look forward to the eventual elimination of Philippine competition.[1]

The effect of the Bell Act was to encourage the re-establishment of the pre-war system of production of a few agricultural commodities for the American market. Even though they would gradually be excluded, profits could be made in the short run. Moreover, it was hard to decide what products should be substituted in order to end the economic dependence upon the United States. Some progress has been made in lessening this economic dependence, but as yet no completely satisfactory alternative has been found. The livelihood of a very large number of Filipinos still depends upon sales in America. In 1957 54 per cent of the exports were still sold there, and it was still essential to the prosperity of the Philippines.

The Agrarian Problem

The most serious agricultural problem in the Philippines is that of land tenures and rural debt, and it is one with political as well as economic implications. In 1939 35.1 per cent of all farmers were tenants, the large majority being share-tenants. In some respects their position resembled that of the American sharecroppers. Since they were unable to support themselves and their families on their portion of the harvest, which was usually 50 per cent, they were forced to borrow from the Chinese shopkeepers or more often from their Filipino landlords. Their natural improvidence, which could lead them to borrow unnecessarily for a wedding or a cock fight, added to the burden, and the usurious rates of interest ensured that they were hopelessly in debt for the rest of their lives. A man might repay more than he had originally borrowed, and be more heavily in debt than ever. A share-tenant in this position was legally free but in actuality a debt slave. His Filipino creditor-landlord could call on him for extra unpaid farm labor such as road-making, and he was unable to leave his holding. Sometimes the creditor could compel him to vote as he dictated. This combination of land-owner *cum* money lender *cum* local political boss, was called the *cacique*, and in many rural areas he was the directing force in Philippine democracy. The situation did not exist everywhere, and it was at its worst in the overpopulated plains of central Luzon where over half the cultivated land was farmed by tenants. It was most widespread in areas which grew rice, sugar cane, corn, or tobacco, and least serious where the crop was coconuts and abaca.[2] The result was bitter agrarian discontent and periodical peasant revolts, such as that of the Sakdals in 1935, and the Hukbalahaps after World War II.

The beginnings of the system of land tenure went back to the period of Spanish rule, when the Spaniards made use of the former aristocratic rulers or *datos* as village headmen and tax collectors. This enabled the latter to preserve their power over the people and gave them the opportunity to acquire more and more land and reduce freeholders to

277

the status of tenants. The failure to introduce an effective system of survey and land titles also helped them to take over the land of the powerless and ignorant peasants. Thus many of the leading families of pre-Spanish days kept their dominance, and often strengthened it by intermarriage with the Spaniards. This same group improved their position during the American regime. They had the wealth and power which the possession of land gave in an agricultural country, unlike the peasants they could afford to give their children an American education, and when democracy was established they won control of national as well as local government. Hayden wrote of

the "common *taos*" [peasants] who as tenant farmers, renters or virtually landless workers eke out a miserable living from the rich Philippine soil . . . Astonishingly ignorant, for the most part unable to use effectively any language save their local dialect, and economically helpless, it is they who are the most complete victims of the local *cacique*, the remorseless usurer and the exploiting political or religious charlatan. It is they who . . . have suffered the most from the increase in the cost of living that has occurred during the American regime and benefited the least from the economic advantages of the American connection.

Hayden went on to speak of "the chasm between the classes in the Philippines, and the danger of revolt that is faced by the minority of 'haves' that rule the majority of 'have nots.' " [3]

The American government tried to increase ownership of the land by the peasants and protect them from fraudulent seizure of their farms by the wealthy landowners. The measures introduced such as surveys, the issue of land titles, and the offer of free grants of land were a failure because they were never properly carried out. The population increased two and a half times, but the number of farms worked by their owners decreased by about half between 1918 and 1939, while the number operated by tenants increased. In 1939 only 49.2 per cent of all farmers were owners of their farms, 15.6 per cent owned part of their land and rented the rest, while 35.1 per cent were tenants, the large majority being share-tenants. Francis Sayre, the last American High Commissioner before the war, wrote that the bulk of the wealth created during the American regime went to the government, landlords and urban areas, "and served but little to ameliorate living conditions among the almost feudal peasantry and tenantry." "The gap between the mass population and the small governing class has broad-ened, and social unrest has reached serious proportions."[4] Shortly after this was written the Hukbalahap revolt broke out.

The government of the Philippine Republic showed itself as reluc-tant as those of the pre-war period to introduce effective agrarian reforms. Both parties, the Liberals and the Nationalists, were con-trolled by landowners, *caciques*, and their supporters, and only a sturdy optimist would have expected them to sanction measures which would lessen their incomes and their political power. In 1946, when the seri-ousness of the Huk revolt was becoming clear, a law was passed which ostensibly provided that the tenant was to receive 70 per cent and the landowner 30 per cent of the crop. Several ambiguities in the act fa-vored the latter, and in many parts of the Philippines it was not en-forced. Some tenants were ignorant of their legal rights: others could not afford the cost of an appeal to the courts: and in overpopulated districts where there were more peasants than farms the landowner had only to threaten to eject a tenant who demanded his rights to secure his submission. The other measures adopted to help the peasants only touched the fringe of the problem. Banks were established to make them loans, but in practice almost all loans were made to land-owners because they had clear titles to their land, whereas many of the peasants did not. Titles could not be issued until their farms were sur-veyed, and the Bureau of Lands was understaffed and hopelessly in arrears with its work. So the peasant continued to borrow from his landlord or the Chinese. Rural cooperative societies had existed since 1915, but they had been only moderately successful. As in other coun-tries of Southeast Asia, the peasant lacked thrift and foresight and did not understand a money economy. Furthermore, those managing the societies were not adequately trained and supervised by the govern-ment cooperative department, and the landowners and money lenders were opposed to the whole policy.[5]

Another method of attack on the agrarian problem was by directed emigration. Though Luzon was overpopulated, other islands and par-ticularly Mindanao were greatly underpopulated, and various govern-ment schemes were launched to transfer part of the surplus population there. Only about fifty thousand Filipinos were resettled between 1913 and 1950. The very limited success was due to a combination of

279

causes — ineffective execution of the plans, political interference, and the reluctance of the peasants to leave their native villages.[6] The funds voted were very small, and much of them was dissipated by poor planning and corruption. "It is extremely doubtful if all past funds spent on agrarian reform projects equal a single annual budget which now must be expended fighting the Hukbalahap."[7]

Magsaysay was the first Filipino leader to make the interests of the peasants the main point in his policy. He did not work miracles — the hostility of the *caciques* in his own Nationalist party as well as in the Liberal opposition was too strong — but he made some progress in the few years before he was killed. It is doubtful whether he permanently altered the traditional relations between landowner and tenant. He knew that the prime cause of agrarian discontent was land hunger, and that it would not be removed until the peasant was given assured possession of a farm of his own. He broke the Hukbalahap revolt as much by agrarian as by military measures. Rebels who surrendered were settled with government help on their own farms. This was as important as Magsaysay's intelligence service which gave him advance information of the rebel plans, or the military reforms which made an effective striking force out of an inefficient collection of marauders who were looked upon as a plague of locusts by every peaceful peasant — and effectively closed all avenues of information about Huk intentions.

Magsaysay energetically supported the program of moving landless peasants to vacant land in Mindanao and other islands. He at least lessened the intolerable delays of the Bureau of Lands in making surveys without which no land title could be issued. He reformed the government management of the agricultural colonies which had been corrupt and inefficient, and he resettled several thousands of families on them. The number was too few to have any appreciable effect in islands like Luzon where there was a serious amount of overpopulation. He also built side roads so that the peasants could bring their crops to market, and did something to extend the irrigated area. The Philippines were markedly deficient in this respect. The importance of irrigation is that it enables two crops a year to be raised instead of one, and thereby increases the income of the peasant. Rural health was improved by, for example, sinking six thousand artesian wells out of the sixty thousand estimated to be needed. As late as 1945 eighty per cent of the villages drew their water from polluted wells. Magsaysay had not much success in improving farming methods, and in 1960 the output of rice per acre was still little more than a quarter of what it was in Japan. He realized that the ownership of land was not enough: unless the peasant could get loans at a reasonable rate of interest he would soon be heavily in debt to the money lender and quite possibly lose his farm through foreclosure. With financial help from the United States, rural banks and credit cooperative societies made a considerable number of loans, and some of the share-tenants were freed from their burden of debt.[8]

The Agricultural Tenancy Act was passed in 1955 in spite of bitter and protracted opposition in the legislature. The peasant was given greater security against illegal actions such as eviction by the landowner, and it was enacted that his share of the crop might be as much as seventy per cent. An organization was set up to inform the tenants of their rights and prosecute landowners who broke the law. Magsaysay also continued the policy which had been begun before the war of compulsorily buying estates and reselling them in smallholdings to the tenants. This measure was opposed in the legislature with far more determination than his other agrarian reforms, because it struck at the root of the landowners' economic and political power. The law was eventually passed, but the landowners were able to introduce so many amendments that not many peasants benefited from it. The former owner was allowed to retain 740 acres, and this considerably limited the number of tenants who could receive farms. Moreover, the government's payment to the landowner was virtually restricted to cash, whereas Magsaysay had wished to pay in government bonds. In view of the limited revenue and the high price demanded by landowners, the number of estates which could be bought was much restricted. The agency established to carry out the law would seem to have been more concerned with protecting the landowners than helping the tenants, and it was doubtful whether this part of Magsaysay's program was of much help to the peasant.[9]

President Garcia, who succeeded Magsaysay, did not reverse his reforms, but also he did not show much zeal in carrying them out. They were laxly enforced, and the landowners and money lenders could feel that while their position was somewhat weakened it was essentially intact. The national income was considerably greater than before the war, but most of the increase went to the landowners, and the gap between them and the peasants and laborers was widening. The population was growing rapidly and unemployment was great. The peasants' standard of living was not much higher than in 1939, and in 1957 the per capita income was placed at $180. The taxes fell lightly on the rich and heavily on the poor: the income tax was less than twenty per cent of the total taxes, and there was widespread evasion by the wealthy governing class. Professor Golay considered that the economic function of the farmers' cooperatives was endangered because they were becoming enmeshed in politics. In most parts of the Philippines officials of the societies were using their appointments as a steppingstone to local political office. A government investigation in 1959 showed that loan funds were often diverted to unauthorized purposes, a large part of the loans were overdue, and many cooperatives were operating at a loss. The principal reasons appeared to be inadequate training of their officials, gross negligence, and dishonesty. President Macapagal, who succeeded Garcia in 1961, has been in office for too brief a period to draw firm conclusions about his policy. In his state of the nation message on January 28, 1963, he said that the Agricultural Tenancy Act of 1955 had been ineffective and that about half the peasants were still sharecroppers. He promised an energetic policy of converting them into owners of their own farms. It appeared that only about 2 per cent of the tenants received 70 per cent of the crop, about 76 per cent received 50 per cent, and the remainder even less. Tenants were usually in debt to their landowner. In spite of the law forbidding it, verbal contracts for renting farms were frequent; and the landowner controlled his tenants' votes.[10] Magsaysay's limited success showed that a leader armed with the wide constitutional authority and political influence of the Philippine president and with unprecedented popular support could be effectively checked by the governing class. The Hukbalahaps have been reduced to a nuisance, but the islands' history shows a succession of peasant revolts against intolerable conditions. Usually the Communists do not invent grievances: they prefer to exploit whatever they find and make efficient use of it. The Philippine agrarian situation might have been designed for them.

Indonesia

A decade after Indonesian independence was established the brave new world which the leaders promised seemed as far away as ever. In 1941 the country was roughly self-sufficient in the staple food of rice. In 1958 the harvested area was 12 per cent larger than before the war, but the population had grown by 31 per cent, and in every year since 1950 scarce foreign exchange had to be spent to import several hundred thousand tons of rice per annum. Something had been done to improve farming methods, but the output per acre was still less than half that of Japan. The production of coal was about two thirds of what it had been before the war. Despite the plethora of paper plans there was little to show in the field of industrialization except the traditional cottage industries, textile factories which supplied about a third of the needs, and one cement factory. However more plans were being put in train to establish steel industries in Java, Sumatra and Kalimantan (Borneo). Much of the Soviet economic aid promised in 1960 was to be used to finance this development and the building of the largest atomic reactor in Southeast Asia. Transport especially by road was inefficient and uncertain, and inter-island communications continued to be crippled by the government's elimination of the Dutch K.P.M. in 1957. Scarce foreign aid was used to buy or charter some additional ships, and in 1958 a five-year plan was announced to build nineteen shipbuilding yards and two hundred and twenty ships. The distribution of food and other commodities was chaotic — a simultaneous combination of scarcities and gluts.

Inflation was "severe and practically continuous" from 1953 onwards. By January 1961 the cost of living was nearly four times as high as in 1953, and in 1962 ten times. The official exchange rate of the rupiah in 1963 was forty-five to the dollar, but the black-market rate was a thousand to one. A flourishing black market existed for currency as well as commodities. Prices were so high that wage earners could barely afford to buy necessities. At the bottom of the group with the lowest incomes were several million who lived in a state of near or actual impoverishment, often virtually landless, jobless, and homeless. The unemployed ran into the millions, especially in Java, and it was estimated that the number of underemployed might be thirty or forty per cent of the total labor force. High prices and inadequate salaries were reasons for the prevalence of corruption and bribery in the army and civil service. Inflation and the progressive devaluation of the rupiah were caused in part by deficit financing to cover the deficits of anything up to a third of the expenditure which occurred every year from 1951 on. The government borrowed from the Bank of Indonesia and printed paper money.[11] The inflation seriously interfered with plans for economic development because the cost of projects often greatly exceeded the estimates, owing to the rapid rise in prices. Reduction of expenditure to balance the budget was difficult, since for one thing it would have been politically unwise to dismiss a few hundred thousand of the superfluous civil servants. For another, heavy military expenditure was necessary to cope with the half dozen revolts, some of which had been going on for years. Moreover, the army had become a power in the state, and got whatever equipment it asked for. Still another cause was faulty planning and incompetent execution.

There are no trustworthy statistics, but the estimate was hazarded that while some fifty or sixty thousand were better off than formerly — the political leaders, the new business class, officers of the armed forces, and senior civil servants — for the mass of the population the standard of living was perhaps ten or fifteen per cent lower than before the war. Another estimate was that in 1959 the income per person was $81, but that in purchasing power this was fourteen to twenty-one per cent less than in 1938. In 1956 the governor of the Bank of Indonesia made a report which is at least as true today as it was then. He wrote of "budget deficits" (which have grown larger): of a "propensity to import increases" (including luxuries): "decreasing production" in export crops, food, and industry: "the persistent and precarious monetary situation" (the declining value of the rupiah and consequent inflation): "the higher cost of living in rural areas": "the difficulties encountered by the young industries" (for example, embargoes on the import of essential raw materials): and finally "the investment problem" (the lack of local capital and of encouragement to invest foreign capital).

The condition of planned chaos that characterized the Indonesian economy was not the result of the untrammeled action of economic forces. Ambitious plans were drawn up to guide development, and were wrangled over interminably by rival politicians before their exe-

ECONOMIC PROGRESS AND PROBLEMS

cution was entrusted to an army of one million incompetent civil servants who were periodically overruled by an independent corps of army officers, who were equally incompetent in business affairs. The plans laid down admirable goals but were vague as to how they were to be attained. Those who drew them up did not seem to realize that among the basic conditions for success were the restoration of law and order, an efficient civil service, more hard work and fewer strikes (the labor laws established one of the shortest working weeks in the world), and sound fiscal and monetary policies. Even if the planners had emphasized the vital necessity of these measures it was most improbable that any government would ever have tried to enforce anything so unpopular. There was, too, a belief, not confined to Indonesia, that an imposing paper plan was a substitute for carrying it out.

The Five-Year Plan of 1956–1960 was a typical example. It was drawn up by Indonesians with the assistance of American and United Nations experts between 1952 and 1956. It was an elaborate scheme for the expansion of mining, manufacturing, transportation, hydroelectric power, agriculture, and the social services. Vagueness entered in when the planners explained how their proposals were to be paid for. Fifty-five per cent of the cost was to come from the government and forty-five from private enterprise, but the plan was very hazy as to which of the projects were to be carried out by the latter. There was an equal lack of clarity as to what part of the private enterprise was to be Indonesian and how far foreign investment would be sought. Professor Higgins estimated that unless something like $400,000,000 a year of foreign capital were obtained it would not be possible to execute the plan. Even if it were successfully achieved he was doubtful whether it would do much more than keep abreast of the rapid increase of the population.[12]

The plan was finally approved by the legislature in 1958, two years after it was supposed to commence. Very few politicians had any understanding of economics, or realized that it was essential to get foreign capital if the goals were to be reached. The belief was common that freedom from Dutch rule would automatically bring prosperity. Every government was an unstable alliance of uncongenial partners, and the main purpose of the opposition was to disrupt it and take its place. Under these conditions, the principal aim of the cabinet was to avoid any action which might be in the national interest but would jeopardize its tenure of office. The plan would inevitably expand the field of action of some cabinet ministers while lessening that of others, and this would arouse dangerous rivalries. Then too, a government would win far more popularity by continuing to discriminate against foreign interests than by deciding what sphere in the national economy was to be allotted to them. To attack that problem would entail dealing with questions such as the squatters on foreign estates, the epidemic of strikes, and the short working week. So the evil day of reaching a decision was put off for two years while economic conditions went from bad to worse. In the end much of the plan was never carried out because of the disturbed state of the country, and in 1961 it was replaced by the still more grandiose Eight-Year Plan.[13]

Exports

The exports consist principally of oil, tin, and vegetable raw materials. During the final years of Dutch rule about half of the last were grown on Western estates and the rest on smallholdings. Under the republic, estate production has fallen and has not been counterbalanced by an equivalent rise in Indonesian output. The one important exception has been rubber, the principal export, where the percentage coming from the smallholdings has greatly increased. It seems unlikely that peasant production will replace that of the estates in other export crops. Much discussion has gone on about the future of Indonesian rubber, but it is hard to form reliable conclusions, owing to the lack of accurate information, especially about the smallholdings. It is known that the trees on the smallholdings and the greater part of those on the estates are ordinary seedling rubber, and that a considerable proportion are over thirty years old. It has already been said that the Western estates did not replant on an adequate scale, because of the hostile attitude of the government. The evidence available seems to show that the smallholders have carried out a good deal of planting with ordinary seedling rubber. In Sumatra and Borneo, when the yield of rice on a patch of cleared jungle falls the peasant plants it with seedling rubber and clears another piece for a new rice field. On the older rubber holdings the trees have greatly increased in number by natural seeding, so that as the yield of the old trees fails it is replaced by that of the younger ones. They are of course small and stunted and very close together but they do produce rubber. The rough estimate has been made that the smallholders can produce at least 650,000 tons a year, and it would appear that there is a reasonable chance that the export of their rubber will continue.

Emigration

The excessive population of Java was already a very serious problem during the last half century of Dutch rule. From perhaps 4,500,000 in 1815 it grew to an estimated 48,400,000 in 1940. In 1959 it was believed to be 59,700,000, and it may be as many as 92,261,000 in 1980.[14] The island is about the size of New York State and the overwhelming majority of people are peasants. The increased population and low standard of living are to a considerable extent the result of the fall in the death rate brought about by the Dutch medical and health services. The irrigation works and social services ought to have improved living standards, but the effect was canceled by the growth of population. From this point of view, the result of Dutch rule was to enable ten Javanese to exist at the same low standard of living where one had lived a century before. Pelzer in 1940 wrote that

the growth of population resulted in an increased parcelling of the land into dwarf holdings, in the accumulation of large holdings [in scattered parcels by well-to-do Indonesians] . . . in the formation of a class of landless agricultural laborers, in widespread indebtedness, in the growth of tenancy, in the decline of rural incomes, and in poverty, malnutrition and food shortage; briefly, in over population with all its frightful implications.[15]

In addition to extension of irrigation works and a modest amount of industrialization the Dutch adopted a policy of assisted emigration from 1905 onwards to Sumatra and other islands. By 1940 the annual number had risen to 60,000, but the total settled overseas was only 210,679. This was merely a drop in the bucket when the annual increase in Java was 700,000.[16]

The pressure of population at the present time is worse than it was twenty years ago, but the government of the Indonesian Republic has been less successful in promoting emigration. It claimed to have resettled about 125,000 in the islands between 1950 and 1956, and a plan was drawn up to move 2,000,000 between 1956 and 1960. In 1956 26,000 emigrated, but thereafter the scheme was suspended owing to the outbreak of revolts in Sumatra and Celebes. The reasons for the republic's limited success were similar to those which hampered the Dutch. The Javanese were most unwilling to leave their native villages, and they were dissatisfied with conditions in the resettlement areas, which were different from those to which they were accustomed. It is unlikely that the government will be able to move enough Javanese each year to keep pace with the growth of population. Even if it did succeed, this would only be a stopgap and not a permanent cure, for past experience elsewhere has shown that heavy and sustained emigration is followed by a growth of population which eventually brings back the number to what it was originally. The temporary decrease gives a breathing space in which the government may adopt measures which will permanently lessen the pressure of population.

So far as Java is concerned further extension of the cultivated area could only be carried out by a dangerous decrease of the forest reserves which would lead to soil erosion. Owing to the Dutch irrigation works, considerable areas already produce two and sometimes even three crops a year, and not much extension of them is possible. The best hope for agriculture is to increase the yield per acre by the use of fertilizers, higher-yielding seeds, and better farming methods. In time this could double the crops, but it will be a slow business to persuade millions of conservative peasants to break with custom and adopt new ways. It is doubtful whether Javanese food production can be increased fast enough to keep pace with the growth of population. It is in the Outer Islands that the cultivated area can be extended since they are underpopulated and have large tracts of vacant land. Industrialization gives the most hope of coping with Java's population problem. When one considers its very disappointing progress under the republic, one sees clearly that a radically different policy will have to be adopted if it is to be successful. The only effective and fairly immediate remedy would be birth control, and that is no part of the government's policy.[17]

Foreign Aid

The greater part of the capital exported to the Indonesian Republic since 1945 has been grants and loans from the United States, the United

Kingdom, and, since 1956, the Communist states. Between 1951 and 1962 American government aid amounted to $485,800,000 (including the loan of $163,400,000 from the Export-Import Bank), and $17,089,000 came from the British Commonwealth under the Colombo Plan for help to the states of South and southeastern Asia.[18] In addition Germany and other countries of Western Europe granted credits for the purchase of manufactures which were estimated at about $132,000,000. Japan gave some assistance under the Colombo Plan, and up to 1962 an additional $85,658,000 under the Reparations Agreement which was negotiated in 1957. In 1958 Djuanda, the premier, praised American assistance with faint damns by writing that it was "limited if considered relative to the enormous and growing needs of Indonesia." Communist bloc assistance began in 1956 with the grant of a credit for $100,000,000, and by 1961 it was believed to amount to some $1,000,000,000 for military equipment and about $650,000,000 in economic aid. By far the greater part came from Soviet Russia.[19]

Taking the estimate that $400,000,000 of foreign financial assistance a year was necessary, the help received was far less than was required. For this Indonesia had itself to thank. Holland was the country which was most interested and, as the grants made after the war showed, she would have continued her aid if she had been justly treated. The United States and the United Kingdom had many calls upon them, and there was a limit to what they could afford to give. Both favored the countries which were of most importance to them, and Indonesia came low upon their lists. Moreover, Indonesia deliberately cut itself off from private investment and assumed that foreign governments would carry the whole burden. Sukarno declared that he did not want private investment but only government loans and grants. These should be on a generous scale and made without any conditions. By contrast the Philippines and the Federation of Malaya got the best of both worlds — substantial government aid and also private investment. One might add that Indonesia dissipated part of the funds it received in prestige spending, though in this it sinned in numerous company. With the new states a steel industry and a national airline rank with membership in the United Nations as certificates of respectability — as essential as her marriage lines to a Victorian female. Indonesia has them, as well as a monumental sports stadium which Russia agreed to build.

Indeed Indonesia will soon be ahead of the Joneses, for part of the Soviet Russian credits of 1961 (which have to be repaid) were earmarked for the largest atomic reactor and the only airplane carrier in Southeast Asia. Wiser uses could have been found for the credits in a country where most of the people are still far below the pre-war standard of living.

A competition seems to be developing between the American and Communist governments to win friends and influence people in Indonesia by providing aid. Sukarno realizes the advantage of being wooed by both sides and of getting them to bid against one another for his favor. He admires the freedom from political opposition that is enjoyed by Communist governments and their methods of forcing the pace of industrialization. At the same time he does not want to break with the West because he would then be forced to rely solely on Soviet assistance. Not only would he get less but he might come under Communist control. So his policy is to play off one side against the other and receive aid from both. To date this policy has been successful.

The Eight-Year Plan

An eight-year plan for economic development was inaugurated by President Sukarno on January 1, 1961. The members of the committee which drew up the plan were appointed by him more for political reasons than because of their grasp of Indonesian economic and financial problems. Very little use was made of Indonesian and foreign economic experts. One is tempted to describe their thinking as woolly-minded. The principles of Indonesia's socialist economy were laid down but frequently the exact meaning was vague and obscure. The basic economic data on which the proposals were based were often of dubious validity. On this shaky foundation the planners based their plan to raise the standard of living by an ambitious development of industrialization, transport, and agriculture. On the financial side there were "fantastic expectations" of the amount of revenue which the government could count upon to finance the plan by the exploitation of natural resources in partnership with foreign private business.

The heaviest emphasis was upon industrialization, in which $1,130,000,000 was to be invested at the official foreign exchange rate of forty-five rupiahs to the dollar. Some of the projects were entirely reasonable, such as a great expansion of the production of hydroelectric power, and the building of a fertilizer factory with a $33,000,000 loan from the American Export-Import Bank. There was the inevitable prestige spending such as a blast furnace with a capacity of 1,000,000 tons in Borneo and a steel mill with a capacity of 100,000 tons in Banten near Djakarta, both to be built with Soviet financial help. Railway, road, and air transport were to be improved and enlarged, and merchant shipping was to be increased to 260,000 tons to replace the service provided by the K.P.M. Expansion of the production of textiles was allotted $640,000,000; $560,000,000 were to be spent on agriculture so that consumption could increase by 15 per cent and Indonesia could be made self-sufficient in food by the end of 1962. To accomplish this the production of rice would have to be increased by two thirds. Among the measures contemplated were expansion of the cultivated area, the distribution of higher-yielding seed and fertilizer and the teaching of improved farming methods. This part of the plan was linked with the law of 1960 by which each family of peasants was to receive a five-acre farm at the least. No attempt was made to explain how the law was to be carried out in Java, where owing to the size of the population only about a third of the peasant families could be given farms of this size.

The total cost of the projects was 240,000,000,000 rupiahs, and this at the official rate of exchange of 45 rupiahs to the dollar was $5,300,000,000. Half of this amount was supposed to come from the profits of state enterprises, the sale of capital and consumer goods, and from domestic savings. The planners assumed that the other half of the cost must be in the form of foreign exchange. They considered that Indonesia already had a larger foreign debt than it could afford to repay. (This conclusion was reached before the government contracted an additional debt of hundreds of millions for the purchase of military equipment from Soviet Russia.) The planners therefore decided that the foreign exchange must be obtained from the exploitation of natural resources by foreign private capital. This would work in partnership with the government, and Indonesians would direct all enterprises. It was not clear whether foreign investors were to provide the whole of the cost or whether part of it would come from Indonesian sources, government and private. Foreign companies, however, were expected to furnish a very large part of the funds. At least $1,500,000,000 of new capital was to be invested by the oil companies, and $1,000,000,000 was to be spent in replanting rubber trees. The plan took it for granted that Western companies were so eager to invest that the government had only to make known its willingness to receive their money and they would compete with one another to be accepted. The assumption was made that the government's share of the profits from the sale abroad of oil, rubber, and so on would give it $2,462,500,000 toward the cost of the development plan. This would still leave a deficit in foreign exchange of about $237,000,000 over the eight years.

Sukarno accepted the plan but insisted that he wanted foreign government loans and not private investment. The statistics given were so dubious that they made it very difficult to appraise the plan fairly. The one thing certain was that Indonesia expected an exceedingly large inflow of foreign capital in the form of private investment and/or government assistance. Either alternative would require so complete a change in Western policy as to be highly improbable. It was doubtful whether Russia would be willing to assume the whole burden, in addition to the $367,000,000 in economic aid which she had already agreed to give during the next twelve years.[20] Foreign observers were also very much afraid that the part of the cost which Indonesia itself must provide was impossibly high. They feared that it would be met by deficit financing on a larger scale than ever before and a corresponding growth of inflation.

The carrying out of the plan was neglected in 1961 and 1962 because Sukarno was absorbed in the acquisition of Dutch New Guinea. He himself admitted that 80 per cent of the national revenue was diverted to his New Guinea project and to the suppression of some of the Indonesian revolts against his government. The revenue was less than the expenditure by 34 per cent. The deficit was covered by deficit financing: the supply of paper money increased by 39 per cent in 1961 and even more in 1962, and the result of this was that prices in 1962 rose to ten times what they had been in 1953 and the black-market rate for the rupiah rose to 1,000 to the dollar. This meant that all the eight-year plan's estimates of the cost of the development projects must be sharply increased. Sukarno could not be accused of exaggeration when he said in November 1962 that there was an urgent need of foreign loans "without strings," and that Indonesia was suffering from runaway inflation, falling production, rising expenditure, and a huge outlay on the armed forces. During this same period Sukarno lessened his ability to meet his previous foreign obligations by borrowing $1,000,000,000 from Soviet Russia to buy military equipment. The Soviet government is not a philanthropist: when it gives military or economic aid it exacts an equal repayment in exports. The result is a drastic lessening of Indonesia's ability to repay Western government loans by the foreign exchange earned through the sale of its exports abroad. More than ever before Indonesia needs massive financial aid from foreign governments, and a very charitable attitude toward terms of repayment. It seems unlikely that the Communist bloc will come to the rescue, and Sukarno can argue that to stabilize economic conditions and then carry out the eight-year plan American aid on a large scale is essential. If it were denied, the Indonesian Communist party would grow in strength by capitalizing upon the effects of Sukarno's New Guinea policy upon his people's standard of living. Sukarno had an interview with President Kennedy and the joint communiqué issued on April 25, 1961, announced that an American "top level economic team" would be sent to Indonesia to advise on the methods by which the United States could help to achieve the goals of the eight-year plan. The American mission recommended that additional aid of roughly $200,000,000 be given to Indonesia during the next five years. About three quarters of the amount would be a loan and the remainder a grant. The existing aid which had averaged $20,000,000 per annum during the previous five years should also be continued. The total assistance given by the Agency for International Development (A.I.D.) over the next five years would be raised to $300,000,000 at the annual rate of $60,000,000. This would be exclusive of the supply of surplus food under the Agricultural Trade Development and Assistance Act. The recommendations made by the mission were not formally adopted by the American government, but they "served as a reference in relation to program formulation." What might be described as the normal A.I.D. aid was increased in 1962, but the government considered that Sukarno must show that he intended to put his economic house in order before it contributed an extra $200,000,000 to his eight-year plan. The A.I.D. expressed its policy as follows.

We would be prepared to give increased assistance to achieve economic development in Indonesia if the Indonesian Government adopts and indicates clearly its intentions to implement a realistic stabilization program. Until some progress is made on stabilization and various areas of economic policy reform, there is little to be gained by providing capital development assistance. However, if a satisfactory stabilization program is put into effect, we believe the U.S. and other Free World nations should then provide assistance to a long-term development program. Essentially then we are waiting for certain steps by the Indonesians before considering increases in our assistance.

Sukarno announced that he would improve his country's shattered economy by concentrating upon the carrying out of the eight-year plan.

This was the rational policy, but instead the evidence showed that he assisted in the Borneo revolt against the Federation of Malaysia. In March 1963 his foreign minister, Subandrio, tried to enlist the cooperation of the Philippines in the "maintenance of security" against Malaysia "which endangers this area." [21] Prisoners and documents captured by the British in Borneo proved that Sukarno was feeding the revolt, and in his speeches he urged Indonesians to join the rebels.

Yet again Indonesia's revenue was diverted to an adventure in imperialism when the imperative need to use it for the improvement of the country's economic condition was greater than ever before. This destroyed the prospect of Western financial aid on a substantial scale. In June 1963 the Development Assistance Committee which included the United States and the United Kingdom was favorably inclined toward helping Indonesia, which urgently needed a loan of $390,000,000. The International Monetary Fund was prepared to grant a credit of $50,000,000. Both offers were conditional on Sukarno's carrying out his program of economic stabilization. When he plunged into his Borneo adventure both offers were withdrawn. Soon afterward he forbade all trade with Malaya. This will do more harm to Indonesia than to Singapore. No Indonesian wants to receive payment for his rubber and other exports in depreciated rupiahs when he can sell them for Straits dollars, and years of experience showed that his government was unable to prevent smuggling across the Straits of Malacca from Sumatra to Singapore. Indonesia lost heavily in revenue and foreign exchange when it tried merely to control trade. Now that trade is forbidden altogether smuggling will increase, and the government will lose more revenue than ever. The attempts of the Indonesian navy to stop the traffic could lead to a clash with Malayan or British warships. Indonesian gunboats have shown scant respect for Malayan territorial waters in their pursuit of vessels which they suspected of smuggling. Their habit has been to beat a hasty retreat when they saw a Malayan or British warship, but the time might come when they did not depart fast enough to avoid a naval action. Russia appears to be unwilling to grant further economic aid on an extensive scale, and China is not in a position to give much help. There remains the United States. The American government has been influenced by the undoubted possibility that if further help were refused the economic situation might get so much worse that Sukarno's Communist supporters might be able to take control. As against this, every consideration of prudence and common sense should have told Sukarno that his imperialistic policy toward Dutch New Guinea had so worsened the economic situation that he must concentrate on endeavors to improve it. Instead of doing so he forced a quarrel on the Federation of Malaysia and the United Kingdom, and followed this up by taking control of British investments in Indonesia and forbidding all trade with Malaysia, even though he must have realized that his actions would result in further deterioration of economic conditions in Indonesia. Sometimes there are people whom it is not possible to assist. The Clay Committee advised in 1963 that Indonesia should not receive economic help "unless it puts its internal house in order, provides fair treatment to foreign creditors and enterprises, and refrains from international adventures." This advice seems to be exceedingly reasonable.

Burma
The principal economic accomplishment of the British in Burma was to make it the world's leading exporter of rice. In the lower valley and delta of the Irrawaddy river an almost uninhabited jungle was transformed into fertile rice fields. Of the roughly 12,500,000 acres sown with rice, about 10,000,000 were in this area, and the annual export rose to around 3,500,000 tons. The rice was not grown on large European estates but by Burman peasants on their farms. They worked

about six months of the year and were very averse to accepting the advice of the Agricultural Department to increase the crop by improving their methods. They felt this to be unnecessary since failures were almost unknown owing to the fertility of the soil and the abundant rainfall. The credit needed by the peasants was supplied to some extent by Burman and Chinese money lenders but very largely by the *chettyars,* especially in Lower Burma. They were a hereditary banking caste of Hindus from the Madras Presidency. The combination of astute money lenders and unsophisticated and thriftless cultivators produced the result that was to be expected. The peasants borrowed far more than they required, spending whatever was left over from the cost of farming. Sooner or later the price of rice fell, they were unable to meet their payments and the money lender foreclosed the mortgage. The farmers then became tenants on the land they had once owned or landless laborers. Before the Great Depression the loss of land was gradual, but after it the price of rice fell sharply, with a rapid increase in foreclosures. By 1936 the *chettyars* owned about a quarter of Lower Burma's 10,000,000 acres of rice land, and had heavy mortgages on perhaps as much more. Other farms became the property of Burman and Chinese money lenders. It was estimated that only 15 per cent of the land of Lower Burma was free from mortgage.[22]

Very great damage was done during the war. Owing to the cessation of the export trade and the requisitions of the Japanese army the peasants allowed much of their land to go out of cultivation. By 1945 the acreage under rice was about 45 per cent of what it had been in 1940. Heavy bombing attacks were made by the British and American air forces on the lines of communication, to soften up the Japanese as a preliminary to the invasion which ended in their total defeat. The harbor works at Rangoon, the principal seaport, were destroyed: communications were disrupted by the destruction of 90 per cent of the river steamers, the greater part of the railway rolling stock, and the bridges: and large sections of Rangoon and other cities were wrecked. There was an orgy of looting and scrounging, and respect for property rights and law and order disappeared. Conditions were much worse than in pre-war Burma, which had been outstanding for the number of violent crimes and murders. In 1942 and 1945 first the British and then the Japanese armies were defeated and abandoned their equipment, and firearms could be obtained by practically everyone. Violent crime and dacoity (gang robbery) multiplied, and their suppression and the repair of war damage were made still more difficult by the rebellions which began in 1948. For several years they threatened the very existence of the government, and while today most of the rebels are little more than bandits, lawlessness and insecurity still prevail over considerable areas.

The Five-Year Plan

The Anti-Fascist People's Freedom League (A.F.P.F.L.) which controlled the government after the war was hostile to the British and Indian firms which had developed Burma's natural resources. It was determined to replace them by Burman enterprises, as well as to raise the standard of living and build a welfare state on Socialist principles. Pre-war business men had been Europeans, Indians, and Chinese, and there were no Burmans with the training and experience to take over from them. The few Burmans who had money preferred to invest it in land and urban housing. This meant that the government itself must finance and control economic life, using as its instrument the civil service. As in Indonesia the political leaders and the officials were ignorant of business and finance, and greatly overestimated their ability to cope with them. Ambitious plans divorced from reality were drawn up to revolutionize the whole economy in a brief period of time, with no clear idea of how to transform these visions into reality. Unlike Indonesia, many of the most important officials were Burmans, because British policy since 1923 had been gradually to substitute Asians for Europeans. Of the 3,200 senior civil servants in all branches of government (administration, police, judiciary, and the specialized services such as health, agriculture, engineers) 715 were Europeans and the remainder Asians. Of the 145 who held senior positions in the administrative service 81 were Europeans and 64 Asians. Burma had the advantage over Indonesia that there was a fairly large number of experienced Asians to take over the civil service, since the government of the republic dismissed the Europeans. Its difficulty was that the plans for a welfare state required far more departments and staff than during the British regime, and the nucleus of trained officials was diluted by a very large number of untrained political appointees. More-

297

over, the former were administrators without experience; the natural result: blunders, delays, failures.[23]

An American firm was employed to draw up a Five-Year Plan which was intended to repair wartime damage and increase production to a point which would give a higher standard of living than before the war. It was a comprehensive and very ambitious scheme which covered every phase of the national economy and emphasized industrialization. Prestige spending was represented by a steel mill, an airline, and coastal and ocean-going steamships. The plan, completed in 1953, was severely criticized by the International Bank and by American and British authorities as unrealistic for the following reasons. The planners' estimate of the government revenue was very optimistic: they made no allowance for the acute shortage of administrative and technical personnel without whom it could not be carried out, and the insecurity caused by the rebellions. It looked as if they had drawn up the plan without first making an adequate study of the resources of the country and the characteristics of its people. Decidedly too little attention was paid to agriculture, and industrialization was over-emphasized. The government rejected the advice of the International Bank.[24]

The total cost of the Five-Year Plan was estimated at $1,650,000,000, and success depended on obtaining large amounts of foreign exchange to cover the heavy expenditure on imports. The bulk of it came from the government's monopoly of the sale of rice abroad. In 1954 the price fell much more sharply than the planners had foreseen. The government found it hard to dispose of its rice, and this was one reason for the barter agreement with Russia. The aid received from the United States, the British Commonwealth, and the United Nations was much too limited to fill the gap. Attempts were made to interest private Western capital in investing, but they had little success as was pointed out earlier. The International Bank made a small loan on condition that the plan be cut down to manageable size. Development fell far short of expectations owing to the lack of foreign aid on an extensive scale combined with the very inadequate supply of Burmans with the necessary technical and managerial qualifications. Mismanagement and dishonesty added to the difficulties: in 1954 the Premier, U Nu, stated that 60 per cent of the yearly expenditure was wasted in ill-conceived plans, bribes, and excessive profits. Sometimes projects cost far more than the original estimate, and the output of commodities from the state factories was disappointing. Eventually a revised Four-Year Plan was drawn up which sharply curtailed the expenditure on industry and increased that on agriculture, irrigation, and forestry.[25]

A moderate amount of progress has been made in industrialization. The government operates factories which partly supply the demand for, e.g., cotton textiles, jute sacks, sugar, bricks, and cement. An expensive steel mill was built for making light steel goods, and is run by electricity because the coal is poor and scanty. The derelict equipment of the British and Japanese armies was estimated to provide somewhere between 25,000 and 175,000 tons of scrap steel, and further supplies of steel ingots could be bought from India. In 1960 the output was about 10,000 tons of hardware and steel bars. In 1962 the Chinese Minister of Finance in the P.A.P. government of Singapore made an accurate and unflattering appraisal of the record of government ownership of factories which applies to Burma and indeed to most of Southeast Asia. With the exception of two or three countries all these efforts have ended in costly failures. Factories have been established without due regard for a continuous supply of raw materials: management lacks business experience and even where there is no total collapse, the cold blast of foreign competition quickly puts these state enterprises out of business. The net result of it all is waste of valuable internal resources and a frittering away of scarce foreign exchange in the purchase of machinery which ultimately has to be abandoned.[26]

The production of hydroelectric power is increasing, and harbor works and the railway are being reconstructed. In 1958 the marked improvement in security made it possible to reintroduce trains that ran at night, but the tonnage of river steamships is still less than it was before the Japanese invasion. The production of teak and minerals is still much less than in 1940.[27]

Agriculture

The Japanese conquest in 1942 solved after a fashion the problem of rural debt. Nearly half the Indians fled, thousands being killed by the Burmans or dying of want as they made their way over the rough mountain trails to India. Most of them never returned, and from that time on the Burman peasants made no further payments to the *chettyars* and seized their land. The government of the republic shared the peasants' hostility to the money lenders, and also it had to win their support by outbidding the Communists who advocated the abolition of rent and taxes. In 1947 all agricultural debts incurred prior to October 1, 1946, were canceled, tenants were given security of tenure, and rents were frozen at pre-war levels. The Land Nationalization Act of 1948 authorized the nationalization of all land with the exception of what belonged to the Buddhist monasteries or was cultivated by the owner himself. Each farmer was allowed to keep up to fifty acres. Noncultivators such as *chettyars* were forbidden to own land, and it might not be sold or transferred to anyone who was not a citizen of Burma. The land which was nationalized was to be allotted to Burman peasants by village land committees. The acts abolished the crippling burdens of debt and high rents and ensured that the land would be owned by actual cultivators. The money lender and the landlord were virtually legislated out of existence. This was a heavy blow particularly to the *chettyars*, for the compensation which the government agreed to pay them was, they complained, completely inadequate. Moreover, the payment was indefinitely postponed since the available foreign exchange was needed for other purposes. The intention was to nationalize 10,000,000 acres, but during the following seven years only about 6 per cent was nationalized and divided because of the collapse of law and order caused by the revolts, the lack of trained personnel, and the maneuvers of A.F.P.F.L. local politicians who used nationalization for their own ends. They controlled the party machine in their districts, and granted farms and agricultural loans to the peasants who joined it.[28]

To replace the *chettyar* the government itself provided farm loans. It was and still is hampered by lack of sufficient funds, and especially at first the peasants saw no reason why they should make repayment. At one time half the loans were unpaid, but by 1960 collection had considerably improved. The aim of government was to restore the pre-war export of about three and a half million tons of rice, as well as increase diversification by expanding the area under other crops. To do this it was necessary to reclaim about 2,500,000 acres which had been allowed to go out of cultivation during the Japanese occupation and the subsequent revolts. Systems of drainage and irrigation works must also be restored, and the poor yield per acre raised. Progress lagged behind the goals laid down in the plan owing to lack of funds and trained personnel. By 1960 the acreage under rice had been raised to 83 per cent of the pre-war average, while for all crops it was 91. Owing to a somewhat increased use of fertilizer, the yield of rice per acre was 12 per cent higher than before the war, but it was still barely half that of Japan. The production of rice in 1960 was 93 per cent of the pre-war average, and export had risen to about two million tons. The population was larger than before the war, and the consumption per head was only 85 per cent of what it had been in 1938.[29] The general condition of the people was better than it had been a decade earlier, but it fell far short of the standard of living which was expected to follow political independence. The military dictatorship intends to further the development of farming rather than industry, at least for the next few years. It hopes to bring the production and export of rice back to the pre-war level.

South Viet Nam

The principal area of fighting in the revolt against French rule was in the north, in what today is the state of North Viet Nam. There was however a good deal of guerilla action in the present state of South Viet Nam, and serious damage was done. The extensive irrigation works which the French had built in the delta of the Mekong river had made it the third largest rice exporting country in the world. By the end of the war the export was negligible, and Ho Chi Minh's guerillas had established their control over large tracts of the countryside. The agreement in the peace treaty that they were to be withdrawn was broken, and they have remained as a fifth column which is far more dangerous today than it was in 1954. The resettlement of the 850,000 refugees from North Viet Nam was another serious problem.

The revenue was completely inadequate, and financial collapse would have been inevitable if the new state had not received foreign assistance. A moderate amount of financial and technical help came from France, but by far the largest part was provided by the United States. In 1955–1960 American aid amounted to $1,387,200,000 or around 62 per cent of the total budget. The United States paid for about 90 per cent of the cost of the army of a hundred and fifty thousand men and furnished about $500,000 of military equipment. The estimate was made that at least 68 per cent of American aid was spent on defense. The greater part of the remainder was used to pay for imports, and the rest was spent on economic aid and the resettlement of the refugees.[30]

The typical farmer in South Viet Nam was the smallholder, but in what used to be the French colony of Cochinchina 45 per cent of the area was occupied by estates of varying size. The French favored this development in the rich rice lands which they had created in the delta of the Mekong river. There were about twenty-five hundred landowners of whom some were French and the rest Vietnamese. Writing before World War II Miss Thompson was of the opinion that the Vietnamese landowners and money lenders exploited their compatriots more than any other race.[31] Most of the landowners were absentees and their estates were divided into smallholdings worked by tenants. The usual rent was forty per cent of the crop, and this left the tenant with about fifty per cent after he had paid the expenses of cultivation. In emergencies he had to borrow, and here as elsewhere in Asia a large part of his debt was to meet the cost of funerals and marriages. The main source of credit was the landlord whose interest charges were usurious, or the Vietnamese and *chettyar* money lenders who were worse. The burden of debt was heavy, and the landlord's income depended on usury more than on rents. The government tried to prevent usury mainly by laws forbidding excessive rates of interest, but this method failed as it did elsewhere. Banks were established to make loans at moderate rates, but this policy failed to help the tenants because loans were granted only on better security than they could offer. The result was that the landlords borrowed large sums at ten per cent interest, and re-lent to their tenants at up to seventy per cent. So the richest rice lands of southern Viet Nam became a center of agrarian distress and discontent. Yet another problem was that the yield per acre was low, owing to the reluctance of the cultivators to adopt the improvements in farming methods urged upon them by the French agricultural service.[32]

Ngo Dinh Diem, the President of South Viet Nam, limited to 100 hectares (247 acres) the amount of rice land which could be owned by an individual. In spite of the strong opposition of the landowners, in 1956 he compulsorily bought the remainder and resold it to the tenants at the same price. France provided the money to buy out the French owners. The result was that about 300,000 tenants became freeholders, but between 750,000 and 900,000 peasants continued to rent their farms from landlords. Most of the latter were the owners of smaller estates, with less than 25 hectares (61.75 acres) apiece. The tenants' rent was reduced to at most twenty-five per cent of the average gross crop, and they were given a security of tenure hitherto lacking by the enactment that the lease must last from three to five years. The government also began to provide loans at reasonable rates of interest. The remaining tenants are not satisfied with these improvements in their situation, for what they want is to own their own land. Furthermore, the government finds it hard to enforce its laws because the landlords do their best to evade them. On the whole, the tenants are better off than under the French regime, but they still have grievances which the Communists can use to advantage.[33] Ngo Dinh Diem tried to improve farming methods and encouraged the cultivation of such other crops as cotton to lessen the excessive dependence on rice and rubber for export. As told elsewhere, he favors state rather than private ownership of industry, but his program has made only limited headway.

Cambodia and Laos

In Cambodia tenancy is rare and most of the peasants are freeholders. The government's Five-Year Plan of 1960 emphasizes agricultural improvements — the extension of irrigation works and flood control, for example. A seaport has been built, the roads and railways have been improved and extended, and the education and medical services enlarged. The cost of the program has been far larger than the revenue and most of the funds have been provided by the United States, France, the British Commonwealth, Russia, and China. The government, which is to say Prince Norodom Sihanouk, has been very adroit in obtaining economic help from both sides in the cold war, playing off one against the other with great success. Laos too drew up a five-year plan for extension of the very inadequate system of communications, agricultural betterment, and social services. It was more successful even than Cambodia in acquiring financial assistance, particularly from the

United States, and at any rate the cliques which controlled the government, profited greatly.

North Viet Nam

North Viet Nam inherited a very serious problem of overpopulation in the rich rice-growing delta of the Red river. The French built drainage and irrigation works on a large scale to control the floods and extend the irrigated area, but their efforts were more than neutralized by the growth of population. At the end of World War II about seven and a half million were crowded into six thousand square miles, and the demographic density was over twelve hundred and fifty inhabitants per square mile. Almost all the cultivators were freeholders, but the growth of population led to the subdivision of the farms until a large part of the peasants owned too little land to support themselves. Three fifths of them had less than an acre apiece. The only source of credit was the Chinese or Vietnamese money lender, and the consequence was a crippling burden of debt. Often the legal owner was virtually a tenant, obligated to make heavy payments to the money lender who allowed him to remain on the holding. At other times the money lender built up a large estate through foreclosure of mortgages. Such estates were farmed by sharecroppers "whose wretchedness is increased by their debts." The French tried to lessen the population by sponsoring emigration — the greater part of Indochina is underpopulated — but most of the peasants refused to move because the tombs of their ancestors were generally on their farms.[34]

Ho Chi Minh was studiously moderate in his agrarian policy during the years of the colonial revolt: he wanted the support of the landowners as well as the peasants. The latter were promised ownership of their farms, and a minority were given this by confiscating land owned by the French or by Vietnamese supporters of Bao Dai. Ho Chi Minh also canceled all debts contracted before 1945, and lowered rents and rates of interest. Landowners and money lenders who supported him retained their property. It was not until 1955, after the final defeat of France, that Ho Chi Minh disclosed that his ultimate goal was the Communist policy of collectivization of the land. In 1955–1956 the holdings of landowners and slightly more well-to-do peasants were abolished and many of them killed with great brutality. Such flagrant injustice was shown that it provoked a peasant revolt, which was suppressed by the army. The confiscated land was distributed in very small amounts among the poor peasants and landless laborers; but there were altogether too many people in the Red river delta to give each of them a farm of adequate size. For the time being the Communists felt it expedient not to provoke more opposition by collectivizing the land. Its future introduction was made easier by destroying the more prosperous peasants who would have taken the lead in opposing it. The production of rice seems to be slightly larger than before the war. The Communists have somewhat improved farming methods, and they appear to have repaired irrigation works which were damaged during the fighting.[35] Under the French, North Viet Nam brought in rice from the south to feed its too many people, and Ho Chi Minh has a very practical reason for trying to get control of South Viet Nam. Most formerly French mines and factories have been taken over by the government; those still in private hands are strictly controlled. China, Russia, and Czechoslovakia have sent technical personnel, machinery, and other industrial assistance.

Thailand

Thailand was the only one of the three rice-exporting countries which was unharmed in the war. Its principal exports were rice and tin, and the foreign exchange earned by their sale, together with financial aid which came chiefly from the United States, made it possible to carry out plans for economic development. The government engaged extensively in trade and industry but the International Bank found that most of its enterprises were run at a loss from lack of business experience, inefficiency, and sometimes corruption. Some light industries were established by Thai or foreign capital. Ninety per cent of the people are peasants, and the majority own their own farms, although there is the usual debt to the money lender. Production is low, and the government's plans have emphasized the building of irrigation and hydroelectric works and diversification of crops to lessen the excessive reliance on rice. There has been heavy expenditure on the improvement and extension of port facilities, railways, and roads. In the past the inadequacy of the system of transportation hampered agricultural development.

The Federation of Malaya

Compared with many of the other countries of Southeast Asia the Federation seems to be in an enviable position. The government is stable, law and order are maintained, and the Chinese Communist revolt was crushed. There are no large estates with *caciques* and sharecroppers as in the Philippines. Rubber and tin have been reasonably prosperous, and replanting with high-yielding rubber has on the whole made satisfactory progress. The social services are good for an Asian country, and Malaya has a well-developed system of roads, railways, and port facilities. Investment of British capital is growing, and the standard of living is the highest in South and Southeast Asia. About ten years ago the annual cash income of the peasant was estimated to be around $220. A rough estimate of 1960 put it at about $300 in the Federation and $400 in Singapore.

Under the surface the situation is not so satisfactory. The principal problem is to provide employment for the rapidly growing population. In 1947 it was 4,870,000, by 1959 it was 6,800,000, and by 1980 it is likely to be 14,000,000. The rate of increase, over 3 per cent per annum, is one of the highest in the world. In India it is about 1.9 per cent. The government's solution is the extension of agriculture combined with the encouragement of manufacturing. It has been generally agreed for years that Malaya is far too dependent on rubber and tin, which between them comprise about 80 per cent of the exports. Uneasiness is increased by the competition from the cheaper synthetic rubber. The difficulty is to find profitable substitutes. A moderate amount of palm oil and coconuts is produced, and tea and cocoa can be grown to a limited extent. The area under rice could be largely extended, and this would relieve Malaya from the heavy expense of importing the bulk of its staple food. For thirty years the government has been encouraging the Malays to grow more rice, but with only moderate success. This is harder work and less profitable as a rule than rubber, and the Malay smallholders fail to see why they should leave the more lucrative crop to the other races. As regards mining, Malaya has only tin, some iron ore and bauxite, and a small amount of poor coal. It has quite large potentialities for developing hydroelectric power. The domestic market is small, and this limits the possibilities of manufacturing.

Another economic problem which could cause serious trouble is that the Malays resent the predominance of the Chinese in the business field. Until after World War II the Malays preferred to be subsistence farmers and fishermen and had no share in trade, mining, and estate agriculture. Today they are resentful that they used to be poor men in a poor country, whereas now they are poor men in a rich country. Secretly, too, they are fearful lest the economic power of the Chinese lead to political control. They are demanding that the government give them special assistance to improve their economic position, so that they can hold their own against the Chinese. The difficulty here is the cost, which would have to be paid mainly by the Chinese. They assert their willingness and even anxiety to help, but they are thinking in terms of a few million dollars a year. A decade ago it was estimated that to put the Malays economically on a par with the Chinese would cost about $100,000,000 a year, for ten or fifteen years.[36] Chinese altruism does not contemplate paying this amount in addition to the present taxes. This Malay grievance is one of the factors which might upset the Chinese-Malay alliance on which the stability of the government depends.

The aims of the Federation's First Five-Year Plan (1956–1960) were to expand agriculture, encourage industrialization by providing such basic prerequisites as hydroelectric power, and enlarge the social services. Rubber was given financial help to cover part of the cost of replanting with high-yielding rubber. The degree of success on the estates was described in the chapter on Western investment. It was also essential to persuade the smallholders to replant, since the greater part of their trees were near the end of their economic life. Any property of less than a hundred acres was classified as a smallholding. The number of smallholders and the acreage were not known with any accuracy, but the total area was believed to be between one million five hundred thousand and one million seven hundred thousand acres. The larger smallholdings of twenty-five to one hundred acres were believed to number 6,845, most of them the property of Chinese business men and Indian money lenders. The bulk of the acreage was divided among about 386,000 smallholdings owned by Malays, the majority being between three and six acres. Down to 1956 the attempts to persuade the smallholders to replant were not very successful, but thereafter there was a marked improvement each year. Between 1948 and the end of 1959 the smallholders replanted about three hundred twenty thousand acres and in addition new-planted eighty thousand acres, most of it with high-yielding rubber.

This would be decidedly encouraging if it were not for one thing. It is believed — for no one really knows — that a high percentage of the replanting has been on the large smallholdings owned by the Chinese and Indians, and not on the small ones owned by Malays. A priori this is not very surprising. An official may warn a Malay that his trees will soon be useless, but what impresses him is that they still yield and that if he fells them he will lose all or most of his income for the next seven years. Moreover, it is very hard to replant less than twenty-five acres, for the older trees cut off the sunlight from the saplings and their roots take most of the food from the soil.[37] Apart from rubber the government has stressed the increased production of rice through expansion of irrigation works and improvement of farming methods. Unlike some of the other governments of Southeast Asia the Federation has not itself gone into business. It has resisted the temptation to build a steel mill or establish a line of ocean-going steamers, and instead it has tried to attract private capital.

To finance its economic program the government relied primarily on the revenue from the traditional mainstays of tin and above all rubber. Since their prices have fluctuated violently, the federal treasurer has been rather like the managing director of a corporation who was never very sure how much profit he could count on in the ordinary way of business, but who always bought a few tickets in the Irish sweepstakes because he had an uncanny flair for drawing quite a few winners. Over the past few years the price of rubber has been fairly high and the treasury did well out of it. The government also raised domestic loans, and in addition it received substantial financial and technical assistance from the British Commonwealth and loans from the International Bank and the United States. In these ways the Federation of Malaya was able to find most of the funds needed to finance its First Five-Year Plan. A Second Five-Year Plan has been begun which emphasizes improvement of agriculture and industrialization. It is too early to predict whether the government will be able to create adequate employment, satisfy the economic aspirations of the Malays and raise the standard of living.

308

XII

Foreign Aid

Government aid to underdeveloped countries as a regular part of the annual budget did not exist before 1939. Very occasionally a colonial power might give financial help to a dependency in exceptional circumstances. The almost invariable rule, however, was that it must live within its income, and not expect the taxpayers of the ruling power to subsidize it. The scale of its social services was fixed by the size of the colony's revenue, together with such loans as it was able to float locally or in the money market of the metropolitan power. The first real break with this policy came in 1940 with the enactment by the United Kingdom Parliament of the Colonial Development and Welfare Act. It provided $20,000,000 a year "for any purpose likely to promote the development of the resources of any colony or the welfare of its people." In 1949 President Truman announced the Point Four policy of assisting underdeveloped countries with American capital and technical skill. The following year the British Commonwealth inaugurated the Colombo Plan for South and Southeast Asia. France, Belgium, and other colonial powers had similar schemes for their dependencies, and help was given by international organizations such as the United Nations and the International Bank. In the middle 'fifties the Communist bloc began to develop similar programs.

Foreign Government Aid
The help given by the governments of Western Europe was economic, whereas the bulk of American aid was military and was in-

tended to strengthen the armed forces of the countries which accepted it. Economic aid was both financial and technical. Part of the first category consisted of outright grants of money, and the rest of government-to-government loans. Sometimes the government of the underdeveloped country was free to use loans for purchases anywhere, but usually they were credits which could be spent only in the donor country. The underlying idea was that the underdeveloped country would itself provide the bulk of the funds needed for economic development. Since, however, they were insufficient for the purpose, the Western governments would supply the essential difference. A principal purpose of the foreign contribution was to finance the carrying out of projects which were vital to subsequent developments, such as irrigation works, roads and railways, or harbor works. In the nineteenth and the early twentieth century these were often financed by floating government loans, but for over a generation private capital has not been interested in this kind of investment. Part of the foreign aid was also used for building factories, and the rest was devoted to expansion of the social services, particularly education and health. Technical training was from the beginning a very important part of the plans. One principal obstacle to economic progress has been the acute scarcity of technically trained personnel of every kind. This has limited the amount of capital which an underdeveloped country could use. It was useless, for instance, to build a factory or a hospital if there were not enough trained people to staff it. Extensive programs have been developed to provide the training either locally or in a Western country. A large number of Americans and Europeans have also been sent out to help the underdeveloped countries.

How long the foreign aid should continue would depend upon the length of time required for the country to arrive at a stage of economic development where it could finance further expansion out of its own capital resources. The phrase "economic take-off" has been coined to describe this stage. Before it can be attained, drastic changes must take place in the traditional economy. To name some of them, farming methods must be revolutionized; a good system of transportation must be created so that there is a country-wide market and natural resources can be productively exploited; production must be expanded to the point where exports in conjunction with capital imports can pay for necessary imports of, for instance, machinery and raw materials; a good start must be made in manufacturing; and the government must have effective control of the country. One evidence that the stage of take-off has been reached is a rapid growth in sectors of the economy where modern industrial methods are used. A result and also an evidence of take-off is that the society has enlarged its productivity to the point where there is a sustained increase in the per-capita real income, of which at least 10 per cent is annually put back into productive investment. Once this stage has been reached there would be continued and regular investment of a large percentage of the growing national income, with a concomitant expansion of industrialization.[1]

American Aid

American aid to Southeast Asia was limited until 1950 to reconstruction in the Philippines and assistance to the French and Vietnamese armies in the war in Indochina. Some $400,000,000 were given in payments to private persons and Filipino and American corporations for damage or destruction to their property from war action. An additional $141,000,000 was spent in rebuilding hospitals, schools, roads, government buildings, and the port of Manila. About $100,000,000 in surplus property of the United States was transferred to the Philippine government, which received $40,000,000 from its sale. The government was also granted a loan of $60,000,000.[2] The total amount in grants and loans was $701,000,000. In 1950 the United States began to provide economic aid and military equipment to the states of Indochina and France as assistance in the war against Ho Chi Minh. Aid to South and Southeast Asia began in 1951, with the original intention of contributing "to raising standards of living." As the result of the Korean and Indochinese wars the original economic aim was soon overshadowed by considerations of military strength and collective defense. Foreign aid came to be regarded primarily as a means of enabling economically weak states to maintain stronger armed forces than they could afford from their own resources. It has been estimated that from seventy-five to eighty per cent of American assistance was given for military reasons. By the end of 1955, however, President Eisenhower was beginning to emphasize the need to increase economic aid. Congress was more anxious to reduce and terminate the appropriations

311

than to increase them, and it also showed much greater willingness to vote funds for military than for economic purposes. The result was that expenditures the purpose of which was economic rather than military were often presented to Congress under the more palatable guise of strengthening the military potential of the underdeveloped states.[3] Under the Kennedy administration the policy was to increase the appropriations and put the emphasis on economic assistance.

Economic aid has been of three principal kinds. Grants and loans for capital development, technical assistance and general economic support were distributed by the International Cooperation Administration (I.C.A.), which was reorganized as the Agency for International Development. Foodstuffs from the large reserves of surplus agricultural commodities grown in the United States were paid for in the currency of the country which bought them. A great part of these counterpart funds were used by the government concerned for economic or military purposes approved by the United States. The use of local currencies avoided the difficulty of making payment in scarce dollars. Extra money was also made available for development, and the United States was able to dispose of part of its great stores of surplus food. Between 1954 and 1962 sales of foodstuffs to Indonesia and other countries of Southeast Asia totaled $339,500,000, and $296,400,000 of local currencies were made available for economic development. A third kind of assistance was given through the Development Loan Fund (D.L.F.). This was an American government corporation to finance undertakings which would contribute to economic growth. The scheme must be technically and economically feasible, there must be reasonable prospect that the loan would be repaid, and the amount asked for must not be available on reasonable terms from any other source, public or private. Loans might be made to American or foreign individuals or private businesses, banks, or governments. A very important point was that the D.L.F. could lend dollars and, where necessary, accept repayment in other currencies. This made it much easier for a country with a weak currency to repay the loan. As examples of the types of loans, the Federation of Malaya borrowed $10,000,000 to develop a new deep-water port near Port Swettenham, and $5,000,000 was lent to the Central Bank of the Philippines so that it could make small loans to private industries.

312

The Export-Import Bank, established in 1934, has had as its major purpose the extension of American foreign trade by making dollar loans. They helped Americans to sell goods and services abroad, and also assisted other nations to carry out their development programs by lending them the money to buy American equipment. Indonesia received loans to buy American aircraft, road-building machinery, and equipment for a cement works. Since 1958 the bank has also made loans in foreign currencies to American and foreign firms operating in countries where these were available. Congress authorized the bank to lend up to twenty-five per cent of the local currencies paid for the purchase of American surplus foodstuffs. Up to 1962 the Export-Import Bank had made loans totaling $405,300,000 to Indonesia, the Philippines, and Thailand.

Burma	$ 90,700,000
Cambodia	249,600,000
Indonesia	322,400,000
Laos	296,200,000
Malaya	22,600,000
Singapore and North Borneo	2,100,000
Philippines	346,600,000
Thailand	302,200,000
Viet Nam	1,702,300,000
Total	$3,334,700,000

The economic and technical assistance given by the United States from 1951 to June 30, 1962 inclusive under I.C.A., D.L.F., and the sale of surplus foodstuffs is given in the accompanying table. It includes funds appropriated but not spent and excludes Export-Import Bank loans.[4] The states of eastern and southern Asia which have received by far the greater part of American aid have been India, Pakistan, South Viet Nam, Formosa, and South Korea. India was granted $3,597,300,000 and Pakistan $1,817,500,000. Assistance to Formosa and Korea was on a far more generous scale per head of population, when the number of their inhabitants was compared with that of the first two countries. South Viet Nam was the only state of Southeast Asia which received aid of comparable magnitude, owing to the American policy of building up its strength against Communism. The large amount received by Laos, with its population of approximately 1,500,000, was given for the same reason. Malaya, Singapore, and the British dependencies in North Borneo were looked upon as the responsibility of the United Kingdom. The Philippines and Thailand, American allies, received favored treatment. Government financial aid to the Philippines, like the investment of private capital, came almost entirely from the United States, although members of the British Commonwealth gave some technical assistance under the Colombo Plan. Burma and Indonesia were granted what was left of the limited American funds available for Southeast Asia, surplus foodstuffs constituting a good part of the total.

United Kingdom Aid

Financial and technical aid to the British dependencies has been given under the Colonial Development and Welfare Act, which was first passed in 1940 and has been periodically renewed. Annual expenditure, originally set at $20,000,000 a year, was gradually increased to $53,000,000. Each dependency drew up its development plans, and the amount available from its revenue and loan funds was supplemented by a grant under the Act. When a dependency attained complete self-government it was no longer eligible for assistance under this Act, and had to get help from other sources. For Southeast Asia this has been the Colombo Plan. The Federation of Malaya was given help under the Act until it became completely self-governing in 1957, after which it came under the Colombo Plan. Part of the United Kingdom grants was spent on development schemes such as means of communication, irrigation works, and agriculture, and there was also heavy expenditure for education, health, housing, and other social services.

Dependencies may float loans locally or on the London money market, and since 1959 they may borrow from the United Kingdom Exchequer when unable to sell their bonds to the public. The Treasury has been empowered to lend up to $280,000,000 for the five-year period 1959–1964. Economic development has also been helped by the Colonial Development Corporation, a semi-governmental company like the British Broadcasting Corporation which was created in 1948. It undertook agricultural, manufacturing, or public-utilities projects provided they were economically sound. In North Borneo the *abaca* (manila hemp) industry was developed to broaden the basis of the colony's economy which previously had depended mainly on rubber. As a rule the Corporation has acted in partnership with private enterprise or colonial governments.

Self-governing members of the British Commonwealth in Southeast Asia have received the greater part of their economic and technical assistance under the Colombo Plan. When the scheme originated in 1950 it was confined to the United Kingdom, Canada, Australia, New Zealand, India, Pakistan, and Ceylon. Subsequently it was joined by the United States, Japan, and the states of Southeast Asia. The organ of the Plan is the Consultative Committee representing all the members, which meets once a year. There is no central or master plan to which the separate state plans are expected to conform. Each government prepares its own development program, estimating what part of the cost can be drawn from its own resources and how much must come from outside aid. The plan is presented and canvassed at meetings of the Committee. Progress is noted, difficulties are considered, and suggestions may be made. But each individual country retains full responsibility for both the formulation and execution of its own program. No control is exercised by one member over another. Any members who wish to assist discuss with one another and the author of the plan what help they can give. The assistance is both financial and technical, and the arrangements for it are the sole responsibility of the donor and receiving governments.

As a rule the greater part of the cost of carrying out a program is borne by the state proposing it, the help received being a supplement. One rule of the Colombo Plan is that members which receive aid also give it to the more underdeveloped states, usually in the form of technical assistance. The Philippines has given training in agriculture, education, health, and so on, and has lent its own technically trained personnel to other countries. The United States attends the meetings of the Consultative Committee, and as far as possible her help to the Colombo Plan countries is coordinated with the arrangements made there. United States aid, however, is given direct through American government agencies, since Congress must approve all plans involving financial assistance. All the plans emphasize basic economic development — irrigation, power, communications, railways, roads, and harbor installations. Extension of the cultivated area and improvement of farm-

315

ing methods receive great attention, along with the expansion of manufacturing. Another aim is the improvement of education, health, and housing. Much emphasis is placed on providing technical aid in the form of training facilities and lending technical experts.

Independent members of the British Commonwealth can float loans on the London money market, and their bonds as well as those of British dependencies are listed as trustee (that is, gilt-edged) securities. The United Kingdom, of course, has no control over an independent government, and if it chose to repudiate its loans nothing could be done. The investing public is perfectly sure that Australia, say, would never do this; but it has less confidence in some other parts of the Commonwealth. This attitude explains a statement that owing to the imminent grant of independence the loans floated by the colonial government of Kenya had fallen in value from $135,800,000 to $87,600,000.[5] The inability to float loans of some Commonwealth members which had recently attained independence led to an important modification of policy by the government. It announced in 1958 that the Exchequer would make Commonwealth Assistance Loans for schemes which could not be financed in other ways. The loans must be used for the purchase of United Kingdom goods and services. These loans, which were additional to those given under the Colombo Plan, amounted to $176,700,000 by 1960, and were granted to Malaya, Pakistan, and India. The government also made available $224,000,000 from its sterling subscription to the International Bank for development loans to Commonwealth members. There is no United Kingdom counterpart to the American Export-Import Bank. The sale of goods to countries overseas, including Commonwealth members, is promoted by the guarantee by the Export Credits Guarantee Department of credits extended by the exporter to the purchaser. Economic development in self-governing members of the Commonwealth has been helped by the Commonwealth Development Finance Company, which was established in 1953 with a capital of $73,000,000. It could work in partnership with governments or private companies, but usually the latter. Funds were provided for schemes which were economically feasible, but for which adequate capital could not be raised from ordinary sources, for example, a hydroelectric project in the Federation of Malaya.

Burma was given grants and loans amounting to roughly $210,000,000 between 1945 and 1948. When it seceded from the Commonwealth repayment of $135,800,000 was waived owing to the straitened finances of the A.F.P.F.L. government.[6] Between 1946 and 1949 India, Pakistan, and Ceylon used approximately $952,000,000 of their sterling balances to pay for their imports of British machinery and other manufactures. A large part of this sum came from the war debts incurred partly for supplies bought for use in various theaters of war, and also for the cost of defending the country. When Indian soldiers fought outside India, for example in Burma against the Japanese, the whole expense was borne by the United Kingdom. The rest of the war debt formed a part of the sums allocated by Britain under the Colombo Plan.

The Commonwealth Queue

Grants and loans for capital development under the Colombo Plan have been made only to members of the British Commonwealth, the allocation to India considerably exceeding what was given to any of the others. The non-Commonwealth states of Southeast Asia received aid on a very much smaller scale in the form of technical assistance only, with the exception of small amounts given to Laos and South Viet Nam. In principle the United Kingdom was willing to give help to any state, whether it were a member of the Commonwealth or not. Her financial resources have been limited since World War II, and she has also had to provide for the needs of the parts of the Commonwealth outside Asia. Preference was therefore given to its members, and what might be called the Commonwealth queue came into existence. At the head of the line was India, with a list of demands which grew steadily longer as the years went on. She was followed by Pakistan and Ceylon, and subsequently Malaya. Then there were all the dependencies in Africa and the West Indies which received help under the Colonial Development and Welfare Act. Their demands grew when they became independent. In 1960 the United Kingdom took the lead in organizing a Commonwealth Aid to Africa organization to assist the newly independent countries such as Nigeria.[7] Help was also given to some foreign states such as Jordan. At the end of the queue came the non-Commonwealth states of Southeast Asia. By the time their turn was reached the United Kingdom had not much left to give.

The following table gives the financial help, including funds appropriated but not spent, to Colombo Plan members for capital development from 1951 to June 30, 1962. The figures include both grants and loans, the latter being the greater part. Grants may be spent in any country, but loans can only be used for the purchase of goods from the United Kingdom. The table does not include withdrawals of $705,600,000 from their sterling balances by India, Pakistan, and Ceylon, and investments by the Commonwealth Development Finance Company of $3,100,000 in India and Pakistan and $1,400,000 in the Federation of Malaya.

Malaya and Singapore	$205,632,000
North Borneo and Sarawak	60,133,000
India	441,280,000
Pakistan	98,204,000
Indus Basin Development Fund	58,240,000
Laos	437,000
Viet Nam	574,000

The table below shows the technical aid given to the countries of Southeast Asia as well as India and Pakistan from 1951 to June 30, 1962. Omitting India and Pakistan the total amount of capital and technical aid to Southeast Asia was $273,487,000.[8]

Burma	$1,960,000
Cambodia	246,000
Indonesia	1,145,000
Laos	269,000
Malaya	916,000
Philippines	851,000
Thailand	910,000
Viet Nam	414,000
India	6,994,000
Pakistan	6,860,000

Canada gave Canadian $18,889,000 of capital and technical aid to the countries of Southeast Asia between 1950 and 1962, the largest allocation being $6,191,000 to Malaya. This contrasts with aid to India, Pakistan, and Ceylon of Canadian $358,224,000. Australia during the same period gave $32,014,000 of capital and technical aid to Southeast Asia, the largest grant being $10,023,000 to Indonesia. The amounts given to India, Pakistan, and Ceylon were $64,768,000. New Zealand's contribution was $7,411,000 to Southeast Asia and $16,550,000 to India, Pakistan, and Ceylon.[9]

France is not a member of the Colombo Plan, and her assistance has been confined to her former dependencies of South Viet Nam, Cambodia, and Laos. In 1955 $57,000,000 was granted for capital and technical aid, the largest share going to Viet Nam. Part of the funds was used to buy the 617,500 acres of rice estates belonging to French owners. They were given to the government for division into smallholdings. West Germany is not a Colombo member. Her principal contribution has been to assist German exporters by granting them a government guarantee of the cost of the goods and services sold to underdeveloped countries. She has also made bilateral government-to-government loans which apparently amounted altogether to $547,600,000 up to 1960 for carrying out projects such as road-building in which private capital was not interested. The policy has been that as far as possible assistance should be provided by private enterprise. To promote investment the federal government has begun to conclude protective treaties on the American model. In 1959 the federal government passed a law which gave government guarantees similar to those offered by the United States against the risks of investing in underdeveloped countries. Under American pressure aid was increased in 1961 to $308,000,000.

Since 1954 the Japanese government has given capital and technical aid to Southeast Asia, India, and Pakistan. In addition up to 1962 it has paid $367,986,000 in reparations to Burma, Indonesia, the Philippines, and Viet Nam. Although the purpose was to give partial compensation for war damage, the effect was to promote economic development because much of the payment was to be made by providing technical experts and machinery and other manufactures. Japan has urgent need to expand her sales abroad, and looks upon southern and Southeast Asia as a promising market. A serious obstacle has been the hostility against her which still continues in some countries of Southeast Asia owing to the behavior of her soldiers in 1942–1945. Japan hopes that the illwill will be ended by the payment of reparations, and that this along with Colombo Plan aid will enlarge her market. If a factory is equipped with Japanese machinery and its technical experts have been trained in Japan, the probability is that future orders will be given to Japanese firms.

International Bank

Fourteen loans were made to the countries of Southeast Asia down to 1962. Of these, seven were to Thailand, three apiece to Burma and the Philippines, and one to Malaya.[10] The loans to the Federation of Malaya and the Philippines were for the development of hydroelectric power. One of those to Thailand was for a combined hydroelectric and irrigation project, and the rest were to modernize the railways and open the port of Bangkok to large ocean-going vessels. Burma borrowed to repair war damage to its railways and the port of Rangoon. Half the loans made to Colombo Plan countries were to India.

The International Bank has been of considerable help to Asian countries. Loans may be made to governments or private enterprises. The bank never lends the whole amount of a project, normally financing only the foreign-exchange costs involved in the purchase of imported goods and services. Local costs, usually more than half the total, are met by the borrower from other resources. The bank does not lend the borrowing country's currency, and requires payment in the currency lent. Since a considerable part of the loans are made from funds obtained by the sale of its bonds in Western capital markets, the rate of interest which it charges is what it would itself have to pay to borrow, plus a 1 per cent annual commission charge. The long-term lending rate has varied between 4¼ per cent and 6 per cent, and the average term of a loan is fifteen years. Lending operations are conducted on the basis of three main principles: first, that the borrowing country will be in a position to repay the loan: second, that the project will be of such benefit to the economy as to justify the borrowing of foreign exchange: and third, that the project is itself well designed and capable of execution. Since the loan must be repaid in the currency lent it is necessary to assess the balance of payments prospects and other factors bearing on the borrower's ability to earn adequate amounts of foreign exchange. The inevitable result is that sometimes the conclusion is reached that the proposed loan would add more to the borrower's foreign-exchange obligations than it could safely meet either from its existing resources or out of new production that could be created by the loan. The bank always examines strictly the merits and feasibility of the project, the plans made for its construction, and the provision for management when it comes into operation. While the project is under construction, its execution is inspected by officials of the bank, and the borrower is required to submit regular progress reports.

The necessity of repaying loans in foreign currencies has meant that the bank could supply only a marginal amount of the total capital needed by the underdeveloped countries. In September 1960 the International Development Association (I.D.A.) was established as an affiliate of the International Bank and is under its administration. Its initial resources were to be $1,000,000,000, of which the United Kingdom agreed to contribute $131,300,000 and Germany $55,000,000. The I.D.A. would accept repayment in the currency of the borrower, which would often be inconvertible, and would make loans on more lenient terms than the International Bank. The latter considered only whether a project were economically justifiable and feasible, and did not take into account that it might be unnecessary from the economic standpoint but desirable for political reasons. The I.D.A. could finance any project which was "of high developmental value . . . whether or not the project is revenue producing or directly productive." [11]

The Communist Bloc

Soviet aid is in the main medium and long-term loans which carry an interest rate of 2 to 2½ per cent, much lower than the Western rates of 4 to 6 per cent. Only about 9 per cent of the aid is grants and the remainder is credits for the purchase of Soviet goods, in return for which the borrowing country pays by diverting its exports to the Communist bloc. The West tries to extend its help as widely as possible among the underdeveloped countries, numbering over seventy. The Communist bloc gives aid to twenty states, but the bulk of it is concentrated upon seven of them: Afghanistan, Egypt, India, Syria, Iraq, Yugoslavia, and Indonesia, countries where Russia has long wished to establish her influence. Indonesia is potentially the most important country of Southeast Asia, and one of the most likely to fall under Communist control. Other states markedly favored are Cuba and Guinea, both of which present encouraging prospects. The prerequisite for aid is not that the government should necessarily be Communist but that it should be anti-Western, or, alternatively, not indissolubly committed to the West. Another point worth noting is that though a great parade is made of the amount of Soviet aid, it is less than that of the United Kingdom alone, and still less than that of the United States or the West as a whole. The Soviet Union, however, is far more skillful than the West in advertising its assistance. In Indonesia the United States has merely carried out medical, educational, and agricultural projects which will improve the condition of the people in the long run, but are not obvious to the casual observer. The Soviet Union has built a large Asian games stadium in Djakarta which is seen by hundreds of thousands of Indonesians.

A Communist dictatorship has a very great advantage over a Western democracy with an economic system based upon private enterprise because it has a monopoly of foreign and domestic trade and banking. Political considerations bulk large in Soviet aid, and it can afford to make an agreement that is unfavorable from the economic point of view if it is politically advisable. The low Soviet rate of interest on foreign loans is less than the economic rate and the higher Western rate is often contrasted unfavorably with it. A Western government which makes a loan must borrow the money at the prevalent market rate. It must therefore charge the borrower at least an equal rate of interest, or else lend at a loss and balance its accounts by making its taxpayers pay the difference. A dictatorship, on the other hand, can charge a much lower rate of interest and make good the loss by raising prices to its domestic consumers. Any who protest can be dealt with by withdrawing them from circulation. Similarly, a state economy, able to ignore normal commercial considerations, can accept payment in raw materials or products which it does not need and which are not easily marketable at the time — though it should be noted that the government of Burma protested strongly when rice shipped to Russia under a barter aid agreement was resold at a higher price on world markets, injuring the Burmese government's attempts to sell its remaining rice.

Underdeveloped countries have found that the manufactures they receive are often of poor quality, and that they have to accept what the Communist government chooses to send them. The credits given them can only be spent in the Communist state, so what is sent must be accepted or the credits left unspent. Burma lamented an inundation of Russian cement and Chinese toothpaste. A country which receives so much Soviet aid that a large part of its exports must be earmarked to pay for it may become almost entirely dependent on Communist markets, since former customers will transfer to other sources of supply. The Soviet Union will thus attain a dominant position in the economy, and will not hesitate to use its advantage for political purposes. Thirty years ago Germany used the same tactics to strengthen its control over the Balkan states. Furthermore, Soviet technical experts may carry on propaganda in favor of Communism, and every effort is made to indoctrinate students sent to Russia for training.

Many of the new states are glad to receive aid from the Communist bloc. They want larger amounts than the West has been able to provide: they do not believe that the Communists are imperialists: they are neutral in the cold war: and to receive Communist assistance is soothing to their pride. For although they take it for granted that the West has a duty to help, at the same time they are resentful that they are financially dependent upon it. It gives them a feeling of satisfaction to show the West that they have an alternative source of supply. There is also the technique perfected by Sukarno of playing off American against Communist aid, in order to extract larger amounts from each.

XIII

Western Aid
and Population Growth

Exports and Price Stability

The stage of economic take-off can be reached without outside aid as the United Kingdom achieved it in the late eighteenth century, but the process is much slower. Moreover, Britain had an advantage over most of the underdeveloped countries of today in her possession of a wealthy middle class which had long been accustomed to risk its money in promising ventures, instead of playing safe by hoarding or investing in land. Development is easier and faster if it can be carried out with the help of foreign loans, as in the United States in the nineteenth century or Canada and some other parts of the British Commonwealth in the twentieth. They paid their way by their exports, at first foodstuffs and raw materials and later manufactures, and they suffered from the same fluctuations in price that hamper the underdeveloped countries today. It is unfortunate that some of the latter are becoming hostile to the export of raw materials, because it is not possible to move directly from their present stage of development, during which the pre-conditions for take-off are coming into existence, to full industrialization and the export of manufactures as in the United States. There must be an intermediate stage and unless the Western governments are prepared to make a gift of their aid their loans must be repaid. The aversion of underdeveloped countries to their present form of exports is partly because of the wide fluctuations in price. Another reason is that many of the present export enterprises were

324

created by Western private capital and are reminders of the era of colonial rule.[1]

Something might be done at least to lessen the wide variations in the world price of foodstuffs and raw materials. The attempt was made during the interwar period for rubber and tin, and was only partially successful. International control was unable to maintain a stable price since it could not prevent sudden rises and falls in demand in an economy of free private enterprise. It succeeded to the extent that without it the changes in price would have been even more extreme. Another attempt would be well worth making if the United States would cooperate. There is one obstacle, however, which the pre-war schemes could disregard, and that is Soviet Russia. As a rule the Communists are as anxious to make a profit as the capitalists, but sometimes for political reasons they will sell for less than the world price and disorganize the markets. No one has discovered how to control the Soviet problem child of world trade.

Private Investment

The rapid development of Asia and Africa cannot be financed by domestic capital and the profits of foreign trade. The third source of funds, and the one expected to provide most of the money, is Western private investment. So far as a large part of Southeast Asia is concerned this is not going to take place, and the exhortations of governments and publicists to the contrary arise from wishful thinking. The private investor is not a philanthropist when it comes to investing the money which high taxes and cost of living have left him: he cannot afford to be. Neither are the directors of corporations or banks: they need the confidence of the investing public on whom they depend for additional funds. At times all of them will take a calculated risk, but they insist on a reasonable certainty of profit before they will finance an enterprise. The reasons why business fights shy of newly independent countries have already been discussed; one of the most important is that they have earned a bad name for unjust treatment of private investment. One recent case was rather more flagrant than usual: Indonesia took over the Belgian estates in Sumatra because public opinion was said to be aroused by the death of Lumumba in the Congo. The assertion was made that the motive was to protect the Belgians, followed by the ominous remark "pending further decisions by the central government." Similar protestations followed the seizure of Dutch property. The private investor learnt that it was useless to look for redress to his own government, the International Court, or the United Nations. So he has taken the only remedy left to him: he has been very chary of investing in newly independent states and at the first sign of trouble he has tried to withdraw his money as in Kenya. Meanwhile, the trustworthy states of the world such as Canada have had to discourage the volume of capital thrust upon them.

The American government tried to encourage investment by American companies through the offer of insurance against losses due to expropriation, confiscation, or inconvertibility of foreign currencies into dollars. The scheme was operative only in countries which passed a law ensuring just treatment and then negotiated a treaty to this effect with the United States. Only a limited number agreed to this procedure, and they tended to be countries like the Philippines which were unlikely to behave unjustly toward American companies. The insurance applied only to new ventures and not to existing investments. Moreover, only a few American companies applied for the insurance guarantees. They complained that the premium charged by the government was too high, and that it was not clear whether the insurance covered "the many forms of indirect expropriation which the newer forms of national thievery have recently developed" such as discriminatory taxes, labor regulations which heavily increased operating costs, and import restrictions that made it difficult or impossible for a firm to stay in business. Furthermore, not even the signature of a treaty reassured a large number of corporations as to the reliability of many of the newly independent governments. So the scheme was not very successful in stimulating the flow of private capital abroad. In 1963 President Kennedy proposed somewhat to enlarge the incentives, for example by allowing a tax credit of perhaps double the domestic credit of seven per cent on new industrial equipment. It would apply to new investment, and "to some extent to reinvestments of their earnings" by American firms already operating in underdeveloped countries. He expected that his measures would "substantially encourage additional private investment."[2]

A few years ago a German banker suggested that business firms themselves agree to boycott any country which treated them unjustly. The objection to this proposal is that there will always be some corporation which will try to make a profit out of others' misfortunes. It happened in Indonesia fifteen years ago and in the Congo in 1960. To be effective, the Western governments themselves should announce that they would discontinue all financial and technical assistance to a government which confiscated Western investments or treated them unjustly. The United States carried out this policy against Ceylon in 1963. The Ceylonese government took over a large part of the installations of three Western oil companies, so that its own oil company would have the filling stations and other equipment which it needed to sell Soviet Russian oil. Compensation was promised, but in practice not paid, since the government procrastinated interminably in coming to an agreement on the amount. Congress had passed a law requiring that all aid be stopped if American private property were seized and compensation were not paid in six months. So in 1963 the Bandaranaike government received a most unwelcome shock. Sixty per cent of the installations belonged to the Anglo-Dutch Shell oil company. It is to be regretted that on this occasion Macmillan, the British prime minister, did not follow the American lead. If both the Western powers which had been giving Ceylon most of its foreign aid had simultaneously cut off supplies it might have had a salutary effect. As it was Macmillan's failure to do anything confirmed the opinion of British investors that they could not look to their government for help when they were unjustly treated. The appeal is often made that the Western nations have a duty to help the underprivileged countries, but it can scarcely be argued that they have a moral obligation to encourage theft. For as long as it can be carried out with impunity some states will practice it, and the Western governments can abandon the hope that private capital will play the role that they had designed for it.

The result is that the period before the underdeveloped countries can themselves finance their own economic progress will be greatly lengthened. During the past decade, over half the capital sent to them has come from the governments and not from private business. To cite one instance for which figures are obtainable, the aid given by the United Kingdom government from April 1959 to March 1960 was $366,800,000 and for the financial year 1961–1962 $452,000,000. Private investment in underdeveloped countries was estimated to be something of the order of $280,000,000. Government aid steadily increases, and the complaint is constantly heard that it is inadequate. It is pointed out that the rate of economic progress in Asia and Africa is much less than in the industrialized nations and that the gap between them is widening instead of narrowing. If the governments make grants or loans they must find the money from taxes or by borrowing, and either method increases the load on the taxpayer. Taxes are already heavy and there are limits on the extent to which further burdens can be imposed. If private business could be persuaded to reverse its present attitude the flow of capital to Asia and Africa would be considerably increased. Some deterrents would still remain — the low purchasing power which so often makes heavy investment unprofitable, for example. Nevertheless, if the hostility of the new states were removed there are many openings for profitable investment which business companies would be glad to take advantage of.

The Soviet Bogey

The objection can be made that if the Western governments refuse aid to a state which treats private investment unjustly it will play into the hands of Russia, and that if a country cannot get help from the West it will turn to the Communist states. Western governments have been afraid to do anything which might lead to a growth of Russian or Chinese influence. Asian and African governments have been well aware of this, and have shown themselves perfectly willing to take all the help offered from both sides. One reason they accepted Russian aid was that this enabled them to show the West that they were not solely dependent on it for assistance. It is far from certain that financial and technical help win the friendship of the recipient. The belief is widespread in Asia that its poverty is due to Western exploitation and that grants and loans are merely a belated atonement for the crimes of the past. Most countries regard them as something to which they have a right. The solution for every financial crisis is sought in additional aid, and the demands have grown larger and larger. Many of the plans for development call for an expenditure far beyond the country's resources, and the assumption is that the United States and the United Kingdom will pay the deficit. Meeting the demands may create goodwill of a sort, if this be defined as a strong expectation of greater benefits to come. Again and again it has changed abruptly to vehement criticism the moment the donor did anything the recipient disliked. Asian leaders are well aware that in the United States especially economic aid is regarded as a tactical weapon against Russia in the cold war. A warning that their country may go Communist unless the help is increased has proved to be a very effective argument. Liberality is stimulated by making the flesh creep. Some leaders such as Sukarno have perfected the technique of playing off one bloc against the other and extracting the maximum from both. The competition in offering him aid has become little more than an auction between the great powers in the cold war. The spending of several hundred million dollars has not checked the advance of Communism in Indonesia, but it has enabled the government to continue the economic and financial policies the consequences of which have been described in earlier chapters.

The United States has had plenty of experience that loans do not gain friendship or permanent goodwill. So why is it assumed that Soviet Russia's experience will be the opposite, or that the country helped will become subservient to her? The effect of loans is often to create resentment that the donor is so rich that it can afford to confer benefits. Just as a very good way to lose friends and create envy in private life is to confer favors. Moreover, the purpose of the Western loans is to increase prosperity and thereby lessen the likelihood of the country's going Communist. So why should it be assumed that a Soviet loan must have the opposite effect? Fear is a poor counselor. It is bad policy to rush forward with a loan merely because Russia has done so. There is one aspect of Soviet tactics which seems worthy of imitation. They do not give aid indiscriminately but concentrate upon a limited number of countries which are of special importance in their foreign policy, such as Indonesia, India, and Egypt. Western financial resources are not unlimited, and it would be wise to concentrate them on countries of special political or strategic importance such as India, or on those like the Federation of Malaya which do their utmost to help themselves, and make a wise use of the assistance they have received. Judged by these criteria Laos or Indonesia would come pretty far down on the list.

The Capitalist Pariah

There is general agreement in the West that it is futile to require a recipient country to foreswear socialism or adopt a system of free private enterprise as a condition of being given aid. Most Asian governments have adopted socialism in varying degrees and have no intention of abandoning it. It is understandable that they should insist that the ownership of some basic industries should be national, or that the foreigner should be restricted to certain spheres of industry which the people of the country cannot operate successfully. But the Western governments have the right to insist that the underdeveloped countries shall do all in their power to help themselves before asking for outside aid. There is no reason why the Western taxpayer should be asked to carry an additional burden in order that some Asian natural resources might remain untouched. To exploit them will often mean that their development must be carried out by foreign private capital. A case in point occurred in Iran in 1953. Premier Mossadegh's seizure of the property of the Anglo-Iranian Oil Company and his inability to make use of it had brought the government and the country to the verge of bankruptcy. General Zahedi, who overthrew him, appealed to President Eisenhower for a large loan. The President made only a small grant, and sent the message that the American taxpayer could not be expected to shoulder an extra burden when Iran could find the necessary funds by settling the oil dispute.

Many of the Western-educated leaders in Asia and Africa believe that they can safely indulge their prejudice against foreign private capital because they can get the funds they want elsewhere. If the United States or the United Kingdom will not finance them they can turn to Soviet Russia, or the United Nations, or the new International Development Association which will make loans on easier terms than the International Bank. Eugene Black, the former president of the International Bank, was of the opinion that with these leaders "nationalism is perhaps even more of a motive force than the drive to escape poverty. And often it is a nationalism that is only one part patriotism for every two parts an obsession that their poverty and discontent stem solely from having been held in tutelage by the strong." [3]

Condemnation of private business in the tropics as imperialist exploitation is fashionable both in Asia and the West. It is easy to adduce bad cases such as the Dutch monopoly of the spice trade of the East Indies in the seventeenth and eighteenth centuries or the Culture System in Java in the mid-nineteenth century, or the later eighteenth century when the British shook the pagoda tree in Bengal and Madras. Actions like these are condemned by the descendants of those who carried them out as unreservedly as by Asians. It is not reasonable to judge the actions of two to three hundred years ago by the standards of the twentieth century. The eighteenth century considered bribery and graft, within limits sanctioned by custom, to be the perquisites of power. It was too much to expect British officeholders in Bengal to behave differently from those in Britain, especially when Indians had the same code of official morality. The idea that the economic and political interests of the colonial peoples must take precedence over those of their Western rulers only developed in the last hundred and fifty years, and was not fully worked out until the present century. It might also be pointed out that the Asian governing classes exploited their fellow countrymen as wholeheartedly as any Westerner.

One of the accusations brought against Western private enterprise has been that it drained the country of its wealth by withdrawing the annual profits instead of reinvesting them. This sometimes happened, but then as now most companies realized that it was necessary in their own interests to plough back part of the profits. Furthermore, profits on the whole were very much less than they were popularly believed to be, and it was as true in earlier times as it is now that unless the shareholder were allowed a dividend he refused to invest. Ultranationalists argue that it would have been better to leave their resources untouched rather than submit to The Drain. In that event the newly independent states would be virtually without the social services which today they are so anxious to expand. For their cost in colonial times was not met from the taxes paid by the people of the country but mainly by those levied on the Western companies. This was one reason why the colonial governments encouraged foreign investment, for until taxable assets had been created the social services were rudimentary from lack of money to pay for them. Malaya was a good example of this policy: it produced two raw materials, tin and rubber, essential to the West. The taxes levied upon them were the mainstay of the revenue. The result was that in medical and health services, roads, and railways

Malaya was superior to the other countries of Southeast Asia. The contrast became particularly noticeable when Malaya was compared with Thailand, the only country of Southeast Asia which was politically independent. Thailand also exported tin and rubber, but production was very much less than in Malaya because foreign investments were far smaller. The result was less revenue, and social services which were far inferior to those of Malaya. It is regrettable that so many Asian nationalists brood over the iniquities of private enterprise and close their minds to its benefits. They would succeed faster in their aim of increasing national prosperity if they would allow foreign enterprise to play its part instead of treating it as a pariah. The attitude exists, however, and because it is based on emotional prejudice it will persist. It would therefore be inexpedient to insist on encouragement of private enterprise in return for grants and loans. But since funds are limited and there is not enough for everybody, sound reason exists for favoring the governments which do their utmost to pay their own way by a reasonable encouragement of private investment.

Bilateral vs. Multilateral Aid

The greater part of American and British foreign aid is given after bilateral, government-to-government arrangements have been made. Some underdeveloped countries such as the Philippines and South Viet Nam have no objections, while others like Indonesia and Burma greatly prefer to receive aid from an international agency like the United Nations. The United Nations Assembly passed a resolution calling upon the Western powers to provide it with a large fund for disbursement. The underdeveloped countries preferred this because they as well as the grantors would control allocations. Another reason was that the Western powers were suspected of having imperialistic designs upon the independence of the new states. Even when aid was given unconditionally the recipients suspected that conditions were secretly attached to it. Aid from the United Nations was free from this because the recipient as well as the donor countries were members of the committee which allotted funds. Moreover, this procedure was not offensive to their national pride; it eliminated the mortifying feeling of obligation to one particular country. On the other hand, the bilateral method gives the donor the power to decide which countries are to receive grants and the purposes for which they are to be spent. To cite an actual case, the United States strongly objected to the United Nations' allocation of some $1,200,000 to help Castro's policy of increasing the production of Cuban smallholders. Over a third of the amount came from the American contribution to United Nations funds. There is the further consideration that Soviet Russia carries on its attacks against the West inside the United Nations as well as without. The more Western aid is distributed through the United Nations, the more opportunities Russia will have for frustrating the West's efforts or converting them to its own political purposes. France declares frankly that her assistance is reserved for the friends of France. This does not mean that she demands a military alliance or unwavering diplomatic support, but that a country must not adopt a hostile policy. Her subsidy to Tunisia was ended because it allowed the Algerian rebels to use its territory as a base for military operations. There seems no good reason why a nation should subsidize its opponents. No one has condemned Russia because it has not pressed loans upon, for example, the Philippines and Malaya which are on the Western side in the cold war.

The manner of giving assistance evolved under the Colombo Plan seems to be an acceptable compromise. All the governments, donors and recipients alike, take part as equals in a friendly and critical discussion where plans are set forth, suggestions made for their improvement, and this or that participant describes what assistance it can offer. Moreover, recipients are also donors, for the underdeveloped countries help one another as well as receiving aid. This removes the feeling of being a poor relation which is a psychological weakness in the usual bilateral method. In addition, the secretariat which supervises the execution of the schemes is international and not confined to the donors. The method of operation has created a spirit of cooperation, and the Colombo Plan is highly regarded by its Asian members and has their confidence.

Prospects of Increased Aid

The demands of the underdeveloped countries grow larger with each new plan, and their Western sympathizers complain that the amount given is far too little. From 1961 onwards, President Kennedy pressed the European nations to give more, as well as asking Congress to approve an enlarged program of expenditures for five years, instead of voting annual appropriations. The bulk of the loans must be spent in the United States. The suggestion was made that one per cent of the annual national income should be contributed. It was not clear whether this percentage were intended to cover only government grants, loans, and technical assistance, or whether it would include private investment and export credits through, for example, the American Export-Import Bank and the British Export Credits Guarantee Department. If the first and narrower definition were intended the United Kingdom and still more the American and German contributions would be less than one per cent. If President Kennedy had the second and broader definition in mind, the United States, the United Kingdom, and France were already contributing as much as or more than one per cent of their national incomes. In 1960 some 1.25 per cent of the national income of the United Kingdom and about 1 per cent of that of the United States went to the underdeveloped countries, including both government funds and private investments. France was giving over two per cent, most of it to the former French territories in Africa. The percentage of the German national income allotted to foreign aid was between those of Great Britain and the United States. In 1961 the Organization for Economic Cooperation and Development estimated that the proportion of the gross national product, both private investment and government funds, allotted to the underdeveloped countries was 2.41 per cent for France, 1.32 per cent for the United Kingdom, 1.17 per cent for Germany, and .97 per cent for the United States. In President Kennedy's message to Congress of April 2, 1963, on his foreign-aid program, he gave the American contribution as .7 per cent for government assistance only.

France is unlikely to give much additional financial aid, if any, to the countries of Indochina. She is already contributing more than the suggested one per cent, and her principle is that help should primarily go to her friends. In 1955 the Assembly showed great unwillingness to vote funds for South Viet Nam, on the ground that Ngo Dinh Diem with American assistance was eliminating French influence while accepting that of the United States. French financial help on an extensive scale would be as unlikely as the despatch of a large army if South Viet Nam were threatened by a Communist attack. Moreover, President de Gaulle has undertaken a very expensive program of economic help to Algeria, though in April 1961 he made it very clear that its continuation depended upon whether its people decided to continue friendly association with France. If they determined to break completely with her "naturally we shall cease immediately to sink in a henceforth hopeless enterprise our resources, our men and our money." The general agreed that one probable result would be that Algeria "would straightway fall into misery and chaos until communism took over. That is no doubt what would happen to them; but then we would no longer have any duty toward them other than to pity them." There was the possibility that Russia or the United States or both of them at once would try to take France's place. "My answer is: I wish both of them a lot of fun." The attitude of West Germany has been that assistance was normally given if it promised concrete advantages to German trade. After some months of pressure from the American government, the government gradually agreed to increase its aid to underdeveloped countries. Federal guarantees to promote German exports would continue to play a major part in the program, but the amount of government-to-government loans would be increased. It would appear that the sum offered was less than that suggested by the American government.

During the past nine years the total amount of grants and aid given by the United Kingdom government rose from $170,800,000 in 1951–1952 to $453,600,000 in 1961. Heavy additional demands are being made by the newly independent states of Africa and the West Indies and above all India. The third Five-Year Plan began in 1961 and needed $5,600,000,000 in foreign aid over and above what India herself provided. This was roughly twice as much as was required for the second Five-Year Plan. The United Kingdom agreed to provide approximately $250,000,000 during the first two years. In addition, the United Kingdom is the principal source of capital for overseas investment in the sterling Commonwealth. The exact amount is unknown, but the government estimates that the annual average over the past seven years has been $840,000,000. The amount of government aid and private investment in 1959–1960 was around $1,206,000,000.[4]

The Treasury officials in London consider that "we are at present providing more aid than our balance of payments can carry. This

335

means that we can do no more unless we can either reduce our imports or increase the exports for which we are paid (as against those we pay for ourselves by giving loans or grants to the buying countries), or both." The balance of payments is the difference between the cost of imports and the amount received from the sale of exports together with the income from overseas investments and shipping, banking, and insurance services. If imports exceed exports and the other sources of income the deficit in the balance of payments must be met from the sterling reserves, the United Kingdom's holdings of gold and foreign currencies. They have to maintain the exchange value of the pound not only for the United Kingdom but also for the whole sterling bloc. The United Kingdom's sterling reserves are entirely different from the sterling balances, which are also kept in London. These are the holdings of gold and foreign currencies which belong to India and the other self-governing members of the Commonwealth. They are entirely under the control of their owners and can be withdrawn at any time and freely converted into dollars or any other foreign currency. Ever since World War II the United Kingdom's sterling reserves have been dangerously small for the work they have to do. They have fluc-tuated in amount and have always been precariously balanced on a knife edge. A large excess of outgoings on imports over incomings either in the United Kingdom or in the sterling bloc is enough to threaten the foreign-exchange value of the pound. Such an excess arouses fears that the sterling reserves will be drained away to meet the liabilities, and that there will be another devaluation of the pound. The result is foreign holders of sterling sell it for exchange into a more stable currency, and short-term funds deposited in London banks are hastily withdrawn. India ran down her sterling balances heavily to help finance her second Five-Year Plan, and this was one cause of a crisis of the pound a few years ago.

The relation of the foregoing to foreign aid is that if the aid were too large it might tip the balance of payments against the United Kingdom. It is therefore a liability, like imports, and a potential drain on the sterling reserves which might bring about the results already described. True, half of the aid is usually in the form of loans which must be spent in the United Kingdom on, for example, machinery. But the raw materials from which it is made have to be bought overseas and so add to the cost of imports. Moreover, the finished product is not sold on the world market to swell the total value of exports. Instead, it is an unrequited export for which no immediate return is received. Eventually the recipient country will repay the loan, but only after a lapse of some years. Payment of the 1961 loans to India is spread out over twenty-five years, with the first payment deferred until 1968. So from the point of view of the immediate foreign-exchange value of the pound sterling a loan to an underdeveloped country can mean an increased strain on the United Kingdom's sterling reserves.

The position in 1960–1963 was not very reassuring. In 1960 imports rose sharply, and though exports also increased they did not do so sufficiently to prevent an adverse balance of payments of $963,000,000. The government adopted measures to check the domestic demand and so lessen imports, but the trade returns for 1961 to 1963 gave no grounds for easy optimism. They supported the Treasury view that the times were not propitious for a large increase in aid to underdeveloped countries. The Federation of British Industries warned that if the unfavorable balance continued the United Kingdom would be driven to reimpose import controls or else drastically reduce private overseas investment and foreign aid. Either alternative would have serious consequences. The only way of avoiding them was to increase productivity and exports, and reduce costs to a level competitive with other industrialized nations, particularly Germany. Wages and costs of production have mounted steadily and outstripped the increase in productivity, and the value of exports obstinately lags behind that of imports. Selwyn Lloyd, the Chancellor of the Exchequer, stated that government aid in 1961–1962 rose to $504,000,000. He did not propose to reduce this amount, but he was compelled to make sure that it did "not rise much above the present level . . . even to sustain this level . . . will not be easy."[5] The problem of how to increase production and exports has not been solved, and the improvement in 1963 was not altogether reassuring. In spite of this, it was estimated that foreign aid in 1963–1964 might range from $504,000,000 to $616,000,000. Until the situation changes radically it is hard to see how the United Kingdom can continue to meet the growing demands of the underdeveloped countries.

Opposition seems to be growing in the United States to further increases in foreign aid, with an accompanying strong desire to shift

337

part of the burden to the European powers. In 1962 Congress voted $1,000,000,000 less than the president asked, and in 1963 he himself felt it expedient to reduce his original request by more than $400,000,000. Even this reduced amount, however, was drastically cut down by Congress. The influential Clay Commission strongly advised that the whole foreign aid program should be critically re-examined and decreased. A bipartisan group of senators headed by Senator Mansfield, leader of the Democratic majority, urged a thorough reassessment of the aid program in Southeast Asia. They were doubtful whether the $5,000,000,000 of military and economic assistance spent since 1950 had accomplished very much. They advised that there should be no extension of aid to countries like Burma which were not already in receipt of it, and that the grants made to other states except South Viet Nam should be reduced. The group also argued that the European allies, particularly France and West Germany, should increase their contributions. President Kennedy emphasized in his speech of April 2, 1963, that this was one of the principal aims of his policy.[6] Strong optimism is needed to picture General de Gaulle as amenable to arguments or pressure once he has made up his mind. His policy is to give aid mainly in Africa where it will benefit France as well as the countries which receive it, and this specification no longer includes Southeast Asia. The general can point out that France is spending more than the United States in proportion to her resources, and that the amount needed in Africa is so large that he has persuaded the other states in the European Common Market to contribute to a development fund. The British Conservative and Labour parties are strongly in favor of aid on a generous scale, but neither of them can afford to ignore the unsatisfactory economic position of the United Kingdom. Perhaps Washington may have more success with West Germany. If the United States imitated Soviet Russia and concentrated aid upon a limited number of key states it could lighten the burden. It is hard to see where Southeast Asia is going to obtain more economic aid than at present.

Population Growth and Living Standards

Successful accomplishment of the present Indian third Five-Year Plan was expected to create employment for about an additional twelve million, whereas it was estimated that during the same period the probable net increase of the working population would be four-teen million. This meant that an expenditure of $23,000,000,000 would not provide a livelihood even for the anticipated growth of population, altogether apart from the millions who were already unemployed or underemployed. The census of 1961 showed that the situation was worse than the planners had foreseen. Five years earlier it had been estimated that the population in 1961 would be four hundred eight million, but the census showed that the actual number was about thirty million more, or four hundred and thirty-eight million. The esti-mates in the new plan were already invalidated so far as providing employment was concerned. More alarming than the actual growth was the acceleration in the increase. The 1951 census showed a 13.3 per cent population growth in the previous decade, but the 1961 census showed an advance of 21.1 per cent in the last decade.[7] If the present higher rate of increase were maintained the estimated cost of the plan must be raised sharply, with the likelihood that once again the growth of population would confound all the calculations of the planners. This situation is not confined to India: in varying degrees it is found every-where in Asia except Japan. It raises the question whether Western aid can succeed in raising the standard of living in face of an accelerat-ing growth of population.

The problem of surplus population is quite recent in Asia, apart from China, and did not become very serious until the last half century. Until the nineteenth century population was kept down by the three natural checks of war, famine, and disease. The birth rate was high, though not excessively so, and it was offset by a high death rate. The population was much smaller than today, and large areas were so sparsely inhabited that the slow increase in numbers could find vacant land to cultivate. War produced its effects less by deaths in battle than by interrupting the production of food and spreading disease. Actual famines seem to have caused fewer deaths than chronic undernourish-ment which weakened the ability of the body to resist disease. It is believed that epidemics were less of a killer than the continual deaths caused by such widely prevalent diseases as malaria or tuberculosis. The recent increase in population was not brought about by a rise in the birth rate but by a fall in the death rate. This was one result of

339

Western imperialism, which weakened and sometimes abolished the natural checks.

The European rulers gave a freedom from civil wars and foreign invasions which had been previously unknown. The building of roads and railways made it possible for the first time to bring in food to a famine area. Irrigation works and measures for controlling floods on the great rivers were sometimes important, as in Viet Nam, Java, and Pakistan. The introduction of European medical and health services had a profound effect especially from the last quarter of the nineteenth century onwards. At a conservative estimate, scores of millions of Asians owe their lives to Lister, who was the first to advance the germ theory of disease. A skilled surgeon, he was troubled by the frequency with which the operation was successful but the patient died. He evolved the theory that the incision made by the surgeon's knife was attacked by a malign though invisible organism for which he invented the name germ. To destroy it he liberally anointed the incision with crude carbolic acid. This gave the patients stimulating and blasphemous nights, but the death rate following operations went down sharply. Lister's theory and the microscope resulted in a great period of medical research, when one after another the causes of tropical diseases and how to cure them were discovered. From the late nineteenth century on the Asian death rate began to fall spectacularly and the population grew with increasing momentum. The process was accelerated by such recent discoveries as antibiotics. In the future the death rate will fall even faster since the Asian governments are spending more and more on medical and health services. The result will be that they will combine the high birth rate of the pre-colonial period with the low death rate of a modern Western state. This may have the effect that for some decades there may be no marked improvement in the level of living, because the increase of production will be offset by a growth of population due to the fall in the death rate.[8]

The demographic effect of colonial rule on predominantly agricultural societies was that it greatly increased the pressure upon the land. Millions who formerly would have died in infancy lived to procreate more millions. Since for reasons already explained little manufacturing developed, the increased population had to find a living by farming. The cultivable area was extended until in extreme cases — Java and the

Red river delta, for example — little further expansion was possible. Attempts to promote emigration to underpopulated areas had limited success. The partial decay of handicrafts owing to the competition of machine-made articles meant that millions of handicraftsmen must become farm laborers. This created a surplus of unnecessary labor, which competed for employment and kept down the rate of wages. Farms became smaller and smaller as they were divided among male heirs, and for the same reason fragmentation increased. There was a marked increase in tenancy as peasants lost their holdings to the land-owner and the money lender. The burden of rent and indebtedness grew, and often there was undernourishment. The yield per acre remained low despite the attempts of the colonial governments to persuade the peasants to change their farming methods. All of them tried hard, but success was limited. The principal reason was the force of custom combined with the magnitude of the problem. Another handicap was the poverty of the peasant: even if he were convinced of the utility of fertilizer he could not afford to use it unless the price were very low.

The newly independent states inherited the problem of a dangerously large agricultural population where the death rate was falling progressively faster. The latter is still much higher than in North America, Western Europe, and Japan, which means that the death rate has still got a long way to fall. At the present the mortality rate for infants of under twelve months is 26.3 per 1,000 live births in the United States, 41.7 in Japan, 49.4 in Singapore, 78.8 in the Federation of Malaya, 166 in the Philippines, 192 in Indonesia, and 221 in Burma. The birth rate has not fallen, and the rates of population increase now range between 1.5 per cent in Burma and 3.9 per cent, the highest, in Singapore. For the Philippines and the Federation of Malaya the rate is 3 per cent, and for Indonesia 2.3 per cent. By way of comparison the rate in the United States and Canada is 1.7 per cent.

The effect of these rates of increase is shown by the accompanying table (population in millions). Taking the population of 1950, two estimates were made of its size in 1980. Both assumed that the birth rate would remain high, but the conservative estimate allowed for a moderate fall in the death rate while the modified estimate assumed that the death rate would fall more rapidly.[9] These figures look small

341

compared with conservative estimates for India of 665,700,000, Pakistan 128,000,000, and China 894,000,000.[10]

	1950	1980 Conservative Estimate	1980 Modified Estimate
Burma	18.5	32.3	45.3
Cambodia	3.9	8.7	9.9
Federation of Malaya	5.2	14.0	14.4
Java	50.0	92.3	
Indonesia	75.0	138.5	160.1
Laos	1.3	2.5	2.9
Philippines	20.2	50.8	57.0
Singapore	1.06	3.3	
Thailand	18.6	41.6	47.5
Viet Nam	26.0	44.6	49.1

The apprehension aroused by them is whether the new states will be able to raise the standard of living or whether their own efforts plus the generous foreign aid which they are receiving will be canceled by the increase in population. Very little trustworthy information is available and what there is relates to India. It is based on personal impressions and not on a proved statistical analysis of results. A British journalist states that in the last ten years "some 6,000,000 new industrial jobs have been created, although even this level is too low to counter the steady flow of new entrants into an economy in which population moves inexorably up by over 8,000,000 a year." Agrarian reforms made 30 per cent of the peasants, "the men with five acres or more, probably better off. Another 30% have kept pace. . . . At the bottom of the scale, especially among the landless and the Untouchables, poverty is growing more intense." The conclusion reached by the author is that "the pace is too slow," and that foreign aid must be greatly increased.[11] This is corroborated by the statement already quoted that the third Five-Year Plan will provide work for about 12,000,000, while the net increase of the working population will probably be 14,000,000. This does nothing to help the millions now in the villages who are unemployed or underemployed. Nor does it do much to help the large number of educated and semi-educated who are bitter because they feel that their prospects are so much worse than they had hoped for. They, more than the peasants, are the army of discontent which is most amenable to Communist persuasion.

The foregoing appraisal tallies with the impressions of the government officials who have administered the aid programs. They all emphasize that they do not have accurate statistics on which to base their opinion, but their belief is that to date India's own efforts and the Western aid she received have merely prevented the standard of living from falling. The high birth rate and falling death rate have counterbalanced the increase in national productivity. A few consider that India's second Five-Year Plan has slightly increased the standard of living, and they hope that the present third Five-Year Plan wil' attain its goal of somewhat increasing the living standard. No one is willing to give a positive answer whether India after fifteen to twenty years will reach the point of economic take-off, when from then onwards it can finance its future economic development from its own resources without further need of foreign aid. All the evidence converges on the same point, that the greatest obstacle to raising the standard of living is the unrestricted birth rate and consequent growth of the population.

The reasons for the high birth rate are principally ignorance and obedience to custom, though in Viet Nam ancestor worship is also an important cause. When a man believes that unless he has a son he cannot become an ancestor because the proper rites cannot be performed at his tomb he is unlikely to neglect his spiritual welfare. Hinduism also requires a man to have a son to carry out the ceremonial rites after his death, but this is a minor factor in Southeast Asia, owing to the limited number of Hindus. Much more compelling reasons are the complete ignorance of the great mass of the population that it is possible to limit the size of families, along with the lack of contraceptives which are inexpensive and easy to apply. Custom encourages a high birth rate, for children are a substitute for an old age pension: they are the most certain support for the parents when they are too old to work. Moreover, they make it unnecessary to hire laborers at the seasons when extra work must be done on the farm. Since for centuries the high death rate meant that the majority of the children would die young, it was advisable to have a large supply. Custom has not yet adjusted itself to the lowering of the death rate and still dictates big families. A final reason for large families especially in the villages is gossip, for public opinion despises or at best pities the childless, and every man knows that a small family will lead to embarrassing speculation among his neighbors as to the reasons for it. Birth control is beginning to be practiced by the urban middle class, but this is too small a percentage of the population for it to have much effect.[12]

The European colonial governments were very careful not to advocate limitation of families. They never forgot that they were foreign in race and religion to their subjects, and a guiding principle was not to interfere with native custom and religion. They felt that if some day a local government chose to intervene in these fields it might command enough support to do so successfully. On the whole the new governments have been as loath to meddle as their colonial predecessors. The one Asian country which has taken energetic action is Japan, where the government carried on propaganda in favor of smaller families and legalized abortion. The people took to it with enthusiasm, and within a decade the birth rate fell drastically. Even so, the population is expected to rise until it reaches its maximum of 104,000,000 in 1990. In India private initiative and the government have done something to popularize birth control, but not a fraction of what the gravity of the position requires. Very recently in Singapore the government has begun a vigorous campaign. The other governments of Southeast Asia are indifferent.

The argument is often made that in time the problem will solve itself, as it did in northwestern Europe, the United States, and the older British Dominions like Canada. As they industrialized and the standard of living rose the birth rate which had been high during most of the nineteenth century began to fall faster and faster. The same development was beginning to appear in Japan before World War II. The conclusion is drawn that eventually the countries of Asia will go the same way. Assuming that Asia accomplishes in a generation a change in social customs which took the West about a century, the population will grow prodigiously before the low birth rate becomes established. Raising the standard of living will be much easier if the governments take steps to ensure that there are fewer people. Warren Thompson is of the opinion that if a third or a quarter

of the money and effort being used to establish heavy industry and basic services were devoted to educating the masses in the need for birth control the rate of population growth could almost certainly be reduced in a shorter time than now appears probable, and the level of living could be raised much faster during the next two or three decades than will be possible by following their present plans for depending almost entirely on economic development to achieve this aim. . . . It is basically this relative indifference to intensive efforts to educate the masses regarding the need to reduce the birth rate at a time when the death rate is declining in an unprecedented manner that has led me to conclude that there is little hope of reducing the rate of population growth for about a generation, and that any rise in the level of living great enough to reduce the feeling of

envy of the West "depends even more on the rapid decline of the birth rate than on the rapid improvement of production." [13]

The countries of Southeast Asia are temporarily better able to provide for their expanding populations than India or China. They all have large tracts of potentially cultivable land which are sparsely inhabited. The area varies from one country to another, and exact information is lacking about the amount. The Philippines could probably double its present cultivated area. The Outer Islands of Indonesia but not Java could support the population increase for several decades, if — a very big if — extensive immigration from Java could be organized. The same statement could be made about Thailand, South Viet Nam, Cambodia, and Laos. Burma could probably provide for two to three times the present population, and Malaya has room for a considerably larger number. A combination of extension of the cultivated area, raising the low yields per acre to the Japanese level, and a moderate expansion of manufacturing should be able to cope with the growth of population for about another thirty years. Unfortunately the governments seem to feel that since they have this respite it is unnecessary to concern themselves with birth control until the need for it becomes urgent.[14]

NOTES, SUGGESTED READING, INDEX

Notes

All monetary figures have been converted into American dollars.

Chapter I. Nationalism and Democracy

[1] M. D. Kennedy, *A Short History of Communism in Asia* (London, 1957), p. 289.

[2] W. H. Elsbree, *Japan's Role in Southeast Asian Nationalist Movements 1940 to 1945* (Cambridge, Mass., 1953), *passim*.

[3] *Straits Budget*, April 23, 1958.

[4] R. Emerson, *From Empire to Nation: The Rise to Self-Assertion of Asian and African Peoples* (Cambridge, Mass., 1960), pp. 288–292.

[5] W. Burmeister, ed., *Democratic Institutions in the World To-day* (London, 1958), p. 93.

[6] *Ibid.*, pp. 88, 94. Emerson, *op. cit.*, p. 279. J. M. van der Kroef, *Indonesia in the Modern World* (Bandung, 1954), p. 62.

[7] *Far Eastern Survey*, XXVI, 3, March 1957, p. 39.

[8] E. R. Black, *The Diplomacy of Economic Development* (Cambridge, Mass., 1960), pp. 10–11.

[9] Emerson, *op. cit.*, pp. 284–285.

Chapter II. The Philippines, Burma, and Malaya

[1] J. R. Hayden, *The Philippines, A Study in National Development* (New York, 1942), pp. 370–371.

[2] *Ibid.*, p. 711. R. Emerson, W. H. Elsbree, and V. Thompson, *Representative Government in Southeast Asia* (Cambridge, Mass., 1955), pp. 103–104.

[3] John H. Romani, *The Philippine Presidency* (Manila, 1956), pp. 179–197.

[4] *Ibid.*, pp. 205–207.

[5] *Ibid.*, p. 208. Emerson, Elsbree, and Thompson, *op. cit.*, p. 104.

[6] G. A. Malcolm, *First Malayan Republic* (Boston, 1951), p. 235. G. McT. Kahin, ed., *Governments and Politics of Southeast Asia* (Ithaca, N.Y., 1959), pp. 473–474.

[7] *Ibid.*, p. 484. A. Ravenholt, *The Philippines, A Young Republic on the Move* (Princeton, N.J., 1962), pp. 173–175.

[8] R. A. Smith, *Philippine Freedom 1946–1958* (New York, 1958), p. 137.

[9] Malcolm, *op. cit.*, p. 302. *Pacific Affairs*, XXVII, 1, March 1954, p. 3.

[10] *Ibid.*, pp. 3–4. Emerson, Elsbree, and Thompson, *op. cit.*, pp. 105–108. C. P. Romulo and M. M. Gray, *The Magsaysay Story* (New York, 1956), pp. 150–151.

[11] *Pacific Affairs*, XXVII, 1, March 1954, pp. 4–7. F. L. Starner, *Magsaysay and the Philippine Peasantry, The Agrarian Impact on Philippine Politics 1953–1956* (Berkeley and Los Angeles, 1961), pp. 25–57.

[12] Kahin, ed., *Governments and Politics of Southeast Asia*, pp. 459–460.

[13] Romulo and Gray, *op. cit.*, pp. 204–205, 221–225, and 231–232. *Pacific Affairs*, XXVII, 1, March 1954, pp. 9–13. A. V. H. Hartendorp, *History of Industry and Trade of the Philippines: The Magsaysay Administration* (Manila, 1961), pp. 2–3.

[14] Starner, *op. cit.*, pp. 77–87, 193.

[15] Hartendorp, *op. cit.*, pp. 3–4.

[16] Kahin, ed., *Governments and Politics of Southeast Asia*, p. 449. *Asian Survey*, II, 5, July 1962, pp. 17–18.

[17] *Pacific Affairs*, XXXV, 3, Fall 1962, pp. 271–274. *Asian Survey*, II, 5, July 1962, pp. 17–19; III, 1, January 1963, pp. 41–43. *Philippine Free Press*, February 9, 1963.

[18] H. Tinker, *The Union of Burma, A Study of the First Years of Independence* (London, 1957), pp. 76–77.

[19] G. E. Harvey, *British Rule in Burma* (London, 1946), pp. 87–90. F. S. V. Donnison, *Public Administration in Burma* (London and New York, 1953), pp. 80–86.

[20] J. S. Furnivall, *The Governance of Modern Burma* (New York, 1958), p. 57.

[21] Tinker, *op. cit.*, pp. 49–58, 61.

[22] *Ibid.*, *passim.* Furnivall, *op. cit.*, pp. 58, 111–112. *Pacific Affairs*, XXXI, 4, December 1958, pp. 338–339.

[23] Tinker, *op. cit.*, pp. 67, 138. Kahin, ed., *Governments and Politics of Southeast Asia*, p. 98.

[24] Tinker, *op. cit.*, pp. 89, 92. *Far Eastern Survey*, XXV, 12, December 1956, pp. 181–183.

[25] Furnivall, *Governance of Modern Burma*, pp. 117–123.

[26] *Pacific Affairs*, XXXI, 4, December 1958, pp. 344–347, 372–374.

[27] *Far Eastern Survey*, XXIX, 5, May 1960, pp. 70–74. *Pacific Affairs*, XXXIII, 2, June 1960, pp. 144–157.

[28] Emerson, Elsbree, and Thompson, *op. cit.*, p. 56. Tinker, *op. cit.*, *passim.*

[29] *Far Eastern Survey*, XXIX, 2, February 1960, p. 24.

[30] *Asian Survey*, II, 1, March 1962, pp. 3–8; II, 6, August 1962, p. 25. *Daily Telegraph*, January 18, 1961.

[31] L. A. Mills, *Malaya, A Political and Economic Appraisal* (Minneapolis, 1958), p. 15. The section on Malaya is to a large extent based on the author's previous books, *British Rule in Eastern Asia, A Study of Contemporary Government and Economic Development in British Malaya and Hong Kong* (London, 1942) and *Malaya, A Political and Economic Appraisal.*

[32] L. A. Mills et al., *The New World of Southeast Asia* (Minneapolis, 1949), p. 186.

[33] *Pacific Affairs*, XXXIII, 1, March 1960, pp. 40–47.

[34] *Daily Telegraph*, November 16, 1961.

[35] *Asian Survey*, III, 2 February 1963, p. 79.

[36] *Daily Telegraph*, October 17, November 23, and December 2, 1961. Parl. Pap. Cmnd. 1563 of 1961, *Federation of Malaysia, Joint Statement by the Governments of the United Kingdom and of the Federation of Malaya, passim.*

[37] *World To-day*, 18, 5, May 1962, p. 197. *Daily Telegraph*, August 30, 1962, February 4, 1963.

[38] *Ibid.*, December 14, 22, 1962, January 30, February 14, 1963.

Chapter III. Indonesia, South Viet Nam, and Thailand

[1] *Pacific Affairs*, XXVII, 3, September 1954, p. 245.

[2] Emerson, Elsbree, and Thompson, *op. cit.*, pp. 22–25. Kahin, ed., *Major Governments of Asia* (Ithaca, N.Y., 1958), pp. 539–545.

[3] *Pacific Affairs*, XXVIII, 1, March 1955, pp. 42–48. van der Kroef, *op. cit.*, pp. 110–111.

[4] Kahin, ed., *Major Governments of Asia*, pp. 484, 526; *Governments and Politics of Southeast Asia*, p. 211.

[5] *Pacific Affairs*, XXVII, 3, September 1954, p. 241. *Far Eastern Survey*, XXVI, 4, April 1957, pp. 50–53. Kahin, ed., *Major Governments of Asia*, pp. 522–526.

[6] *Far Eastern Survey*, XXVIII, 2, February 1959, pp. 17–24.

[7] Kahin, ed., *Governments and Politics of Southeast Asia*, pp. 189–191, 210; *Major Governments of Asia*, pp. 527–528.

[8] *Ibid.*, pp. 548–550. *Far Eastern Survey*, XXVI, 11, November 1957, p. 163.

[9] Kahin, ed., *Major Governments of Asia*, pp. 492, 527. F. N. Trager, ed., *Marxism in Southeast Asia: A Study of Four Countries* (Stanford, 1959), p. 226.

[10] Emerson, Elsbree, and Thompson, *op. cit.*, pp. 26–29. Kahin, ed., *Governments and Politics of Southeast Asia*, pp. 200–201. T. Mende, *South East Asia between Two Worlds* (London, 1955), pp. 97–99.

[11] B. Higgins, *Indonesia's Economic Stabilization and Development* (New York, 1957), pp. 96–102. Kahin, ed., *Major Governments of Asia*, pp. 551–559.

[12] *International Affairs*, 34, 4, October 1958, pp. 454–457.

[13] *Ibid.*, pp. 459–460.

[14] *Ibid.*, pp. 460–461.

[15] *Far Eastern Survey*, XXVI, 4, April 1957, p. 57. *Pacific Affairs*, XXX, 3, September 1957, pp. 197–198, 204–208.

[16] Kahin, ed., *Major Governments of Asia*, pp. 540–541.

[17] *Ibid.*, pp. 529–530, 564–566. *Far Eastern Survey*, XXVI, 8, August 1957, pp. 113–114.

[18] *Ibid.*, XXVII, 7, July 1958, pp. 99–101.

[19] *Ibid.*, XXVIII, 12, December 1959, pp. 177–182.

[20] *Far Eastern Survey*, XXIX, 4, April 1960, p. 49.

[21] *Pacific Affairs*, XXXV, 2, Summer 1962, pp. 141–156.

[22] *Foreign Affairs*, 35, 1, October 1956, p. 118. *Pacific Affairs*, XXVIII, 1, March 1955, p. 21.

[23] *American Political Science Review*, LII, 2, June 1958, pp. 437–462.

[24] *Foreign Affairs*, 35, 2, January 1957, p. 285.

[25] *Asian Survey*, I, 2, April 1961, pp. 19, 21.

[26] *Pacific Affairs*, XXX, 1, March 1957, pp. 50–52, 56.

[27] *Ibid.*, pp. 55–57. *The Observer*, March 4, 1956.

[28] *American Political Science Review*, LII, 2, June 1958, p. 458. *Pacific Affairs*, XXXIII, 4, December 1960, pp. 336–344. *Far Eastern Survey*, XXVII, 12, December 1958, p. 179. *The World To-day*, 16, 2, February 1960, pp. 71–79. *Daily Telegraph*, October 6, 1959.

[29] *Ibid.*, November 12, 1960, June 28, 1961. *Asian Survey*, I, 2, April 1961, pp. 19–20.

[30] *New York Times*, March 1, 1961. *Wall Street Journal*, March 21, 1961. *New York Herald Tribune*, April 17, 19, 1961. *Daily Telegraph*, June 26, 28, 1961.

[31] *Asian Survey*, I, 2, April 1961, p. 18. *Daily Telegraph*, June 26, 1961. *Wall Street Journal*, March 21, 1961.

[32] *Asian Survey*, III, 1, January 1963, pp. 48–54. *New York Times*, September 28, October 21, 1962.

[33] Emerson, Elsbree, and Thompson, *op. cit.*, p. 161.

[34] Kahin, ed., *Governments and Politics of Southeast Asia*, pp. 46–47.

[35] *Far Eastern Survey*, XXVI, 8, August 1957, p. 118.

[36] Kahin, ed., *Governments and Politics of Southeast Asia*, pp. 25–29. *Far Eastern Survey*, XXVI, 6, June 1957, pp. 92–96; XXVII, 8, August 1958, pp. 114–117.

[37] *Pacific Affairs*, XXXIII, 4, December 1960, pp. 348–359.

[38] Kahin, ed., *Governments and Politics of Southeast Asia*, pp. 36–40, 54–55.

[39] Trager, ed., *op. cit.*, pp. 66–67.

[40] *Far Eastern Survey*, XXVII, 8, August 1958, pp. 117–118. Kahin, ed., *Governments and Politics of Southeast Asia*, p. 33. W. D. Reeve, *Public Administration in Siam* (London and New York, 1951), *passim*.

[41] Trager, *op. cit.*, pp. 80–81.

[42] *Far Eastern Survey*, XXVII, 8, August 1958, pp. 118–119.

[43] Kahin, ed., *Governments and Politics of Southeast Asia*, p. 57.

[44] Reeve, *op. cit.*, pp. 77, 81.

Chapter IV. The Chinese

[1] V. Purcell, *The Chinese in Southeast Asia* (London and New York, 1951), *passim*.

For other accounts of the Chinese prior to 1941 see W. J. Cator, *The Economic Position of the Chinese in the Netherlands Indies* (Chicago, 1936). R. Emerson, *Malaysia, A Study in Direct and Indirect Rule* (New York, 1937). J. S. Furnivall, *Netherlands India, A Study in Plural Economy* (Cambridge, England, 1939). J. R. Hayden, *The Philippines, A Study in National Development* (New York, 1942). K. P. Landon, *Siam in Transition* (Shanghai, 1939) and *The Chinese in Thailand* (London and New York, 1941). L. A. Mills, *British Rule in Eastern Asia: A Study of Contemporary Government and Economic Development in British Malaya and Hong Kong* (London, 1942). V. Purcell, *The Chinese in Malaya* (London and New York, 1948). A. Vandenbosch, *The Dutch East Indies* (Berkeley, 1941). V. Thompson, *French Indo-China* (New York, 1937).

[2] Mills, *Malaya, A Political and Economic Appraisal*, p. 105.

[3] *Journal of Asian Studies*, XVI, 2, February 1957, pp. 244–246.

[4] V. Thompson and R. Adloff, *Minority Problems in Southeast Asia* (Stanford, 1955), pp. 5–8.

[5] *Daily Telegraph*, March 8, 1953.

[6] Thompson and Adloff, *Minority Problems in Southeast Asia*, pp. 11–13. R. H. Fifield, *The Diplomacy of Southeast Asia: 1945–1958* (New York, 1958), pp. 288–290.

[7] Thompson and Adloff, *Minority Problems in Southeast Asia*, pp. 9–10. Royal Institute of International Affairs, *Collective Defence in South East Asia* (London and New York, 1956), p. 87.

[8] Kennedy, *op. cit.*, p. 380.

[9] D. E. Willmott, *The National Status of the Chinese in Indonesia* (Ithaca, N.Y., 1956), pp. 2–15.

[10] *Ibid.*, pp. 16–21. Kahin, ed., *Major Governments of Asia*, pp. 518–519.

[11] Thompson and Adloff, *Minority Problems in Southeast Asia*, p. 49. Willmott, *op. cit.*, pp. 25, 33–50.

[12] *Ibid.*, pp. 58–59. Thompson and Adloff, *Minority Problems in Southeast Asia*, pp. 52–53.

[13] Willmott, *op. cit.*, pp. 53–54, 60–61. *Far Eastern Survey*, XXIV, 9, September 1955, p. 133.

[14] Willmott, *op. cit.*, pp. 65–73.

[15] Much of the material for this section comes from a long and detailed report by Professor Sheldon Appleton, based upon an investigation which he carried out in the Philippines. Parts of his findings were published in *Pacific Affairs*, XXXII, 4, December 1959, pp. 376–391, and *The Journal of Asian Studies*, XIX, 2, February 1960, pp. 151–161.

[16] *Journal of Asian Studies*, XIX, 2, February 1960, pp. 157–158.

[17] *Ibid.*, pp. 160–161.

[18] G. W. Skinner, *Chinese Society in Thailand: An Analytical History* (Ithaca, N.Y., 1957), pp. 177, 324–337, 365–375.

[19] *Ibid.*, pp. 377, 381. *Journal of Asian Studies*, XVI, 2, February 1957, p. 247.

[20] E. H. Jacoby, *Agrarian Unrest in Southeast Asia* (New York, 1949), pp. 237–238. Skinner, *Chinese Society in Thailand*, pp. 216–220.

[21] *Ibid.*, pp. 347–360. *Journal of Asian Studies*, XVI, 2, February 1957, pp. 248–249. G. W. Skinner, *Leadership and Power in the Chinese Community of Thailand* (Ithaca, N.Y., 1958), *passim*.

[22] *Ibid.*, p. 145.

[23] *Ibid.*, pp. 132–136.

[24] C. Robequain, tr. Isabel Ward, *The Economic Development of French Indo-China* (London and New York, 1944), pp. 37–41. V. Thompson, *French Indo-China* (New York, 1937), pp. 167–169.

Chapter V. Communism

[1] Kennedy, *op. cit.*, pp. 361–367.

[2] Royal Institute of International Affairs, *op. cit.*, pp. 57–60.

[3] Kennedy, *op. cit.*, p. 358. J. K. King, *Southeast Asia in Perspective* (New York, 1956), pp. 90–92.

[4] W. L. Holland, ed., *Asian Nationalism and the West* (New York, 1953), pp. 230–242.

[5] B. Fall, *The Viet-Minh Regime: Government and Administration in the Democratic Republic of Vietnam* (Ithaca, N.Y., 1954), pp. 6–16, 34–42.

[6] J. H. Brimmell, *Communism in South East Asia, A Political Analysis* (London and New York, 1959), pp. 279–283.

[7] W. Burmeister, ed., *op. cit.*, p. 93. L. W. Pye, *Guerilla Communism in Malaya, Its Social and Political Meaning* (Princeton, 1956), p. 38. *Pacific Affairs*, XXXV, 2, Summer 1962, pp. 116–127.

[8] Pye, *op. cit.*, pp. 128–135, 148–154.

[9] *Pacific Affairs*, XXIV, 3, September 1951, pp. 231–233.

[10] *Ibid.*, pp. 229–231.

[11] Mende, *op. cit.*, p. 101.

[12] Kennedy, *op. cit.*, p. 505. Fifield, *op. cit.*, p. 292.

[13] *Pacific Affairs*, XXIV, 3, September 1951, pp. 234–235. W. MacMahon Ball, *Nationalism and Communism in Eastern Asia*, 2nd ed. rev. (Melbourne and New York, 1956), p. 12.

[14] While the Dutch law of 1870 forbade the sale of land to aliens there was no prohibition on its transfer from one Indonesian to another. No large contiguous estates owned by Indonesians existed which would correspond to the *haciendas* in the Philippines. However, in Java there were some natives who, by Indonesian standards, owned a considerable amount of land in scattered parcels, acquired by foreclosure of mortgages. Javanese landowners leased their land to tenants, taking one to two thirds of the crop as rent. (K. Pelzer, *Pioneer Settlement in the Asiatic Tropics* (New York, 1945), pp. 168–169.)

[15] Kennedy, *op. cit.*, p. 471. *Far Eastern Survey*, XXIX, 1, January 1960, pp. 5–13.

[16] A. H. Scaff, *The Philippine Answer to Communism* (Stanford, 1955), pp. 7–24.
[17] Mills *et al.*, *op. cit.*, pp. 70–71. Scaff, *op. cit.*, pp. 27–29.
[18] *Ibid.*, pp. 30–31. *American Perspective*, IV, 1, Winter 1950, pp. 86–91. Romulo and Gray, *op. cit.*, pp. 123–124.
[19] *Report to the President of the United States by the Economic Survey Mission to the Philippines*, 1950, p. 49. Scaff, *op. cit.*, pp. 31–35.
[20] *Ibid.*, pp. 36–45, 65–75, 133–137. Romulo and Gray, *op. cit.*, pp. 125–146.
[21] Trager, ed., *op. cit.*, *passim*.
[22] For accounts of Communism in Malaya see V. Thompson and R. Adloff, *The Left Wing in Southeast Asia* (New York, 1950), pp. 123–162. L. A. Mills, *Malaya, A Political and Economic Appraisal*, pp. 43–70. L. W. Pye, *Guerilla Communism in Malaya*, *passim*. A. Campbell, *Jungle Green* (London, 1953). Brigadier M. C. A. Henniker, *Red Shadow over Malaya* (London, 1956). The last two give a vivid first-hand account of the jungle war.
[23] Mills, *Malaya, A Political and Economic Appraisal*, p. 53.

Chapter VI. International Relations

[1] Mills, *Malaya, A Political and Economic Appraisal*, pp. 162–163.
[2] *Orbis*, IV, 4, Winter 1961, pp. 452–466.
[3] *Daily Telegraph*, February 26, 1962.
[4] A good account of American policy is given in King, *op. cit.*, pp. 106–172.
[5] *Ibid.*, p. 140.
[6] *Ibid.*, pp. 173–185.
[7] R. H. Fifield, *op. cit.*, pp. 58–59, 496–500. This is by far the best and fullest account of the foreign policies of the states of Southeast Asia.
[8] *Ibid.*, pp. 76–84.
[9] *New York Times*, March 7, 1962.
[10] Fifield, *op. cit.*, p. 386.
[11] *Pacific Affairs*, XXXIV, 4, Winter 1961–1962, pp. 364–371.
[12] *Orbis*, IV, 4, Winter 1961, pp. 458–463.
[13] *Asian Survey*, I, 1, March 1961, pp. 41–42. *Pacific Affairs*, XXXIV, 2, Summer 1961, pp. 178–183.
[14] Fifield, *op. cit.*, p. 228.
[15] *Daily Telegraph*, March 2, April 5, 10, 1961.
[16] Paul W. van der Veur, *West New Guinea: Irian Barat or Papua Barat*, mimeographed, pp. 6–9 (Canberra, 1962).
[17] *Asian Survey*, III, 2, February 1963, p. 73.
[18] *Daily Telegraph*, July 10, 11, 1961. *Asian Survey*, I, 1, March 1961, pp. 13–21.
[19] *Pacific Affairs*, XXXIV, 3, Fall 1961, pp. 286–290. *International Journal*, XVI, 4, Autumn 1961, pp. 366–367. *World To-day*, 17, 11, November 1961, pp. 496–501. *Daily Telegraph*, January 13, 1962.
[20] *Asian Survey*, III, 2, February 1963, p. 69.
[21] *New York Times*, November 29, 1961.
[22] *Asian Survey*, III, 2, February 1963, p. 70. van der Veur, *op. cit.*, pp. 10–16.

Chapter VII. The Economic Effects of Colonial Rule

The following authors describe the colonial period in Southeast Asia: J. H. Boeke, *Economics and Economic Policy of Dual Societies as Exemplified by Indonesia* (New York, 1953). G. H. Bousquet, *A French View of the Netherlands Indies* (New York, 1940). J. F. Cady, *A History of Modern Burma* (Ithaca, N.Y., 1958). J. L. Christian, *Modern Burma* (Berkeley, 1942). M. Collis, *Last and First in Burma*

(1941–1948) (London, 1956). W. C. Forbes, *The Philippine Islands,* 2 vols. (Boston and New York, 1928). J. S. Furnivall, *Netherlands India: A Study of Plural Economy* (Cambridge, England, 1939). J. S. Furnivall, *Colonial Policy and Practice: A Comparative Study of Burma and Netherlands India* (Cambridge, England, 1948). G. E. Harvey, *British Rule in Burma* (London, 1946). J. R. Hayden, *The Philippines, A Study in National Development* (New York, 1942). K. P. Landon, *Siam in Transition* (Shanghai, 1939). L. A. Mills, *British Rule in Eastern Asia* (London, 1942). C. Robequain, tr. I. A. Ward, *The Economic Development of French Indo-China* (London, 1944). Sir F. Swettenham, *British Malaya* (London, 1920). V. Thompson, *Thailand, The New Siam* (New York, 1941). A. Vandenbosch, *The Dutch East Indies* (Berkeley, 1941). H. J. van Mook, *The Stakes of Democracy in Southeast Asia* (New York, 1950). B. H. M. Vlekke, *Nusantara, A History of Indonesia,* rev. ed. (The Hague, 1959).

Chapter VIII. Financial Problems of the Underdeveloped Countries

[1] B. Higgins, *op. cit.,* pp. 48–49.
See also P. T. Bauer and B. S. Yamey, *The Economics of Underdeveloped Countries* (Cambridge, England, 1957). F. Benham, *The Colombo Plan and Other Essays* (London and New York, 1956). P. Talbot, ed. *South Asia in the World Today* (Chicago, 1949). Warren S. Thompson, *Population and Progress in the Far East* (Chicago, 1959). M. Zinkin, *Asia and the West* (London, 1951). M. Zinkin, *Development for Free Asia* (Fair Lawn, N.J., 1956).

Chapter IX. Private Investment Abroad since 1945

[1] U.N. Economic and Social Council, *Economic Development of Underdeveloped Countries: Interim Report,* E/3258, 1959, *passim.* U.N. Economic and Social Council, *The International Flow of Private Capital 1956–1958,* E/3249, 1959, pp. 9, 11, 20, 47. U.N. Economic and Social Council, *International Flow of Private Capital 1958–1959,* E/3369, 1960, *passim.*
[2] *Ibid.,* p. 22.
[3] U.S. Department of Commerce, *U.S. Business Investments in Foreign Countries,* 1960, pp. 89, 92.
[4] R. F. Mikesell, *Promoting Private United States Investment Abroad* (Washington, D.C., 1957), p. 2 and *passim.*
[5] *New York Times,* April 3, 1963.
[6] A. R. Conan, *Capital Imports into Sterling Countries* (London, 1960), p. 82. The author analyzes in great detail investment in the sterling bloc since 1945, and compares pre- and post-war trends. Unfortunately he is least useful for Southeast Asia, largely because the lack of authoritative and detailed information about the British dependencies forces him to content himself with approximations. Moreover, countries which do not belong to the sterling bloc are not discussed, and this excludes the whole of Southeast Asia except Malaya, the dependencies in Borneo, and Burma.
Information about the investment abroad of private capital from the United Kingdom is vague and often unreliable. Government statistics estimate that since 1952 private investment overseas has averaged $840,000,000 a year, of which something like a third has been in underdeveloped British territories. No attempt is made to subdivide these totals, and the information is not very enlightening when one tries to discover how much is invested in any particular area. The most detailed survey of United Kingdom foreign investment is the *United Kingdom*

Overseas Investments, published annually by the Bank of England. The estimates, however, are incomplete since they cover only the investments of residents of the United Kingdom in securities dealt in on the London Stock Exchange and in American and Canadian dollar securities quoted abroad. More important, they quote only the nominal value of the securities and not their current market value. Furthermore, the estimates include among United Kingdom registered companies only those which operate entirely or predominantly abroad and exclude, e.g., insurance and shipping companies altogether. As a result the estimates omit an important part of United Kingdom investments overseas, and underestimate seriously their extent and contemporary value. But the Bank of England estimates are useful to some extent because they show the areas favored by United Kingdom investors, and whether their holdings have increased or decreased during the past fifteen years.

[7] Conan, *op. cit.*, pp. 33, 85.
[8] Lord Chandos in *Journal of the Royal Commonwealth Society*, II (New Series), 6, November–December 1959, pp. 222–223.

Chapter X. Western Investment in Southeast Asia

[1] Helmut G. Callis, *Foreign Capital in Southeast Asia* (New York, 1942), *passim*. Callis tried his best to arrive at certainty in a problem where no certainty exists. In his analysis he sometimes quoted several contradictory estimates, all authoritative, and finally gave a figure which might or might not agree with any of the preceding statistics.
[2] F. H. Golay, *The Philippines: Public Policy and National Economic Development* (Ithaca, N.Y., 1961), pp. 241–245.
[3] *Ibid.*, pp. 254–263, 317–335.
[4] Hartendorp, *op. cit.*, pp. 348–383, 415–417.
[5] *The Colombo Plan for Co-operative Economic Development in South and South East Asia. Sixth Annual Report of the Consultative Committee, 1956–57*, p. 107. H. G. Callis, *op. cit.*, pp. 13–17. S. Jenkins, *American Economic Policy Toward the Philippines* (Stanford, 1954), p. 38.
[6] U.S. Department of Commerce, *Investment in the Philippines* (Washington, D.C., 1955), pp. 5–8; *U.S. Business Investments in Foreign Countries* (Washington, D.C., 1960), p. 89. Hartendorp, *op.cit.*, pp. 431–481.
[7] B. Higgins, *op. cit.*, pp. 82–94.
[8] G. C. Allen and A. G. Donnithorne, *Western Enterprise in Indonesia and Malaya* (New York, 1957), pp. 278–279.
[9] U.S. Department of Commerce, *Investment in Indonesia* (Washington, D.C., 1956), p. 10. Callis, *op. cit.*, pp. 26–34.
[10] U.S. Department of Commerce, *Investment in Indonesia*, p. 13; *Survey of Current Business*, September 1958, p. 18.
[11] Higgins, *op. cit.*, pp. 65, 78.
[12] U.S. Department of Commerce, *Investment in Indonesia*, pp. 6, 52–55. Higgins, *op. cit.*, pp. 70–78. Allen and Donnithorne, *op. cit.*, pp. 257–260.
[13] *Ibid.*, pp. 238–239. *Pacific Affairs*, XXVII, 1, March 1954, pp. 36–37; XXX, 3, September 1957, pp. 202–203.
[14] Allen and Donnithorne, *op. cit.*, pp. 175–180. U.S. Department of Commerce, *Investment in Indonesia*, pp. 12–13.
[15] Massachusetts Institute of Technology, *Stanvac in Indonesia* (Washington, D.C., 1957), pp. 28–34.
[16] *Ibid.*, pp. 39–44, 92–95. Allen and Donnithorne, *op. cit.*, p. 179. *Far Eastern Survey*, XXIX, 4, April 1960, p. 53.

[17] *Daily Telegraph*, November 2, 1960. *Pacific Affairs*, XXXIV, 2, Summer 1961, pp. 126–130.

[18] *Daily Telegraph*, January 26, 1962.

[19] *The World To-day*, 12, 9, September 1956, pp. 353–354.

[20] *Daily Telegraph*, December 19, 1957. *Pacific Affairs*, XXXII, 4, March 1959, p. 66.

[21] *Nederlands Tijdschrift Voor Internationaal Recht*, VI, Extra Issue, July 1959, pp. 217–310.

[22] *Pacific Affairs*, XXXIV, 4, Winter 1961–1962, pp. 344–351.

[23] Callis, *op. cit.*, p. 94. *Pacific Affairs*, XVII, 1, March 1944, p. 93. Tinker, *op. cit.*, p. 303.

[24] *Ibid.*, pp. 93–95, 115–118.

[25] *Ibid.*, p. 116.

[26] *Daily Telegraph*, December 28, 1962.

[27] *Ibid.*, February 25, 27, April 5, 1963. *New York Times*, April 5, 1963. *Asian Survey*, II, 6, August 1962, pp. 26–31.

[28] Callis, *op. cit.*, pp. 51–57.

[29] *Straits Budget*, August 6, 1958.

[30] L. A. Mills, *Malaya, A Political and Economic Appraisal*, pp. 173–184, 199.

[31] Some rubber estates had unused reserves of land. When this was planted it was called new planting, to distinguish it from replanting, which involved felling the old seedling and replanting with high-yielding rubber.

[32] U.N. Department of Economic and Social Affairs, *The Population of South East Asia 1950–1980*, p. 11.

[33] International Bank Mission, *The Economic Development of Malaya* (Baltimore, 1955), p. 40.

[34] *Far Eastern Survey*, XXVI, 11, November 1957, pp. 170–175. *Pacific Affairs*, XXXIV, 2, Summer 1961, p. 159. Bundit Kantabutra, *The Economy and National Income of Thailand* (Bangkok, 1959), pp. 11–12. *A Public Development Plan for Thailand. Report of a Mission Organised by the International Bank for Reconstruction and Development at the Request of the Government of Thailand* (Baltimore, 1959), pp. 12, 89–97, 114.

[35] *Pacific Affairs*, XXXIV, 3, Fall 1961, p. 251.

[36] Lord Heyworth, *Capital Investment*, p. 8.

Chapter XI. Economic Progress and Problems

[1] P. E. Abelarde, *American Tariff Policy towards the Philippines, 1898–1946* (New York, 1947), *passim*. S. Jenkins, *op. cit.*, pp. 64–67.

[2] J. E. Spencer, *Land and People in the Philippines* (Berkeley and Los Angeles, 1952), pp. 123, 128. Pelzer, *op. cit.*, pp. 89–96. Hayden, *op. cit.*, pp. 378–400.

[3] *Ibid.*, pp. 378–379, 391. Pelzer, *op. cit.*, pp. 88–89.

[4] *Ibid.*, pp. 86, 109–113. Jacoby, *op. cit.*, pp. 179–180, 191. Spencer, *op. cit.*, pp. 116–127.

[5] *Ibid.*, pp. 129–136. *Pacific Affairs*, XXVII, 1, March 1954, pp. 41–50.

[6] Pelzer, *op. cit.*, pp. 127–159. *Far Eastern Survey*, XXIV, 2, February 1955, p. 29. Spencer, *op. cit.*, pp. 137–138, 147.

[7] *Ibid.*, pp. 233, 239–240.

[8] R. A. Smith, *op. cit.*, pp. 172–182. *Pacific Affairs*, XXVII, 4, December 1954, pp. 353–363. Pelzer, *op. cit.*, pp. 52–54, 96.

[9] *Far Eastern Survey*, XXVII, 1, January 1958, pp. 7–15; XXVII, 2, February 1958, pp. 23–30. W. M. Ball, *op. cit.*, pp. 92–96. Golay, *op. cit.*, pp. 275–277. Starner, *op. cit.*, pp. 127–199.

[10] *Far Eastern Survey*, XXVI, 11, November 1957, pp. 161–169. Golay, *op. cit.*, pp. 278, 288–289. *Philippine Free Press*, February 9, 1963.

[11] *Far Eastern Survey*, XXIX, 8, August 1960, p. 116. *Malayan Economic Review*, VII, 1, April 1962, p. 39. *Asian Survey*, III, 2, February 1963, p. 73. *New York Times*, April 5, 1963.

[12] Higgins, *op. cit.*, pp. 123–125. *Pacific Affairs*, XXXIV, 2, Summer 1961, p. 125.

[13] Higgins, *op. cit.*, pp. 41–46, 101–105.

[14] U.N. Department of Economic and Social Affairs, *The Population of South East Asia (Including Ceylon and China: Taiwan) 1950–1980*, Report III, Population Studies No. 30, p. 89.

[15] Pelzer, *op. cit.*, pp. 160–174.

[16] *Ibid.*, pp. 155–231. *Pacific Affairs*, XXIV, 3, September 1951, p. 275.

[17] *Ibid.*, pp. 274–277. Higgins, *op. cit.*, pp. 61–63. U.N. Department of Economic and Social Affairs, *The Population of South East Asia 1950–1980*, pp. 86–90.

[18] *The Colombo Plan, Eleventh Annual Report 1962*, pp. 190–241.

[19] *Asian Survey*, III, 2, February 1963, p. 73.

[20] *Ibid.*, I, 1, March 1961, pp. 14–22. *Ibid.*, I, 4, June 1961, pp. 5–11. *Pacific Affairs*, XXXIV, 2, Summer 1961, pp. 115–130.

[21] *Asian Survey*, III, 2, February 1963, pp. 73–75. *Daily Telegraph*, February 11, 1963. *Straits Times*, March 8, 1963. *New York Times*, April 5, 1963.

[22] Christian, *op. cit.*, pp. 104–108, 116–119. Jacoby, *op. cit.*, pp. 77–88. Furnivall, *Colonial Policy and Practice*, pp. 84–89.

[23] Furnivall, *The Governance of Modern Burma*, p. 111. Harvey, *op. cit.*, p. 31.

[24] Tinker, *op. cit.*, pp. 101, 113. F. N. Trager, *Building a Welfare State in Burma 1948–1956* (New York, 1958), pp. 95–105. Government of Burma, *Pyidawtha, The New Burma, A Report from the Government to the People of the Union of Burma on Our Long-Term Programme for Economic and Social Development, 1954, passim.

[25] Robert I. Crane, *Aspects of Economic Development in South Asia* (New York, 1954), pp. 15–18. Tinker, *op. cit.*, pp. 102, 120–125. T. Mende, *op. cit.*, pp. 158–165.

[26] Quoted in *Malayan Economic Review*, VII, 1, April 1962, p. 32.

[27] Tinker, *op. cit.*, pp. 303–305. Government of Burma, *Economic Survey of Burma 1960* (Rangoon, 1960), *passim*.

[28] Tinker, *op. cit.*, pp. 228, 229, 238–245. Thompson and Adloff, *Minority Problems in Southeast Asia*, pp. 83–86.

[29] Trager, *Building a Welfare State in Burma*, p. 36. Tinker, *op. cit.*, pp. 231–235. Government of Burma, *Pyidawtha*, pp. 33–45; *Economic Survey of Burma 1960*, *passim*.

[30] *Pacific Affairs*, XXX, 3, September 1957, pp. 229–230; XXXIV, 3, Fall 1961, pp. 243–246.

[31] Thompson, *French Indo-China*, pp. 143, 159.

[32] Robequain, *op. cit.*, pp. 84–86. Jacoby, *op. cit.*, pp. 143–153.

[33] *Far Eastern Survey*, XXV, 2, November 1956, pp. 163–164; XXIX, 1, January 1960, pp. 1–5.

[34] Jacoby, *op. cit.*, pp. 140–148. Robequain, *op. cit.*, pp. 82–86.

[35] Kennedy, *op. cit.*, pp. 434–435. Fall, *op. cit.*, pp. 101–104. *Pacific Affairs*, XXXI, 1, March 1958, pp. 45–46. *Far Eastern Survey*, XXVI, 1, January 1957, pp. 12–14; XXVIII, 8, August 1959, pp. 113–126.

[36] T. H. Silcock in *Asian Nationalism and the West*, W. L. Holland, ed., p. 328.

[37] Mills, *Malaya, A Political and Economic Appraisal*, pp. 186–188.

Chapter XII. Foreign Aid

[1] W. W. Rostow, *The Process of Economic Growth*, 2nd ed. (Oxford, 1960), pp. 313–318; *The Stages of Economic Growth, A Non-Communist Manifesto* (Cambridge, England, 1960), pp. 4–72.

[2] *Report to the President of the United States by the Economic Survey Mission to the Philippines* (Bell Report) (Washington, D.C., 1950), pp. 102–103.

[3] King, *op. cit.*, pp. 155–159, 234.

[4] *The Colombo Plan, Tenth Annual Report, 1961*, pp. 213–215, 224–225. *The Colombo Plan, Eleventh Annual Report, 1962*, pp. 228–230, 241.

[5] *Daily Telegraph*, January 31, 1962.

[6] Tinker, *op. cit.*, p. 98.

[7] *Daily Telegraph*, September 15, 1960.

[8] *The Colombo Plan, Eleventh Annual Report, 1962*, pp. 226–227. Parl. Pap. Cmnd. 974 of 1960, *Assistance from the United Kingdom for Overseas Development*, passim.

[9] *The Colombo Plan, Eleventh Annual Report, 1962*, pp. 195, 199, 217.

[10] *International Bank for Reconstruction and Development*, Annual Reports, passim.

[11] Parl. Pap. *Cmnd. 965 of 1960, International Development Association, Articles of Agreement*, passim.

Chapter XIII. Western Aid and Population Growth

[1] Black, *op. cit.*, pp. 50–53.

[2] *New York Times*, April 3, 1963.

[3] Black, *op. cit.*, p. 14.

[4] Parl. Pap. *Cmnd. 974 of 1960*, p. 6.

[5] *Daily Telegraph*, July 26, 1961.

[6] *New York Times*, April 3, 1963.

[7] *Daily Telegraph*, March 28, 1961.

[8] Thompson, *Population and Progress in the Far East*, passim. Zinkin, *Asia and the West*, passim. P. M. Hauser, *Population and World Politics* (Chicago, 1954), pp. 245–257. Bauer and Yamey, *op. cit.*, pp. 61–63.

[9] U.N. Department of Economic and Social Affairs, *The Population of South East Asia 1950–1980*, pp. 11, 18, 89.

[10] U.N. *Economic Bulletin for Asia and the Far East*, X, 1, June 1959, p. 21.

[11] *Foreign Affairs*, 39, 2, January 1961, pp. 259–263.

[12] Thompson, *Population and Progress in the Far East*, p. 314. Zinkin, *Development for Free Asia*, pp. 226–227.

[13] Thompson, *Population and Progress in the Far East*, p. 400.

[14] *Ibid.*, pp. 302–353.

Suggested Reading

General

Allen, G. C., and Audrey G. Donnithorne. *Western Enterprise in Indonesia and Malaya*. New York, 1957.
Benham, Frederic. *The Colombo Plan and Other Essays*. London and New York, 1956.
Black, Eugene R. *The Diplomacy of Economic Development*. Cambridge, Mass., 1960.
Emerson, Rupert, Willard H. Elsbree, and Virginia Thompson. *Representative Government in Southeast Asia*. Cambridge, Mass., 1955.
Fifield, Russell H. *The Diplomacy of Southeast Asia: 1945–1958*. New York, 1958.
———. *Southeast Asia in United States Policy*. New York, 1963.
Kahin, George McT., ed. *Governments and Politics of Southeast Asia*. Ithaca, N.Y., 1959.
Mikesell, R. F. *Promoting Private United States Investment Abroad*. Washington, D.C., 1957.
Purcell, Victor. *The Chinese in Southeast Asia*. London and New York, 1951.
Thompson, Warren S. *Population and Progress in the Far East*. Chicago, 1959.
Vandenbosch, A., and R. Butwell. *Southeast Asia among the World Powers*. Lexington, Ky., 1958.
Zinkin, Maurice. *Asia and the West*. London, 1951.

Communism

Ball, W. MacMahon. *Nationalism and Communism in East Asia*. New York, 1956.
Brimmell, J. H. *Communism in South East Asia: A Political Analysis*. London and New York, 1959.
Kennedy, Captain Malcolm D. *A Short History of Communism in Asia*. London, 1957.

Burma

Cady, J. F. *A History of Modern Burma*. Ithaca, 1958.
Christian, J. L. *Modern Burma*. Berkeley, 1942.
Harvey, G. E. *British Rule in Burma*. London, 1946.
Tinker, Hugh. *The Union of Burma, A Study of the First Years of Independence*. London, 1957.

Indonesia

Feith, H. *The Decline of Constitutional Democracy in Indonesia*. Ithaca and Toronto, 1962.

Furnivall, J. S. *Colonial Policy and Practice: A Comparative Study of Burma and Netherlands India*. Cambridge, England, 1948.

————. *Netherlands India: A Study of Plural Economy*. Cambridge, England, 1939.

Higgins, Benjamin. *Indonesia's Economic Stabilization and Development*. New York, 1957.

Vandenbosch, A. *The Dutch East Indies*. Berkeley, 1941.

van Mook, H. J. *The Stakes of Democracy in Southeast Asia*. New York, 1950.

Vlekke, B. H. M. *Nusantara, A History of Indonesia*. The Hague, 1959.

Malaya

Gullick, J. M. *Malaya*. New York, 1963.

Mills, L. A. *British Rule in Eastern Asia: A Study of Contemporary Government and Economic Development in British Malaya and Hong Kong*. London, 1942.

————. *Malaya, A Political and Economic Appraisal*. Minneapolis, 1958.

Swettenham, Sir F. *British Malaya*. London, 1920.

Philippines

Forbes, W. C. *The Philippine Islands*. 2 vols. Boston and New York, 1928.

Golay, Frank H. *The Philippines: Public Policy and National Economic Development*. Ithaca, N.Y., 1961.

Hayden, Joseph R. *The Philippines, A Study in National Development*. New York, 1942.

Pelzer, Karl J. *Pioneer Settlement in the Asiatic Tropics*. New York, 1945.

Ravenholt, Albert. *The Philippines, A Young Republic on the Move*. Princeton, N.J., 1962.

Spencer, Joseph E. *Land and People in the Philippines*. Berkeley and Los Angeles 1952.

Thailand

Landon, K. P. *Siam in Transition*. Shanghai, 1939.

Skinner, G. William. *Chinese Society in Thailand: An Analytical History*. Ithaca, 1957.

Thompson, V. *Thailand, The New Siam*. New York, 1941.

Viet Nam

Fall, Bernard B. *The Viet-Minh Regime: Government and Administration in the Democratic Republic of Vietnam*. Ithaca, 1954.

————. *The Two Viet-Nams: A Political and Military History*. New York, 1963.

Honey, Patrick J. *Communism in North Vietnam*. Cambridge, Mass., 1963.

Robequain, Charles, tr. Isabel A. Ward. *The Economic Development of French Indo-China*. London, 1944.

Index

362